UNDER THE SPHINX

the Search for the Hieroglyphic Key to the Real Hall of Records

MANU SEYFZADEH

HUGO HOUSE PUBLISHERS, LTD.

ISBN: 978-1-948261-63-0

Library of Congress Control Number: 2021910974

Cover Design: Maryann Sperry
Interior Layout & Formatting: Ronda Taylor, HeartWorkCreative.com
Graphics by Anthony Sturmas, Mrsturmas@gmail.com
Graphics and Photography by Manu Seyfzadeh

Some photos with rights obtained from Agfafoto, Alamy, Oriental Institute of the University of Chicago, Tony Hallas, AGE Fotostock America, Inc., Phoebe A. Hearst Museum of Anthropology, University of California, Berkeley, Karim Iliya Photography, KHM-Museumsverband, Edfu Project, Art Resource, Inc., Blog, Podcasts & More, Lepsius-Project, Sachsen-Anhalt, agefotostock, The Metropolitan Museum of Art, New York, NY, Manna Nader, Gabana Studios Cairo, Egypt, bpk Bildagentur, the Robert and Frances Fullerton Museum of Art at California State University, San Bernardino, and John Lundwall.

Some graphics and photos used with Creative Commons License or marked as Public Domain; unmodified unless noted in caption.

Quotes: I would like to thank the following individuals and entities for permitting me to quote them:
  Graham Hancock
  Thomas Brophy
  Edgar Cayce Readings © 1971, 1993-2007 The Edgar Cayce Foundation. All Rights Reserved
  James Peter Allen
  Michael Brown
  Konstantin Batygin
  Liverpool University Press
  ARCE Sphinx Project, Sarah Whitcher Kansa, alexandriaarchive.org, opencontext.org

To send correspondence to the author use the contact form at www.cheopspyramid.com

Hugo House Publishers, Ltd.
hugohousepublishers.com

Dedication

To the memory of my dear cousin, Dr. Ahmad Samsamshariat, who died in July, 2019 after a long fight with brain cancer.

Contents

Acknowledgments

SINCE I BEGAN RESEARCHING NUMBERS AND WORDS OF ANCIENT EGYPT, I have made several dear friends with whom I have had some of the most interesting conversations you could ever wish for. This list of friends includes some of the most creative, intelligent, spiritual, brilliant, and warm folks I have ever met. Thanks to their incredible insights during presentations and discussions, I have learned much from them. With this introduction, I want to thank with great respect and admiration the following five people: Robert Schoch, Jean-Paul Bauval, Robert Bauval, Alan Green, and Gary Osborn.

Robert Schoch and I have collaborated on several papers and a film. I have gotten to know him well over the last few years. To me he personifies the fearless scientist, unencumbered by dogma and agenda to whose attitude and posture all scientists ideally should aspire. On behalf of an entirely new generation of fearless researchers, I would like to thank him and acknowledge his own sacrifice and struggle dealing with widespread rejection, ridicule, and condemnation of his work. Robert reminds me to keep the theory walking behind the evidence and not in front.

Jean-Paul Bauval is a most brilliant architect and has taught me many things. The most precious of them is to ask the big questions instead of looking for the small answers.

Robert Bauval inspired me to learn about the many things I have studied since I first read *the Orion Mystery*. It is his style, in the immanent spirit of Egyptian science, which taught me to learn not from lectures, but from stories.

Alan Green has given me a most important lesson of looking for hidden truth: That if something isn't right, it may be so by design, or of our own ignorance. We learn from pardoxes. Alan, if anyone, has made a carreer out of taking this to masterful perfection. I would also like to acknowledge Alan's review of and feedback on parts of the manuscript for this book.

Gary Osborn impresses me with his breadth and balance. It is the polymath in Gary, which brings out the same in me.

I am greatly indebted to Graham Hancock for his exceedingly valuable review of, and critical comments regarding, the structure of the argument and thought process I have presented in this book. Without Graham's superb insights as a writer, I could not possibly have laid out the case as effectively as possible.

My developmental and copy editor, Linda Carbone, who made great suggestions to make this a better book. Thank you, Linda.

I also owe special thanks for helpful discussions to Stephen Brabin, the author of the book *The Incomplete Pyramids*, John Legon who years ago proposed a compelling design theory of the Giza Pyramids, and Jean-Pierre Houdin, the architect who proposed the Internal Ramp Theory to explain how the Great Pyramid was built.

Among my old friends stands out Tassos Polydoros, who with great interest has always helped with useful questions and comments discussing the various projects on which I have worked.

Over the last couple of years, I have met several of the world's most brilliant and scholarly Egyptologists, some in person and some through e-mail contact. I would like to thank Drs. Mark Lehner, Eidan Dodson, Salima Ikram, Bob Brier, James Allen, Peter Der Manuelian, Okasha El Daly, Wael Sherbiny, Zahi Hawass, Hratch Papazian, Petra Goedegebuure, and Florence Dunn Friedman for their valuable advise and help with my questions.

A great book needs great graphics. I cannot praise enough the incredible talent of storyboard artist Antony Sturmas who produced some of the incredible drawings in this book. Anthony collaborated on my first book in 2016, and it was with great pleasure that I asked to return for this one.

A great book also needs a superb publishing team. I found that team with Hugo House Publishers, Ltd. Dr. Patricia Ross, Publisher and Senior Editor, has been my ultimate critic and fan at once. Without her, this book could not have been presented on the linguistic platter that my readers will receive it. Ronda Taylor, Design Director, performed nothing short of magic, to put the final words and images into a work of art. And George Gluchowski, the CEO of Hugo House Publishers, provided the robust infrastructure to bring this book to market. To my fellow authors: Give Hugo House a consideration. I am as happy as can be that I did.

I want to thank the following people for how they have shaped my path, with whom I have shared some special moments, or who have somehow inspired. In no particular order, they are Marcus Bergmann, Ralph Fischer, Christian Riep, Annette Kniepkamp, Horst Depping, Dirk Bischof, Philippe Caillat-Grenier, Rene' Rennefeld, Greg Petrie, Haydeh Khamneian (dec.), Rowland H. Davis (dec.), David Walters (dec.), Masayasu Nomura (dec.), Neda Alalhessabi, James Matthews, Sabe Molloi, Monica Todd, Leila Sharifian, Mike Bloom, Ronald Cotliar, Milind Ambe, Cyrus Mirsaidi, Ali Sabbaghzadeh, Arlena Beane, Jamie Levenson, Elia Gutierrez, Bahare Samsamshariat, H. Thomas Tadayon, Alan Degrandmont, Howard Murad, David Yellin, Shirin Bagheri, Oliver Nikpour, Mohamad Reza Nikpour, Amir Lajevardi, Peyman Forooghi, and Nagui Guorgui.

My cousins Ahmad, Masood, Mehdi, Reza Samsamshariat, my uncle Aziz, and all of their families are my extended family who have been with me at every stage in my life. I have been blessed to have them with me on this journey through the ups and downs and there are so many memories with them which make up the canvas of which it is still being painted.

There are two people without whom I would not have come to the United States. They changed my life most profoundly. Commander Roland and Marion Petrie are living legends of the greatest generation. They embody to me all that is virtuous, righteous, and good.

I want to thank my parents, Dr. med. Hassan and Gunda Seyfzadeh and my brothers Bijan and Sam for being the best family I could have ever hoped for in which to have come to this world and grow into who I am today.

Finally, to Nereyda Aguirre: I love you.

Foreword

By Graham Hancock,
author of *The Message of the Sphinx* (1996)

THERE HAVE ALWAYS BEEN MISGIVINGS ABOUT THE VIEW OF PREHISTORY PRO-moted by mainstream archaeologists; there has always been dissent and a feeling that something important is absent from the picture. However, it was not until the early 1990s that strong and compelling evidence began to be put forward that gave real substance to the doubts. This evidence focused initially on ancient Egypt and drew on the hard sciences of astronomy and geology to raise uncomfortable questions about the age of the Great Sphinx of Giza, the ultimate emblem and symbol of the high civilization of the Nile Valley.

According to Egyptologists, the Sphinx was carved out of the bedrock of the Giza plateau on the orders of Khafre, a pharaoh of the Fourth Dynasty who reigned from 2558-2532 BC. Students are therefore taught that the Sphinx is a little under 4,600 years old. But the geological perspective, first suggested by rogue scholar John Anthony West and soon thereafter supported and refined by Dr Robert Schoch, Professor of Geology at Boston University, confronts the mainstream Egyptological case with hard scientific evidence that the monument must be much older than that. To cut a long story short, Schoch quickly recognized that at some point after its body was hewn from the bedrock, it was subjected to around a thousand years of extremely heavy rainfall. Such rains did not fall in Egypt 4,600 years ago, or for a millennia before that, and Schoch is today confident that the origins of the monument that we know as the Sphinx go back more than 12,000 years to an epoch of cataclysmic climate change, known by geologists as the Younger Dryas, that occurred near the end of the last Ice Age.

Schoch's work has continued to unfold, producing ever more evidence in support of his thesis, since he first began to investigate the Sphinx in the early 1990s. His conclusions, though thoroughly reasoned and supported by an impressive array of facts, have never been accepted by mainstream Egyptologists.

Interestingly enough the same holds true for Robert Bauval whose 1994 book *The Orion Mystery* first explored the implications of the peculiar layout of the three great pyramids of Giza—a layout that mirrors the three stars of Orion's Belt. Robert and I went on to write a book together, titled *Keeper of Genesis* in the UK and *Message of the Sphinx* in the US. Published in 1996, it presented evidence that the remarkable mirroring of the belt stars of Orion with the pyramids of Giza is matched by a second "mirroring" phenomenon involving the Great Sphinx and the constellation of Leo. In both cases—Orion's Belt and the pyramids; the Great Sphinx and Leo—computer simulations of the ancient heavens reveal a sky-ground match that would have been obvious in any epoch but that was only perfect around 12,500 years ago, the epoch of the Younger Dryas.

I feel privileged to have known the late great John Anthony West and to have worked and travelled extensively with my good friend Robert Bauval and with Robert Schoch. Thanks to these three, the field of "alternative Sphinx studies" has been bolstered with archaeo-astronomical and geological breakthroughs of real merit that add substantially to human knowledge.

Since the 1990s we have continued to plow our own furrows, all of us elaborating in various ways and filling out with new details and in new contexts the implications of what we'd already understood.

The discovery of Gobekli Tepe in Turkey, an immense megalithic site almost 12,000 years old and thus belonging to the same Younger Dryas epoch in which we situate the origins of the Sphinx, provided new impetus and energy to the archaeological heresy we advocate, namely that an advanced civilization must have flourished somewhere in the world during the last Ice Age and then mysteriously vanished—but not before its survivors had left their fingerprints at the Giza plateau and at other ancient and mysterious sites on many continents.

Another development of great relevance to our heresy concerns growing scientific understanding of exactly how cataclysmic the Younger Dryas climate episode really was. It lasted from about 12,800 years ago until about

11,600 years ago and witnessed sudden sea-level rises, wildly fluctuating global temperatures and the mass extinction of the famous megafauna of the Ice Age—mammoths, mastodons, sabre-toothed tigers, dire wolves and so on. In this context, the mysterious disappearance of an advanced human civilization of the Ice Age, "Atlantis" by any other name, no longer seems so heretical. Moreover there is growing recognition today of how fragile a thing civilization is and how easily it can be lost. Were our own 21st century civilization with its much vaunted advanced technology to face rapid climate change on the cataclysmic scale witnessed during the Younger Dryas, it is unlikely that we would survive. Why then should it seem implausible that a civilization, as yet unrecognized by prehistorians, failed to survive the Younger Dryas?

So important progress has been made by our heresy in the past thirty years, with pieces of the jigsaw puzzle falling into place all around the world. Concerning ancient Egypt itself, however, our initial assault on the mainstream paradigm for a long while lacked a satisfactory follow-up. We had presented both geological and archaeo-astronomical evidence that the Sphinx was vastly older than Egyptologists believed; we had made the case for a connection to a lost civilization of prehistory, and we had even indicated where records proving the existence of that civilization might be stored—in a chamber hewn out of the bedrock beneath the Sphinx itself. But without access to the location—fiercely-resisted by the Egyptian authorities—it seemed that there was nothing further we could add, or that ever could be added.

I'd grown completely resigned to this state of affairs when Manu Seyfzadeh contacted me late in 2019 and asked me to read the first draft of a book he was writing about the Sphinx. He suggested that his findings added support to my work and to the work of John Anthony West, Robert Schoch, and Robert Bauval. This is something I've heard many times from many would-be authors, so I only agreed to read Manu's draft because I'd met him before, liked him, and knew him to be serious-minded. I honestly didn't expect to be confronted by any earth-shaking new information, but out of respect for him I was willing to take a look.

Imagine my surprise, therefore, when Manu's book, for which I'm glad to have been asked to provide this Foreword, turned out to be the first substantial and significant addition to human knowledge concerning the Sphinx since the breakthroughs of 1990s.

I'm not going to foreshadow at any great length the labyrinths of evidence, argument, and erudition in the pages that follow. But here, to whet your appetite, are a few brief hints:

Under the Sphinx proves, beyond reasonable doubt, that:

A massive lion statue stood at Giza long before the Fourth Dynasty, at which point—roughly around the accepted date of 2550 BC—it was re-carved with a human head to take the form of the Sphinx.

An archive of prehistoric documents was stored in a portable wooden container in a chamber beneath the lion predecessor of the Sphinx.

After a breach, this archive was later removed to another place, but certain priestly officials continued to have access to it.

Reproduced in art and hieroglyphs on the coffin of a high-ranking ancient Egyptian nobleman, information leaked from the archive reveals that the records once held beneath the Sphinx contained exact scientific knowledge of the workings of the solar system–knowledge that was far in advance of anything possessed by the ancient Egyptians and that the ancient Egyptians themselves did not understand.

I'll not say more here except to add that Manu is a gifted and determined researcher who left no stone unturned in the investigation that led to *Under the Sphinx*. You will find yourself in the safe hands of a brilliant historical detective as he builds his very intriguing case.

I

Paradox

IT STARED AT ME AS IF IT HAD BEEN IMPATIENTLY WAITING FOR THOUSANDS OF years to be set free. New truth is sinking in. Everything we thought we knew—. It's like sand running between my fingers into the sea, washing it away as if it had never been.

What I see there haunts me. It calls to me as if it were an omen embedded in me from who knows when. Fate, I feel, has somehow led me to where I am about to take you: on an investigation that begins with a surreal piece of ancient art and ends in the unimaginable time and place from where it came. But my story does not end down on some lonely beach where the sea washes away the sand from our eyes. It begins above—in the sky, in a place where we can stare at the past and find the records of history before history. That is, if you know where to look and what to look for.

But what if such prehistoric records confront us with a paradox, one so titanic it shatters a paradigm we have nervously clasped like the shifting sand on the shore? Why are we so sluggish to let go of it, so blinded by its allure, even when faced with that which goes against it?

The paradox of which I speak has to do with none other than our solar system. It took us two thousand years to come around to the model that put us out of the center and the Sun in it. Why is that? The problem is not just one of discovery but also one of inertia. We prefer to stay in the comfort zone of our dogmas, enamored with the facts which feed them, yet ignorant and dismissive of evidence which threaten them.

This is when the architects of paradigms, the ones inside, cannot pierce the next outer layer of the dogmas they created. It takes an outsider to do this, someone not burdened by the view from the inside. I am such an outsider.

I cannot claim credentials of the type which have created the dogma of history in which we currently reside. My sole credential is that I am *not* an insider. I am a self-taught, multidisciplinary, independent researcher with a special love for ancient Egypt. As many before, I have stared at the Great Sphinx in wonder and have asked to know her secret. Yet, from all the many places I might have searched to learn it, I least expected this: that her secret was tied to the prophesies of the famous American psychic Edgar Cayce, who spoke in trance-like sleep of a *Hall of Records*, an archive of history before history.

But Cayce' recorded accounts of the many journeys he took into his own subconscious to cross a bridge into the distant past in 10500 BC, and connect with his former self Ra Ta, making Cayce himself the maker of the *Hall of Records*, belies a hard and fast reality. When I looked for evidence for a real *Hall of Records*, I found it, *written* in the hieroglyphic language of the ancient Egyptians. That's when I stared at a real paradox of history, one that would lead me back to her, the mysterious, enigmatic Sphinx, and who she really was.

In this book, I tell the story of this investigation and what I found under the Sphinx. Once the sand was washed away by the sea, I had to come to terms with my own discovery: Our history is but the newest chapter in a book of cycles of civilized human cultures who wrote, designed, studied, and recorded for posterity that which they felt was a legacy worth preserving. This legacy I speak of was their knowledge of the sky. Our history began long after theirs ended, but this archived knowledge is what made possible the growth anew of civilization's seed: recorded images and symbols referring to the sky.

The Paradox in the Sky

Nowadays most people sooner or later learn that it is we who move, while the sky, the stars, and the Sun are relatively still. It only looks to us as if the sky moves because our senses are tuned to fool us into the illusion that we stand on solid, stationary ground. No wonder that the experience of an earthquake is surreal and unsettling to our core. But on any normal day, we never question this illusion of steadiness. It is hardwired into our sense of living on Earth. It is only by detachment from this sense of comfort, coupled with a healthy dose of intellectual curiosity, that we know by now that we are encircled by our Moon and our fellow planets together with their moons. All then move around the Sun as the Sun moves around the center of the Milky Way.

This is our heliocentric sun-in-the-center solar system, the truth of which is now unquestioned. Our blue globe not only rotates about itself, but it also wobbles like a tabletop, and the whole Earth races around the Sun at a breakneck speed of almost thirty thousand meters per second—faster than twice around Earth in an hour. Yet we do not feel any of it. On the contrary, we live in this bubble inflated by our senses taking advantage of our small size compared to the enormously big place we call Planet Earth, our home.

This illusion of inertness into which we are born explains why the ancients believed that Earth was at the center of the universe they knew. They believed that what is in the sky moves about Earth on defined paths blazed into the deepness of the dark—the cosmic sea. We know that this is so because the ancient Egyptians, for example, believed that the Sun travels across the sky in a boat floating on an imagined river, what we now know to be the ecliptic. The Moon, the planets, and even the constellations can be seen on Egyptian reliefs and paintings to float across the sky. Even the sky itself, they imagined, revolved around the Earth. This view of the universe by the ancient Egyptians persisted well into Plato's time in the fourth century BC, and history teaches us that this world view was *always so* up until this time. Neither the ancient Egyptians, nor any other people would have, or could have, known what we know today before the dawn of scientific inquiries during the era of antiquity. At least, that is the dogma dictated from within our current paradigm of history.

But this "earth-centered" view entrapped us for centuries longer. World views and *Zeitgeists* unopposed by reason could be used and abused to exert power over the people. This is when order over chaos also ruled over hearts and minds. Like our ancestors, we abhor chaos. We may go to great lengths to entrap ourselves with what we want to believe and not what reason tells us. We yearn inside for stability and order. The ancient Egyptians were no different. To them, nature's orderly rhythm observed as repeating cycles of time meant there was harmony after all, blooming from the scary chaos of the cosmic waters that had given rise to their world. The thought that Earth herself, the very place on which they built their motionless, timeless monuments, could be a rotating sphere racing with eight others on a nine-lane highway around the Sun would have been as uncanny as unbearable.

Cosmic order was their comfort zone. We still share this deeply held desire for an orderly comfort zone. This is what protects us from what chaos new knowledge may hurl our way.

But the fact remains: it is not us, but the sun, at the center of our solar system, itself nowhere near any center of our galaxy, the Milky Way, which, in turn, is nowhere near any center of an ever-expanding, universe-creating deep space. Is it any wonder then that to the tide of ages and eons of thinking required a paradox in the sky that would shake the Earth? For only such a paradox could set into motion those forces, tiny doubts at first growing into a small cadre of dissent and eventually into a loud enough unified force to tear down the old "earth-centric" paradigm. That our ancestors had to grapple with that paradox is a known fact. But what many may not know—or do not want to see even when presented with the evidence—that paradox presented itself far earlier than Copernicus in 1508 AD, long before maybe even the Ancient Egyptians.

Strange Behavior in the Wrong Model

As far as we think we know, the ancient Egyptians were aware of the five planets nearest to us: numbers one, two, four, five, and six—Mercury, Venus, Mars, Jupiter, and Saturn. They knew of course the Sun and the Moon. But with an unaided eye, they could not have known of seven, eight, and nine: Uranus, Neptune, and Pluto. Neither did they realize that planet number three was Earth itself, the center of their universe. When you consider these seven known bodies in the sky, which were so different from the millions of stars everywhere around, it is remarkable that in one of their main three creation stories, the one taught at the City of the Sun Heliopolis, it was the Sun that created the other eight to make "The Nine" at the beginning of time, not "The Seven." How curious that today, from Sun to Neptune, we also count to nine when asked to list the main bodies we call our solar system.

Ancient sky watchers must have been quite perplexed, witnessing strange behaviors of the planets they knew, so different from the vast number of stars everywhere else. Strange, that is, when viewed from within the paradigm that dictates Earth is in the center of the sky and everything therein. Take Mars for instance. This easily spotted, red dot of light moves like no other. It may wander first from west to east relative to the map of stars made up by the Zodiac constellations and then, as if by whim, returns towards the west. Stranger yet, it seems to take a few days of rest in between, dwelling in a place on this map as if in a total standstill. Mars, indeed, must have looked to the ancients as if he had a mind of his own. Yet, this was not the only planet to act in such disorderly ways. Look at Venus. For months she hovers like a dazzling light in the east and then disappears. Then, as if by magic, she reappears and hovers in the west.

While it looks as if Mars and the other planets shift direction, or leap across the sky, we know better now. What scientific observations have taught us is that it's only an illusion generated by our own orbital movement and position relative to that of our planetary companions, which is turn is all relative to the Sun. The leaping is really caused by conjunctions, and this illusion is called retrograde planetary motion. The planets, and we on Earth, orbit the Sun in the center, but we complete our laps faster than Mars and the outer planets. And so, it is our own shifting perspective which fools us into thinking that the planets are acting in erratic ways. The same illusion can be witnessed on the road from behind the wheel when we pass and are passed by other cars, but a bystander by the side of the road will see all the cars move forward all in one direction some faster, some slower. And so, what seems natural and rational from one perspective in the right model looks strange and chaotic from another model observed through the wrong lens.

We can learn an important lesson from this one simple fact in terms of how we advance our knowledge. A wrong model can create paradoxes and strange phenomena that are not at all strange in the right model. Perhaps it was such observations of the Red Planet that prompted Aristarchus (living around 200 BC) to question the validity of the Spindle of Necessity—the idea that the cosmos is represented by this Spindle and is attended by sirens and the three daughters of the Goddess Necessity known as the Moirai (the fates). Their job was to keep the rims of the spindle revolving. Would the Moirai suddenly turn the orbit of Mars the other way and defy their own mandate to control the course of time in foreseeable ways? Could the fates get confused?

Paradoxes, then, may serve as warnings that a paradigm has become too dogmatic and too comfortable for its own good. Yet will we be ready to handle an expanded new truth that springs from a new way of thinking, especially if it shakes us down from the ladder of history, if it turns upside down our idea that progress in how we live and what we know is a one-way climb up alongside the vector of time?

Many years ago, I remember watching an American movie with my parents and brothers. In those days, the 1970s, many American movies shown in Germany tended not to have happy endings. This movie's ending was so sobering that it haunts me to this day. It tells the story of an astronaut called Colonel George Taylor who travels through space in deep sleep with two others for two thousand years. He awakes and lands on a planet ruled by apes who hunt humans as slaves. Yet, this paradox of evolution means he cannot possibly be on Earth. It must be another planet.

Yes, I am referring to the original *Planet of the Apes* (1968). The movie ends with Taylor, played by Charlton Heston, and his mate, Nova (Linda Harrison), riding into the unknown on the strangely beautiful, deserted shore of the Forbidden Zone to be free from the apes. They remind me of Adam and Eve, but what they end up finding is not a new paradise to live in freedom and peace. Instead, they discover a half-buried, damaged Lady Liberty (figure 1).

Figure 1: "Painful Truth" based on the 1968 film Planet of the Apes. Graphic by Anthony Sturmas, Asturmas Studios.

Taylor realizes he is in New York. The painful truth hits him: Earth was destroyed by a human nuclear war, and it is now two thousand years in the future. He has landed back on Earth. He falls to his knees, into the sand and sea of this lonely beach of truth, staring in agony at his devastating discovery. Humanity, full of excess and arrogance, has finally destroyed itself—and on that decimated beach, as if sifting the sands of history through his fingers, he learns that history on Earth is not what he thought. He was in fact deceived by the dogma that ruled the planet of the Apes. But it begs the question: just because it's not "there," not present for the eye to see, and no matter how vehemently denied, does that by necessity mean it never existed?

To me, *The Planet of the Apes* illustrates the two-edged sword that epic shifts in knowledge and paradigms of thought represent. We want to know, yet we don't. We are conflicted because knowledge both liberates and enslaves us. Even though I was young, I took away from this the reason why we make bubbles and want to live in them. The lies we live ease our discomfort from the chaos of knowing the new, so we prefer to live those lies than to know the truth and lose our grip on some illusion of order. This state of comfort persists until we—or those who come after us, even when ourselves are long forgotten—are forced to reconsider. The lies wash away like the sand on the shore of truth, somewhere on Earth, sometime tomorrow.

The History of What We Know about Our Solar System.

Such drama of discovery, and then drawn out endlessly, was the Heliocentric Revolution. It represents one of the most drastic, most epic upheavals in our view of things. It began in antiquity and ended during the Renaissance, but it took a two-thousand yearlong span of time for us to come to terms with it. Why, you may ask, *why so long*?

In the final part of his famous *Republic*, Plato tells the *Myth of Er*. It is a lengthy, didactic argument that being just and good pays off in the end. Er is a man who has a near-death experience. He returns to life nine days later. During his colorful journey yonder, he witnesses the virtuous souls from the sky and some of the sinning souls from the Earth who meet in the gates between. From here, they get to choose where they want to go next: to whence they came or somewhere new and unseen. On the way, the souls experience the *Spindle of Necessity*, kept in motion, as I noted above, by the three goddesses of fate (figure 2).

Figure 2: "Spindle of Necessity" from Plato's *Myth of Er*. Graphic by Anthony Sturmas, Asturmas Studios.

All these themes of the afterlife, the gates, and an encounter with the planetary paths in the sky have their origin in the 4,000-year-old hieroglyphic texts of the ancient Egyptians. They were written onto the coffins of the privileged who wanted to be equipped with spells to attain immortality. Yet even the people alive by the time of Plato, between the fifth and fourth century BC some 2,400 years ago, still did not know they were not in the center of the universe. Only few thinkers must have questioned this claim to the center. One such visionary we know from the writings of Archimedes.

In one of his third century BC writings to King Gelon, we are told that Archimedes speaks of a certain Aristarchus from the Greek Island of Samos, alive during his own time:

... Aristarchus has brought out a book consisting of certain hypotheses, wherein it appears, as a consequence of the assumptions made, that the universe is many times greater than the 'universe' just mentioned. His hypotheses are that the fixed stars and the sun remain unmoved, that the earth revolves about the sun on the circumference of a circle, the sun lying in the middle of the orbit ...

According to Archimedes, who himself discovered and invented many things, Aristarchus "invented" the heliocentric model of the universe, which put the Sun, and not Earth, at the center. Aristarchus, it turns out, was two thousand years too early for his time (figure 3).

Figure 3: The Heliocentric Solar System as known since 1930. The Sun is in the center. The rocky planets Mercury, Venus, Earth, and Mars are on the inner four orbits. The asteroid belt divides the inner planets from the four outer gas planets Jupiter, Saturn, Uranus, and Neptune. The rings indicate the axis of planetary spin. Pluto is an icy dwarf planet in the Kuiper Belt made up of both rocky and gaseous asteroid bodies. As of 2006, it is no longer considered a planet. ©, Science Photo Library; Alamy Stock Photo FFFBNH.

Only the scientific power trio of Copernicus, Kepler, and Galilei, alive during a period of rebellion and awakening in the fifteenth through the seventeenth century AD, would prove what the ancient scholar had long before suspected. It would still take another hundred years before the world at large would be allowed to learn about it and, at last, uneasily accept it. That was only four hundred years ago. Why so long? Because the truth was too uncomfortable, too dangerous, too chaos-spawning. The very fabric of world order was at stake. Epic discoveries take epic times to change the course of history. Compared to the true center of our solar system, the number of planets in it may seem much less of an epic task to know and accept.

But there is a catch to that conundrum no one really expected. At first there were eight, then there were nine, then there were eight again. And now, it could again be nine. The only problem is we cannot see it. *Yet.*

The Mystery of the Ninth Planet

Unlike the stars, planets visibly move along the ecliptic, the celestial highway in the sky lined by the twelve Zodiac star constellations. The light they send us really comes from the Sun and that explains why the ancients initially noticed the five bright ones and missed the other three much dimmer points of light. After centuries of observations made by Babylonian and Egyptian astronomers and likely others across the ancient world, Number Seven, Uranus, was finally noticed.

We can only presume this discovery happened with an unaided eye, sometimes in antiquity, but relics like the 3,000-year-old burning glass found in Nimrod's palace by British archaeologist Sir Austen Henry Layard[1] should caution us: We should not presume that magnifying lenses to view the sky could not have been made in remote ancient times, even if we have not archaeologically retrieved them. If Nimrod's planoconvex cut and polished rock crystal is used as a light focusing lens, it magnifies objects three times their real size.

Be that as it may, Galileo must have observed Number Eight, Neptune, through one of his light concentrating telescopes, since he recorded it.[2] Whether he knew it or not, the telltale sign of a planet vis-à-vis the stars is its changing position, forwards or backwards, but sometimes still in between, as if a star: Yes, the very same retrograde planetary motion I mentioned earlier.

Only ninety years ago, on February 18, 1930, a young astronomer by the name of Clyde Tombaugh discovered an icy dwarf called Pluto and it, at last, became Planet Number Nine in our solar system. Pluto, without a doubt, would not have been detected without a telescope, for it lies beyond Neptune inside a gigantic ring around our solar system called the Kuiper Belt.

But in 2006, Pluto was kicked off "The Nine." Suddenly, it was declared too small to make the planet cut. We were back to the Sun plus eight.

In yet another feat of science, two Caltech astronomers, Konstantin Batygin and Michael E. Brown, published evidence in 2016 of a new, more refined scientific model of our solar system. It predicts that a large planet some five-thousand times more massive than Pluto yet might lurk in the darkness of even deeper space around us. If it exists, its massive presence will explain the lop-sided cluster of orbits travelled by the Sednoids. These cousins of Pluto in the Kuiper Belt encircle the Sun on elliptical paths thousands of years long.[3] In the words of K. Batygin:[4]

Although we were initially quite skeptical that this planet could exist, as we continued to investigate its orbit and what it would mean for the outer solar system, we become increasingly convinced that it is out there ... . For the first time in over 150 years, there is solid evidence that the solar-system's planetary census is incomplete ... .

And Michael Brown, referring to Uranus and Neptune, said this:[5]

This would be a real ninth planet. ... There have only been two true planets discovered since ancient times, and this would be a third. It's a pretty substantial chunk of our solar system that's still out there to be found, which is pretty exciting.

The authors propose that this Sednoid "perturber" is the long-suspected missing Planet Nine[6] in our solar system with a mass about ten times that of Earth and a long orbital axis, a whopping 700 astronomical units long, seven hundred times the distance from us to the Sun. But despite its enormous size, we cannot see it today. If Batygin and Brown are correct, it currently travels on a part of this extreme orbit which keeps it in the dark.

Based on these parameters, an orbital period of circa 20,000 years is not out of the question. If Planet Nine, the Sednoid orbit perturber, exists, it would have been visible from Earth in 10,000 BC So even though we cannot see it now, it could have been seen in the past, and will be seen again in the far distant future.

As incredible as these discoveries are, I want to make one thing clear: The biggest obstacle in putting together the heliocentric model of our solar system was neither technological, nor imaginative. The biggest obstacle in the way of discovering our current version of the truth was our self-imposed dogma of Earth centricity, and the organized effort for centuries to enforce what was false for reasons that have nothing to do with scientific exploration, but, for example, with the need to rather keep order in society than deal with the unrest some discoveries might cause. As sobering as it is to those with purely scientific motives, wide-spread comfort and other unscientific priorities, at times, may trump the unsettling truths they seek.

The correct model of nine planets orbiting a Sun in the center required the insight that the sky has depth, something you realize when the Moon shifts in front of the Sun during an eclipse, and that some lights moving on the path of the Sun and Moon within such sky space, the ecliptic, did not act like the stars. With nothing more than a 30x magnifying lens, all eight of our currently accepted planets could have been discovered, and, if Batygin and Brown are right about the Sednoid Perturber, even Planet Nine. At this point, it requires all but the imagination of someone like Aristarchus, to come up with the right idea, a Sun orbited by nine "strange stars".

Despite of what has stood in the way of mankind's inborn curiosity to learn the truth, science never stops its relentless advance into the unknown. Given the increasing speed with which we learn new things about us, our universe, and beyond, we should expect to be confronted with another revolution of thought of epic proportions—epic like our place in the universe near and far, like the relativity of space and time, and like the uncertainty of where the elements of existence dwell within us at any given moment. Will we be able to embrace such revolutionary knowledge more quickly this time, or will we fall back into the comfort zone of our familiar paradigm? Will this idea be forgotten, as if erased from memories?

Or will it be recorded and archived away to be unsealed and revisited by those long after us, a future-distant humanity who will hold it up in the proper light to recognize its value in giving us a more correct view of us and that what is around. Or will it be reinterpreted beyond recognition through the prism of the prevailing, but less correct paradigm of that future time?

This question about our future I ask about our past in *Under the Sphinx*, for this book is about questioning such an existential paradigm: our history and the origins of what we know. Did we steadily climb the ladder of civilized history on the steps of material progress for only the last five thousand years, or did we, at times, have help to lift us up when we slipped and slid down a few rungs? And if we had help to lift us up, how did that get to us?

To answer this question, we need to take a deep dive to search for the kind of paradox I mention at the beginning on this chapter. What if there was, among the vast archaeological records of ancient Egypt unearthed and catalogued over the last few centuries, relics that do not fit into their place and time? What if there exists a written document, a carved relief, a painting, a sculpture, a monumental building, or a tool— anything in all ancient Egypt—that cannot be explained from within the state of art and knowledge of the ancient Egyptians or anyone else, and before? It seems, so we are told by historians, that after centuries of Egyptological investigations, no such paradoxical things have emerged.

Sure, there are people who question how the pyramids were built, how hard stone was cut with soft tools, and how the numbers that appear here and there tell a story of scientific knowledge, not known to yet have been known. But none of these mysteries can be solved beyond a shadow of doubt without written proof, for or against, left to us by the ancient Egyptians. Nothing so clear, so unmistakably can express an idea and intention for it to be understood by others, as a written document. Yet in the known body of Egyptian writing, no scholar has thus far presented us with evidence of unusual knowledge that might confront us with a paradox of history. What we need is such as a mind-boggling problem that we truly cannot explain it from within the prevailing paradigm of the time, the time of the ancient Egyptians. Perhaps however, old evidence was never seen in the proper light.

The Odd Painting

Let us assume for a moment what some may claim is ridiculously absurd. Let us say that there were *some* ancient astronomers in Egypt who secretly knew that the Sun was at the center of their known universe and that they were on a floating body (Earth), along with eight others, orbiting this solar center. For a significant period of their history, they worshiped the Sun's manifest incarnation, which they called Re-Horakhty, a falcon who carried the Sun disk over his head. They also worshiped The Nine, also called the Ennead, a pantheon of nine gods, according to the creation of the world taught at Heliopolis.

How, then, might these ancient scholars have visualized their universe? I asked graphic designer Anthony Sturmas to create something for me to show you what this might have looked like, and he came up with this (figure 4):

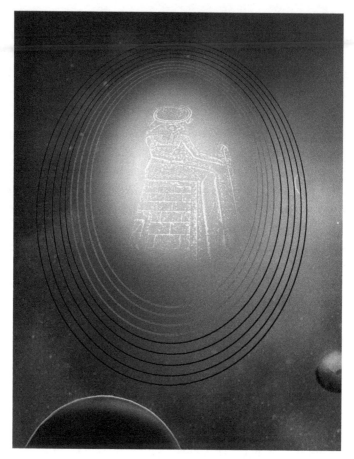

Figure 4: Illustration showing a fictitious "what-if" case of how the ancient Egyptians may have depicted the Heliocentric Solar System had they known it. The seated Sun God R^c-Horakhty surrounded by nine elliptical orbits representing the Ennead, the pantheon of gods according to the Heliopolitean Cosmogony. Red indicates the paths of the rocky planets and black that of the for gaseous ones. Graphic by Anthony Sturmas, Asturmas Studios.

Yet, here is a paradox of history that I have discovered: this idea of the Egyptian Sun God in the center surrounded by nine elliptical bands exists in the records of ancient Egypt in a painting on a little-known sarcophagus some 4,000 years old. Most Egyptologists probably have never seen or known of it, but this relic is not only unique in ancient Egypt but also very much out of place (figure 5).

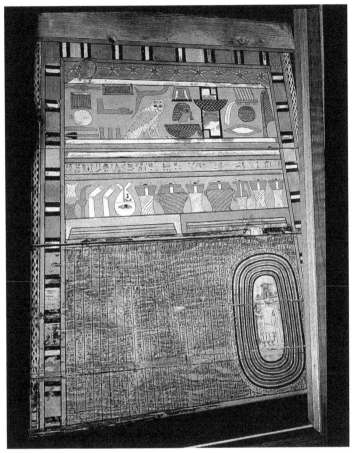

Figure 5: Decorated headboard of the interior of the sarcophagus of ***jmj-rˁ-mšˁ zpj***, General Zepi. Inserted into the right lower Coffin Text columns is the so-called Vignette of ***Rˁ***, also known as the *Roads of Mehen*. ©, Werner Forman/Universal Images Group; agefotostock® UIG 951-05-55401709.

All major discoveries begin with a good paradox, one which causes consternation even by those who would know best. The existence of this strange painting harmlessly called the Vignette of ***Rˁ*** has confounded the few scholars who know of it. They have attempted a read, but their interpretations understandably stay confined to the limits of the current paradigm of history. They cannot quite pierce the dogma, even if they may be tempted, for they risk being wrong and ridiculed, never to be taken seriously again. The paradox of a painting that appears to show the Heliocentric Solar System on a coffin, as expected, has thus remained unresolved.

Peter Robinson, the Trustee of the Canadian Society for the Study of Egyptian Antiquities (SSEA), webmaster of the *Friends of Nekhen,* and Topographical Editor of *Ancient Egypt Magazine,* for example, interestingly calls the painting a "cosmogram," but reinterprets ostensible ovals of space instead as maps of time:[7]

> *It might be reading too much into this enigmatic Cosmogram, but we might be seeing here an attempt to define a map, not of linear but temporal space, mapping time as a unit in preference to physical space.*

Björn Billson gives the following comprehensive review in his 2010 University of Birmingham Master of Philosophy Thesis under mentorship of Martin Bommas, Professor of Egyptology, archaeology, and philology, Museum Director at Macquarie University in Sydney, Australia, and Director of the Qubbet el-Hawa Research Project (QHRP) in Aswan, Egypt [emphasis added]:[8]

> ***The vignette depicts Re enthroned and surrounded by concentric circles, which the text makes clear are four roads of fire depicted in red and five black roads.*** *These roads are guarded by **nine gates** and protected by **Re** (CT VI 387a–m). A deity referred to as **Mehen** is described as both the roads themselves (CT VI 390k) and the one who sails along them in his barque (CT VI 387c–d). References to this deity are also found in CT sp. 493 and 495, both only found on B3L (CT VI 73/77). Both spells refer to the 'st3.w mḥn' (CT VI 73j/77f), translated as the "**Mysteries of Mehen**," and the implication of this phrase is **that secret knowledge existed concerning this deity**. CT sp. 759 in fact deals with the importance of knowledge of the 'roads of Mehen', with repeated assertions that **the deceased knows particular features of the roads** (CT VI 389c–d). CT sp. 758–760 have been interpreted, for the reasons mentioned above, as a part of initiation rituals which were undertaken during life (Piccione 1990:44). If this is the case, then **the texts have been transferred from one context to another**. Important to this study is that the theme of the 'roads of Mehen' is not seen elsewhere, and that **the use of the vignette is quite unusual for the Coffin Texts**. These spells were **not part of the established Coffin Texts tradition**, and even if they were not produced specifically for the individual, they are indicative of the ability of the individual **to choose unusual spells** to be placed on his or her coffin.*

He recognizes that ancient reinterpretation of texts related to the painting may have been at work and cites an inscription written around the painting which states that the ovals as roads.

A "cosmogram" that maps time on four roads of fire and five black ones, guarded by nine gates on which a mysterious god called Mehen sails who possesses secret knowledge useful in the afterlife—all this is unique in the corpus of Egyptian texts and transferred from another context involving initiation rituals? *What?* This is exactly the kind of evidence that needs a fresh look to see if a transfer of recorded and archived knowledge occurred from one civilization whose past existence can no longer be traced to another whose records exist and were written down.

My original quest to search for an archive under the Sphinx began with a question many of you would also ask about what may lie under one of the forepaws of the Great Sphinx: *What hidden knowledge might it contain?* This question would, of course, be based on Edgar Cayce's prophecy that within this fabled library was sealed the lost knowledge from Atlantis, the same 12,000-year-old legendary Atlantis about which Plato wrote. Such sealed and hidden recorded knowledge, if unsealed and rediscovered today, would truly be a much older history before our known history, which we think only began with the invention of writing in Egypt and Sumer 5,000 years ago. Remember, Cayce predicted the *Hall of Records* had *yet to be unsealed!*

However, when by happenstance I came across the Vignette of R^c and the hieroglyphic text that accompanies it both archived away at the Cairo Museum of Egyptian Antiquities, I realized I had asked the wrong question. I had assumed that the real of *Hall of Records*, if it existed, would still be sealed where it was hidden because that is what Edgar Cayce predicted. But if the ancient Egyptians did not discover the Heliocentric Solar System, and that is what we have been led to believe, then how did they come into possession of the information recorded on this painting? It would mean that contrary to his prophecy, the *Hall of Records* had long been unsealed and breached, its content taken and likely reinterpreted. And so, the better question I really had to ask was one to put Edgar Cayce to the test:

If the Vignette of R^c is in fact anachronistic to ancient Egypt, does its existence prove that a prehistoric archive also once existed, made by a civilized culture we no longer know, and was that archive under the Sphinx?

Modern archaeologists and explorers alike have tried their fortunes to prove the *Hall of Records* existed because this is where a potentially paradigm-busting revelation has long been suspected to hide: Proof of a lost civilization with whose preserved knowledge we recovered after an epic disaster on Earth. This lost civilization is what Plato called Atlantis, condemned to the depths of Earth for its immorality. Its legacy—the Soul of Atlantis, so to speak, to borrow the idea of soul cycling from Plato's *Myth of Er*—however, allegedly survived in the form of archived knowledge of a past people who vanished without a physical trace. Edgar Cayce predicted that it would reemerge from the halls beneath Earth and resurface when its time has come, when the right key is turned to unlock the door that seals it. If, or when, we learn of it, our world view will not be the same, for we, like Taylor and Nova in *The Planet of the Apes*, will realize how fleeting, how short-lived, how finite, like Atlantis, we and what we call our history are.

This is where the excitement of discovery and cultic beliefs are met with derogatory ridicule and dogmatic dismissal. Canonical scholars scoff at all those like me who believe that this is far more than a didactic myth created by Plato and popularized by Schools of Mysticism, Edgar Cayce, and what they call pseudo-historians.

But I am not one to believe without proof. I am an outsider, but I am not one to categorically scoff back at those scholars on the inside, unless I have proof. One day, when we get to look under the Sphinx, in the right place where no one has looked, we may find an archive—or something else? As so often in science, the answer may prove to be what no one expects. What I do know is that once breached, a surprise awaits us there one which may take us to a new frontier no one could have known about, not even a psychic prophet.

But I get ahead of myself. My investigations had revealed to me a paradox of history. That paradox is the Vignette of R^{ς}. It stared at me as if it had been patiently waiting for me to set it free, to resolve the paradox of its meaning, and its origin.

II

Breach

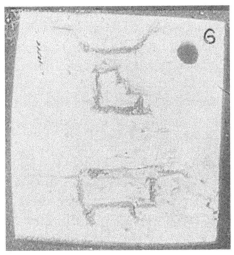

Figure 6: Ivory tag from the tomb of Horus-Djer (circa 3000-2900 BC). The three symbols from top to bottom stand for *wp*, *st*, and likely the earliest example of the word for coffer/chest/archive *ꜥfdt*. Petrie (1901), *Extra Plates*, Plate VA. [6]

ALTERNATIVE HISTORIANS ARE A LOOSELY ASSOCIATED, INTERNATIONAL GROUP of unorthodox rebel researchers who tend to be non-academics with few exceptions. Among them are independent scholars, investigators, authors, and adventurers who believe that cultural and technical evolution has not been a straight ascent up the ladder of history. They believe that civilizations have risen and catastrophically fallen without leaving a trace of their wiped-out existence archaeologists have been able to find, except— and this is a key element in their theories—that some of what these lost civilizations knew must have survived. It is this relic, esoteric, and high knowledge, according to alternative historians, that may explain the gaps left by the dominant narrative of how primitive prehistoric humans in the wild became the civilized people about whom history is taught and told.

Anyone who espouses such unorthodox views is nowadays labeled as a believer of the banner themes associated with this group and thus becomes a member, willingly or not. They are further lumped together with others from groups who believe in aliens or a flat Earth, for example. All these people, the rebels, the heretics, the lunatics, and the independent, non-academic researchers are dismissed wholesale with disdain by some university-based, academic historians and archaeologists, and their prolific proxies. Alternative historians have thus come into the unwanted and undeserved possession of labels such as pseudo-archaeologists, pseudo-scientists, fringe authors, and even racists to dissuade the knowledge-seeking public at large from reading their publications in an act of academia-sanctioned demagoguery. The study of history cannot be easily separated from ideological and moral thinking and be only focused using the scientific method. That's the problem. The irony is, history, if real or invented, has long been used to teach us morals and subject us to dogmas.

The idea of a fallen civilization that only left a non-material trace of its high culture know-how and knowledge, sending the stumbling human cause back up the ladder of history, is captured by one of the chief banner themes associated with alternative historians: Atlantis, the mythical, lost island described by Plato who allegedly merely invented it as a morally decaying counterpart to the virtuous city state of Athens.

Merge these themes, an American psychic predicting a secret library in Egypt containing written records of advanced knowledge hidden there by people from a mythical island invented by Plato, and you may get a feel for why independent researchers of history are fighting an uphill battle against the officially organized outlets of historical narratives that stake a claim to sanity against lunacy.

It seems to me that what is billed as this fight by reason against irrational belief, however, is a turf war for who controls the popular narrative that explains anthropological and archaeological discoveries. This is not always about finding out what really happened. Sprinkle on it a dose of moral indignation and the battle of the narratives becomes a war for the power of moral dogma held over heresy. This is when the scientific pursuit of things gets caught up in normative thinking, what should be instead of what is and was.

Remember though: In science, no model, however improbable, is invalid until it is proven impossible. Let's then ignore the noise and talk science and evidence.

The Mystery of the Void

Most alternative historians believe that a void exists under the Great Sphinx. It would be relatively easy to confirm or falsify this proposal with a drilling experiment if you could get a permit from the Egyptian authorities and probed the right place. Yes, there have been drillings in various spots around the Sphinx and her temple, but not where the most promising location is based on prior non-invasive probes.

Most alternative historians also believe that the void contains an archive that stores records of an unusually advanced, prehistoric civilization whose other material remnants have thus far evaded archaeological discovery.

And most alternative historians would probably base these beliefs on the most famous theory of such esoteric knowledge left by a lost civilization—of course, I speak of Edgar Cayce's prophecy of the *Hall of Records*. He foretold that this library lies hidden in bowels of the cave-riddled Earth somewhere under Giza, Egypt, and the entry to it would be somewhere under the Great Sphinx. This still-sealed archive is where the lost civilization of Atlantis allegedly left its legacy for a new civilization to unearth it and resurrect the spirit of Atlantis to seed a new age of civilization.[11]

At about the same time as Cayce began to mention the *Hall of Records* in the 1930s, the same theme of a lost archive of ancient knowledge was also championed by Harvey Spencer Lewis, the founder of the Ancient Mystical Order Rosae Crucis. In contrast to Cayce, who knew of these things psychically, the A.M.O.R.C. claimed its knowledge came to it from ancient Egypt.

Regardless, it is Cayce who caused the *Hall of Records* to become widely popular through his foundation's outreach. Ask anyone today if they have heard of the *Hall of Records*, and, if they have, they will probably bring up Edgar Cayce.

Not surprisingly, this legend has long become a quintessential banner theme of the Alternative History camp, which also commonly identifies it with the Edgar Cayce brand. This unfortunately has severed this archive from its potentially historic connection and tainted any serious effort to investigate if it really existed. Looking for the real *Hall of Records*, in the eyes of serious scholars of history and Egyptology, is like looking for the Holy Grail, the Ark of the Covenant, or El Dorado: It's madness and baseless lunacy.

But no matter what the experts say, the undeniable, hard fact remains: There is a seismically measured void under the Sphinx. Could there be a library inside as Edgar Cayce and Spencer Lewis insisted? Let's look at it logically.

To prove this claim, three what ifs need to be considered:

- *if* the void is still sealed,
- *if* whatever was in it has not decayed,
- and *if* whatever can be recovered is knowledge incompatible with what the ancient Egyptians knew.

The biggest *if* of these three is the first. If the void was breached at any time after it was originally sealed, then whatever was in it may no longer be there and lost forever. However, there is a silver lining. If the archive was breached in this hypothetical scenario, the knowledge contained within would most likely be found in traces, in written records of unquestionably esoteric and anachronistic knowledge, but also possibly adapted and modified knowledge in the records of ancient Egypt that were reinterpreted and absorbed by the prevailing paradigm.

If such records existed, they had to have come from somewhere and sometime else. If found, they could lead us back to whence they came.

Traces of Knowledge

To put it in simpler terms let's say that whatever was in that void was taken to a secure place to preserve it. There it may have left its esoteric footprints on the culture and science of the people alive at the time of the breach, in this case, the ancient Egyptians.

But why have such footprints not been found? Is that because the hypothetical scenario is baseless, or is it because these traces are there, but we have missed them? What if we have ignored the evidence because it presents the paradox I noted in the previous chapter? Like us, could this be what the ancient Egyptians may have done with information foreign to their own belief system and knowledge base? Remember what we sometimes do with paradoxical information not compatible with our own beliefs and knowledge base? The ancient Egyptians may have done the same. But what if instead of bending any anomaly into a predetermined shape and adapt it to what we believe to be true, what if we—what if *I*—looked at it in a different light?

A presumptive breach of the presumptive archive, I decided, may be a blessing in disguise, depending on who opened it and when. If we cannot look inside the archive to prove it contained esoteric knowledge of a lost civilization, we may instead be able to recover such lost knowledge taken away after a breach and trace it back to that place. The logic of the investigation is thus reversed.

While we wait for Egypt to permit another drilling under the Great Sphinx, we can hunt for lost knowledge strange enough to stare at us from above the massive stack of ancient Egyptian records, unearthed by archaeologists to date. If we find it, we can confirm a breach occurred. Then, we look for the written trace to walk us back to its origin, the elusive archive under the Sphinx.

Myth as Scientific Fact

Today, we view myths as fairy tales. But ancient stories are not free inventions creatively dreamed up by ancient authors with no real-life reflections. Ancient Egyptian mythical texts often contain colorfully expressed scientific observations. Dismissing this is as fiction is largely based on a grave misunderstanding of what the gods about whom these texts were written were to the ancient Egyptians: the actual forces of nature. As James Peter Allen explains:[12]

Egyptian gods and goddesses are nothing more or less than the elements and forces of the universe. The gods did not just "control" these phenomena, like the Greek god Zeus with his lightning bolts: they were the elements and forces of the world. We recognize this quality by saying that the Egyptian gods are "immanent" in the phenomena of nature.

In other words, there is a real, physical, material, and scientific aspect to the content of ancient writing about the gods. Unless one understands this concept, it is easy to dismiss myth as fiction, when it is rather a more imaginative way to describe reality than how we do it, having separated the sciences from religious themes.

That Egyptian religious texts have a real, material basis is well demonstrated in the Pyramid Texts, which first appeared in the Old Kingdom. In them, vivid mythical metaphors describe the motions of the Sun, Moon, and stars cast into a world of sky gods and goddesses navigating heaven's waterways by day and night.

Another example from the New Kingdom speaks of Thoth's hieroglyphic legacy kept under the feet of the god *R*ꜥ-Harmakhis. In this passage of the *Hymn to Shu* from the magical papyrus of Harris, you can recognize the idea of a *Hall of Records* under the Great Sphinx:[13]

A will hath been done into writing by the lord of Khemenu (Thoth), the scribe of the library of Ra-Harmakhis, in the hall of the divine house (or temple) of Anu (Heliopolis), stablished, perfected, and made permanent in hieroglyphs under the feet of Ra-Harmakhis, and he shall transmit it to the son of his for ever and ever.

Automatically, we may be inclined to write such texts off as myth and fictional storytelling. However, when we also read the excavation notes of Egypt's first Director of Antiquities, Auguste Mariette, describing a chamber[14] he observed at the bottom of the major fissure which splits the Great Sphinx ("... *se termine par une chamber*"),[15] we begin to get a taste of how this story could be based on a physical reality, not far away from Heliopolis across the Nile on the Giza Plateau.

Histories of travel and exploration accounts reporting voids, chambers, and corridors in and around the Great Sphinx over the last three centuries has been covered in detail by Robert Bauval[16] and Robert and Olivia Temple.[17] Suffice it here to say, these accounts validate the so-called myths of the ancient Egyptians hinting at secret, subterranean places where written records of a divine character were kept. Not just any places I should like to point out: We are being led directly to the Great Sphinx by the ancient Egyptians themselves.

Reading the Great Sphinx

*R*ꜥ-Harmakhis was the Greek name for none other than Horus-in-the Horizon, Hor-em-akhet,[18] one of the two names given to the Great Sphinx on the Dream Stele placed between its paws by Thutmose IV. The other name given to the Great Sphinx was Horakhty, later also R^c-Horakhty, proposed by Robert Bauval to be the celestial Sphinx appearing as the constellation Leo and depicted as a west-facing second statue on the Dream Stele.[19] An interesting correlate to this proposal by Bauval is an account by the historian Sarem Ibn Duqmaq (1349-1407) describing a granite-made, east-facing, second Sphinx across the Nile in a line of sight with the Great Sphinx. This statue was destroyed in 1311, and large blocks of stone found beneath it were allegedly used as column bases in the Nasiri Mosque in Cairo.[20]

Texts and physical reality on the ground begin to align. We have an ancient Egyptian text speaking of a will by Thoth written in hieroglyphic, hidden in the *Hall of the Divine House* at Heliopolis under the feet of what can only have been the Great Sphinx—or a similar statue once, or still, residing under Heliopolis. Two other, fairytale-like narrations also make more sense now: The first is a short note by the Roman historian Pliny the Elder about the Great Sphinx:[21]

In front of these pyramids is the Sphinx, a still more wondrous object of art, but one upon which silence has been observed, as it is looked upon as a divinity by the people of the neighborhood. It is their belief that King Harmaïs was buried in it.

The second is an account cited by the Arab historian Al-Maqrizi about two brothers of the biblical tribe Misr, Atrib and Ashmun. When Atrib dies, Ashmun buries him on an island. Demons, however, carry the body where now stands the Sphinx, Abu Al-Hol.

The synthesis of all four written records, seemingly unrelated at first, sums up to an underground chamber beneath the feet of a statue of Horus in the Horizon, a.k.a. the Great Sphinx, containing a written will by Thoth and a tomb of a king.[22]

Thanks to Edgar Cayce's persona and life, we are already in hot pursuit of the *Hall of Records* near the Great Sphinx, where it is said to be hidden. However, we do not need a modern prophet to inform us about an idea explicitly mentioned in writing at least as far back as the New Kingdom of Egypt, more than three thousand years earlier. The legend of the *Hall of Records* under the Sphinx storing records by Thoth came to us first and foremost from the writings of the ancient Egyptians themselves, not the Persians, not the Greeks, not the Romans, not the Arabs, and not modern era archaeologist,[23] historians, storytellers, or psychics.

The foregoing example of rereading historical texts in a new light also illustrates the task at hand. The grains of truth from various texts must be assembled, dots must be connected, and corroborated with physical evidence on the ground. Only then will it be possible to find the real *Hall of Records* and its esoteric content.

It is important to note here that, because of what these ancient Egyptians' records say about an archive under the Sphinx, I am detaching completely from the Cayce readings, their association with it, and the *Hall of Records*.

The Language of Astronomy

An example of a quest to locate the contents of a real *Hall of Records* at Giza is the theory proposed by Graham Hancock and Robert Bauval in 1996[24] that the lost knowledge inherited by the ancient Egyptians from a prior civilization was astronomical in nature. The authors begin their argument by pointing out a paradox: The Great Sphinx faces due east towards the equinoctial sunrise position on the horizon, but during the Pyramid Age the constellation Leo, Horakhty in their reconstruction, emerged from beneath the morning horizon on the point of the summer solstice. That is a three month shift away from due east.

When one realigns Leo with the Sphinx by turning back astronomical time, a match occurs around 10,500 BC. This match is further corroborated by the alignment of the three Giza pyramids with the orientation vis-à-vis the meridian of the belt stars of the constellation Orion, and the fact that this constellation then reaches its lowest point above the horizon during a full precession cycle. Temple inscriptions complete the picture painted by the physical and astronomical evidence, because they mention the First Time during the dominion of Osiris, Orion in the sky.

Here again, the myth matches what we see on the ground. The paradox prompts us to consider that the ancient Egyptians of the Pyramid Age knew about the phenomenon of precession—the change in the orientation of the rotational axis of a rotating body. It's what a gyroscope creates—both sideways along and up-and-down below the ecliptic. The authors conclude that the *Hall of Records* under the Sphinx is the physical counterpart to the sun beneath the horizon at dawn, with Leo just above. The knowledge it contains may be numerical in nature and relate to precession.

Knowing it serves the initiate on his or her way to Osiris, represented by the Giza pyramid field itself. The authors draw a parallel between the *Book of Two Ways* and the two roads to Rostau commonly attributed to it. One, they propose, led through the causeway that ascends past the Great Sphinx up to the Pyramid Temple in front of the Pyramid of Khafre. The other travelled through passages under the Great Sphinx and towards the Great Pyramid, where resurrection is consummated in the physical unification with Osiris.[25]

With esoteric knowledge of precession at hand, Egyptian priests and architects were also able to compute vaster cycles of time than the Egyptian civil year of 365 days, or the Sothic cycle of 1,460 Egyptian years. To commemorate precession, the three Giza pyramids were added to the much older Great Sphinx to create a megalithic map. The map unlocks by aligning it with the corresponding sky map of starry constellations. The pyramids were built, so to speak, like a crooked painting relative to the orientation of the belt stars of Orion in 10,500 BC.

Computing the number of years to align pyramids and stars amounts to rebalancing the painting. This alignment produced the time passed since the first mythical kingdom of Egypt ruled by Osiris, the so-called First Time, Zep Tepi. With certain numbers only to be revealed to the resurrecting Horus king, he became "equipped" to perform this computation of the time since the First Time, Zep Tepi, and by having observed the prevailing astronomical conditions of his era.[26]

All this information, according to the theory presented in *The Message of the Sphinx*, was stored in the *Hall of Records* under the monument and is architecturally embedded as a numerical code in the many dimensions of the Great Pyramid.

What I find compelling about this theory is that the lay-out and architecture of the Giza monuments could indeed reflect the astronomical theme of precession, suggesting there was a master plan. The Great Sphinx is like the hand on the celestial dial. Leo on the horizon marks the top of the hour. The pyramids' orientation and alignment with Orion's belt stars symbolizes the message we are to be told: There is something about the First Time that should matter to us. It begs the question: why precession is important, then and now, and what was important about Zep Tepi? Are we to learn something new from this or do something differently about how we mark time or space? What is the message of the Sphinx? The past, the future, or both?

Precession and Climate Change

One way to look at this is climate change. Earth's axial precession is one of three major factors besides Earth's axial tilt and the eccentricity of Earth's orbit in determining how much sunlight the northern Artic ice cap receives during the northern summer. This matters because ice formation on land is a self-reinforcing cycle. Land's heat capacity is lower than that of water. On land ice forms more easily. When ice forms it tends to cool the globe, including and the polar regions. This causes even more cooling because sunlight is reflected away from Earth. Only a prolonged and intense period of sun warming will cause the northern ice cap to reverse this runaway cooling cycle. Earth likes to be icy, but when enough northern ice melts, the whole globe enters a prolonged warm period. The vicious northern ice cycle is temporarily broken.

These conditions occur when the Earth's land ice-heavy northern hemisphere is maximally leaning towards the Sun at the same time Earth also happens to be at its shortest orbital distance from it at perihelion (the point in orbit when a celestial body is closest to the Sun). In other words, precession is the smallest wheel in a gigantic three-wheel clockwork that determines our long-term climate on Earth. Is it possible that prehistoric people wanted to alert posterity that such a climate super-cycle exists? Was the First Time that time when Earth was finally able to escape the perma-frost of the last Ice Age? These changes would be slow and thus difficult to observe by one generation.

While the cyclical climate cycle discovered by astronomer Milutin Milanković can predictably explain Earth's climate over multiples of thousands of years, other factors sprinkle a dose of chaos on this order, though they, too, are run by hidden clockworks. These catastrophic events include earthquakes of Earth's sliding tectonic plates, eruptions of super volcanoes, and extraterrestrial bombardment with rocks and radiation. Did prehistoric people witness such catastrophes during the First Time and send us a warning in the form of a count-down to the next time? These changes would be fast.

Whichever pretext for prehistoric monuments we invoke, celestial order or celestial chaos, the moral of the Atlantis story, whether fact or fiction, is a story about moral decay and catastrophic demise. It is a message from the past to the future, woven into a fabulous story from which we can learn, if we choose. For one thing is certain: Earth is constantly changing and so is life on Earth. To not stay nimble in the face of a proven, violent past is living in a bubble to stay comfortable, but it will not keep us safe.

Yet, we are anything but nimble. The mainstream model of history ignores the possibility of cyclical civilizations because there is no physical evidence for it in the archaeological records, it is claimed. The archaeological record is a layered-cake mountain of material culture whose sequence has been interpreted as a one-way street from sticks and stones to cranes and steel and continues through mountains of plastic waste and pollution to virtual reality, quantum computing, and artificial intelligence. It is thus inconceivable within this paradigm that there could have been prehistoric people who knew more than their descendants. But what if that prehistoric layer in that cake got wiped without a trace? Would there be any other way to prove it?

Dating the Decay of Stone

This is where megalithic evidence comes into play. Stone cannot be unequivocally dated, and stone decay needs a good standard for comparison. The methods used to build stony monuments are often difficult to reconstruct. In the case of the Giza monuments, even if one agrees that they were substantially built when Egyptologists tell us, we are still left arguing about the ideas behind the undertaking. Were these ideas of the same time or a time more ancient? And why on Earth would there be such a vast effort to see them come to life?

To critics of the conventional paradigm such as John Anthony West, Robert Schoch, Graham Hancock, and Robert Bauval, the answer may be summed as this: It is the deeply held human desire to preserve one's legacy and not be forgotten. Next to being fruitful and multiplying, this type of legacy drives us, as it evidently drove ancient people, to do things which are incredible, then and now.

Egyptologists, however, have pushed back against all the major elements of this theory,[27] including the idea of a masterplan and the authors mentioned have published their rebuttals.[28] In an interview with Kmt Magazine in 1997, for example, Zahi Hawass was asked about a room found under the Sphinx reported by Graham Hancock and Robert Bauval.[29] He flat-out denied anything of this sort. He cited scientific tests that refuted any notion of a *Hall of Records* and alleged that Hancock and Bauval were following in the footsteps of Edgar Cayce's ideas. I only paraphrase the essence of Hawass' comments here, because neither Kmt's editor Dennis Forbes, nor Zahi Hawass, responded to my asking for their permissions to quote the interview verbatim.

The statements made by Hawass to Kmt are factually contradicted by the findings of a Japanese research team from Waseda University in the late 1980s and of Thomas Dobecki and Robert Schoch in 1991. Nevertheless, my purpose is not to weigh the evidence for and against, but to highlight the fact that Egyptian texts and architecture still allow room, and not implausibly so, for the idea that esoteric knowledge came into Egypt from a time before ancient Egypt existed as a unified kingdom and even before prehistoric nomads settled in the Nile Valley. This evidence will not be properly examined by unbiased researchers if it gets tossed into a bucket together with the pyramid and Sphinx lore of classical antiquity and modern times, usually dismissed as pseudo-history.

Unfortunately, this is exactly the treatment it has received. But when viewed without such bias, these records tell a completely different story than the biased narrative will have us believe. What I will show you is visible, clear and unshakable proof of inexplicable knowledge possessed by the ancient Egyptians. In the face of these records, it rather is this presumptive narrative that is no longer defensible.

To entertain the idea that esoteric, prehistoric knowledge was kept in a *Hall of Records* guarded by a couchant megalithic statue resembling a lion, physical evidence was needed. It came in April of 1991 when Thomas Dobecki and Robert Schoch measured the extent of subsurface weathering of the ground around the Great Sphinx. During this experiment, they discovered several voids. One of them, Anomaly A in Dobecki and Schoch's designation (figure 7), is under the left paw of the Great Sphinx. It appears to be bound by artificial borders.[30] The void's ostensibly rectangular dimensions are estimated to be nine by twelve meters long, at an approximate depth of five meters below the surface of the Sphinx ditch.

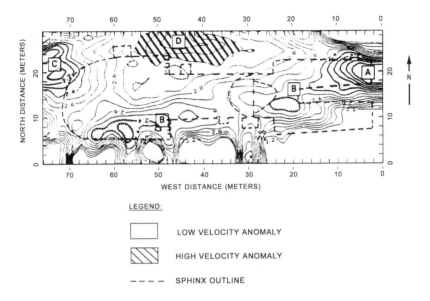

Figure 7: Seismic map showing areas of low activity possibly reflecting subsurface voids. Anomaly A is under and east of the left forepaw of the Great Sphinx. ©, Robert M. Schoch.

The data collected by Dobecki and Schoch also quantitatively corroborated the qualitative assessment of the degree and cause of erosion on the enclosure wall of the Great Sphinx by rain and rainwater runoff. They pointed to a much older age than the Old Kingdom.[31] This was a bona fide scientific investigation, yet it was treated as if the data had been procured in a psychic reading.

Ask Robert Schoch today, and he will tell you that he feels comfortable with dating the original carving of the monument to the eleventh to tenth millennium BC. This conclusion harmonizes well with the astronomical argument made by Bauval and Hancock that the Giza monuments are a massive shrine dedicated to winding back the precessional clock to the First Time when the people lived who knew about precession and archived this knowledge under the Sphinx. Mark Lehner and Zahi Hawass' rebuttal is well summarized in their most recent collaboration[32] and Robert Schoch's comprehensive response to their rebuttal was published in 2017.[33]

Not surprisingly, the debate over the age of the Sphinx and who built it is not new. George Reisner believed he clinched the truth in 1912, when he found an alabaster bust of Menkaure and noticed how it showed the king

31

wearing a triple-pleated headdress (the so-called nemes), exactly like that worn by the Great Sphinx. *Cosmopolitan* announced:[34]

> *Professor Reisner has found in the desert sands the clue to the Sphinx's mystery, and the traveler can now say to the watcher by the Nile, I know you.*

But do we really know you, Mr. or Mrs. Sphinx? The next major battle over the age of the Sphinx began in 1993, when John Anthony West and Robert Schoch were featured on prime time American television hosted by Charlton Heston, the very same who played Taylor in *Planet of the Apes*.[35] The documentary laid out the case for an older Sphinx to a wide audience of over thirty million viewers, many of whom are still alive today. They have lingering doubts about when the Great Sphinx was really built, by whom, and why.

At this point, it might appear obvious what the next step would have to be to solve the impasse between the orthodox position held by Egyptologists and the unconventional position held by alternative historians: Probe the void defined by seismic Anomaly A. Alas after almost thirty years and more than a dozen drillings around the Sphinx ditch and temple by various parties, the most promising place found by Waseda University and Dobecki and Schoch has not been probed. It appears as if this spot is to be avoided, as if it is cursed. The last known drill in 2009, just north of the left forepaw of the Great Sphinx, may have missed the westmost extension of Anomaly A by a couple of meters.[36]

The Importance of Provenance

This beating around the bush, avoiding the eight-hundred-pound gorilla in the room—or is it walking on eggshells? —pushes us back to the main purpose of this book. In order to make the case for a scientific probe of Anomaly A, the "Dobecki-Schoch Chamber" (figure 7), more compelling, whatever evidence amassed to date is obviously not enough for the authorities to act, if they would only be willing to extend such a permit once more. What is needed to raise the stakes? The crown jewel of Egyptological evidence: written evidence in the language of the ancient Egyptians. This may seem like a daunting task; however, there is one shred of hope. The texts discovered and translated over the last two centuries were not viewed considering the possibility of lost esoteric knowledge, passed forward to the ancient Egyptians by a lost civilization. Remember, narrow-minded paradigms create comfort zones within which paradoxes become conveniently brushed over and dismissed.

But let us live out an explorer's dream for a moment. Let us assume Egypt's Ministry of Antiquities were to permit a decisive drilling experiment in the right spot to probe Anomaly A. What are we likely to find inside? For starters: sewage water. As far back as 1979, on July 7 and 11 of that year, Mark Lehner probed the subsurface of the Sphinx ditch, where it is cracked open by the so-called Major Fissure.[37] At a depth of 4.5 meters, he found ground water indicating that the Sphinx and its enclosure were a floating island. Add to that water the ever more encroaching limits of Cairo's suburbs closing in on the Giza Plateau and the sewage to go with that expansion of the city. It likely seeps into the ground by the tons every day. This means that Anomaly A, if indeed it is a man-made chamber under the Sphinx, has been flooded to the ceiling with a toxic sludge for decades, if not centuries. If there ever was an archive in it, anything written remaining of a perishable nature like papyrus, clay, wood, or even limestone would likely be destroyed by now, unless the water level has been steady without repeated drying and wetting cycles of any such relics.[38] There may be some bad news here for all those who expect a movie moment when that void gets finally probed.

Nevertheless, there is a much more exciting possibility in disguise. First, one especially important reason why this probe is still necessary is to confirm that Anomaly A is an artificial void such as a human-made chamber. This, in and of itself, would compel us to reconsider when and why the monument above it was created. A well-designed drilling experiment will put this interpretation of the seismic data collected by Dobecki and Schoch, corroborated by textual evidence I will present in this book, to a decisive test. We may not find remnants of records inside Anomaly A, but this is also where the good news begins as my investigation intends to demonstrate. The textual traces I have examined suggest that these records were taken away to a safer place a long time ago, after the archive was breached. In fact, had they not, they may have been destroyed inside such archival vault under the Sphinx, without a chance for them to ever be recovered.

In a recent interview, I was asked if I believed that Dr. Zahi Hawass, the former Minster of Antiquities in Egypt, might have already entered the *Hall of Records*. The rumor that the chambers, corridors, and hallways under the Sphinx have been breached is as old as the idea of chambers, corridors, and hallways under the Sphinx itself. However, the textual, symbolic, and artistic evidence left to us by the ancient Egyptians hints that an archive of significance was opened not in modern times, or in the middle ages, or in antiquity, and not even during pharaonic Egyptian times, but as early as the very beginning of dynastic Egypt five thousand years ago, and probably even earlier than that.

Such an event of high significance was recorded during or before the life of Horus-Djer on an ivory label (figure 6). The symbols read *wp st ꞽfdt*, "Opening of the Place of the Chest." The word for chest here, as I will show, specifically refers to a portable coffer, an ark(hive) if you will, in which written records were kept. The event of opening a chamber, chest, or cave containing a chest of written documents sometime during the First Dynasty of ancient Egypt was of such significance that the scribes felt compelled to preserve the essence of this memory. It can be found in various versions recounted as part of funerary and medical documents, e.g., Papyrus Turin and Papyrus Ebers, written a millennium and a half later.[39]

The Vignette of Rꜥ

Egyptian texts initially led me on two parallel paths of investigation. One, in pursuit of an archive breached, and the other, on the textual trail of a monument guarding an archive. Both were centuries older than the Old Kingdom, when Egyptologists tell us the Great Sphinx was created. These two investigative paths began to converge when I found the Vignette of *Rꜥ*. Its uniqueness and strangeness made me wonder if there might not be a connection with the archival breach in the recorded distant memories of ancient Egypt on the one hand, and a prehistoric monumental lioness associated with writing and archiving. In the Vignette of *Rꜥ*, I had found a possible paradox of history whose solution would lead me to consider that a prehistoric archive left by an unknown culture once existed under what became the Great Sphinx. I had found a candidate for a real, the thus far elusive, *Hall of Records*.

With the Vignette of *Rꜥ*, the emergence of esoteric, anachronistic knowledge in the written records of dynastic Egypt suggests that an earlier, prehistoric culture with advanced scientific knowledge must have existed, and the ancient Egyptians came into possession of it.

My mission in this book is to show that this knowledge was stored in a portable archive originally housed in a chamber under Mehit, a prehistoric stony lioness at Giza that would eventually become the Great Sphinx. This portable archive later ended up in a library called the *House of Life* in the city of Thoth at Hermopolis magna in Middle Egypt. Be it fate or serendipity, without this journey from a secret royal library to an archive of mysticism and funerary rites opened to a select few of the non-royal elite, we may have never learned that such esoteric knowledge existed. If the *Hall of Records* were still sealed and intact, its content could not possibly have leaked into the culture and science of the ancient Egyptians, an idea a relic like the Vignette of R^c and the Roads of Mehen written around it seemed to contradict. I knew I had to leave the prophecy of Edgar Cayce behind, for I was now on my own in a pursuit of something completely unknown and unpredicted.

What I want to show you are the details of this investigation of the hieroglyphic evidence for what once was under the Sphinx, and how that confronts us with a paradox of history. It is only this written kind of evidence—revealing the intent, beliefs, thoughts, and ideas of this fascinating civilization—that will force critics, sceptics, and cynics alike to not be able to casually dismiss the findings. With written evidence, they will not be able to explain it away as the mutterings of a psychic or the creation of fiction tellers, or what they call pseudo-historians.

The path on which I take you now is a step-by-step detective story of what I discovered and how I did it so that you can see what I saw, learn what I learned, weigh the evidence for yourself, and then draw your own conclusions: We must first step into the den of the old lioness. We must learn to read between her symbols. Equipped with this hieroglyphic magic, I will introduce you to the context you need to interpret the mysterious Vignette of R^c. This will take us to the city of Thoth in Middle Egypt, where the elite had their coffins decorated with spells from the *House of Life* to help them on the path to immortality in the afterlife. I will show you the evidence which proves that this illustration was meant to show the Heliocentric Solar System and from where this esoteric knowledge came to Hermopolis. We will trace the portable archive containing the arcane records of Thoth back to its original place under the Great Sphinx, and then to, ultimately, under a stony lioness called Mehit from whom she was remodeled. I will show you that this original lioness was built by an unknown prehistoric civilization predating the ancient Egyptians.

Ultimately, this "history before history," peopled by a civilization we know nothing of, I believe may have seeded the "new" civilization of ancient Egypt with the spark of higher knowledge of the sky and symbolic writing imitating the ultimate act of creation.

III

Heka

" ... *for to me belonged all before you had come into being, you gods; go down and come upon the hinder parts, for I am a magician.*"

—FAULKNER, R.O. "COFFIN TEXTS SPELL 261," 1973.

W E STRUGGLE TO DEFINE GOD, THE SINGULARITY OF OUR UNIVERSE, AT ITS instance of creation, before who or which nothing else supposedly existed. To the ancient Egyptians, the most primordial power of nature, nature at its origin, that what was in the very beginning was Heka. But what is Heka? The best way to sum up what this power entailed is the company it kept: Perception and Idea. From these came the purest form of divine action, the spoken word of creation.

To understand how ancient scribes captured in writing that which could not easily be described that which could not easily be shared, and that which could not easily be used in vain, I must introduce you to the Egyptian art of phonetic mimicry and insinuation. Without it, you cannot see the deeper layer of the texts, the realm of hieroglyphic where the secrets lie, the semantic layer intentionally invoked to reinterpret that which could not be fully understood nor expressed conventionally because it was sacred, because it came from another time and place.

The best way to explain how Heka worked is to practice it with a few examples.

Hidden away in one of the many display cases of the Cairo Museum is a piece of wood carrying some of the oldest known written records of the ancient Egyptians (figure 8).

Figure 8: Ebony wooden tablet from the reign of Horus-Aha showing the *jmjwt* symbol. The Museum of Egyptian Antiquities, Cairo, Egypt, 2018.

This was found by famous British surveyor and archaeologist extraordinaire Sir William Matthew Flinders Petrie in the five-thousand-year-old tomb of Horus-Aha, the likely real person behind the mythical Menes.

Horus-Aha was Egypt's first king after unification following the conquest of the northern Delta region by Narmer. The central scene on this broken piece of a bigger tablet has been interpreted as a human sacrifice. But that explanation does not consider what is on the right: a pole wrapped with a feline skin. This is the symbol for the word *jmjwt* [i-my-oot]. On this commemorative tablet, this all-important hieroglyph is being coined and inaugurated.

While I cannot be completely certain that *jmjwt* is a certified act of phonetic mimicry to conceal a single word, or rather two words in this case, I will let you make that determination.

The Phonetics of Heka Magic

The evidence for my argument—that a prehistoric people understood, wrote about, then buried their knowledge of the heliocentric universe—lies in the form of texts written in the language of the ancient Egyptians, called *mdw nṯr* [medoo-neter].

There are a few basic tenets of hieroglyphic you need to know to stand on your own feet and appraise the evidence I present.

In the Appendix, I introduce *mdw nṯr* for those interested, but there is only one feature of the language to remember here: Its symbols were largely read phonetically, not pictorially. As easy as this *sounds*, it is exactly the hypnotic, *visual* effect of the hieroglyphic symbols that confused scholars from antiquity, through the Middle Ages and into the nineteenth century. They tried to make sense of the images staring back at them instead of hearing the once-spoken words they spelled.

It turns out that as bedazzling as hieroglyphic is, it is really a phonetic script. A phonetic script needs fewer symbols to express more ideas because they do not all need to be displayed as distinct and unique images. The sound of the words which express them can be spelled out with a small set of sound symbols, an alphabet, if you will.

That's simple enough. But with phonetics came a fascinating feature: the ability to insinuate or invoke one word that sounded like another. In a nutshell, this was Heka magic.

Heka was a ritualistically, hence magical, method to say a sacredly held taboo word and bring its meaning to life without casually uttering it in vain. To do that, such a word, person, ritual item, or name of a god, or goddess, for example, would be embedded in another ordinary, even mundane word, or sometimes a string of words, to conceal it to all those not initiated in this formulaic way to speak.

Here is an example in English—if I say the words "the arc I've drawn," you may imagine me drawing an arc. However, the word phonetically hiding within "arc I've" is *arch-ive*. By uttering, or ritually invoking, "the arc I've drawn," I am *activating* the idea of an archive in the minds of all those who know what I am doing without uttering the word in a way that its meaning might be revealed.

In ancient Egyptian religious tomb texts, to *be equipped* meant knowing how to activate certain words in the right circumstances with magical spells. This skill was believed to be indispensable to face the challenges of the journey through the afterlife to reach resurrection and immortality.

The art of producing these disguised, phonetic gateways to other intended meanings must have been a full-time occupation because there was an entire guild of high priests devoted to it. These priests were the shaman *sm* [sem] and the ceremonial *ḥrj ḥb* [hery heb]. As Robert Schoch and I have shown based on initial insights by Wolfgang Helck, the *sm* is phonetically activated in the Mouth Opening Ceremony of the Pyramid Texts with the phrase *jsmn.j n.k ꜥrtj.k* [ay-se-me-ny en-ek aah-re-tik], "I have fixed your jaws."[40]

Activating the shaman priest is the first verbal action in the invocation of an archaic, probably prehistoric, ritual. First, a wooden or ivory figurine was prepared to represent a deceased person. Then, it was animated with the dead person's shadow, ritually captured from the netherworld by the *sm* shaman in a self-induced trance and symbolically imbued into this figurine. From this ritual, it would have been a small, easy step to place a written scroll of shadow-like outlines, symbols in other words, inside the statuette, or under a statue to create this animation.

All the verbal components of the Statuette Making Ritual are phonetically hiding in the text of the Mouth Opening Ceremony, as initially suggested by Wolfgang Helck.[41] The first known instance of this famous passage of the Pyramid Texts is inscribed into the north wall of the sarcophagus chamber of King Unas' pyramid. The concealment of one message within another greatly complicates the proof that it was done with intent. Only when you have a series of phonetically concealed words line up to into a coherent story, such as is the case for the Statuette Making Ritual, such proof can be obtained. However, when it comes to individual words, the task is more difficult unless the scribe spells out the word to be concealed nearby in an act of brazen boastfulness, knowing all too well that only the initiate would catch the pun regardless.

Writing Within Writing

The act of inventing a word and then stamping it onto a royal inscription was the way scribes in this early phase of writing marked a certain year. And this leads me back to the piece of wood with which I opened this chapter.

Instead of counting the years like we do, Egyptian "historians" identified them with significant and memorable events. In this case, you could say it was "the reign of Horus-Aha in the year of the sacrifice of so and so, during which the *jmj-wt* symbol was coined.

The hieroglyph *jmj-wt* is a contraction of two words, which literally translate as "that which is in the bandage," for example, written with the owl symbol, is the Egyptian word for English "in" or "from." This type of word, which describes location, is grammatically classified as a preposition. *jm* is a word derived from *m* which means "inside" in English. *jmj* is a preposition turned into an adjective by adding the ending "j" for masculine, or "t" for feminine. In English for example, we casually add the letter "y" to the noun "taste" to make the adjective "tasty." That is the basic idea of an Egyptian nisbe,[42] except that the Egyptians did this also to prepositions such that *jm* would become *jmj*. Thus, "inside" became "insidey," which amounts to saying "that/he/she/it, which is inside," for lack of a better way to say it in English.

The word *wt*, the other part of the outlier hieroglyph, translates to "embalmer," "bandager," and "bandage." The phonetically close word *twt* means "image," "statue," and "assemble." The ideas behind *wt* and *twt* merge in the context of mummification. The embalmer hollowed out a dead corpse, dried it with salt, preserved it with resins and oils, and then wrapped it with linen bandages, effectively making a statue from a dead body. It served as a vessel that could regain the life force lost with the shadow and the *k3* when the person died. But is it also a phonetic play that tells us that Heka is hiding in a statue?

The Phonetic Significance of Mehit

You need one more piece of information to see how clever this word riddle is. *m3j* [my] is an Egyptian word for lion. It is phonetically embedded in *jmj* [i-my]. What I suspect is that the words *m3j-twt*, which together mean "lion statue," are hiding inside the word *jmjwt*.

To prove this, I needed both versions in the same written text. Fortunately, this text exists. It is called the Papyrus Jumilhac, also known as pJumilhac (figure 9). Now split into 23 sheets, it was written sometime during the Ptolemaic period of Egypt (305-30 BC) and possibly even somewhat later during the Roman period, after Cleopatra and Marc Anthony succumbed to Octavian.

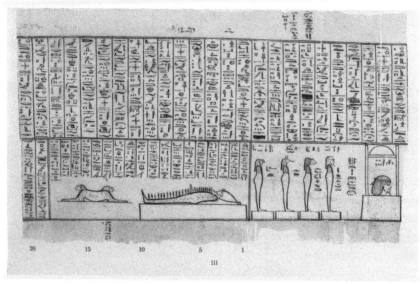

Figure 9: The four sons of Horus on the bottom right and the mummy of Osiris on the left, guarded by the double lion Aker. pJumilhac, sheet III, Louvre, Paris. ©, François Olivier.

One of the two main themes of the text deals with the story of the jackal god Anubis, the embalmer who prepares the body of Osiris for resurrection while he is being conned by his evil antagonist Seth. Isis and Horus are the other protagonists.

I was led to this papyrus originally because it contains a couple of instances of the Egyptian word and context sign for coffer, *ʿfdt.* [af-det]. When I scanned the text before and after one of these occurrences on sheet IV, the sheet after the one shown here, I was shocked to read a name I knew too well: Mehit. What was she doing here in pJumilhac?

I have much to say about her later, but suffice it to say for now that Mehit was one of Egypt's earliest lioness goddesses. Right after her name in the text of the papyrus, I saw the word symbol for *jmjwt*, but I did not right away recognize it as such (figure 10).

Figure 10: Text columns 23 and 24 from sheet IV of pJumilhac. The hieroglyphic words Mehit and *jmjwt* are framed. ©, François Olivier; modified.

Initially, it did not make sense. *Jmjwt* was an epithet of Anubis, not Mehit. Rather than seeing the feline skin wrapped around the pole (figure 11), I imagined a bird on an arrow. My perplexion made me look deeper and that was the scribe's intent.

Figure 11: Osiris in the Underworld with the *jmjwt*. From *Amduat for Amenophis, priest of Amun.* Thebes, Egypt, 21st dynasty (1070-946 BC). ©, bpk-Bildagentur/Aegyptisches Museum und Papyrussammlung, Staatliche Museen, Berlin, Germany/Sandra Steiss/ Art Resource, NY.

What was Anubis' epithet doing here next to the name of a couchant lioness? I already had a paradox on my hands that no one else may ever wonder about. But my training had only begun.

To my good fortune, I found a clue to my little mystery on sheet XI of pJumilhac, where the coffer word and symbol also appear. This sort of discovery process, by the way, is how ancient texts must often be deciphered, even by the experts. One needs a context to interpret unknown words and that context comes from other passages where the same or similar words are being used.

The problem of missing cross-references and context was the main reason, for example, why the Edfu Project was launched. The now thirty-four yearlong mission has been to tackle the massive volume of text written in

Ptolemaic hieroglyphic. This late phase of the language used thousands more symbols than the basic set of 700-800 used up until the New Kingdom.[43]

Let us now look at the three relevant segments of sheet XI in columns 12 and 14.

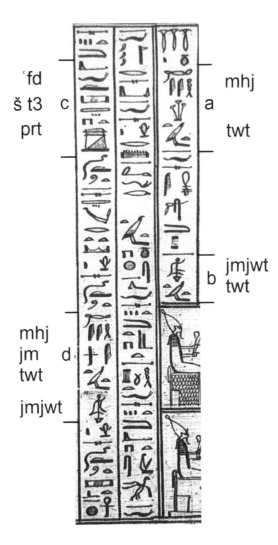

Figure 12: Text columns 12-14 from sheet XI of pJumilhac. The relevant segments, labelled a-d, are discussed in the text. ©, François Olivier; modified.

In (a), *mhj* alludes to Mehit, the northern lioness, but the papyrus stalk symbol signifies the Delta of Egypt, also in the north. Hence, this could just be a reference to that region. The word *twt* means image. At face value, (a) means "northern image," phonetically alluding to the "image of Mehit."

In (b), we get "image of *jmjwt*," or "the *jmjwt* of the image." Both are possible. Here, the scribe is taking us to a place where we see and hear the word *twt* embedded within the word *jmjwt*. Already alerted to such sound plays from (a), we are now also able to associate with these two words the name Mehit, or, alternatively, the concept of north.

The ultimate flaunt is in (d). It is so obvious here, it made me laugh. But was it so obvious because I was prepared by (a) and (b)? That is the brilliance of phonetic Heka. To leave no doubt, it seems the scribe wanted to hold the answer right in front of my face, just short of explicitly mentioning it in writing:

mhj jm-twt jmjwt

Was I to realize that *jm-twt* is the same as *jmjwt*? The words hiding here are "Mehit inside the lion statue," a completely different meaning than what *jmjwt* normally designates: embalmer and bandager. Did the scribe cryptographically try to tell the Heka-initiated reader that anubis embalmed and wrapped the mummy of osiris inside the statue of the lioness Mehit in the tomb of Osiris?

Becoming Equipped

Let me show you one more example of the playfulness and ingenuity Egyptian scribes put into practice when composing some of their most mysterious texts. Imagine I wrote the same word three times in the same sentence, spelled once as *imagenie*, as I just did. Surely, you have noticed the misspelling in *imagenie*. Without doubt, you also noticed that I used only two different spellings of "imagine," not three as stated. Your reaction might be, "Manu made a spelling error in his book, and does he not know how to count?" Then you just move on. But what if I wanted to say something else to you, something to make you stumble and alert you to a hidden message by triggering a phonetic resonance first and an association second? What if I really wanted to say, *"Imagine I'm a genie,* and you have *three* wishes"?

We find this method used in the text written around the Vignette of R^c which talks about the Roads of Mehen. It is divided into two columns. In each, the word "confused" is used once (figure 13). This word is spelled in two different ways: *ztnm* [ze-the-nem] and ***stnm*** [set-e-nm].

While it was common for Egyptian scribes to use different spellings for the same words at different times, it is harder to explain, however, why the same word would be spelled two ways within the body of the same text. It seems impossible to explain why the same word would be spelled in two

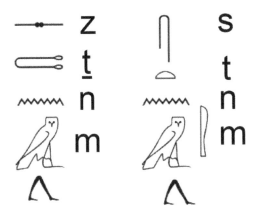

Figure 13: The hieroglyphic word for the verb "confuse," spelled two different ways.

different ways in a caption to an illustration where it is the key semantic bridge which connects two mirroring phrases into one passage—unless we were meant to stumble, become alert, and thus become equipped to slide aside the veil of the first semantic layer and look at the layer hiding behind it. That hidden layer is the god *zwnt* [zun-thoo].

Yes, as incredible as it seems, this is an anagrammed, phonetic insinuation of a relevant deity in the context of this inscription, one whom we will meet again. There is good evidence for this stunning display of scribal play with words.[44] *sm* shamans were true masters of this cryptographic craft, and you are now *equipped* to enter their mysterious world of symbols, signs, and insinuations.

Speaking of being equipped, I must not omit a fascinating metaphor from the Pyramid Texts of King Unas that refers to acquiring magical knowledge: eating.[45] In the so-called Cannibal Hymn, the resurrecting king devours the gods and his divine ancestors—but this apparent act of kin-consumption is only code for learning the magical spells required to ascend into the celestial realm from the bowels of the pyramid under the Earth. The two utterances, 180a/PT273 and 180b/PT274, not surprisingly are inscribed onto the walls of the antechamber, immediately before the spiritually symbolic exit towards the sky from the pyramid.

Hieroglyphic's lexical ambiguity in this regard further underscores this equivalence of eating and learning with which we are also familiar, when we say we *devour* knowledge: the word *ꜥm* can mean "eat" and "know" or "be aware."[46] In the later *Book of the Dead*, a faint remnant of this metaphor is preserved in the devouring of the heavy heart by the netherworld monster *ꜥm mwt* [am-mwt], the avenger, so to speak, who screens out the sinning souls when if he or she fails the "Weighing of the Heart" test.

This is but a sample excursion into the hidden layer behind hieroglyphic, and it is meant to convey to you what modern translators have been facing in their attempts to make sense of this language. The impression I have gotten from studying ancient Egyptian texts is that the scribes heard and saw a symphony of linguistic overtones when they deployed these bewildering symbols onto palm leaves, papyrus, wood, leather, bone, and stone. Today, we miss most of these resonances in our translations. However, this does not mean that we cannot understand some of the themes.

Egyptologists have been able to penetrate past the first semantic layer across two big interpretative barriers: The first is the immanent character of the observational science content of some texts hiding behind what we initially think of merely colorful metaphors. The second is the phonetic mimicry of Heka that reveals content, at times, completely unrelated to the first layer's meaning one encounters.

My level of attention has been sharpened as I have learned from these ancient scholars. When I look at a hieroglyphic translation nowadays, I look for concrete content wrapped in metaphors. I look for sounds of words that may hide in the symbols used to write others, such as the name of the god *zwnṯ* hiding in the hieroglyphic word for confused *zṯnm/sṯnm*.

But what might have been the purpose of this hidden phonetic bridge? It turns out that this wordplay is a crucial piece of evidence needed to understand the Vignette of *Rꜥ* on the Middle Kingdom coffin of one General Zepi. He is the only person ever known to have been given this painting to decorate his final place of rest. Not only does this painting not exist on any other coffin, but it also doesn't exist anywhere else. I knew I had to inspect it, and the writing around it, with my Heka-sharpened lens to detect any clues as to its meaning and origin.

I admit, I cringe at the thought of a coffin. I am claustrophobic. But there is a trick I learned from my mom: Close your eyes and think of floating in the sky with the stars. That was great advice, both once in the MRI scanner, and for what I am about to show you.

A Description of the City of Atlantis Based on *The Critias* by Plato—Scene One

"Tell me," said Solon to the priest at the Saite Temple of Neith, the goddess of the Red Crown of Egypt's kings and queens, "How do your texts describe this forsaken place you call the City on the Island of Atlantis?"

"It was the one you call Poseidon who built his throne on a low mountain. He surrounded it with three moats of water and two rings of land in between. One hundred water spirits encircled his temple statue. He built waterways across the rings to the outer zones carrying the pure water from this mountain. He carved tunnels beneath the Earthen rings for the ships.

Their walls he laid out in black, red, and white. He set out guardians in front of these gates, the most trusted ones he kept near his palace. On the outer zone, he built a concourse for the horse-drawn chariots to race. This sanctuary he built to protect him and his beloved Cleito, with whom he had ten sons.

To the one you call Atlas he handed his rule. His brother was *Sheepfold*, and he ruled the straits. The other *eight* he sent to the rest of this once magnificent island, and they ruled from there to the far reaches of the world, even *as far as Egypt*."

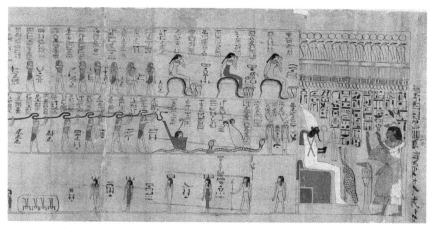

Figure 14: From *Amduat for Amenophis, priest of Amun*. Egypt, Thebes, 21st dynasty (1070-946 BC). ©, bpk Bildagentur / Aegyptisches Museum und Papyrussammlung, Staatliche Museen, Berlin, Germany/ Sandra Steiss/Art Resource, NY.

IV

Coffins

Prehistory
>3000 BC
Early History
~3000-2700 BC
Old Kingdom
~2700-2200 BC
First Intermediate
Period
~2200-2000 BC
Middle Kingdom
~2200-1700 BC
Second Intermediate
Period
~1700-1500 BC
New Kingdom
~1500-1100 BC
Third Intermediate
Period
~1100-700 BC
Late Period
~700-300 BC
Greco-Roman Period
~300 BC-400 AD

Mediterranean Sea — Levant

Buto

rst3w/Giza — Sinai

E G Y P T — Arabia

ẖmnw/Hermopolis — Deir El-Bersheh

z3jwtj/Lycopolis/Asyut

tnj/Thinis — Naqada — w3st/Thebes — Red

nḥn/Hierakonpolis — bdt/Edfu

3bw/Elephantine Island — Aswan — Sea

Nabta Playa

Sahara Desert

Figure 15: Map of ancient Egypt and historical timeline. ©, AdobeStock 111793774; modified.

THERE IS ONE, AND ONLY ONE, COFFIN IN ALL OF EGYPT ON WHICH IS PAINTED a most unusual image. The coffin belonged to a general named *zpj* [ze-pee] once laid to rest in a four-thousand-year-old cemetery of the elite called Deir El-Bersheh (figure 15). No doubt, this general enjoyed special access at the local library called the *House of Life* because no one besides him, as far as is currently known, adorned his burial boxes in this way.

The interior of the headboard of the outer coffin is painted with an image of the Sun God directly facing the head of the dead general, but physically still separated by the inner coffin wall. This painting is the Vignette of *R^c* (figure 16).

Figure 16: The Vignette of *R^c* also known as the Roads of Mehen. Painting on the interior of the sarcophagus of *jmj-r^c-mš^c zpj*, General Zepi, discovered in Deir El-Bersheh. ©, Werner Forman Archive/ agefotostock® HEZ-2571859.

It is as unique as it is strange. The Sun God is surrounded by nine concentric elliptical circles of alternating red and black color. He sits on a throne with an inscription translated as "myriads of years." Surrounding the ellipses is a white band of hieroglyphic text annotating the eerie image it encircles. It is written in two opposing reading directions.[47] Around the right side of the ellipses from bottom to top, the first part of the inscription—translated by English hieroglyphic expert and disciple of Sir Alan Gardiner, Raymond O. Faulkner (1894–1982)—reads (emphasis added):[48]

The paths of fire. These paths guard the larboard side of the bark of the Coiled One, who makes a circle in a myriad after a myriad (of years). **The gates are confused**, *the bow of the bark of the Coiled One has swung round. This is the seat of the Shining Sun which these gates guard; it is a myriad of a myriad after a myriad (of years).*

Around the left side, from bottom to top, the second part reads:

The gates are confused, *the starboard side of the bark belongs to the right side of the Coiled One. The paths of fire go round about the seat of the Shining Sun, who guards the paths for the great bark of the Coiled One, who makes a circle for myriad after myriad.*

This inscription is Spell 758 of a body of spells called the Coffin Texts, variously inscribed on coffins from the Middle Kingdom. Their purpose was to aid the deceased in his journey through the afterlife to attain immortality.

Ultimately, their origin dates to the Old Kingdom Pyramid Texts, which were also "spells", though not inscribed on coffins but carved into the walls of the chambers and corridors inside the royal pyramids. Both, Pyramid and Coffin Texts deal with the afterlife, but there are two principal differences: The first difference is that the Pyramid Texts played out in the sky, but the Coffin Texts played out both in the Netherworld under the Earth and the Skyworld above. The second difference is that the Pyramid Texts were written for the royals, but the Coffin Texts were custom-made for powerful and wealthy commoners, such as the General Zepi. He is the only known person whose coffin was inscribed with the strangest spell of them all: Spell 758.

In this chapter, I am going to demonstrate that these few cryptic sounding lines of text wrapped around the Vignette of *R*ʿhide the key needed to unlock the true meaning of this odd illustration of nine elliptical bands surrounding the Sun God. I will show you how this hidden key works and then prove that the bands were meant to be nine planetary orbits. What I presented to you in the last chapter is what we must now look for with utmost alertness: Heka. Whoever wrote this annotation must have been a master scribe and Heka magician par excellence. Like all seasoned masters, s/he disguised the design as a clumsy error, something most of us would carelessly pass up—unless, of course, we have been first initiated to understand that we are to stumble first to then be alerted that a deeper message hides in the text.

Confusion upon Confusion

The Heka is well hidden. The text of the annotation in the Vignette of R^c begins at the seven o'clock position, but the symbols are on their heads in this orientation, even though the Sun God is right side up. So, to be able to read more easily, you must first flip the paining on its head. Now the text begins at one o'clock and the symbols are right side up. The first part runs clockwise down to six o'clock (figure 17).

To read the second part, you must go back to the one o'clock position, but now read it in a counterclockwise direction. Part Two ends at six o'clock where it meets the end of Part One, the terminal symbols meeting in a bottom-to-bottom orientation. The lay-out seems clumsy and cumbersome. *But what if that was intentional?*

The confusing way in which the text was written did not make sense to me until my designer Anthony Sturmas and I tried to reproduce the symbols to make a graphic of it. I only then realized—and I may be the first to point this out—that the text was intentionally written in a counterintuitive way. The inscription states that "The gates are confused." In order to amplify this statement the Heka master made the text confusing to read. Imagine the ghost of General Zepi turning the painting, let alone the entire coffin, around and around in a haste to read the spell he needed to pass a gate in the afterlife. The idea to use the reading direction of the text to augment its main theme, confusion, is ingenious, is it not?

What is also seemingly clumsy, at first, are the two different ways to spell the hieroglyphic word for "confuse" in the two parts of the text I mentioned in the previous chapter: *zṯnm* and **stnm**. The goal, as I stated before, was to alert you and make you take a closer look at what other words were being phonetically activated, words like *zṯwn* for "navigate",[49] *zn* for "open" and "reveal",[50] and *zni* for "pass by",[51] and finally the name of a mysterious ferryman mentioned in the more archaic Pyramid Texts called *zwnṯ*/Zunthu.[52]

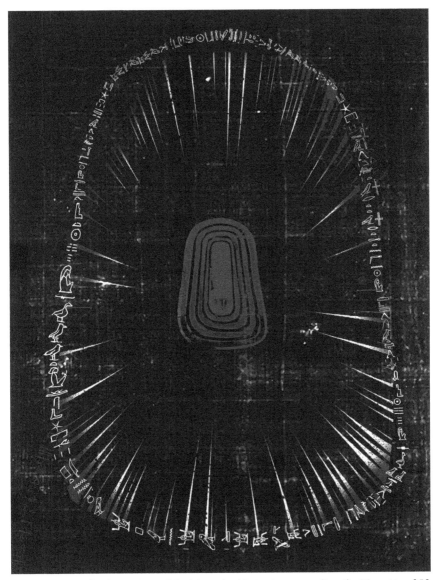

Figure 17: Upside-down view of the hieroglyphic text surrounding the Vignette of *R*ꜥ, based on the original transcription by de Buck (1956). For orientation, the painting is faintly shown in the center. Graphic by Anthony Sturmas, Asturmas Studios.

In other words, the text around the vignette was both spatially and lexically designed to invoke the idea of confusion, redirection, and, at once, point to this strange deity associated with navigation and path finding in the sky.

And if you're not looking closely enough, it is very easy to miss the reference to Zunthu.

It turns out that Zunthu is the key to understanding that the elliptical bands in the Vignette of R^c are nine sky orbits reserved for nine sky gods called the Ennead. But I am getting ahead of myself. At first, I admired the cleverness of these master scribes at the *House of Life* in the city of Thoth, but I was still struggling with the hidden meaning of Spell 758. Yet, my first impression of the painting had been immediate: This had to be an image of the Heliocentric Solar System with the Sun in the center and nine elliptical orbits around it. I just needed to prove it.

Nonwithstanding my better sense, I knew this interpretation would be rejected based on its implausibility. Any reasonable interpretation acceptable to scholars of history "must be plausible" and "conform to the existing paradigm of history," which dictates that the ancient Egyptians did not know the Sun is at the center of our solar system. They certainly had no idea that there were nine planets.

An argument based on plausibility alone, however, will never break a paradigm: it can only preserve it. What is plausible is based on expectations generated from within a paradigm, not based on the unknown. Plausibility, therefore, should not be the yard stick used to appraise evidence that is contrarary to prevailing theory.

In order to prove beyond a reasonable doubt that the Vignette of R^c depicts the Heliocentric Solar System, plausible or not, I had to prove that what is shown in the center is the Sun, and what is shown around it are nine one-way sky orbits. I needed textual proof that the bands in the vignette were indeed meant to represent nine planetary paths.

It is relatively easy to prove that it is the Sun shown in the center of the painting. Spell 758 is unequivocal: "This is the seat of the Shining Sun." It is far more difficult to prove that the oval rings represent nine unidirectional, one-way orbits. Complicating this proof is the texts must be read from the perspective of ancient Egyptian astronomy, not ours. Obscuring this even more is the the vocabulary available to an ancient Egyptian scribe with which to express the concept of an orbit. We may not immediately understand how that would have been put into words. Why is that?

Remember that an astronomical concept obvious to us—a planet on a continuous, counterclockwise, elliptical orbit around the Sun—would have made no sense to ancient Egyptian astronomers. They may have interpreted an image such as the Vignette of R^c from within their own paradigm. It may have been analogous to the way modern scholars have interpreted it from within ours: as a cosmogram of travelled time, for instance. In other words, the ancient Egyptians would have explained what they saw in terms they understood from within their familiar geocentric view of the solar system in which the sky is circumnavigated by planets on boats along meandering waterways.

This then begs a question: how would have ancient Egyptian astronomy explained retrograde planetary motion? In its simplest terms, it is something we explain as passing and being passed. What if they explained it as if they were in a chariot race of planets on a celestial one-way hippodrome around the Sun—to use an analogy from antiquity.

The key concept to know, then, is how the ancient Egyptians conceptualized the celestial mechanics at play causing the planets to move in discrete orbits and yet suddenly change direction. The explanation of these erratic workings and confusing machinations of the orbital paths in the sky as understood and recorded by ancient Egyptian astronomers can be found embedded in the Coffin Texts, divided by Lacau, Breasted, Gardiner, and de Buck into 1185 total spells. Within this body of spells is a section of 157 spells called the *Book of Two Ways*. Contrary to its original interpretation, these illustrated texts deal with paths in the sky—not on the ground. To see why this is so, and to understand the origin of the confusion, I must first take you back in time to a golden era of Egyptology, the early twentieth century.

Zweiwegebuch

It was a last-ditch effort before his money and his sponsor Lord Carnarvon's patience was to run out. But it paid off in gold for British Egyptologist, Howard Carter, in November 1922. He had discovered the tomb of King Tut. It was undisturbed and full of priceless Egyptian royal treasures as he would come to know a few months later when he opened the burial chamber. Meanwhile, a much less glorious, underappreciated, and hardly known project was about to begin in Cairo. It would end up consuming the careers of some of the most well-known Egyptologists in the history of its discipline. The history of these events has been well covered by Egyptologist and hieroglyphic writing expert, Wael Sherbiny.[53] I will only highlight a few details as they matter to my investigation.

Pierre Lacau, the third chief of Egyptian Antiquities after Auguste Mariette and Gaston Maspero, had already spent twenty-two years on publishing two catalogs, one entitled *Sarcophages antérieurs au Nouvel Empire*, of over one hundred First Intermediate Period and Middle Kingdom coffins in the Cairo Museum, and another entitled *Textes réligieux égyptiens* covering the vast amount of hieroglyphic texts and illustrations with which many of them were decorated (figure 18).

Figure 18: Exterior of a Middle Kingdom Coffin. The Museum of Egyptian Antiquities, Cairo, Egypt, 2018.

But Lacau needed help with the monumental task of cataloging all such coffins, including those that had been discovered and shipped to museums in Europe and America. Help in the form of expertise and money came from the United States and England with James Henry Breasted and Alan Henderson Gardiner who agreed to continue what Lacau had started. Both Breasted and Gardiner took turns traveling to Thebes to examine the inscriptions discovered in King Tut's tomb. This put their own work studying the Cairo coffins on hold for a few weeks to get this work done.

After beginning the arduous task of photographing, transcribing, and sorting the texts from Cairo, Boston, London, Berlin, and Paris, Breasted had to resign from the project to attend his new Oriental Institute in Chicago. Gardiner was overwhelmed. But help came with Dutch Egyptologist and theologian, Adriaan de Buck, a young, motivated, recent graduate who would have never thought then that even he would never see the end of this project alive. Not until 1961 would all volumes of the Coffin Texts be published by the Oriental Institute under the title *The Egyptian Coffin Texts*.[54] De Buck died in 1959.

This understandable but long delay is the chief reason why the interpretation of the 157-spell segment called the *Book of Two Ways* in the Coffin Texts became monopolized by a much earlier publication in 1903. Its German title was *Zweiwegebuch*, written by Count Hans Schack zu Schackenburg (1852-1905), a self-taught Egyptologist from Dresden, Germany, with an interest in hieroglyphic. The count had at his disposal the *Zweiwegebuch* from one coffin at the Berlin Museum. He also knew of a related map from similar Cairo coffins Lacau had previously cataloged. Based on this limited information, Schack-Schackenburg published his interpretation. It would become gospel. The problem is so pronounced that one cannot help but keep calling these texts by their erroneous name for fear that other Egyptologists may not know what is being referenced. Sherbiny's solution is to call it the "so-called *Book of Two Ways.*" If there was ever a book not to judge by its cover title, it is this one.

Schack-Schackenburg had basically concluded that the *Zweiwegebuch* deals with two paths through Rostau, the abode of Osiris, one on water and one on land. The map segment accompanying most versions of this Coffin Text episode shows two serpentine bands, one blue and one black. This, deceivingly, seemed to support his idea. The *Zweiwegebuch* is key to understanding the nine bands around the Vignette of R^c. It is thus upon me to briefly enumerate the main reasons why Schack-Schackenburg was most likely in error. This critique is entirely based on an excellent, detailed analysis by Wael Sherbiny.[55]

First, there is no mention of the waterways of Rostau in the upper register of the map segment of the book, despite it being traversed by a blue serpentine band. Second, the phrase "ways of Rostau on water and on land," is also not mentioned anywhere on the map. But it is mentioned in the next segment, which is textual and not illustrated. The phrase "two ways of Rostau" is not mentioned anywhere in the "book." Third, Schack-Schackenburg assumed that these phrases were relating to two prior illustrated segments of the book he was studying, but when compared with other coffins, it shows that there is no spatial connection between similar segments in these other book versions. Fourth, Schack-Schackenburg had assumed that one could interpret this Middle Kingdom text using ideas learned from

New Kingdom netherworld book-like texts such as the *Amduat* or the *Book of the Heavenly Cow*, which refer to a journey through the underworld and mention alternative paths on water and land. In other words, he felt justified to extrapolate his textual interpretation back in time, which is risky business given that the meaning of texts can change over time, as later scribes reinterpret older versions.

Finally, he misinterpreted the word *mḏ3t* [me-jat] at the end of one of the final segments he had artificially created to organize the book to mean the word "book" ("Buch" in German), as opposed to an alternative, more plausible meaning in that context as text medium, meaning the wooden floorboard of the coffin on which the book was most often inscribed.

The take-away is that whoever studies the *Zweiwegebuch* with these erroneous presumptions generated by Count Hans Schack-Schackenburg in 1903 will conclude that it narrates a journey on a terrestrial path. Wael Sherbiny has convincingly demonstrated that this is wrong.

Sherbiny's analysis leads to three key conclusions: that the two bands on the map of the *Book of Two Ways* were likely both waterways like rivers, canals, or lakes,[56] and that they were but only two of several others like them. Most importantly, these waterways were imagined *in the sky*, not on the ground.

Of course, no blame goes to Schack-Schackenburg. He did the best he could with what was known at the time. The problem really lies in the monopolization of how new information is disseminated in Egyptology on a first-come, first-call basis in the absence of proper vetting when new data may take decades to become available. False ideas can linger, which is why outside vetting by researchers from other disciplines can help.

Hancock and Bauval, for example, recognized the problem with interpreting netherworld texts because of their astronomical interpretative approach to the Pyramid Texts. The authors had this to say about the *Book of Two Ways* and other Netherworld books which came after:[57]

We suspect that the history of ancient Egypt, to the extent that it was written down at all in papyri and tablets and inscriptions, was frequently expressed in a kind of "cosmic code" ritualistically and symbolically linked—like the Pyramids themselves—to the ever-changing patterns of the sky. From this it follows that we must look to the sky, just as the Egyptians did, if we wish to understand the ideas that they were trying to communicate in their (on the face of things) extremely strange and problematic religious writings. These writings include mysterious and archaic texts aimed at guiding the afterlife journey of the deceased, such as the Book of the Dead (which the ancient Egyptians knew as Per-Ém-Hru, the Book of 'Coming Forth By Day'), the Book of Two Ways, the Book of Gates, the Book of What is in the Duat and the Coffin Texts.

To further support this concept, I will repeat here something I mentioned in the beginning: To the ancient Egyptians, their gods were the phenomena they observed. The many gods of Egypt did not send the forces of nature from afar; they *were* the forces of nature. Not appreciating this leads to grave misunderstandings of their texts. What you read is a personified—or, rather, deified—account of events that have no visible actors other than the moving lights in the sky, or the wind that blows against our faces, or the aroma of scents and incense that enthralls our nostrils. The gods in Egypt did not make these experiences of the senses happen from a distance; to the ancient Egyptians, they were one and the same.

That is why there were so many gods. Those who accuse them of polytheism fail to understand the difference between reverence and respect for the many aspects of nature and worship of one creator God. In that sense, the Egyptians too only worshiped one creator God in the Memphite cosmogony with Ptah or in the theology of the Aten at Amarna.

One aspect of the unfortunate legacy of Schack-Schackenburg's *Zweiwegebuch* has been that many Egyptologists have continued to neglect the sky and look instead on the ground for a concrete expression of what they otherwise read as just another mythical story with no real basis. This did not go unnoticed by Hancock and Bauval. They likewise looked for an on-the-ground mirror image of the sky myth of two ways as part of their theory of the Duality Dictum that the sky must have a mirror image on the ground.[58]

They proposed, for example, that the causeway leading up to the Pyramid of Khafre must be the way on land and that a water channel underground must be the way on water that leads under the Sphinx and up to the pyramids.[59] This model was based on Bauval's earlier proposal that the Giza pyramids are a concrete recreation on the ground of the starry image of Osiris in the sky, the constellation Orion. Therefore, if Giza, what the ancients knew as Rostau, was the on-the-ground abode of Osiris, this model appears reasonable. After all they knew of a Middle Kingdom book about two earthly ways on a path to unite with Osiris in Rostau, which the authors suspected to really play out in the sky. As above in the sky, so below on the ground. But if the premise is wrong, the dictum cannot produce a correct correlate. In this case, the premise was that there were only two paths, one on water and one on land.

Along the same lines dictated by the theory of Sky-Earth duality, Bauval's reconstruction in *Message of the Sphinx* of the eastern sky during the Zep Tepi era at 10500 BC, led him to propose that the Sun beneath the imaginary hind paws of the constellation Leo over the horizon dawn of a vernal equinox was the celestial counterpart of the *Hall of Records* some hundred feet beneath the Great Sphinx,[60] a location very different from the one proposed by Robert Schoch.[61]

Even though I think Bauval may have become another victim of Schack-Schackenburg's *Zweiwegebuch* myth, finally dispelled now by Sherbiny, this insight by Bauval is essentially correct, but with an unexpected twist. The main takeaway for now is this: There is an undeniable correlation between the sky and the ground when it comes to Egyptian architecture, but when the wrong textual interpretation is projected onto the ground as part of this duality paradigm, it creates a likewise erroneous interpretation of the monument's meaning.

In this sense, the so-called *Book of Two Ways* should really be called *Traveling Safely on the Winding Waterways* to clean the slate and give the text a more fitting title since it dealt with the sky and with paths of water. And because it is about celestial waterways and not about earthly land ways, I hypothesized it could bring me closer to understanding how the ancient Egyptians had reasoned why bodies in the sky move on these highways in the sky the way they do.

Before I take you to the Skyworld of the Coffin Texts, a few words must be said about the Netherworld, because it is here, inside the bowels of Earth, where the overall mission and purpose of the composition is explained. The overall mission is the needed context to understand what happens in the sky.

Netherworld

We are told what the mission is in the first spell (Spell 1) of the main body of the Coffin Texts' 1128 spells.[62] Let's enter the Netherworld together with the deceased, generically called N. We are in Rostau, the gateway to this Egyptian idea of the Underworld.

Here begins the book of vindicating a man in the realm of the dead. Ho N! You are the Lion, you are the Double Lion, you are Horus, Protector of his father, you are the fourth of these four gods who are powerful and strong who bring water and make the Nile through the power of their fathers. O N, raise yourself on your left side, put yourself on your right side.

The idea of this and the next ten spells is that N must pass a test and overcome being judged by his enemies to receive his/her soul and shadow, without which there is no afterlife. S/he takes the role of the lion and the double lion, either *rwtj* or Aker. S/he also takes the role of Horus. In this way, N becomes god-like and must then descend into Earth-Geb on a stairway to reach the city of Horus' father Osiris. There, s/he unifies with him and resurrects. Then, s/he must face a tribunal following which s/he is vindicated in a replay of the judgment of Thoth over the feuding Horus and Seth. The deceased is then greeted by Seshat, the goddess of archives. Upuaut the jackal, a symbol of secrecy when depicted couchant atop a shrine, opens a path for the vindicated N. N encounters a statue and takes possession of Earth-Geb's thrones.

Even though it is difficult to prove that these spells are speaking of the archaic origins of a real *Hall of Records* under a lion statue at Giza, the elements of it are there. Nevertheless, from these powerful opening salvos of the Coffin Texts, it becomes clear that access is given to secrets only after transformation and vindication of the deceased's afterlife spirit. These secrets are written within the spells themselves and are kept in an archive. Only when equipped and proficient with these spells can N succeed on the treacherous journey about to begin to achieve the final goal.

The generally accepted mission described in the Coffin Texts is for the deceased to attain immortality in the afterlife and dwell among the immortal gods as one of them, as one of the imperishable stars. To achieve this, he or she had to reenact the events in the Osiris story where the son Horus avenges the murder of his father by his uncle Seth. N is aided by help from Osiris' sister-wife Isis, the embalmer and Netherworld guardian Anubis, and Thoth the Moon to prepare a proper, mummification burial for Osiris so that he can live forever in the Netherworld of his Father, Earth-Geb, thus becoming the natural force of regeneration and resurrection of life.

But to reach Osiris, the deceased N was put to the test, having to pass several guarded gates and survive the trials and tribulations s/he encounters. Honing his/her skills on the way, s/he becomes a capable ritualist. From this initiated level of consciousness and skill, s/he can slip into the role of various gods, for example Isis, Horus, and Thoth, and it is this ability to transform which ultimately is key to saving and healing the mortally wounded Osiris. This heroic deed earns N a favor in return, granted by the revived Osiris, that s/he needs to attain immortality in the afterlife.

Yes, you read that right. This is basically a quid pro quo, I-scratch-your-back-if-you-scratch-mine mission on which the deceased nomarchs and their wives, doctors, generals, priests, and stewards of the Middle Kingdom believed they were embarking after death. I can only speculate that they were willing to pay for this ticket to eternity with an absolution fee. This forgiving of sins in life began with vindication and ended with a divine transformation of the deceased to become equipped. The first phase of the afterlife thus takes place in the Netherworld to become prepared to then enter the Skyworld in the second phase.

Skyworld

The sky is N's ultimate destiny once a vindicated, transformed, and equipped shadow spirit. There are three places and two entities that matter to the correct interpretation of the text around the Vignette of R^c: the Winding Waterway, the Lake of Fire, the Gates, The Nine (also known as the Ennead), and the Coiled One, Mehen. All of these are colorful metaphors for things in the sky. At last, we enter the world of ancient Egyptian astronomy.

Let us again join N who is now vindicated and ready to ascend to the Skyworld.

1) The Winding Waterway, Spell 18: [63]

Ho N! You shall cross the sky and traverse the firmament, those who are in the Winding Waterway shall worship you and see you when you arise in the eastern horizon, those who are in the Netherworld having permitted your beautiful appearing; you shall come forth from the Night-bark and go aboard the Day-bark as Horus Lord of Patricians himself commands you.

Ho N! You shall go up upon the great west side of the sky and go down upon the great east side of the earth among those gods who are in the suite of Osiris, in peace, in peace with Re who is in the sky.

The metaphoric language of the Coffin Texts is often difficult to pin down, but in this case, the Winding Waterway is unequivocally in the sky. We also learn from this spell that the Egyptians believed that the bodies in the sky were floating on these celestial rivers as if they, on Earth, were still. It helps to look at the actual hieroglyphic text to be able to confirm the location of the Winding Waterway.

The following analysis is based on German Egyptologist and astronomer Rolf Krauss' excellent article on the topic.[64] Help comes here from the Old Kingdom's Sixth Dynasty Pyramid Texts (PT), where the same word is spelled in three different ways in the pyramids of Pepi and Merenre (figure 19).

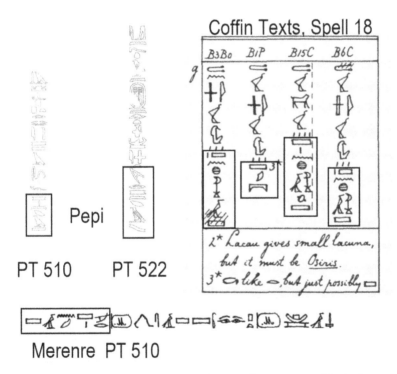

Figure 19: Variant hieroglyphic spellings for "Winding Waterway" in the Pyramid Texts (PT) and the Coffin Texts. Left, in the pyramids of Pepi and Merenre. Right, in Spell 18 from four Middle Kingdom sarcophagi. ©, Allen (2013). Courtesy of the Oriental Institute of the University of Chicago, de Buck (1935); modified.

The Egyptian words for Winding Waterway are *šj-nj-ḫ3* and ***mr-nj-ḫ3***. The literal English translation is Lake or Trench of Lotus. Hieroglyphic context symbols visually clarify the meaning of words, spelled phonetically. To highlight the common idea among the various hieroglyphic versions of the Winding Waterway, I compared four samples from the Pyramid and Coffin Texts (figure 20).

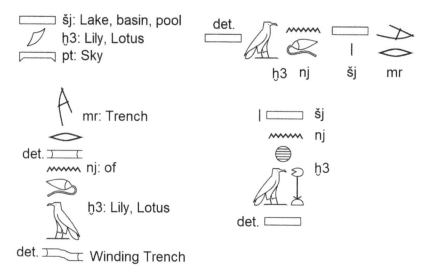

Figure 20: Hieroglyphic synonyms for "Winding Waterway" with phonetic transliterations and English translations. Det. stands for determinative symbol, which provided context only, it was not pronounced. The word ***mr*** is spelled with the hoe symbol to which the mouth symbols for the consonant *r* was added as a pronunciation aid (see Appendix).

For example, in PT 522 of King Pepi, the Trench of Lotus is contextualized with the silent symbol resembling a bending canal or a winding trench. On Middle Kingdom Coffin B1P, the sky symbol *pt* clarifies that this Lotus Trench is in the sky. The pool symbol is used both as a word and as a context symbol. It specifies that the trench is filled with water and that it is a water channel or waterway for boats and ships. The upshot of Rolf Krauss' analysis is that the ancient Egyptians imagined that the Lotus Trench flows across the sky meandering through a bed of Lotus flowers.

Furthermore, Krauss concluded the place in the sky believed to be this Winding Waterway was in fact the ecliptic, and not the Milky Way, which was rather believed to be the goddess Nut, consort of Geb.[65] For example, in the Pyramid Texts, the Winding Waterway must be crossed by ferrymen called Eyes-Forward and Eyes-in-the-Back to reach the northern stars zone from the southern bank. These are names of the waxing and waning Moon phases. The Moon does in fact wander above and below the ecliptic.

R^c, on the other hand, floats along its length from east to west, as one might expect from a sky path taken by the Sun.[66] According to Krauss, the past confusion of the Winding Waterway with the Milky Way came about because the Sun and Moon transit through areas in the sky where the ecliptic crosses the Milky Way, twice per year in the case of the Sun, and twice a month in the case of the Moon.[67]

2) As to the Lake of Fire, Krauss agrees with German Egyptologist, Hartwig Altenmüller, who identified the ecliptic not only with the Winding Waterway but also with the later Island of Fire and the Lake of Knives.[68] However, the Lake of Fire has an even more precise location marked on the map section of the *Book of Two Ways*. At first sight, the map does not look anything like an illustration of the sky. Only when taking account of how the ancient Egyptians modeled the sky does the map make sense.

Most scholars influenced by Count Hans Schack-Schackenburg's interpretation believed, and still believe, they are looking at a terrestrial map with two alternative routes, one on water and one on land. To dispel this misconception and prove that what was meant to be illustrated is the ecliptic in the sky, we must first review the ecliptic in modern astronomical terms. Then, we will attempt to recreate the view from the perspective of an ancient astronomer to make sense of the strange map drawn on the floorboards of coffins from Deir El-Bersheh.

The ecliptic is the invisible path the Sun travels during the day from sunrise to sunset. By night, we can trace its path alongside the twelve Zodiac constellation. Wherever the Moon and planets dwell, the ecliptic is nearby. In summary, it encompasses that part of space visible to us that contains orbital paths of the planets in our solar system as well as our Moon.

If you were to draw a line to trace it, you would be drawing an imaginary arc with its summit somewhere between right above your head and due south, or due north on the horizon, depending on where on Earth you are (figure 21).

Figure 21: Intersection and cross-over zone between the ecliptic/Winding Waterway and the Milky Way/the goddess Nut. Orion/Osiris and Canis Major/Isis are in the south. The so-called Imperishable Stars of the circumpolar region are in the north. The Moon in the right lower field is moving towards the east past the cross-over zone when it in two pathways at once. Graphic made with Stellarium 0.14.3.

The legs of this arc fall north or south of due east and west, depending on the season and the date. In astronomical terms, the ecliptic is the plane of our orbit around the Sun. The reason why the ecliptic path is in the shape of a tilted arc is that our Earth rotates around an axis that is not perpendicular to its orbital plane.

To the ancient Egyptians, the Winding Waterway was the band of stars we know as the Zodiac constellations. They observed how the planets and the Moon wandered within this starry band, sometimes near its northern bank, sometimes near its southern extreme. These excursions were imagined to be the crossings between the banks of the channel. The wandering Moon gave rise to the idea of a ferryman. He alone could carry the star spirits from the southern zone, the abode of Osiris and the Field of Reeds, *sḫt j3rw*, to the northern zone, where the Field of Offerings, *sḫt ḥtp*, and the Imperishable Stars dwelled. As a now Heka-initiated reader, you may recognize the words *j3* and *rw* in the name of the former field, Moon-Lion. *In the lion the Moon is born!*

The initial difficulties in deciphering the metaphoric Pyramid Texts of the Old Kingdom in terms of Egyptian astronomy was, in part, due to the absence of charts and illustrations. Translators such as Kurt Sethe, Gustave Jéquier, Alexandre Piankoff, Raymond Faulkner, and James Allen had various levels of awareness of the intricate details of observational astronomy at their disposal which compounded the problem. In addition, the topographical arrangement of the texts inside the pyramids and the still refining lexical and grammatical knowledge of hieroglyphic further complicated a deeper understanding.

All this changed with the discovery of the Middle Kingdom Coffin Texts inscribed on coffins from Deir El-Bersheh. The importance of the map section embedded within the 157 spells of text Count Schack-Schackenburg had called *Zweiwegebuch* can be gleaned from the fact that the mummy of the deceased was laid to rest on top of it (figure 22).

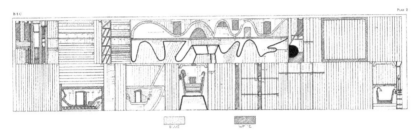

Figure 22: Hieroglyphic text columns and illustrations schematic of a representative floorboard from coffins found in Deir El-Bersheh containing the Book of Two Ways/ *Zweiwegebuch*. In this example (Coffin B3C), the map section is in the middle of the upper register. Illustration by de Buck (1961). Courtesy of the Oriental Institute of the University of Chicago.

Let's study the details of this map. The map of the *Zweiwegebuch* was variously drawn either in the top or the bottom half of the coffin's floorboard (figure 23).

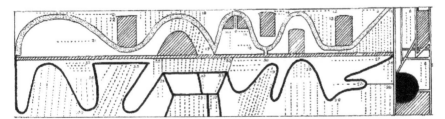

Figure 23: The Map section enlarged. The stippled lines are texts that refer to the details of the subsections on which they are written. From Deir El-Bersheh coffin B3C. Illustration by de Buck (1961). Courtesy of the Oriental Institute of the University of Chicago.

There are two registers. Through the top register, a blue, serpentine band snakes its way from right to left, i.e., west to east.[69] Through the bottom register, a black band is tethered to the barrier between the upper and lower map registers. Between these two anchors, it too runs a winding course. On the right end of the map is a subdivided compartment with inscriptions.

The reason why Schack-Schackenburg and others believed this was meant to be a terrestrial map with roads over land and sea is the color of these two bands, black and blue. Not having the benefit of the annotations compounded the problem leading to the fateful misinterpretation. When the texts are restored to their illustrated context, however, the black band is captioned as a lake, not a land route.[70]

In fact, the reason for the black color of the curved path through the lower register becomes obvious when reading these captions. It was meant to represent a dangerous path taken during the night. This night-sky path was believed to be guarded by a knife-wielding demon who could spew fire. It is this demon that gives the lake situated between the two registers its name, *Lake of Fire*. Connected to this lake is the black band. This further supports the idea that it, like the blue serpentine path in the upper register, was meant to show a watery path.

What I have reviewed here is only a part of the evidence cited by Sherbiny that effectively falsifies the Schack-Schackenburg interpretation of two terrestrial paths shown on the map. Instead, the map of the *Book of Two Ways* marks the *Lake of Fire* to reside between two serpentine watery paths, one apparently representing daytime; the other, nighttime. But what about the names of the black and blue winding paths?

A hint as to their names appears in the texts immediately before the map section. There is a mention of the so-called Lakes of *Šw*.[71] The word for "lake" is *šj*. The word for "lakes" is *šw* or *šjw*. In other words, this may be another case of phonetic mimicry in the text suggesting a Heka insinuation. I suggest the bridge to the two bands is established in the following way: The word "lake" is written both in the top register referring to the blue path and a spirit who dwells beside it.[72] "Lake" is also written in the bottom register referring to the black path and one of its bends.[73] There is even a more indirect mention of sailing on the black path demonstrating that it, in fact, is a waterway.[74]

The evidence sums up to this: The two winding paths shown in the map of the *Book of Two Ways* are made of water. Both are in the sky. Separating them is the *Lake of Fire*. The conclusion was an eye-opener for me: The ancient Egyptians conceptualized the ecliptic as a band of discrete, compartmentalized, sectors traversed by meandering water channels and separated from each other by liquid fire.

Why this imagery? What astronomical observation led the ancient Egyptians to visualize things in this way? Why did they believe that the bodies in the sky meandered? This was the key question to the entire mystery of what the elliptical bands, and the text around them were originally meant to be in the Vignette of R^c.

3) The Gates. A few details from the *Book of Two Ways'* map section animate the ancient Egyptian's idea of the guarded gates and way stations encountered by N. This will help us to understand the interpretation of astronomical observations captured by this map.

The text segments annotating the map describe how N gains safe passage on either sky path, light or dark. Successful passage requires the use of protective spells appearing as captions labeling stations along the bands through the upper and lower registers of the map.

At the entry to the two realms, for example, the deceased is in possession of R^c's regalia and becomes one with the Sun. S/he faces the Gate of Darkness made up of walls of fire and a zone of darkness. The gate's guard is He-Who-Repels-the-Demolishers. The hint embedded in this name is that this guard is the personified mechanism that prevents collisions between different objects floating in the sky on the same path of water. The Gate of Darkness opens the way to both realms, light and dark. A caption hints that N has been here before to treat Osiris and has therefore earned a dignity attribute of the air god, Shu.

Two other captions written behind the wall of fire in the gate hint that N has previously gained access to the light realm. We are informed of the reason for N's return here: to check a second time on the corpse of Osiris. Praise is mentioned and received in Buto and Rostau. There, we learn, is the place where N attained both Spirit Power by Re-Horakhty, a name of the Great Sphinx, and respect for his service guarding the gods on their mounds in Rostau. The overall impression being conveyed is that N has become a skilled and equipped afterlife spirit, a ritualist who can act in the role of various gods to perform services such as embalming, resurrecting, gaining access to forbidden zones, and repelling enemies.

What the texts of the map section clarify at this stage of N's journey is that the mission is to return to the abode of Osiris *after a prior visit*. What is not clear is whether that abode is on this map or elsewhere not shown. Sherbiny notes that there is no definitive statement on the map to clarify this question.[75] The basic premise, regardless, is that to safely pass by the towns of demons guarding the way in either the light or dark realm, these threats must be stood down using ritualistic spells, utterances, and invocations.

The implication is that these are one-way stations and gates that direct the path of the deceased on a trajectory from west on the right towards east on the left. This direction is the same as that of the general reading direction of the texts on the floorboard. And this is the key take-away from the annotations left for us at the Gate of Darkness.

A return to Osiris' abode means that this is a path once traveled. How and from where did N return to the beginning of the map where the Gate of Darkness is? Did s/he go backwards or did s/he circle around to find another way forward. Another caption answers the question: N circumnavigates alongside Thoth-Moon.[76] This confirms that there is no going backwards once N passes a gate. *The gates are one-way.*

This, in a nutshell, is the mechanism of one-way orbital motion as understood by Egyptian astronomers. The guarded gates were personified celestial flow valves restricting the movement of the wandering bodies in the ecliptic. They prevented collisions and demolitions.

The map section of the *Book of Two Ways* mentions two gates: 1) The Gate of Darkness, and 2) The gateway guarded by He-Who-Gains-through-Robbery. In addition, there are seven gates mentioned in two text boxes, four written vertically[77] and three horizontally. Like the Gate of Darkness, they are made up of darkness and fire.[78] They are 3) The Outer Gateway, 4) The Second Gateway, 5) The Third Gateway, 6) The Fourth Gateway, 7) The First Gate, 8) The Middle Gate, and 9) The Third Gate. The total number of gates is therefore *nine*. These nine gates sort into three groups of two, three, and four. Sherbiny points out that there is no consensus as to the total number of gates mentioned but cites nine as most likely[79] and concludes that at least some of these gates can be localized to the sky.[80]

Likely, therefore, the *Book of Two Ways* mentions nine gates and gateways in the sky. A common characteristic appears to be that a gate is an obstacle created by darkness and fire. Combined with the Winding Waterway and the Island of Fire, I concluded that what was being imagined here was the entire bandwidth of distinct celestial highways running along the starry ecliptic.

The gates apparently were also believed to be guarded crossings between these highways in the sky. Just like it is illegal to cross to the opposite side of a freeway on the ground, this was also forbidden in the ancient Egyptian concept of the celestial circuit of lanes on which the planets moved, at times, in strange and perplexing ways.

I concluded that the map of the *Book of Two Ways* is an illustration of the orbital mechanics as understood by the ancient Egyptians. They would have been able to observe seven bodies in motion with the unaided eye: the Sun and the Moon, and the planets Mercury, Venus, Mars, Jupiter, and Saturn. Their observations must have led them to conclude that these seven bodies meander along dedicated compartments dividing the Winding Waterway, i.e., the Lakes of Shu, separated and isolated by gates to prevent collisions. But if indeed the gated waterways were the Egyptian concept of orbits within the ecliptic, then why did these orbits meander?

I finally came to realize that the Winding Waterways meandered because the bends of the water channels explained what looked like retrograde planetary motion. The sight of a planet gradually climbing along the ecliptic day by day, to curve downward again and then disappear under the horizon for a few days, only to reemerge, must have been truly bewildering. The best way to appreciate this is to see it in a time lapse. I have made a video of a two-year time lapse showing the meanderings of Venus in the western sky using Stellarium. This video can be viewed on my YouTube channel.[81]

The final question which remained was which part of the ecliptic did the map of the *Book of Two Ways* represent? The captions in the map mention that N is on the way to Osiris. It is reasonable to conclude that the map is near the constellation Orion/*s3ḥ*, a constellation long associated with Osiris since the Pyramid Texts (figure 24).

Figure 24: Star zones north and south of that segment of the arc-shaped ecliptic lined by the Zodiac constellations Leo, Cancer, Gemini, Taurus, and Aries. Orion with Canis Major are marked in the south, and the Big and Small Dippers are in the north. Graphic made with Stellarium 0.14.3.

The lower register with its meandering waterway through the darkness of the night would then represent the southern extent of the ecliptic band near the constellation Orion and bordering on the Field of Reeds, the *sḫt-j3rw*.

There are no unequivocal road signs "To Orion" to help us on this side of the map, but, interestingly, there is a compartmented trapezoid structure that immediately reminded me of the shape of this constellation (figure 25 B). One caption written into this structure refers to a marshy basin. Sherbiny sees four purification basins here, symbolic of an embalming ritual.[82] This is also consistent with a fragmented, starry corpse of Osiris, represented by Orion whose place of mummification this represents.

In the upper register, before the last bend, there is an area devoted to agriculture and bread making from where offerings to Osiris are made (figure 25 A). This area of offering aligns with a synonymous area in the northern star zone called the Field of Offerings, the *sḫt-ḥtp*. The blue meandering waterway is therefore an illustration of the northernmost extent of the ecliptic bordering on the northern star zone and the circumpolar stars.

74

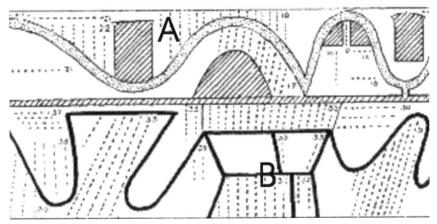

Figure 25: Enlarged view of the map section showing the northern (A) and southern (B) zones of the ecliptic. From Deir El-Bersheh coffin B3C; illustration by de Buck (1961). Courtesy of the Oriental Institute of the University of Chicago.

I had finally deciphered the meaning of the map of the *Book of Two Ways*.

The ecliptic is a crowded place and somehow the lack of collisions in the sky had to be explained as well as the erratic movement of the planets relative to the stars lining the ecliptic. The way this was understood by ancient Egyptian astronomers was the one-way traffic restriction and compartmentalization imagined to be enforced by the guards and gates. The gate concept of the Coffin Texts can thus be understood as an attempt to model the universe known to the ancient Egyptians based on what they observed in the sky. In their model, they were at the universal center and the Sun, Moon, and planets moved about on defined circuits seen as winding waterways separated by guarded gates of fire and darkness.

Transfer between the lanes along the ecliptic was possible only by those spirits properly equipped with spells. That is what kept order in the sky. Appropriately, the horizontal line defining the upper limit of the trapezoid structure is labelled the Road of Maat.[83]

In the Vignette of ***R ͨ,*** the Sun God is surrounded by nine elliptical bands. To prove that these were orbits, and that, in fact, nine were intended to be shown, I had to find the evidence in the text written around the painting, Spell 758, the *Roads of Mehen*. What now made sense about this inscription was the turning around of the barque and the mention of *gate confusion*. It means that keeping the planets on a one-way course was not working. This I thought, must have been the description of retrograde planetary motion illustrated as meandering on the map of the *Book of Two Ways*. In other words, what was shown in the painting and what the ancient Egyptian knew as shown in the map of the *Book of Two Ways* conflicted. That is why the text written around the vignette had to be written. It was designed to reinterpret the confusing image of one-way, concentric ovals instead of the meandering paths the ancient Egyptians had imagined.

But the final proof that the Vignette of *R*ᶜ was originally meant to represent our Heliocentric Solar System depended on the number nine. Was it a coincidence that the Sun God is depicted encircled by nine red and black bands or was that number specifically chosen?

I needed evidence that the vignette was intentionally painted with nine bands because that was also the number of gated orbits the Winding Waterway accommodated. Awareness of nine orbits, and thus nine planets was not compatible with the knowledge base we attribute to the ancient Egyptians. This proof was important. It turns out that the number nine appears prominently in the writings that refer to some of ancient Egypt's most important gods.

4) The Nine. In hieroglyphic writing, the word for The Nine (Greek: Ennead) is ***psḏt***, which might have been pronounced something like the Coptic word for the number nine ***psit***, or ***psijit***. There were multiple spellings, some phonetic, and some pictorial (figure 26).

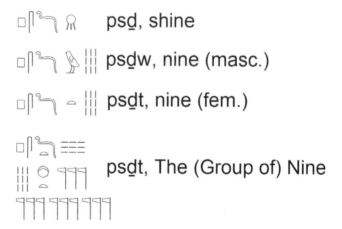

psḏ, shine

psḏw, nine (masc.)

psḏt, nine (fem.)

psḏt, The (Group of) Nine

Figure 26: Various hieroglyphic spellings for The Nine including the nine flag symbols used in the Pyramid Texts, and its alternative use as the word for "shine".

Multiple references appear in the Coffin Texts to The Nine and The Ennead, even the plural form Enneads.[84] It cannot be assumed, unfortunately, that only one and the same entity was meant each time and that complicates the matter a lot. Evidently, several groups of deities were known under this name. I will give a brief review on this confusing subject and then focus on one specific entity called The Nine that mattered to my investigation.

In the Heliopolitean Cosmogony of Lower Egypt, The Great Nine *psḏt ꜥꜣt* [pes-jet aah-ut] are the great gods of ancient Egypt: Atum *jtm*, Shu *šw*, Tefnut *tfnt*, Geb *gb*, Nut *nwt*, Osiris *wsjr*, Isis *jst*, Seth *sṯ*, and Nephthys *nb-ḥwt*. But there was another Nine.

A short compilation of attributes of The Nine in the Coffin Texts paints the following picture (spell numbers in parentheses): They are in mysterious places (33). They place the foes of the deceased under him, and Osiris is their Foremost (42). Geb is ahead of them (69). Geb sees, The Nine hear (74). They cannot see Shu (76). They grant a boon (306). They encircle the sky, are in the west, and in the lower sky (all 306). They accept natron and incense as offerings (306). The deceased knows their names, shapes, and modes of being (306). Mystery surrounds these nine, that much is clear, but who are they?

Surely, these Nine were in the sky because that is what they encircle. Coffin Texts Spell 78 unequivocally separates them as a distinct entity from the Great Nine and another group called the Chaos-Gods. Their esoteric character becomes clear when one realizes that they are not being called by their real names, but only cryptically invoked with a Heka insinuation. Let me explain what I mean.

The context of this spell is N assuming the role of Shu asking this mysterious group of nine to be recognized. N pleads with them to bow their heads and reach down to Earth from the sky to help N ascend:[85]

I am the soul of Shu who ascended on the wings of Shu the father of the gods. O you bowmen of Shu, regard me, for I am eternity, the father of the Chaos-gods; my sister is Tefenet, the daughter of Atum, who bore the Ennead. O you gods, bow your heads, extend the arms of Shu until I go up upon the ladder, regard my father Atum in these his processions with the wrrf-crown forever. I am he who fashioned the Chaos-gods, whom Atum repeated, and this my sister is eternity.

Let me emphasize, first, that the Bowmen of Shu cannot be same group as the Chaos-Gods, separately mentioned in the same sentence. The Chaos-Gods refer to eight primordial beings in existence before creation, collectively called the Ogdoad in ancient Greek, The Eight in English, and the ḥmnw [khe-me-noo] in hieroglyphic. They, famously, were part of the Hermopolitean Cosmogony. In this spell, N, as Shu, is their father, himself one of the Great Nine. This means the Bowmen of Shu are neither from Hermopolis nor Heliopolis.

To confirm that the Chaos-Gods are the Ogdoad, we can look to Spell 80. It begins with "Oh, you eight Chaos-Gods… … ." In de Buck's hiero-glyphic transcription of this spell, you see eight, not nine, bars and the symbol of a seated god with his forearms raised above his head.[86] The eight bars confirm that the Chaos-Gods are indeed identical with the Ogdoad.

However, here is the problem: The seated god with forearms raised is *ḥḥw* [he-hoo], the personified concept of eternity called myriad (figure 27). You have seen this god. He is painted in the plural triplet form, meaning myriads, onto the throne of the Sun God in the Vignette of *Rꜥ*. The Ogdoad, on the other hand, were four couples of snakes and frogs, not eight *ḥḥw*. Is this a mistake? Hardly. It is meant to trip you and raise your awareness that Heka is at play here.

Before I explain this mystery, let me first dispel any doubt that N is really addressing eternity and the *ḥḥw* when he calls on the bowmen of Shu because what he says to them is this: "regard me, for I am eternity … " N wants to be in the sky, eternally. He needs the help of the *ḥḥw* to help him ascend into the sky. Neither the Ogdoad not the Great Ennead can do that for him or her.

It turns out that the hieroglyphic word for "bowmen" *pḏtjw* [Pe-je-teeoo] is a phonetic allusion to the word for nine, *psḏt* [pes-jet]. This is a Heka word play on the similar sounds of these words used here to invoke a com-plex concept, that of nine sky gods, the *ḥḥw,* who personify eternity in this spell in the same way that they do in the Vignette of *Rꜥ*. What looks like a confusion between these nine and the Ogdoad is really the idea that the *ḥḥw* were primordial, from a time before creation, just like the power of Heka, and just like the Ogdoad. In fact, one of the eight Ogdoad was called *ḥḥw*.

This was a break-through. I had identified a group of nine primordial and esoteric sky gods mentioned in the Vignette of *Rꜥ* and in the surrounding

Figure 27: *ḥḥw*, the Egyptian god Eternity representing a Million, or Myriad of years. Photo taken at the Temple of Isis, Philae, Egypt, 2019.

text. This was strong evidence that the nine red and black bands in the painting were, in fact, meant to be nine paths in the sky. The fact that the composer of this spell employed a Heka insinuation to allude to the nine *ḥḥw* is an indicator for their esoteric nature further linking them with the esoteric vignette.

There is yet more information about these eternity gods hidden in another Heka insinuation, in this case the word for "New Moon," *psḏntjw*, literally "The Nine-ish Ones" or "The Shining Ones." An allusion to nine makes no sense astronomically, or does it? The ancient Egyptians believed that the stars were souls. The "souls of the New Moon" were stars near the ecliptic and near the horizon, one could see best when the Moon was invisible. In other words, they were planets, nine of them, as the name implies.

In Coffin Texts Spell 155, we learn that knowledge of these New Moon souls, i.e., planets, relates to having access to a case of documents. The deceased N presents himself in the guise of Thoth, greatest of the scribes and magicians. He is in a dialog with a guardian, so that he may be permitted to gain access to the House of Osiris. This very much appears to be related to what we learned from the map of the *Book of Two Ways*. N is now the New Moon floating on the Winding Waterway, near Orion [notes in brackets added]:[87]

> *Knowing the Souls of the New Moon, entering into the House of*
>
> *Osiris of Djedu.*
>
> [gate guard:] *Who is he who enters, whence comes he who comes forth because of this soul, on whom the earth is high? Such a thing is unknown.*
>
> [N:] *Open to me, for I am a saviour, I am one who keeps secrets, and I belong to the House of Osiris. I am the god in charge of the document-case in the room which contains the ritual robes...*
>
> *... I KNOW THE SOULS OF THE NEW MOON: THEY ARE OSIRIS, ANUBIS, AND ISDES.*

From these examples we can glean the idea that there must have been a group of nine Eternal Ones (*ḥḥw*) in the sky and at least some of them, but not all, were visible as star-like objects. The name, myriads, as in eons, suggests even an awareness that these had long orbital periods.

This is startling knowledge in possession of the ancient Egyptians. It means they knew that the planets do not emit light on their own. More incredible yet, they knew of nine planets but could only observe five. How could this be possible in our current paradigm that says they could only have known of those they could see with the unaided eye, i.e., Mercury, Venus, Mars, Jupiter, and Saturn? Or else they did not understand these ideas but had gained access to them. Since the knowledge was unintelligible from their Earth-in-Center perspective, it was written about in enigmatic ways using Heka. Encryption was a way to enhance complex ideas.

When making such claims, one can never have enough proof. I needed more evidence that what was shown in the Vignette of *R*ᶜ was a solar system of nine planets. I was close, but the stakes of this incredible possibility were too high not to pursue this all the way. Little did I know, I was already in possession of the smoking gun, but let me show you how I got there.

Zunthu

Earlier in my investigation, when the search for the definitive Nine travelling the Winding Waterways in the sky had almost become hopeless, I had come across one mysterious use of both the number nine and a mysterious group of nine mentioned in the Pyramid Texts. This strange passage comes from Pepi II's pyramid. In it appears a mysterious god you have already met: Zunthu.

For context, I am showing both the hieroglyphic text and the phonetic transliteration (figure 28).

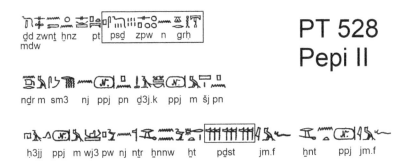

**PT 528
Pepi II**

Figure 28: Pyramid Text (PT) 528 from the corridor of the Pyramid of Pepi II. Hieroglyphic text from left to right and the phonetic transliteration below.

The mention of "nine times" and "The Nine" are framed.

In English:

Words to be spoken: Zunthu who traverses the sky nine times per night, hold onto the braid of this Pepi and may you ferry Pepi in this lake. May Pepi board this divine bark, in which is the body of The Nine. May Pepi be in it as well.

The fact that this passage has caused much ado with Egyptologists attempting to understand it is a great clue that it contained information the ancient Egyptians themselves had encrypted. Perhaps that action was due to its esoteric nature, either because it was too sacred or because it was not well understood. Encryption was in fact a way to express difficult concepts not necessarily to conceal information (see Appendix).

In Rolf Krauss' discussion of this passage, he cites Kurt Sethe's interpretation of Zunthu as German "Sternschnuppe," in English, shooting star or meteorites, but dismisses it as implausible.[88] Instead, Krauss cites PT 511, which clarifies that Zunthu moves in the sky with Sothis-Sirius[89] and that this movement is indeed a circumnavigation of the sky.[90] He dismisses the "nine times per night" as implausible and concludes that Zunthu must be a phase of the Moon given the ferrying function.[91]

We have a paradox, do we not? Sethe could not wrap his mind around the idea of anything up above traversing the sky nine times per night and neither could Krauss. Sethe tried to explain it with shooting stars. Krauss decided to simply dismiss the paradox by dismissing the "nine times," even though there can be no mistake here: Both the word and the number nine are written out.

This is what chapter 1 is all about: When we work from within a certain paradigm and we cannot explain this or that paradox, we tend to dismiss it because it just does not fit. This is much more convenient than challenging the paradigm. Too much is at stake; credibility and acceptance by the peers are part of a categorical, hyper-skeptic stance.

I greatly respect Rolf Krauss for his superb work decoding the astronomy hidden in the Pyramid Texts, but here he landed a small faux pas. At least Sethe was willing to let his imagination run to find a way to explain what Zunthu might represent. But in all attempts, no matter how seemingly ridiculous, something useful may be found, which is why outright dismissal of implausible explanations is a bad habit in science.

What Sethe was trying to imagine is a physical entity that may have been interpreted by the ancient Egyptians to *sequentially* revolve around the sky nine times per night. Since there is not anything even known today that could do this for us to watch, he came up with the idea of shooting stars. He reasoned that the ancient Egyptians may have believed that this is simply one and the same shooting star that keeps shooting many times a night, every night. According to him, the number nine was merely a vague reference to the varying frequency of such common events.

Herein lies the value of Sethe's idea. It is so off-the-wall that it should challenge anyone to question whether the premises are correct. Why must we assume that Zunthu circumnavigated the night sky nine times sequentially *in a row*? PT 528 refers to the *body* of The Nine in the barque, does it not? Zunthu ferries The Nine *together* as a group. What sort of movement was implied by ferrying?

Krauss cites the following passage from Pyramid Text 506, just a few spells upstream from PT 528 inscribed into the corridor of several Sixth Dynasty Pyramids (Figure 29):

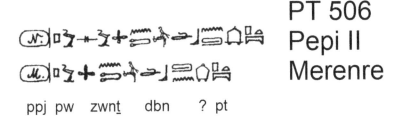

ppj pw zwnṯ dbn ? pt

Figure 29: Above, hieroglyphic Passage read left to right from Pyramid Text (PT) 506 from the corridor of the pyramids of Pepi II and Merenre. Below, the transliteration of the text.

It is Pepi/Merenre as Zunthu, who encircles [the box] *of the sky.*

I placed a question mark under the box icon because its pronunciation and meaning are unknown. It is clear, however, that the sky is being orbited, captured by the word *dbn*. The appearance of the box icon suggests that this was believed to be the structure of the space around Earth: *a box surrounded by nine orbits.*

Whoever composed these two passages of the Pyramid Texts wanted to express the idea that there is a celestial transport mechanism that ferries The Nine as a group around this sky box. In that sense, one circumnavigation transports nine individual gods. Instead of nine sequential circumnavigations, we have a nine-for-one ferry trip on the celestial circuit.

This idea is well captured by the nine red and black bands encircling R^f shown on the vignette painted on the coffin of General Zepi. The text around the vignette proves that this is so:

*The paths of fire go round about the seat of the Shining Sun, who guards the **paths for the great bark of the Coiled One**, who makes a circle for myriad after myriad.*

This no longer leaves any doubt that the four red and five black bands around the Sun God in the Vignette of *R* were meant to illustrate celestial orbits and that they are the paths of The Nine, confirming that there are *nine in number*, the paths of fire.

But if there is still a doubt left, I submit the best of all the evidence here at the end, because I only found it a couple of months ago even though I had looked in its direction every time I looked at the Vignette of *R* and the written text around it (figure 30).

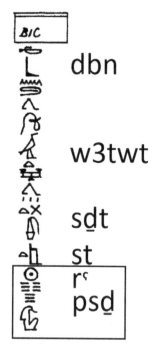

Figure 30: The Seat of the Sun of Nine. Hieroglyphic Spelling from the *Roads of Mehen*, Coffin Texts Spell 758. The word **psd** [pe-sej] has a double meaning, either "shine" or "nine". Here it is spelled in the number version as nine bars together with the word for the Sun God **R** but was translated by R. O. Faulkner as "shining Sun", instead of the "Sun of The Nine". From de Buck (1956); modified. Courtesy of the Oriental Institute of the University of Chicago.

What Faulkner had translated as "The Seat of the Shining Sun" was actually, and quite literally, "The Seat of the Sun of the Nine."

For lack of a sensical way to read the nine bars under the Sun symbol as The Nine, Faulkner used the other known meaning, "shine." There are two occurrences of this number nine symbol in this text of the *Roads of Mehen*, and both are in the context of the seat of the Sun. What a beautifully poignant way, is it not, to call our solar system the Seat of the Sun of Nine? I even had a name for The Nine: The *ḥḥw* ... The Eternal Nine.

The Power of Paradigmatic Prisms

When we take away our modern, reductive prisms and view their texts through ancient lenses that fuse natural phenomena and divine forces, we no longer see fancy mythology; we see science and models to explain the world and universe. In ancient Egypt, the gods were the powers of nature. The stories about the gods were not fairy tales, they were scientific treatises. When Egyptologists accept this concept, they will at last begin to understand the messages we think are hiding behind the colorful metaphors, even though they were never really meant to be concealed.

When in the past, I looked at the frieze high up on the enclosure wall of the Edfu Temple and saw two bull-headed falcons facing each other, I now see the planet Mars headed in opposite directions after a U-turn on the Skyway through the Zodiacs. When in the past, I read about the Winding Lotus Waterway, I now imagine the planets appearing from below the horizon from within the cosmic waters and climbing up the celestial ladder, sometimes meandering off to the east and at times to the west of the path of the Sun. And when I tried to understand the purpose of the demons who guarded the gates in the afterlife, I now understand that these were the rules of celestial motion that governed how the cosmic chaos became order.

When you see Egyptian texts for what they are, when you begin to see things through their lens, not ours, then you begin to see the paradoxes of their time and how they tried to resolve them from within their paradigm of how the world fit into the universe *as they saw it*. Once I saw how you could pass and lane-shift through horizontal and vertical gates, I became more fluent in their scientific lingo.

In science, there is a mantra called "wreck and check." To learn about a complicated system, you disable one aspect of it and see how that affects the rest. I thus began to wonder what a gate violation may look like.

A gate violation could be to traverse a gate, horizontal or vertical, in the opposite direction, basically sneaking up behind the guard and moving outwardly on the coil and moving against traffic on a given lane. But a gate violation would also be a model that would be inconsistent with the apparent movements observed and explained by the gate model of the coil. After all, the need for the gates concept arose merely because Egyptian astronomer-priests assumed that the Earth was in the center of the universe, not the Sun. If an observer believed s/he on Earth was at the center of everything, a heliocentric model would not explain why planets would turn around and fly backwards or why the Moon was sometimes above and sometimes below the star figures lining up by its path.

Therefore, the model of a Sun in the center surrounded by elliptical orbits would be inconsistent with the view of the universe of an ancient Egyptian. The inconsistency would be viewed in the fact that the planets cannot keep going around the Sun on their dedicated orbits, always obeying the same directional movement in a counterclockwise sense. That, to an Egyptian, would be a gates violation, where the gate guardians were being spoofed. Instead of directing one-way traffic through the gates along a coiled path, the guardians would allow continuous traffic on the same elliptical waterway. The gates would be corrupted. *The gates would be confused.*[92] We are left with two mysteries: How can concentric elliptical orbits become a coil? Who was the Coiled One in relation to Zunthu?

The name Zunthu relates to *znt*. Zenet is an old Egyptian board game played on a wooden box with thirty squares in three rows and figurines (figure 31). The rules of the game and how to win are unknown, though some have attempted to reconstruct them—for example, Peter Piccione.[93] Based on the meaning of the word *znt*, the game involved *passing*. Zunthu then can be understood as the personified gate crosser, literally the *passenger*, he who can pass the celestial gates that separate the orbits. By passing these gates, one by one, an inward spiraling motion is created, the goal of which was for none other than a king or a queen in the Old Kingdom, or for a privileged private person in the Middle Kingdom, to reach the place of resurrection, the place of Osiris in the zone south of the ecliptic. *Could concentric rings have been transformed into a coil?*

This is where the dogmatic power of a paradigm produces a lens through which paradoxical information is filtered to make it conform with what is known. Since the Heliocentric Solar System of nine planets was not compatible with the ancient Egyptian's view of the sky, and their place within, the knowledge enshrined in the painting known as the Vignette of *R*ᶜ, was reinterpreted. What was meant to be a solar system of independent

Figure 31: The Zenet gaming board circa. 1938-1700 BC. Faience. The hieroglyphic spelling of the name of the game is in the upper left corner. Charles Edwin Wilbour Fund/ Brooklyn Museum. ©, Creative Commons-BY (Photo: CUR.36.2_36.3.6-.12_erg2.jpg).

planetary orbits became a spiral path made by bridging these orbits with the opened gates. The result of this reinterpretative transformation was a model of passing time instead of a model of space. That model of passing time was the celestial super-cycle we know as precession, and its symbol became the coil.

I had been perplexed by Faulkner's seemingly awkward description of the elliptical concentric rings in the Vignette of R^{ς} as coils based on his translation of the relevant Coffin Text spells. Then, I came to realize that ancient Egyptian theologians had devised an entire body of funerary spells to magically escape the restriction imposed by the guarded gates. The gate concept, I concluded, had been devised by the astronomer-priests to explain the spatial confinements of concentric orbits to prevent collisions between gods, for example the planets. The success of an afterlife in eternity, however, was based on being granted passage through these boundaries. The effect of being granted passage amounted to transforming nine closed-loop concentric circuits, *The Roads of Mehen*, into a path along an inward-coiling spiral. But how?

Given what I had already encountered, I now suspected the answer was hiding in plain sight. *The gates are confused.* The hieroglyphic translation of the English word confused, *ẕṯnm/sṯnm*, was an anagram for Zunthu, as I demonstrated in Chapter III. The secret of how to violate the boundaries of the sky imposed by nine concentric orbits to venture to their center had been phonetically embedded into the text surrounding the Vignette of **Rˁ**: *Become a passenger and pass the gates!*

The gates had now been swung open for me, but the next question already stared at me: Who was the Coiled One?

V

Coils

A SK ANYONE TO SHOW YOU WHAT THEY THINK IS THE OLDEST AND MOST PRI-
meval symbol known to mankind, and they will make a circle. But
in ancient Egypt, an almost equally
primordial sign was the coil. I'm
certain that the coil imagery must
have come from a circle, but what if
it wasn't just one circle, but a series
of concentric, oval rings like those
shown in the Vignette of *R$^\varsigma$*? If so,
how and when did this transforma-
tion occur?

In this chapter I describe how
far back in time this symbol transformation possibly took place. This,
it turns out, was crucial evidence
which I thought might help me to
place in time when the original
archive that contained the Vignette
of *R$^\varsigma$* must have been breached.

A Lion's Game of Astronomy

The Four Dog cosmetic slate
palette (figure 32) dates to before
3000 BC, to ancient Egypt's

Figure 32: The Four Dogs Palette (Naqada
III, circa 3300-3100 BC). An ibis above a
lion sprinting on a circle. Louvre Museum,
Paris. Petrie (1953), Plate B.

predynastic era. It shows a ring and a sprinting lion above, as if on a running wheel. Opposite the lion, a lion-like, flamingo- or snake-necked fantasy beast hovers over the ring. I had seen the palette, but never took the time to study these details. Without some needed context, one could write this off as whimsical art if it were not for an ancient Egyptian board game called Mehen. The game action took place on a spiral board made up of a checkerboard-like, slotted snake wrapped into a coil. On it, six couchant ivory lions and lionesses—or six dogs in a variant version of the game—and thirty-six marbles made their moves based on how three throw sticks landed when cast like dice (figure 33).

Figure 33: Reconstructed early dynastic game boards. The Mehen game is shown in the foreground, its playing pieces to the right: three lions and three lionesses. Another version was played with six dog figurines. In the left upper corner is the Zenet game. The Museum of Egyptian Antiquities, Cairo, Egypt, 2018.

The rules of Mehen are unknown, but the goal seemed to be to advance the lion figurines from the outer coil to the center along the game slots. Perhaps the player who made it first won the game though this, too, is unknown.[94]

A wall painting of the game's coiled snake board and playing figurines was discovered in the tomb of the Third Dynasty high official at Djoser's court, Hesy-*Rᶜ*, Master Scribe of the king and master of a mysterious, hitherto untranslated, function symbolized by a couchant lioness deity called Mehit. This lioness had a neck characteristically adorned with rings.

Similarly, a neck ornament details the lioness figurines used to play Mehen (figure 34). Was this game connected to the Roads of Mehen mentioned in the text wrapped around the Vignette of **R'**, and both to Mehit?

Figure 34: Game pieces used in Mehen. The lioness figurine has an ornamental neck band. The Museum of Egyptian Antiquities, Cairo, Egypt, 2018.

Like the Four Dog Palette, Mehen dates to predynastic times, before 3000 BC. Apparently, the iconographic theme of a lion running on a ring or advancing down a coil had already pervaded the culture of the Nile Valley before it became unified with the Delta region by the conqueror Horus-Narmer.

At first, rings and coils may seem only vaguely related without the necessary context given by other, similar artifacts. For example, on the Two Dog Palette—a ritual slate object of the kind originally used to prepare cosmetic make-up found in Hierakonpolis and dated to 3300-3100 BC—snake-necked lions or panthers girdle a ring (figure 35).

On the later Narmer Palette, also discovered in Hierakonpolis and dated to circa 3000 BC, their necks contort into a ring (figure 35). The common iconography shared between these palettes and the game Mehen comprised rings, coils, and lions. Why these two symbols were used interchangeably in Egyptian art made no sense until I reviewed Timothy Kendall's excellent paper on the history of the Mehen.

Strangely, it did not seem to matter to the game if it were rings or coils. In the tomb of Second Dynasty's King Seth-Peribsen, four Mehen boards

Figure 35: Two Dog Palette (left) and Narmer Palette (right), both verso. From Petrie (1953), Plates F16 and K.

were found. One of them is not a coil but made from a set of concentric rings. Kendall speculates that a specially painted, colored slot in each ring may have served as an access bridge to move the game pieces over to the adjacent inner or outer circle.

Another board has four parallel, spiraling tracks. Yet another has five non-spiraling, concentric rings. In each ring, a game slot acts like a portal to transfer from one ring to the next. The various versions of the game provided the decisive clue how the ancient Egyptians had made the leap from concentric rings to a spiraling coil: with bridges and gates.[95]

I realized what this game was really about. I was looking at the playful version of Zunthu's barque passing a sky gate to leap from one orbital waterway to the next on the way to R^c. *Mehen was a game about observations in the sky.*

This was a major leap forward in my investigation. Prehistoric Mehen players reenacted the imagined, perilous journey undertaken by Middle Kingdom elites as told in the Coffin Texts over a thousand years later. In the texts, N the deceased, armed with spells, ventured inwards on the Roads of Mehen, across guarded gates first to Osiris and then towards R^c, the Sun. These gates were placed between the parallel, concentric Winding Waterways which formed the ecliptic border zone between the Field of Reeds to the south, the abode of Orion-Osiris, and the Field of Offering to the north. As I concluded in the previous chapter, the gates preserved the integrity of the celestial traffic, and in this way also guarded the holy path to resurrection reserved to only those equipped to pass, like Mehen, Zunthu, and the ritualist N.

In the game, similarly, a lion(ess) figurine made its way in, or out, of a coil. The name of the game was the same as that of the elliptical bands in the Vignette of R^c, the Roads of Mehen. It made sense. The game illustrated an ancient Egyptian astronomical concept: The mechanics of overcoming the confinement of an elliptical orbit and moving to the next, and then the next one, all the way to the center, where the Sun dwelled on its throne. The gated bridges had turned concentric orbits into a spiral, both in the sky and in the game.

So yes. Mehen was a game about the sky. But what concept of astronomy was being reenacted on this coiled game board? It could not possibly have been anything to do with the Heliocentric Solar System, which has nothing to do with a spiral. I should point out as a technical side note, however, that the circular motion of objects around the Sun are in fact spiraling considering that the entire solar system moves in unison through space.

I was faced with the real possibility that as early as the dawn of civilization in Egypt and Sumer, the idea to journey across nine orbits towards the center of the known universe culminating in an encounter with the Sun God, an idea alluded to in Spell 758 written around the vignette, was a fantasy played out on a game board. This boggled my mind. Naturally, I wanted to know where and when this concept had originated, but it was surely older than the civilization of ancient Egypt and therefore also what was shown in the Vignette of R^c. I had suspected this based on its esoteric, anachronistic content, but now I had evidence. Mehen took me back in time much further than I had foreseen.

The idea that bridged and gated concentric rings could became a coil had evidently left a profound imprint on the culture of ancient Egypt from its predynastic beginnings. The coil icon appears in the earliest set of Egyptian hieroglyphs found thus far. These symbols were carved into bone tags discovered in the tomb of Scorpion, Tomb UJ, dated by the German Archaeological Institute to circa 3200-3100 BC (figure 36).

Figure 36: Number and coil symbols on bone tags, found in Tomb UJ. ©, DAI/Dreyer (1999).

The origin of the celestial gate mechanics described in the Coffin Texts and the Mehen game must have been based on a primordial astronomical concept known long before Egypt became a unified kingdom, long before 3000 BC. This much older concept was that of a Sun encircled by nine planetary orbits illustrated in the vignette. The original image had been copied as a painting onto the headboard of general Zepi's coffin by a scribe from the Hermopolitean *House of Life*. It had been annotated with a text whose design and word choice insinuated and phonetically invoked Zunthu, the gate-crossing ferryman known from the earlier Pyramid Texts. What this means is that the text represented a reinterpretation of the idea shown in the vignette. Concentric ellipses had become the Roads of Mehen, a spiraling coil—just like in the game Mehen.

Such coils feature prominently on several painted pots and jars from the predynastic Decorated Pottery Era (figure 37). What could have been on the jar painters' mind at a time that remote? It had to be something more profound than fancy pot ornaments.

Figure 37: Decorated Ware with spirals, Roger Fund (1910). ©, The Metropolitan Museum of Art, New York, NY. Public Domain.

The reinterpretation of anachronistic knowledge must have occurred long before dynastic Egypt came to be. That means this knowledge came into possession of prehistoric people near the Nile at least that far back in time. If it was hidden in an archive, that archive was breached long before Egypt was unified. I had not expected this. The guarded gates of the afterlife, like the specially designed slots on the coil and rings of Mehen, had converted an illustration of heliocentricity into an image of a spiral celestial path to the Sun. What explained the initially confusing, paradoxical equivalence of rings and spiraling coils were these gates.

But in the Coffin Texts these gates are also an astronomical concept of celestial mechanics to explain the motions of the heavenly bodies, identified with the gods. The gates were part of the ancient's concept of the ecliptic, the Winding Waterways.

Something had prompted prehistoric sky watchers to imagine these gates that turned concentric elliptic paths into a spiraling coil. But why did these astronomers imagine the coiled celestial path as a snake, and who was Mehen? What was the meaning of the lion figurines? The answers had to depend on the astronomy at play, the key to this fascinating riddle.

Coil and Snake

In later dynastic Egyptian iconography, coils and snakes became symbols of the Sun cult of R^c and divine kingship. The coil was part of the *dšrt* [desh-er-et], the Red Crown of Lower Egypt, already worn by Egypt's founder king Narmer (figure 35). The cobra snake can often be seen to form a protective ring around the Sun God during his journey by day and night (figure 38).

Figure 38: The coil attachment to the Lower Egyptian *dšrt* [De-she-ret] Red Crown, shown here combined with the Upper Egyptian *ḥdt* [He-jet] White Crown to form the *sḫm-ty* [Se-khem-tee], the Dual Powers Crown. The cobra snake is a protective, and regenerative symbol of the divine Sun Kings. Portal relief at the gate to the inner sanctuary of the mortuary temple of Hatshepsut. Deir El-Bahari, Egypt, 2017.

But even the earlier, more primordial iconography I had been studying suggested that the coil and snake were astronomical symbols. They invoked the celestial highway along the ecliptic around the Sun God and an inward, spiritual path departing from it towards the center to be with him, the creator.

This merging of astronomy and religion may seem strange to us because we separate science and religion into distinct quarters. Hence, the immanent, scientific character of Egyptian theology can escape us. Religious texts were, in part at least, scientific treatises describing the workings of the forces of nature—in this case, celestial mechanics. I was now looking at an astronomical concept represented by a spiraling coil that was more ancient than recorded history and that had been modified from an original which appeared to be older still. This original idea had been reworked and transmitted in the form of a pictographic coil icon that would become a symbol seeding two pillars of civilized people: science and art.

The reinterpretation of the original primordial, though anachronistic, astronomical concept, concentric elliptical rings surrounding the Sun, led to its transformation into another based on what was familiar at the time. This familiar astronomical concept was represented by a coiled snake and a wandering lion. These two symbols become iconized and acquired theological importance.

The model I envisioned crystallized out as such: A prehistoric people who lived in the Nile Valley had come into possession of, to them, esoteric astronomical knowledge. They could not explain it with what they knew. They did what we would do in part: They scientifically adapted it according to how it fit into their own knowledge base. But their science was also theological; they iconized it as a power symbol and expressed it in the form of a theological theme. Since it originally came to them from a source they could not explain in secular terms, for example from an archive guarded by a monumental stony lion statue, its origin had to be divine. This religious theme must have revolved around resurrection and immortality because that is the central theme of the later Pyramid and Coffin Texts, in whose context the original idea suddenly reappears in the archaeological record.

I thus suspected that the underlying astronomical foundation of religious ideas dealing with resurrection must have been a recurrent astronomical event—a celestial cycle symbolized by a coil. *But which?*

Since the movement of the ivory lion game pieces on the coiled board of Mehen reenacted a journey in the sky to the game board's center and back, this could have been the constellation Leo. I must add here that Egyptologists and archaeo-astronomers do not accept that Leo was a recognized constellation before Egypt's New Kingdom, some 1500 years after Egypt became a unified kingdom.

But if prehistoric people could see what we see today, a lion-like figure recognized in the starry outline of the constellation Leo, then the concept of resurrection and immortality could have been imagined as the recurrent cycle of time. One way to imagine this cycle is that of an iconic image in the sky, like a lion, periodically reuniting with the rising Sun in a certain position on the horizon. Such a recurrent meeting of the Sun with a certain group of stars near the ecliptic after a period of many years is caused by Earth-axial *precession.*

Was Mehen a game of immortality in the afterlife played to reenact observations of the Precession of the Equinox? And if so, why was this represented as a coil?

Of course, the idea that the ancient Egyptians might have known precession wasn't new. As I mentioned in Chapter II, Hancock and Bauval proposed that the monuments of the Giza Plateau were a precession clock calibrated to time the spring equinoctial rising of the constellation Leo above the due east horizon.

And so, I now asked myself if the lion in the Mehen game was based on an equally ancient, east-gazing, gigantic stony lion at the foot of the Giza Plateau long before it was remodeled into a sphinx?

To tie the coil to precession, I needed a text which made a connection between this symbol and astronomical time. Indeed, the Pyramid Texts give us a clue what the coil might have meant in terms of the sky. In Utterance 175, also known as Pyramid Text 268, written on the south wall of the antechamber inside the pyramid of Unis, we read:[96]

The portals will act for him, the (Red Crown's) coil will be tied on for him, and this Unis will lead the Imperishable Stars.

We are being told that the coil on the *dšrt* empowered the king to be at the head of the stars which revolve around the celestial north pole. These circumpolar stars were believed to be imperishable, and hence immortal, because they never cosmically set below the horizon. They could be observed in various positions around the northern celestial center throughout the year.

By contrast, the periodic appearance and disappearance, called cosmic settings and heliacal risings, of prominent stars, planets, the Sun, and the Moon south of the circumpolar stars were explained in terms of dying in the west and resurrecting in the east. The sky was therefore conceptually divided into a small zone of immortality in the extreme north and a big the zone of dying and resurrection south of it. This large southern zone was further divided into the Field of Reeds and the Field of Offering by the Winding Waterway, what we know to be the ecliptic and the band of the twelve zodiac constellations which line up with it.

What the two zones had in common was the circular motion around an axis which extended from the observable celestial north pole above the horizon to the unseen celestial south pole below it from the perspective of people living in the northern hemisphere of Earth. The symbol of that motion, I initially wondered, could be a turning coil representing the nightly merry-go-round of the stars around the north pole. This is what PT 268 initially seemed to suggest.

However, as I have noted, the coil originated from the idea of bridged, concentric ellipses, a concept originally meant to show the solar system of the Sun in the center and nine planets around.

How had a model of the solar system become a model for the daily motion of the starry sky? This did also not seem to fit the theme of a lion traveling into a spiral or a ferryman embarking on a rendezvous with the Sun God. Further arguing against a daily cycle was the length of time, as the text around the vignette informs us, it took to travel the Roads of Mehen: not hours but myriads of years.

Precession and Coil

Something was missing, unless, of course, the coil represented a much longer period, like the precession of the celestial north pole along a ring made up of the imperishable stars. This effect is caused by the same forces that cause ecliptic precession observable, for example, on the eastern horizon where the Sun rises in the morning. One precession cycle is almost 26,000 years long. Is the message of PT 268 that the northern, red crown empowered the king to run the precessional motor of the sky on the eastern horizon by turning the northern circle of the Imperishable Stars?

The Pyramid Texts, again, help make the connection: The imperishable stars were also thought to be the rowing crew of the bark of $R^{ς}$.[97] The ancient Egyptians recognized that there was a connection between what turned the ecliptic in the south and the Imperishable Stars in the north.

In their theory of a master plan at Giza, Graham Hancock and Robert Bauval proposed that the Great Sphinx and the pyramids were a megalithic, precessional clock waiting to be wound back to Zep Tepi. In astronomical terms, this was the ecliptic star-epoch when the lion on the ground stared at the due east equinoctial Sun rising into the starry lion on the horizon. In the same epoch, the three pyramids more perfectly aligned with the belt stars of Orion. Could a spiraling coil represent this astronomical super-cycle generated by precession?

Initially, I did not understand how Mehen might have been played to completion in this context—did the lion arriving in the center on the head of the coiled snake represent the constellation Leo? Or was it a lion statue on the ground, returning to a certain alignment with the observable sky after circa 26,000 years?[98] Was the coiled snake the symbol of this precessional journey that ended where the game ended: in the center with the Sun? I could not yet see the astronomical underpinning of the coil symbolism if it were indeed meant to be an icon of precession.

Things were getting complicated visually. I had to study the movements of the night sky during thousands of years using simulation software called Stellarium.[99] The first part was easy. Is there a snake-like constellation near Leo? The answer is in the affirmative: the magnificent constellation Hydra, nestled along the ecliptic uncannily extending below Leo (figure 39). This could explain why the coil was thought of as a snake. The snake was in the sky near the lion.

The second part, however, was difficult. Not until I let Stellarium run through many simulations did I make the connection to the coil. But the idea was much simpler than I expected. Instead of tracking the slow westward march of the Zodiac constellations barely visible due east in the predawn sky during hundreds of spring equinox sunrises, it is much easier to follow just one constellation's wander on the horizon as its appearance shifts with the seasons. Indeed, this way to track precession explains how ancient people

Figure 39: Above, southeast view of the night sky at dawn showing the constellations Leo and Hydra. The ecliptic is simulated with an arc. Graphic made with Stellarium 0.14.3. Below, photo of the same region. ©, Andrea Scuderi.

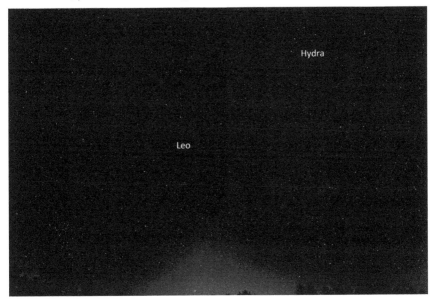

could have observed and symbolized the phenomenon as a coil. Imagine for example, how Leo might wander along the eastern horizon during a full precession cycle, when one follows the place of its heliacal risings[100] over a few centuries.

The full range centers on due east; from there it extends north- and southward on the horizon to the extremes of the solar year, the solstices. Precessional wander is an almost imperceptible effect visually (only about 1/72 of a day per year) to observe with unaided eyesight over a few years' time.[101] Over the entire cycle of circa 26,000 years, (365 days per year/[1 day/72]) there are four visually discrete horizontal stations, each successive two circa sixty-five centuries apart.

These four points are at the two extremes and center of the total horizontal range of sunrises during a year: the solstices at the northernmost and southernmost ends, and the equinoxes centered on due east (figure 40).

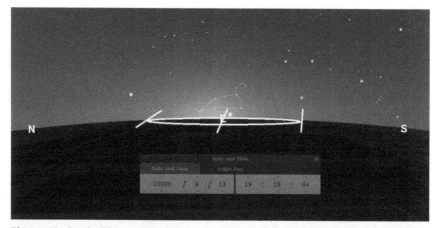

Figure 40: Gradual horizontal wander of heliacal risings of Leo after visual absence during a precession cycle, centered around due east. The four stations are spring equinox, summer solstice, fall equinox, winter solstice. The entire cycle lasts circa 26,000 years. Approximate ecliptic angles to the horizon indicated in red. Graphic simulation with Stellarium 0.14.3.

Arbitrarily the cycle could of course be construed to begin at either of the solstices or equinoxes, or at any position in between these. To recreate Mehen, I assumed a starting position on the spring equinox, with Leo hovering immediately above the predawn horizon like a couchant lion over the due east vernal point, where the center of the Sun rises on that day. This is day one in my simulation. Leo has just arisen heliacally moments before a sunrise due east.

As the cycle commences, Leo initially continues to appear in the pre-dawn hours near due east on the horizon. It always disappears near due west no matter what time of the year except during a two-month period when it cannot be seen at all after its cosmic setting. As the centuries pass, the arc of Leo's appearance and sky path on the ecliptic to the point of its disappearance in the western sky widens as it wanders northward on the horizon towards the summer solstice station.

Sixty-five hundred years into the cycle, when Leo heliacally rises at the summer solstice, that arc is now much broader, its legs displaced maximally north of due east and west. Another sixty-five hundred years later, at the fall equinox, the legs of the arc return to due east and west. Having reached the fourth station at the winter solstice, yet another sixty-five hundred years have passed, the legs intersect the horizon more closely spaced together, south of due east and west. The precessional cycle completes with Leo returning to the spring equinox with the vernal point at due east. The entire journey has taken about 260 centuries.

We thus have a set of four major precessional epochs, demarcated by four seasonal transitions. Their corresponding ecliptic arcs range from wide at, or near, the summer solstice to narrow at, or near, the winter solstice. Intermediate arcs in between these wide and narrow extremes occur at, or near, the equinoxes of spring and fall. The entire set of arcs does indeed look like a coil (figure 41).

A near-ecliptic star like Regulus in Leo, an asterism like the head and neck of Leo, or the entire constellation Leo that looks like a couchant lion could have served as markers to track precession along this epochal timeline. The specific event to track would have been the complete reappearance over the horizon of that ecliptic constellation, asterism, or star after its annual period of absence— about two months in the case of Leo.

This reappearance is called a heliacal rising. We cannot see stars behind, or near the Sun, until Earth orbits forward such that the observer's view of the horizon blocks the Sun enough for the star's weaker light to again become visible. Could this disappearance and reappearance have been interpreted as passing a gate to bridge one ecliptic arc to the next?

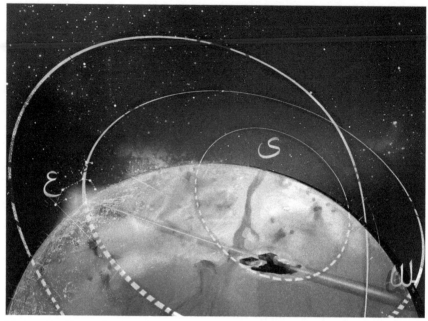

Figure 41: The path of the Sun during the years when Leo appeared immediately above the horizon due east, at the vernal point on Spring Equinox. Mehit at Giza in Egypt by the Nile is the monumental marker. Graphic illustration by Anthony Sturmas, Asturmas Studios.

Suppose then a hypothetical observer tracked the bright star Regulus forming the "heart" of Leo. This marker appears near the spot where the Sun rises, circa twenty minutes later than in the prior year. With each successive year, the star's appearance seems more delayed. After seventy-two years, the lifetime of only a fortunate person in prehistoric times, Regulus rises a full day after the equinoctial sunrise, having now slightly drifted away from the vernal point on the horizon. This horizontal drift of an ecliptic star marker, when measured and recorded over generations' time from equinox to solstice and solstice to equinox, takes 91 x circa 72 years: circa 6,552 years. One full precessional cycle through four transitions is four times longer, circa 26,000 years. I am using rounded figures here to only illustrate the principle with an accuracy of no better than a century or two.

Whether prehistoric people could measure such small changes and record them for their descendants, who after generations of such recorded observations would eventually recognize the vast cycle of time during which these astronomical events would repeat themselves, is obviously not widely accepted by historians. It seems that this is difficult to accept without archaeological evidence for astronomical surveying equipment and many generations of astronomical records.

Yet in the middle of the northeastern Sahara, the southwest of Egypt, prehistoric nomads did just that. They tracked the slow wander of certain stars and marked this movement with megalithic rows of quarried stone blocks. I speak of the early Neolithic, pastoralist cattle culture whose cultural remnants were discovered at Nabta Playa. This idea is not far-fetched.[102] To me, this had the tell-tale signs of an organic, observational, gradual process of slow discovery, not a leap in knowledge based on inherited information. I began to ask myself, if awareness of precession had been empirically discovered, rather than based on inherited knowledge, like other, misunderstood information about the Heliocentric Solar System. This mattered if I wanted to date the breach of the archive after I which I was hunting.

Something else came to me much unexpected: After I had developed the spiral model of precession by tracking the horizontal wander of the constellation Leo over a 26,000-year cycle, I suddenly realized that this could be the original astronomical basis for the story of the Wandering Lioness, rather than the yearly excursions of the Sun on the horizon. I had just come across Barbara Richter's 2012 University of California, Berkeley Ph.D. thesis that deals with word plays used in the *pr wr* sanctuary of Hathor at her temple in Dendera. Richter focused on three themes, Hathor as creator goddess, Hathor as a cause of cosmic disorder, and the king's role in restoring this order by appeasing and reuniting her with the Sun from whom she ran away.[103] This function of the king and its successful execution was one of Ptolemaic Egypt's most prominent festivals, called the Return of the Wandering Goddess. In the Middle and New Kingdom, a similar theme revolved around the Tekh Festival, also known as the First of Drunkenness.

From the New Kingdom also comes a statue kept at the British Museum of a scribe called Hati.[104] On the statue, originally from Thinis, is an inscription that mentions Anhur/Onuris-Shu, and Mehit. Anhur, *jn-ḥrt*, is the hunter who "brings that which is apart," but also "brings that which is in the sky," an allusion to his escaped consort Mehit and the Wandering Goddess Story. What matters here most is that the wandering goddess in the stories of ancient Egypt was not only a *lioness*, possibly seen in the sky, but she was also, originally, Mehit, or should we say Mehen?

The model of precession I had simulated, that of a heliacally appearing lioness slowly wandering on the horizon, suddenly made perfect sense as the real phenomenon underlying this story. Richter herself draws a connection between the Wandering Lioness story and astronomy, specifically the yearly wander of the Sun southward on the horizon towards the winter solstice.[105] My model of precession more directly applies to a lion figure made up of the stars of Leo whose positional wander on the horizon, back and forth, and centered on the equinox position, takes place over millennia. I can even explain the cobra on the head of the Sun God and kings: That was the rising of Hydra together with Leo.

My research, thus far, had led me to formulate a prehistorical model in which concentric rings depicting orbits of planets had been reinterpreted as a coiled snake and had been combined with a lion-march into the spiral center of the Mehen game. I had concluded that this was a prehistoric, playful reenactment of an equinoctial precession cycle of time.

I could not be sure at this stage. However, based on the text around the vignette painting, I concluded that the gate model and the coil that results from it were a reinterpretation of the concentric orbits model of heliocentricity. This left me wondering if the Vignette of R^f had been reinterpreted based on preexisting, empirical knowledge of precession since remote, prehistorical times or if knowledge of precession was an idea born out of interpreting the vignette.

Inherited or Discovered Knowledge?

Let us now assume the other case though. Let's say knowledge of precession was part of the inherited stash of esoteric, anachronistic information which fell into the hands of predynastic Nile Valley dwellers. Would the coil symbolize a precessional message form a more remotely prehistoric people to commemorate an epic Earth event: An event, for example, which gave the Earth a push to finally escape from the permanent frost and begin to warm?

If such were the case, then these prehistoric people also knew that the Sun is at the center, knowing precession would be the lesser feat because they would then also know the composite nature of Earth's motion around the Sun, both orbital and axial. They would have understood that precession is an Earth-tilting effect, independent of its orbital period around the Sun—if knowledge of precession depended on knowledge of heliocentricity, we would have to conclude that both insights would be anachronistic to the ancient Egyptians and their immediate prehistoric ancestors who lived by the Nile.

The other case to consider is this: Knowledge of heliocentricity was inherited by prehistoric cultures near the Nile, but they did not understand it. Since it could not be explained from the Earth-centric view of the time, it was reinterpreted as a model of then already recognized precession, as evident from Nabta Playa where straight megalithic stone lines target Orion, Sirius, and Arcturus over many centuries of time. These stone vectors radiate from one of the thirty so-called complex structures, Complex Structure A.[106]

All these impressive megalithic creations were built as ovals over naturally carved rocky outcroppings of the Nabta lakebed with a central stone lying in the center. Complex Structure A is the largest of these. There were ovals at Nabta Playa, which is interesting, but no concentric ellipses, or spiraling coils, or were there?

I had to be sure. I contacted the one person who would know the answer as best as I could hope for, and that is astrophysicist Dr. Thomas Brophy who has visited Nabta Playa. He is an expert on the archaeoastronomy of the site having written *The Origin Map* (2002), *Black Genesis* (2011), and *Imhotep the African: Architect of the Cosmos* (2013), the latter two with Robert Bauval. During our phone conversation, Dr. Brophy had two startling pieces of information for me: He had interpreted the fashioned surface of the bedrock, called the Table Rock,[107] over which the cow stone had hovered in the sedimental soil, to be a spiral.

I gasped when he mentioned this. The context of this buried spiral, if that is what was meant to be carved into the bedrock of Complex Structure A, was a precessional dial above ground made from gigantic stones, something Brophy and Bauval had already proposed. But things got even more exciting.

Dr. Brophy and I had already finished the conversation and he promised to send an e-mail with a few photos from Nabta Playa. Then came another e-mail. He had almost forgotten to tell me about the even bigger find: There is a megalithic structure called X-1 at Nabta Playa. I had read about it in the past, but there is a crucial detail he mentioned I would have never appreciated on my own not having been there. It sits atop a gigantic man-made stony mound shaped like a spiral measuring some seventy-five meters across.[108]

This discovery by Thomas Brophy was immensely important to my investigation. At this prehistoric site, predating the beginning of dynastic Egypt by several thousands of years, archaeoastronomical evidence exists that Neolithic, nomadic desert pastoralists understood the slow wander of the star map, enshrined this knowledge using megalithic stones, and used a spiraling coil to symbolize something in relation to these insights. This was the missing piece.

It made much more sense to me now why Egyptian astronomers had reinterpreted concentric ellipses in the Vignette of R^f as a spiral coil of precessional time. The slow wander and return of the sky had long had a profound impact on the people alive in predynastic times thousands of years before Egypt became a unified land under one royal power. No wonder a strange new idea about the sky had to be assimilated into that which had been engrained for so long as a sign of order in a sky otherwise full of chaos.

And since the insight to model precession as a coil did not require knowledge of the Heliocentric Solar System, I feel I can conclude with confidence that while the idea of the Heliocentric Solar System was likely inherited knowledge passed from an unknown time and place, knowledge of precession was discovered. I vote for case number two above.

Sky Motor

That dynastic Egyptians could have also known the effect of precession on how they saw the sky is suggested by the positional lay-out of the Giza pyramids and Sphinx. This was the central idea proposed by Hancock and Bauval in *Message of the Sphinx*. In their model, the Great Sphinx tracks the slow, sideways wander of stars near the ecliptic, as centuries and millennia flow by. They also pointed out that stars below the ecliptic, or above, precess by slow-shifting more vertically, for example the up and down, over a 26,000-year-cycle of Orion. In yet another pattern, precession of the north pole in the sky tracks along a ring of constellation. Sideways, vertical, and around a ring. The effect of precession on the way we see the stars depends on where in the sky we look.

The coil mode of precession I propose the ancient long defined, incorporates all these into one. That is why it is the coil was a symbol of power.

The force which turned the sky to make precession happen in the first place rested with the king. It is he who was symbolically empowered by the coil on his crown to turn the firmament. But remember PT 268: The driving force of the precessional sky motor was applied in the northern star zone. This is where the coil was being turned. But why there? Why in the north? Because the north is where the star souls were immortal. *He who controls mortality controls time.*

Theologically speaking, the ancient Egyptians distinguished between repeated resurrection after dying and immortality. The Imperishable Stars around the north pole were believed to be immortal. They did not keep dying and reviving every year, such as the other stars to the south. The circumpolar stars near the celestial north pole were always visible from Egypt. Since these stars never disappeared below the horizon, they attained their exceptional, imperishable attribute.

Rarely, however, would a once-believed immortal star would dip below the horizon and thus feared to have perished, especially when observed from the lower, more southerly latitudes of Egypt. This temporary absence was, of course, rather caused by precessional shifting of the northern map of stars. The so-called hoof-star Alkaid in Ursa Major, for example, may have disappeared below the horizon for Upper Egyptian observers during the early Old Kingdom, the early Fourth Dynasty.[109] This likely unsettling discovery correlates with a new choice of star targets in the sky to orient the pyramids as is evident from their new orientations.[110] It is even possible that this observation may have triggered a fundamental shift in the theological focus from immortality to resurrection, from the northern star zone to the ecliptic.

Egyptologists like James P. Allen have pointed out the Pyramid Texts of the late Old Kingdom appear ambivalent as to where the king wanted to go, north or east.[111] One way to explain that ambivalence in where salvation could be found is that to resurrect in the east as a theological doctrine had not yet fully replaced the more archaic aim of a king to become immortal in the north. Indeed, both concepts remained represented in the texts, though ritually and architecturally separated in terms of where their corresponding spells were inscribed: *offering* and *insignia* on the north wall and *resurrection* on the south walls of the burial chamber and antechamber.[112]

Of such importance then was the predictability of recurrent events in the sky that only the king was vested with the power to control the cycle of time measured on the map of the stars. The symbol to project that power was the coil.

I had reconstructed a scenario that began with prehistoric knowledge of heliocentricity that had been passed forward and reinterpreted as a coil model of precession, from within the prevailing, geocentric view of the world. The original knowledge was thus not lost but assimilated into a form which made it less recognizable as anachronistic and foreign to the ancient Egyptians. This was the likely reason why its significance has been overlooked by those Egyptologists who studied it.

The next step in the process of assimilation was how this, now modified, esoteric knowledge became weaponized so to speak: in other words, how it was used to claim and project royal power to control the people of Egypt.

This transformation of knowledge to power must have involved a new theology based on which the new rulers claimed their authority, and whose symbols organized the formation of a new civilization. As these symbols became stylized, their origin became ever less obvious. The key aspect of this transformation of reinterpreted knowledge into influential symbols is the fact that the original knowledge came from an unexplainable source. The mystery of it imbued it with a divine character.

It turns out, as you will see, that Egypt's main power symbols have their origin in the same astronomical theme I just developed. The reason why they became so powerful and instrumental in forging a cultural identity for the people living by the Nile was that they were based on something dynastic Egyptians could not possibly have been able to reconcile with what they knew. In other words, the mystery of the knowledge and its impenetrable origin created its divine aura. By that token, the idea represented by the Vignette of R^c had a profound impact on the symbols of royalty and the nature of the afterlife in ancient Egypt.

Power Symbols

Egypt's most iconic symbols of royalty: the ring, snake, and cartouche, along with the coil and the cobra, can all be traced back to the central idea represented by the Sun inside the oval bands in the Vignette of R^c and the coil of the snake in the Roads of Mehen. The first stylizing transformation

I think was the representation of the elliptical bands as a ring first and then as a tied rope. Already, the astronomical origin was thus obscured. A royal symbol was born from the sheer mystery of it.

Nevertheless, there is a hieroglyphic symbol which proves that the tied rope symbol referred to the sky. This symbol is prominently displayed as a pair, for example, behind the image of King Djoser on the six wall reliefs that commemorate his Heb Sed jubilee run underneath his Step Pyramid complex at Saqqara (figure 42). The dual symbols depict a corner of the sky *pt*. Nestled beneath is a rope tied into a ring thereby identifying it as part of the sky.

Figure 42: Relief of Djoser from his Step Pyramid complex. Behind the king, two sky corner symbols can be seen together with tied-rope rings. Photo by Juan R. Lazaro, cc by 2.0 <https://creativecommons.org/licenses/by/2.0>, via wikimedia commons.

The earliest association between the coils of a snake, the Sun, and a signet ring resembling a tied rope can be seen on an ivory box found by Flinders Petrie in the tomb of Horus-Den (circa 2900 BC) at Abydos (figure 43). The Sun's golden color is symbolized here by the golden necklace.

Figure 43: The royal palace icon banner of Horus-Den from the First Dynasty showing a coiled-up cobra snake, the necklace symbol for gold, and a tied-rope ring. From the tomb of Horus-Den. Petrie (1901), Plate VII #12.

As early as, if not earlier than, the First Dynasty of Egypt, astronomical symbols became the icons of royalty. The last king of the Third Dynasty, Huni, alive around the end of the twenty-seventh century BC, was the first Egyptian ruler to have his name inscribed inside of an elliptical oval called a *šnw* [shen-oo] rope, known in French as a cartouche. Up until this time, the names of the kings had been exclusively placed inside of a banner containing an iconic sketch of a palace, the so-called *sḫt* [se-khet].

But even on this pre- and early dynastic icon of rulership, the same idea of a protective enclosure around the king is evident. The texture of the banding of the palace façade suggests that the cobra's skin was the model here just as the cobra represented the protective rope of the cartouche.

With Khufu's son Djedefre, the name of the Sun God was appended to that of the king. He was no longer an emissary of R^c, he was now R^c incarnate on Earth. The symbol of the Sun was placed off-center inside the cartouche, and the king's name was next to it (figure 44).

Figure 44: The cartouche of Fifth Dynasty King Sahure. The symbol of the Sun is off-center to the left inside the oval. It honorifically precedes the name of the king, when written. Thus, the name is spelled, from left to right, *R^c-s3ḥ-w*, but read *s3ḥ-w-R^c* [Sa-hoo-raa]. The cartouche is preceded by the Sedge and Bee title, translated as the "King of Upper and Lower Egypt." The Museum of Egyptian Antiquities, Cairo, Egypt, 2018.

This new titular designation became established at the time of a major theological shift during the Old Kingdom, according to, for example, Zahi Hawass, former Secretary General of the Egyptian Supreme Council of Antiquities, former Minister of Antiquities of Egypt, and Egypt's most vocal Egyptologist.[113]

I have previously proposed that this shift might have been triggered by an almost complete solar eclipse over Memphis in the year 2568 BC, one month before the summer solstice (Stellarium 0.14.3, J.D. 783632). I thought there had to be a major astronomical event to cause a religion so deeply rooted in the sky to drastically shift its focus of worship. It was now the Sun, off-center, inside an ellipse, as if borrowed from the drawings of Johannes Kepler.

The irony is that, beginning with the Sun kings of the Fourth Dynasty, the royal house projected its divine nature using a symbol that represented the true, heliocentric order of the universe. This, even though the ancient Egyptians of this era could not possibly have known that the Sun is at the center of the universe and is surrounded by elliptical orbits. They believed they were the center.

How then is it possible that the symbol of heliocentricity, an oval with an off-center Sun, could have been wedged anachronistically into the royal insignia of a culture at the dawn of civilization? Where did it come from? How was it understood? How was it transformed and assimilated almost beyond recognition by the prevailing dogma of the time?

The paradox of this iconography has been staring at us ever since we figured out what a cartouche is. All the evidence, all of what we came to discover about what the ancient Egyptians believed points in one direction: They believed that the Earth, in fact Egypt, was the center of the universe and everything else including the Sun, the Moon, the planets and stars revolved around the land of the River Nile. And so, the idea that the Sun could be at the center of the universe would have been an alien, esoteric concept. It would have been a paradox no one amongst the priestly astronomers would have been able to explain, unless it was of divine, inexplicable origin—but that is exactly the sort of stuff from which rulers forge the emblems of authority. No one can question their power since *no one can explain them.*

In 2017, I walked up the stairs to the mountain tomb of Thutmose III in the Valley of the Kings near Luxor, Egypt. KV 34 is at the southernmost end of this famous New Kingdom necropolis. When you enter the mountain and descend the ramp down south and then east towards the sarcophagus chamber, you first think this is not too different from other tombs of the valley. But the sarcophagus chamber has a unique feel. At first you don't know what's different, but eventually you realize that the entire room is a big oval. The coffin rests not in the middle but near the eastern end of the oval. There are two pillars in the center. You are basically standing inside of a giant cartouche symbolic of the Heliocentric Solar System Thutmose III could not possibly have understood. The ceiling is full of stars. When you realize what kind of place this is, you take a deep breath. It is an awe-inspiring experience because it feels like you are standing at the center of the universe.

The entire wall is inscribed with haunting images from the ***jmj dw3t*** Amduat, the netherworld book whose original title is *Book of the Hidden Chamber*. The Amduat describes and illustrates the twelve hours of the Sun's underworld journey after sunset before rising once more in the east at dawn. The twelve hours are sectioned off along the oval based on instructions provided by the texts. There is no other tomb like this one in all of Egypt.

No doubt, the idea here is the flow of time in keeping with what I mentioned earlier: In the reinterpretation of the Vignette of R^c as a precessional coil of ecliptic wander, the ellipses are thought of as time curves, even though the original idea was orbital spaces. But here is the catch: Time does not flow sequentially on the curved surface of the oval wall around the sarcophagus chamber inside KV34. If you follow the sequence of the hours from one to twelve, you are in fact moving along a coiled loop along the oval wall.

In her interpretation of the architecture of KV34, University of California, Berkeley Egyptologist, Dr. Barbara Richter,[114] points out that the timeline followed by the texts on the oval wall that encloses the entire chamber is, in fact, a spiral schematic.[115] What this means is that the Sun physically goes backwards on the time map laid out on the wall during the fourth and fifth hour where the Sun God resurrects through Osiris, before he continues with his journey forward in the sixth through twelve hour. Where did this idea of going back in time to resurrect come from?

Only one group of prominent objects in the sky seems to defy the map of the stars as they relentlessly rotate with time between the limits set by the horizon: the planets. If the ecliptic was a time dial, they did in fact go forwards and backwards, not just in the space of the Winding Waterways but also on the dial of time during retrograde planetary motion.

This was astutely pointed out by Brendan Crawford, an independent researcher who recognized that the spiral pattern of the *Amduat* inside KV34 is reminiscent of the spiral like motion of a planet (Saturn in his example) along the ecliptic as it proceeds through its orbital cycle relative to us.[116]

This was why the *ḥḥw* I introduced in the last chapter as The Nine who encircle the Sun in the Vignette of R^c were given the time attribute of cyclical eternity, i.e., myriads in the reinterpretation of the idea as a precessional coil. They were immortal by virtue of going around and around a circle of time. But as planets, they seemed to be able to defy time like no other object in the sky and that is why they became associated with the primordial universe and the beginning of time, just as the all-pervasive Heka magic power.

If you think about it, the ultimate power in defeating mortality is to beat time. And so, to the ancient Egyptians, the *ḥḥw*, like Heka, were the ultimate power concepts to control space and hence time, forwards and backwards. This is how they had reinterpreted the Heliocentric Solar System and retrograde planetary motion.

Imagine Leonardo da Vinci had known about the Heliocentric Solar System and wanted to secretly embed this knowledge in a painting of Jesus Christ? That's what I believe he did in his Salvator Mundi. By depicting the axial tilt of Earth as a tilted cross on the robe, by showing Earth as a globe on its elliptical orbit coursing counterclockwise around the left shoulder of Jesus, and by hinting at the circumpolar constellation Draco with a split thumb he later concealed (figure 45).

Figure 45: Salvator Mundi. Note the split thumb on the right hand. Leonardo da Vinci, Salvator Mundi, 2006-07 photograph, after cleaning, before restoration. Public domain, via Wikimedia Commons; modified.

116

This model of the solar system, which is the correct one we believe, would have been both unintelligible and sacrilegious during his lifetime, when most people still believed in the geocentric universe. How would they have interpreted the information had it been pointed out? They would have likely seen it as divine symbolism of sanctimonious, benevolent power—as people still do today when they see this painting. The painting is called *The Savior of the World*, after all.

Power Over Time

Essentially, this is what I think happened with the astronomical information embedded in the Vignette of R^c and the coil. The astronomical symbols became the power symbols of the Egyptian kings, displayed as cartouche and crown, as iconic as divine, as mysterious as anachronistic. These symbols were revered beyond question, beyond scientific inquiry, beyond intellectual embrace.

The coil became symbolic for the ultimate power of the Egyptian king to control the motion of the universe and its recurrent, cyclical order. If the king possessed the power to control this coil of the clock of the universe, essentially the power to control time, his rule on Earth would be unquestioned. The symbol of this power to turn time in the form of a coil was physically displayed like a horn on the crown of the king. This crown was the *dšrt* [De-she-ret], the Red Crown of Lower Egypt in the north of the country (figure 46).

I should interject a clarification here: One of Egypt's oldest female deities called Neith also wore this crown. Her other emblems were the bow and arrows. Her sanctuary was in *z3wt*/Sais/Sa El-Hagar in the Delta of Egypt. Recorded references to her are among the oldest known writings.[117] A temple dedicated to Osiris at Sais was called *ḥt-ḥbjt*/House of the Bee.[118]

Based on these associations, some researchers have proposed that the crown is fashioned in the shape of a bee while the coil represents the antennas or the bee tongue, which, indeed, is coiled.[119] However, this idea is not supported by the way bees were portrayed in Egyptian relief—without coiled protrusions. The conflation between Neith's crown and coil on the one hand, and bees on the other, may be based on a mix-up between the temple of Osiris[120] at Sais and that of Neith, based on a description by Wallis Budge.[121]

Figure 46: The king of Egypt wearing the Red Crown with the coil. The *w3s*-scepter [waas] is a power symbol made in the shape of a windpipe or throat *wsrrt* [oo-ser-ret]. This word is a phonetic hieroglyphic word play on *wsr jrt* [oo-ser Ay-ret], the Power of the Eye, which is the creative power of the Sun God *R*ᶜ. The solar cartouche is immediately next on the right. The Museum of Egyptian Antiquities, Cairo, Egypt, 2018.

Another source of confusion is a few instances of superstitious, falsely equivalent substitution.[122] Regardless, the older textual evidence from the Pyramid Texts is clear: The coil was associated with the circumpolar star zone where the sky revolves around a central focus. We know this celestial center is the true north pole of our planet's rotational axis. Originally, the coil was a symbol of time.

Since coiling was also an escape from the confinement of the orbits dictated by the guarded gates, this liberating power represented Zunthu, playfully simulated in the game Zenet. Zunthu was the force of nature enabling its possessor to pass these obstacles using Heka magic. Therefore, Egyptian kings and queens were endowed with the originally astronomical, then divine and magical powers to turn the universe and to keep its recurrent, cyclical order.

A stunning relief informs us as to the origin of this power: The northern star zone of the *dw3t*.

In KV11, the tomb of New Kingdom's Ramses III, we see how this power is handed off by the star gods of the north and transferred to the mummy of the dead king on his path to resurrection (figure 47). The tomb's wall images and captions illustrate the symbols of the royal powers to create and keep timely, universal order. Horus holds the *w3s* scepter in the form of a jackal's windpipe, the *wsrt*, a wordplay on *wsr jrt*/*Power of the Eye of R*. The crocodilian deity Heken represents one of the circumpolar constellations.[123] He holds the royal coil of time. Horus and Heken can be seen to pass these powers to Hekaw, Heka Magic materialized in her primordial universe form as a snake. She carries the powers to the mummy of the king on his journey through the depths of the Netherworld in his afterlife.

Figure 47: Illustration and captions from the *Book of the Dead* in the tomb of Ramses III in the Valley of the Kings. ©, John Lundwall, Valley of Kings, KV11, 2019.

This haunting imagery even alludes to the connection of the coil with Neith's Red Crown. She was the mythical mother of the also crocodilian Sobek. Archaeoastronomers agree that the Egyptians saw a large hippopotamus figure carrying a crocodile in the immediate vicinity of the snake-like Draco, which certainly explains the imagery in figure 47.[124]

In the shape of the *dšrt*, I recognize Ursa Minor, the Little Dipper sign in the northern star zone (figure 48). How fitting this is since the Red Crown was the king's emblem of his reign over Lower Egypt, the northernmost part of his land.

What all this means is that the Red Crown and coil represented the royal power of immortality harnessed from the imperishable stars and used to turn the sky. This power was thus imbued into the northern headdress. From here to the bee is now no longer a leap. The royal association with bees in ancient Egypt finds its explanation with the waggle dance.[125] Bees seem to imitate the revolving motion of the sky and the universe, likely observed by ancient keepers. That could have meant to them that they too possess this power—or emulate it rather.

Figure 48: Circumpolar northern star zone. Ursa Minor is shaped like a ladle. Graphic made with Stellarium 0.14.3.

The caption immediately left of the coil in figure 49 identified the origin of this power: The *dw3t!* *ʿb stp n dw3t* [aab setep enn doo-ut] means The Chosen Horn of the Netherworld. The king displayed the magical power to control universal time in the form of a symbolic horn on his Red Crown.

The astronomical concept of a solar center inside of a shell of orbits also made its way into the priestly mystics' circle, a world where theology and science were one, and where language was used didactically not just to inform the mind, but also the heart and intuition.

The secretive and secluded layer of ancient Egyptian society is difficult to penetrate by nature of its clandestine activities. The scientific research and its composition into written records played out behind the scenes of the widely visible performance stage on which the kings and queens acted as the rulers of their people. We are therefore fortunate that some of these

Figure 49: The Northern star zone. The crocodilian deity *ḥkn* holds the coil. Horus holds the *w3s* scepter, symbol of divine power. The caption reads: *ʿb stp n dw3t* [aab setep enn doo-ut], The Chosen Horn of the Netherworld. ©, John Lundwall, Valley of Kings, KV11, 2019.

secrets leaked from the vaults of the *House of Life* at Hermopolis and into the tombs of the upper middle class where archaeologists were able to recover them.

The Vignette of *Rʿ* on the coffin of General Zepi had led me via its inscription to the ancient Egyptians' understanding of the orbital mechanics in the sky in the Middle Kingdom according to their geocentric perspective of the world. But I still had no good clue when someone first laid their eyes on the original of this painting, after the original, still elusive archive that stored it had been breached. I knew it had to have happened before the Middle Kingdom. *But when?*

From the Sphinx to Hermopolis and Back

The astronomical knowledge illustrated in the Vignette of R^c is the Heliocentric Solar System. We only learned of it five centuries ago. We do not accept that it was known by the ancient Egyptians, or any other known ancient civilization as far as our linear model of history predicts.

But if the *House of Life* in Middle Kingdom Hermopolis magna was in possession of such paradoxical, anachronistic knowledge, how did it get there? So far, what I had found was a vague reference from the First Dynasty to a significant, year-defining past event when an archive was opened. Was this the breached archive from where the Vignette of R^c had come? Where had it been? Was it guarded by a monumental Sphinx or something else? And who had made it to leave this knowledge of the sky behind?

To answer any of these questions I had to find a textual trace that would lead me from the City of Thoth back to the land of Osiris, under the hills and valleys of the Giza Plateau, through the Mouth of the Caves, and into the mystical Netherworld realm of Rostau. I already knew of one important clue: The coil, which had become a rope, was the *st3* Hieroglyph in the name of this mystical place: r-*st3w*.

What I was to find there would not be rooms filled with shelves for books or scrolls. What I found instead was likely a single chamber called the *pr-dw3t* and in it stood a portable archive. Its hieroglyphic name, I would come to learn, was *'fdt*.

VI

Coffers

I N HIS EXCELLENT BOOK, *THROUGH HERMOPOLITEAN LENSES*, WAEL SHERBINY spends fifteen pages on the possible meaning of *one* hieroglyphic word: *ꜥftt* [awf-tet].

Sherbiny's book is nearly seven hundred pages, 8 x 11 inch, and those fifteen pages comprise 2 percent. And rightly so. Previous translators of the Coffin Texts, such as Raymond O. Faulkner, did not know what to do with this word. It appears disproportionally often on coffins from Deir El-Bersheh comprising twelve instances of seventeen total in the entire body of the Coffin Texts, half of these alone in the *Book of Two Ways*.[126] No wonder these lexical statistics, because it, and its origin *ꜥfdt*, are the words for "archive," but not just any archive: *The* archive of mysterious knowledge used by the mortal dead in the afterlife to attain immortality.

When I first realized this, I knew I had to find out if *ꜥfdt* was also the word for a real archive in a real library in ancient Egypt.

Even though the remnants of no ancient Egyptian library have ever been excavated, from various inscriptions it is evident that one name used to refer to such a place was *House of Life*. In the case of the cemetery at Deir El-Bersheh, the nearest population center was Hermopolis magna/ *ḥmnw*/ [khe-me-noo], the mysterious city of Thoth, named after a group of eight primordial chaos gods from which the universe was believed to have been created in the Hermopolitean Cosmogony.

It is from the *House of Life* at Hermopolis that the Vignette of *Rꜥ* had leaked. How else could it have appeared on the coffin of the General Zepi who was entombed at Deir El-Bersheh? If there ever was a real *ꜥfdt*, I should be able to trace it back to this real library.

Little did I know at the time, but this part of my investigation would eventually take me back to where it had all begun.

The *House of Life*

My focus on the *Book of Two Ways* relates to the fact that it was used as a coherent unit only on coffins recovered from the cemetery of Deir El-Bersheh. The way to explain this unusual concentration of its use in one locale is that nearby Hermopolis was the quintessential city in all of Egypt, where esoteric knowledge related to the sky was being studied and stored. This was also the place where a library called *pr ʿnḫ* [per-onkh], the *House of Life*, had evidently leaked a piece of esoterically themed art, the Vignette of *Rʿ*. The Vignette, the *Zweiwegebuch*, and the *ʿfdt*: It all began to point to a unique archive of unusual astronomical knowledge in the City of Thoth.

The evidence for a *House of Life* in Hermopolis during the Middle Kingdom comes from the tombs of two individuals laid to rest at Deir El-Bersheh, *jḥ3* [ee-ha] and *dḥwtj-n3ḫt* [djc-hootee-nakht] where it is mentioned.[127] I had to become familiar with this facility to see if it contained an archive of esoteric knowledge about the sky. I wanted to know why this undoubtedly secret knowledge had escaped from a presumably secured archive and find its way into a local cemetery—but nowhere else in Egypt. Why did the library scribes give away esoteric art to the provincial non-royal elite?

It is fascinating how economic, climatic, sociological, and cultural currents sometimes conspire to bring about what we might otherwise call serendipitous outcomes. The cause of the case of the secret-leaking *House of Life* is basically a story of the declining power of the royal class in Egypt, and the rising status of the upper middle class. Thus, in the Middle Kingdom (circa 2030–1640 BC), a real market grew for secret and arcane knowledge from libraries like the *House of Life*, because that knowledge, it turns out, was expected to be a ticket to a better, eternal, afterlife.

In the Old Kingdom (circa 2649–2150 BC), secret, sacred texts were property of the kings. Only they could travel to the sky to become immortal spirits. During the last phase of the Old Kingdom, however, the Sixth Dynasty, the land of Egypt transformed from a centralized state to a centrally ruled federation of provinces. The kings began to cede power to the provinces along the Nile Valley, called nomes, governed by the nomarchs. This diffusion of power ended up splitting the land into two kingdoms. Egypt entered a dark age called the First Intermediate Period (circa 2150–2030 BC). As a result of the loss of the royal grip on power, the provincial governors first, and later also military officials, doctors, and other high society members, were able to equip their lavish tombs with expensive sarcophagi, decorated with texts and illustrations.

Now, they too could gain immortality in the afterlife, previously the prerogative and privilege of kings and queens who had built themselves lavish Sun temples and pyramids and whose inner chambers and corridors were decorated with the Pyramid Texts.

This is the historical context from within which the demand for customized coffin inscriptions can be understood. It means that no two sarcophagi had identical inscriptions. It also means that any given sarcophagus preserved to date is an archaeological record of a personalized relationship between a scribe from the *House of Life*, or any other similar facility at the provincial power centers of the time, and a private, though high official, client. The extra special privilege enjoyed by the elite of Hermopolis, however, was their proximity to the *House of Life* and its incredibly special content. I could come up with several scenarios in which its scribes may have made secret arrangements for high-profile clients willing to pay a special price. And what were these coveted arrangements? Unique magic spells.

Laboratory

An analysis of unique spells on coffins from Deir El-Bersheh by Billson found that the proportion of spells unique to only one coffin among the thirty-one studied ranged from 0 to 20 percent.[128] The owners were nomarchs and their immediate family, doctors, generals, royal scribes, a treasurer, stewards, and a priest. Interestingly, the owner's status and wealth appeared not to determine the number or type of unique spells on their coffin.[129] Instead, it appears that, for unknown reasons, only certain individuals like Chief Physician *gw3* and General Zepi, whose coffin uniquely features the Vignette of *Rꜥ*, had special access to a larger number of magical spells and uniquely illustrated inscriptions. The mention of Thoth appears more often in unique spells than expected, which is explained by the proximity to Hermopolis. If you wanted esoteric spells, Hermopolis was the place to be in Egypt to get your custom-designed coffin.

A comparison between Coffin Texts in general and the older Pyramid Texts shows a clear and extensive connection, indicating that the former were not first invented during the First Intermediate Period or the Middle Kingdom, but are deeply rooted, if modified, in their older predecessors.[130] Since the astronomical nature of the Pyramid Texts is undeniable, the Coffin Texts must have had an astronomical basis just the same.

The ongoing text modifications, however, suggest that scribes in the *House of Life* were actively creating new material based on traditional sources to make unique, new spells requested by their wealthy clientele. While there was a basic corpus of standard Coffin Texts mostly on the inner coffin shell, there were new, custom-made texts more so on the outer one. The scribes were thus not simply copying standard texts onto coffins. They were splicing elements from different spells into new spells, just like molecular biologists cut and splice together DNA pieces using recombinant DNA technologies to create new genes.[131] The resemblance between the original Pyramid Text passages and the modified Coffin Text versions has allowed Egyptologists to make this connection.

Billson cites one example that I want to use to highlight something remarkable about what these scribes were really doing. If Billson himself noticed this, I don't know, but he made no mention of it.[132] In this example, Adriaan de Buck saw a resemblance between the beginning lines of Pyramid Text 284 (PT 284), lines a-b, and Coffin Text 717 (CT 717), lines a-c (figure 50).

He was able to deduce that the former was the original spell that gave rise to the modified latter. However, things change drastically in the ending lines, PT 284/425 d-e, which seem to have nothing to do with the end of CT 717. The beginnings matched but the ends did not, not even close. The deceised person is here generically called N:

| PT 284/425d | *pf rw m ẖnw pn rw*/That lion is within this lion |
| CT 717f | *m 3m N tn*/Do not grab this N |

| "/425e | *ꜥẖ3 k3wj m ẖnw tẖn*/Two bulls fight within the ibis |
| "/g | *m 3m j3m.s*/Do not grab and bind her. |

Or are they? The trick is to realize that the word for lion in PT 284, *rw*, is hidden in CT 717f as the word *3m*, translated by de Buck as "grab/seize,"

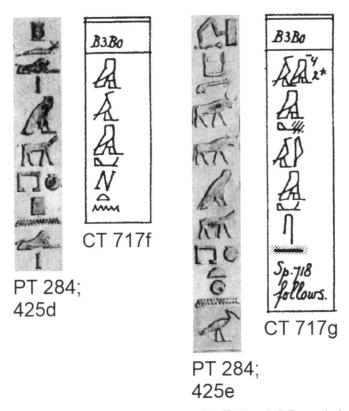

Figure 50: Comparison of Pyramid Text 284 and Coffin Text 717. Transcriptions from Allen (2013) and de Buck (1956); modified. Courtesy of the Oriental Institute of the University of Chicago.

but it also means *lion*. The word for ibis in PT 284, *thn*, is an allusion to *thj* the architect, an aspect of Thoth, the Moon God in its crescent shape. The word for Moon is hidden in CT 717g as *j3m.s*, because *j3h* or *j'h* mean Moon and *m.s* sounds like *ms* for birth. In other words, what we have is an allusion to New Moon. The word game played here is, of course, Heka magic. The scribes of the *House of Life* were embedding what they really wanted to say in otherwise unrelated, possibly even meaningless phrases. The transformation is now revealed:

That lion is within this lion. The two bulls fight within the ibis.

became

In the lion is this N. In the lion the Moon is born.

"In the lion the Moon is born," is key. In other words, N has transformed into Thoth at first crescent Moon within the lion. Astronomically speaking, this is quite a spectacle: a new month, visually identified with new crescent Moon, arising within the constellation Leo. A brilliant feat of phonetic mimicry, is it not? Egyptologists and archaeoastronomers who insist there is no evidence that the ancient Egyptians recognized the constellation Leo before the New Kingdom should take another look at the Coffin Texts through the prism of Heka Magic, through *Hermopolitean Lenses* so to speak—the well-conceived title of Wael Sherbiny's book.

N, in this case was the wife of the Hermopolitean nomarch *ḏḥwtj-n3ḫt/* [Je-hoo-tee nakht]. She was the owner of the coffin on which this custom spell was placed. The spell transforms her into Thoth in the afterlife while on the Osirian barque called *3kr*/Aker, the double lion cleverly invoked here by the double bull *k3wj* in an anagrammatic truncated form. In her role as Thoth, she helps Osiris come back to life. In exchange, she herself receives immortality and eternal sustenance. The visual connection between crescent Moon and Aker is the sickle shape.

The veiled meaning phonetically encrypted by CT 717 catered to the desire of high officials who wanted their coffins to be magically imbued with Coffin Texts. The idea was for the deceased to play the part of a Heka magician and ritualist who was able to safely travel the treacherous and perilous paths while variously transformed into Thoth, Osiris, or *R*ᶜ to attain immortality in the sky. This transformation required the deceased to be equipped with magic in the form of Heka. They had to be able to phonetically invoke a god, goddess, sacred item, or other needed aid without deliberately pronouncing it. And so, it must have been the skill to be equipped with Heka that the spell-splicing scribes secretly supplied to the rich and powerful from the spell lab of the *House of Life*.

The example from PT 284 gives us but a hint as to what was going on in the library of Thoth at Hermopolis: It was a Heka Laboratory that used innovative, phonetic ways to invoke old theological teachings related to astronomy. In the process, new textual content was created, which previous translations by Egyptologists may have missed.

It is important to note here that these scribes did not invent this art of magical spell creation called Heka. The exact same process can be seen in the *Mouth Opening Ritual* from the Pyramid Texts of the old Kingdom into which embedded lies the more archaic, prehistoric *Statuette Making Ritual*. The scribes of the *House of Life* were doing what scribes in ancient Egypt had likely been doing since writing was invented: preserving recorded traditions from decay by copying, archiving, and creating new texts based on classic sources. Unlike in the old times, however, when these activities were all conducted in the secrecy of the royal library, in the Middle Kingdom the newly formed non-royal, upper middle class was able to either buy or earn its way past this veil of secrecy.

Anachronism

For my purpose, this was a perfect scenario. Via the Coffin Texts, I had found leaked traces of information stored away in an archive of the arcane, which really seemed to be stored, ancient knowledge of astronomy. Thus, this was the perfect place to search for esoteric, anachronistic, paradoxical knowledge not originally discovered in ancient Egypt.

Anachronisms are things from another time that look out of place, for example, an early twentieth century Ford Model-T car in a science fiction movie, or a DeLorean in the American Wild West of the late nineteenth century. Note how only the former case is a possible scenario, not the latter, which is a movie fantasy. We have no widely accepted evidence yet that big things can travel back in time or that more advanced things existed before their time.[133]

Anachronistic knowledge, likewise, makes sense only when old-fashioned thinking appears in more modern records. More advanced knowledge before its time is implausible in the current model of history. Anachronistic knowledge in the records of ancient Egypt would be knowledge inconsistent with what we think they knew then. A paradox of history does not appear when anachronisms come in the form of old-fashioned, obsolete, or outdated knowledge. A paradox of history arises only when this knowledge is out of place because it is *more advanced*.

While the bulk of the almost twelve hundred spells of the Coffin Texts were used on coffins across Egypt, it seemed to me that texts dealing with astronomy like the so-called *Book of Two Ways* only found on coffins made in Hermopolis would bring me closer to such a paradox that cannot be reconciled with the state of astronomical knowledge in ancient Egypt during the Middle Kingdom. Our current, well-established paradigm of history reconstructs human progress as a straight line, the so-called linear model of cultural and material evolution from sticks and stones to quantum computers and artificial intelligence. This model predicts that throughout human history and prehistory, more advanced and more correct knowledge cannot possibly have come before less advanced, incorrect knowledge. The ancient Egyptians, for example, believed the Earth was in the center of their universe.

Yet, if they were in possession of records whose authors unequivocally demonstrated awareness of heliocentricity, the linear model of history cannot be correct. This would then be a compelling paradox of history, suggesting that historians might have been getting it wrong and their linear model is false. Instead, we would have to conclude that the evolution of knowledge has been cyclic, with at least one phase of a more advanced culture replaced by a less advanced culture from which our modern culture eventually emerged.

It was at this stage in my research that I had originally found a reference to the Vignette of *R*ˤ. My own bewildered reaction to what I saw staring at this bizarre painting was confirmed by how Egyptologists had viewed it: something strange and one-of-a-kind. My bewilderment began immediately with the face-to-face stare by the Sun God, a highly unusual appearance for an ancient Egyptian god. There are very few deities in Egyptian art that stare directly at you, certainly not the principal god the nation worshiped. Usually, gods and goddesses were shown in profile. Add to that the unmistakable ellipses, the fact that there are nine of them, and this vignette becomes a prime candidate for an anachronism in ancient astronomy. *What else other than to illustrate a solar system might have been intended here?* I initially wondered whether this might not be a modern forgery—I was that incredulous. Other explanations did not seem logical, however. For starters, the translator Raymond O. Faulkner, who had learned hieroglyphic under Sir Alan Gardiner, wrote in his annotation to the vignette:[134]

> *The enthroned god enclosed in a series of ovals is Reˤ within his coils; cf. 'Reˤ who is in his coils' in Th.T.S. I, Pl 37, middle horizontal band.*

But coils are not concentric rings, I thought. Was it possible that an ancient Egyptian scribe could confuse a set of closed ovals with a coil? I hoped that any lingering doubts as to what I was dealing with would have to be erased by the text around the vignette.

With what I know now based on the discoveries I described in the previous two chapters, the Vignette of R^c illustrates an idea that is anachronistic in the times of the Middle Kingdom of ancient Egypt, or any time before that. The text written around the vignette was an attempt at explaining this idea in terms then understood, a coil-like precession of the ecliptic arc along the horizon. What were meant to be orbital ellipses of the nine planets encircling the Sun, became concentric loops of time connected by gates turning them into a spiral coil. The concept of guarded gates was the prism of the ancient Egyptian view of celestial orbital mechanics through which they had reinterpreted the idea of the Heliocentric Solar System shown in the Vignette of R^c.

With evidence of an anachronism, I was staring at a haunting paradox. Where did the original painting copied onto General Zepi's coffin come from? I already suspected it came from the *House of Life*, but how had it gotten to Hermopolis in the first place?

I had my hands on a piece of esoteric art looking for an esoteric archive in which it might have been kept like the real *Hall of Records*. That is exactly what I found when I came across the name of just such a place, except there was an unexpected twist: It was neither a hall, nor a chamber, not a room, or a shelf even, it was a portable chest.

Portable Archive Under the Arm

In *Through Hermopolitean Lenses*, Wael Sherbiny meticulously establishes that *ꜥftt* was just another way to write *ꜥfdt* [awf-det], the word for box, chest, or coffer. The former appears to be a variant spelling of the latter, given that the sounds "t," "d," and "th" are similar.[135] Copying mistakes are one explanation given by Egyptologists for different spellings in different versions of the same text. My objection to that idea, at least in this case, is that this would implicitly assume the less likely scenario that the scribes were writing something which was dictated to them rather than copied from a written original in front of them. While this may be so, I would consider that the choice of "dt" instead of "tt" may have been an intentional allusion to the *dw3t* [doo-ut], the name of the netherworld in the afterlife. My reason: It turns out that this peculiar coffer was kept in an underground location.

Sherbiny's later discussion of other examples of *ʿftt* in Middle Egyptian inscriptions[136] supplies the lexical bridge between a vault and an archive it houses: the hieroglyphic name of a subterranean vault, crypt, or chamber under a temple—a concrete, not mythical "Netherworld House" *pr-*dw3t [per-doo-ut] so to speak—and the coffer kept inside, the *ʿfdt*. I think there is a vocal bridge here connecting the hieroglyphic words for coffer, *ʿfdt*, with that for Netherworld, *dw3t*. The scribes in the *House of Life* may have later altered the spelling from *ʿfdt* to *ʿftt* to obscure this link. Or, it no longer made sense. The latter would be true if the coffer had long been taken from the vault.

Indeed, the true origin of the Netherworld House became obscured through stylization and ritual formation, but hints remain as to the original meaning. In chapter IV, I showed you an excerpt from Coffin Text Spell 155:

> *I am the god in charge of the document-case in the room which contains the ritual robes...*

The "room which contains the ritual robes" was probably one and the same as the House of Morning Adoration, which has been identified with the *pr-*dw3t, [137] although I think that is a later function of it, not its original archaic origin. What is significant however, even in the late Greco-Roman imagery of this place, is that it involved pouring a wave-like stream of water over the king such that it surrounded him exactly like the elliptical bands surround the Sun God in the Vignette of *Rʿ*. The streaming water is represented with a chain of life and power symbols.[138] This stream of symbolic purification, I propose, is the "magician's robe" after which the chamber is named in Spell 155, and which housed the *ʿfdt,* a chest of documents used to attain immortality in the afterlife. Not surprisingly, the gods performing the purification ritual on the king in the Netherworld House are Horus and Thoth.

That coffer and vault were verbally connected becomes apparent in another way: The words *ʿn* and *ʿf* are prepositions that refer to the two gates to and from the *dw3t*.[139] This would be similar to saying "the yonder" and "the after" in English. In his superb analysis to decipher the meaning of *ʿfdt*, Sherbiny, in disagreement with this idea, dismisses any connection between this word and *ʿf,* "the after." He also does not draw a link between *dt* and *dw3t*. This was my own insight. I would even go as far as to say that *ʿf* and *dt* are words, not only syllables. They were contracted by a scribe into the fusion word *ꜥfdt*, specifically so chosen to identify a coffer inside of a Netherworld chamber containing useful knowledge for the afterlife. An English analogy is the word "archive." Imagine it to be a contraction of "arc," a vaulted ceiling silhouette, and "hive," a stack. The word "arc-hive," then, could signify a stack of records inside of a vault.

Despite my departure from his analysis in this one respect, I completely agree with Sherbiny's final conclusion that an *ꜥfdt* was an archival coffer. I think that my reconstruction of its origin does not subtract from his but rather adds a layer of relevance he may just have overlooked. And so, I suspect, the name of the original chamber that housed the *ꜥfdt* coffer was the *pr-dw3t*: The House of the Netherworld, if you will.

When I first stumbled upon this connection, all I knew was that this "coffer" was a mythological item. It appeared in funerary texts dealing with the afterlife. This begged two obvious questions: *Did it actually exist? And if so, what was in it?*

Reviewing what I knew at this point, I had a vague association between this archival coffer from the netherworld and hints of a real counterpart in Egypt's temple culture. I had also identified a suspiciously esoteric, astronomical acumen leaving an imprint on ancient Egyptian phonetic spell magic. However, I did not yet have the needed textual evidence to connect either to the Great Sphinx.

What had brought the coffer and the knowledge embedded in the vignette into a context of exclusivety and secrecy for me was that both appeared within the archaeological record of the Egyptian cemetery at Deir El-Bersheh. It made sense that such knowledge would have been kept secure in the nearby *House of Life*. This context was so compelling to me that I asked myself, if it were even likely that the original record of the Vignette of *Rꜥ* and astronomical records of heliocentricity and precession would *not* be stored in an *ꜥfdt* sitting in a vault called *pr-dw3t* under that library.

In the end, I would have to return to the so-called *Book of two Ways*. It brought together astronomy and magical knowledge kept in secret places. If the *Hall of Records* really existed, I could not think of a better textual trace to follow. When I did, it led me forward in time and forward to later texts.

During Egypt's New Kingdom and Late Period, the meaning of *ꜥfdt* degenerated, as likely did the meaning of the Netherworld House. Its use broadened to include the name of the cabin hiding *Rꜥ* on the solar bark, a shrine of a god under whose feet documents were hidden, and even a temple crypt, chamber, or cave housing records.[140] Evidently, *ꜥfdt* was indeed the hieroglyphic word for an arcane archive of esoteric records, but the English word does not quite do it justice.

In chapter III, figure 12 (c), for example, I showed an instances in the Papyrus Jumilhac where *ꜥfdt* appears in the context of a shrine-like facility with a descending ramp or staircase. Despite two thousand years, the essential meaning of the word endured. It still invoked an underground archive of records. Now though, it could be either "coffer" or "vault." *But what was in it?* For that, I had to follow the textual trace back in time.

Continuing with Sherbiny's analysis, in that part of the Coffin Texts called the *Book of Two Ways* the word *ꜥftt* occurs six times.[141] This statistical prominence of the word is matched by its importance in this part of the afterlife. The *ꜥftt*, identical with *ꜥfdt*, contains the divine knowledge required during the deceased N's dangerous journey on a mission to save and serve Osiris, and to be resurrected in return. This context further raised my suspicion that the *ꜥfdt* was a secret stash of records. What kind of records? Likely, they had to be of the arcane, esoteric, and, even of the anachronistic type. This meant I had to continue following Sherbiny's trail and examine the known instances of *ꜥftt* in the Coffin Texts. My ultimate hope was that these references would help me trace these records back to their original location.

Before delving into the specifics, I would like to bring back, once more, Edgar Cayce. As I earlier demonstrated, the idea of an archive under the Great Sphinx did not originate with him. I doubt even he would have made this claim. A couple of years after founding the Association for Research and Enlightenment (A.R.E.) on October 29, 1933, he gave a reading to an executive of Protestant faith.[142] In his reading, Cayce referred to "record chambers" and the "sealed room of records." When asked about this sealed room and what it contained, Cayce responded that it was not in the Great Pyramid.

In other readings, he placed the records inside the *Tomb of Records*, itself inside the *Hall of Records*, located on the way from the Sphinx to the temple or pyramid.[143] Elsewhere yet, Cayce also called this tomb a pyramid, a store house, and a record house.[144]

Regardless, he did not locate this archive directly under the Sphinx. Instead, the Sphinx is only at the entry to the *Hall of Records*, which is reached through a chamber or passage or the connecting chambers. According to Cayce, this archive contains the records of the history of Atlantis from its beginning to its destructive end and the ensuing diaspora of the surviving Atlanteans. They constitute the copies of Atlantis. Once the room, chamber, tomb, pyramid, or house is unsealed and reopened, the temple of Atlantis can be resurrected.[145]

As to the precise location of the sealed room, Cayce said this:[146]

This in position lies, as the sun rises from the waters, the line of the shadow (or light) falls between the paws of the Sphinx, that was later set as the sentinel or guard, and which may not be entered from the connecting chambers from the Sphinx's paw (right paw) until the TIME has been fulfilled when the changes must be active in this sphere of man's experience. Between, then, the Sphinx and the river.

Thus, the content of this archive, according to Cayce, was the will of the perished Atlanteans, from which their legacy could be revived. For comparision, I would like to cite a few Eygptian texts to demonstrate that the Atlantean *Hall of Records* under the arm of the Great Sphinx is in principle, if not by name, really the same idea as an *ꜥfdt*.

In Chapter II, I cited Harris' *Magical Papyrus*, discovered decades before Edgar Cayce was alive. In the *Hymn to Shu*, Thoth the scribe in the *Hall of rꜥ ḥr3ḥtj*[147] [rah-hor-akh-tee]/Re-Horakhty at Heliopolis has composed a will. This will is hidden "under the feet of Re-Horakhty," also the name of the Great Sphinx in the New Kingdom when pHarris was written. The *Hymn to Shu* is three thousand years older than Edgar Cayce's prophecy about an archive guarded by the Great Sphinx. But the evidence for an archive "under an arm" is even older.

In 1933, when Cayce made this prophecy, the Middle Kingdom's Coffin Texts had not yet been published. Adriaan de Buck and Alan Gardiner were still transcribing the originals and collating copies in Cairo and elsewhere. In Spell 695, it says that the unknown god *mrš.f*,[148] the one in charge of litters, is being asked to deliver the following message to Osiris in Abydos:

"Open the chest of writings so that you may hear the word of this god whose face is hidden, ..."[149]

First, what the translator Raymond Faulkner overlooked here is that the word "litters" literally translated from hieroglyphic *ḥwdt/ḥwdwt* [khoo-det/khoo-doot], litter/litters,[150] makes little sense, except that it invokes the idea of protecting the young. Phonetically read instead, *ḥwdt* embeds the sound *dt*, reminiscent of *dw3t*, and *ḥw*, in fact, means "protect," just as it does in the Egyptian name of Cheops, *ḥw.fw—He, the protected one.*

As I reconstruct this, *mrš.f* protects the *dw3t* which is important to the passage I cite here, since a chest of writings is also mentioned. The hieroglyphic spelling of "chest of writings" is *ꜥfdt ḫrt-ꜥ* (figure 51).

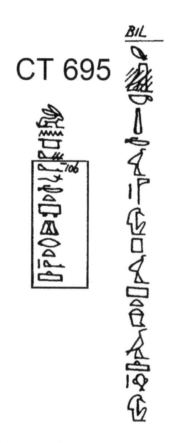

Figure 51: Hieroglyphic excerpt from Spell 695, coffin B1L. The phrase *ꜥfdt ḫrt-ꜥ* is framed. From de Buck (1956); modified. Courtesy of the Oriental Institute of the University of Chicago.

The literal translation is "the coffer under the arm." Since the *ꜥfdt* was kept in the the Netherworld House, I thus gained a crucial additional piece of textual evidence that further describes the location of the *ꜥfdt*: It was in an underground chamber called the Netherworld House located "under the arm."

Egyptian names for things, including natural and supernatural beings, were often epithets of defining attributes. This is how I view the words *ꜥfdt* and *ẖrt-ꜥ*. They describe the physical location of the coffer. That description became synonymous with what we would call a sealed coffer containing secret knowledge stored below ground.

In other words, two hieroglyphic words written almost four thousand years before Edgar Cayce, encompass the key detail of his prophecy from the October 29, 1933, reading that deals with the location of the sealed room under the arm of the Great Sphinx.

The Book of Thoth

Yet there is even more evidence to inform us about this coffer. In CT Spell 225, the deceased is being hailed as vindicated from judgment (figure 52). He is to enter the sky realm and be near Hathor.

The spell then continues:

> ... may you sit under the branches of the myrrh-tree near Hathor who is pre-eminent in Itnws when she travels to On bearing the script of the divine words, the book of Thoth.

Here, at last, we learn that the writings inside the coffer—which Sherbiny pieced together from other texts—to be the *Book of Thoth*, another often quoted, yet commonly misunderstood idea, usually misattributed to later eras. In addition, this book is somehow related to the cattle and Sycamore Tree goddess, Hathor, and the Myrrh Tree. Here, I want to reproduce this important and relevant hieroglyphic text, transliterated for other researchers as a reference. It reads:

> *zšw n mdw nṯr mḏ3t nt ḏḥwtj nb ḥmnw*, "the writings of divine words, the "book" of Thoth, master of Hermopolis."

The word *mḏ3t* is liberally translated as "book" here, but the real meaning is closer to any medium used on which to record hieroglyphic writings,

sd̲3.s

r

jnw

ḫr

zšw

n

mdw nt̲r

md̲3t

nt

d̲ḥwty

nb

ḫmnw

Figure 52: Hieroglyphic spelling and transliteration of an excerpt from Coffin Texts Spell 225 on coffin B1L. From de Buck and Gardiner (1947); modified.

for example a papyrus scroll. Spell 225 documents two important facts: The ꜥfdt coffer contained divine words written by Thoth, and it was portable.

To further paint the semantic canvas behind this important word, I am going to briefly summarize all other associations of ꜥftt Sherbiny found in the Coffin Texts.[151] Out of seventeen, there are six instances in the context of "being equipped" and four mentions of "coffer snakes" as guards. In one case, the coffer is carried "on the arms of Thoth." In another, it "houses" **Rꜥ** and "four" protective spirits which can be "falcons." There are also hints that a jackal may have guarded over the shrine, symbolic of the secrecy of its content.[152]

In Spell 208, there is mention of the "roads of the coffer," an indication of chambers and corridors which lead to its subterranean location. This association also occurs in the slightly later dated *Westcar Papyrus* where ꜥftt is used three times.[153] In Spell 259, it becomes clear that the coffer is opened by an assistant to Thoth called **m-ḫnt-jrtj**, he-whose-eyes-are-in-the-front, an allusion to the crescent Moon during the waxing phase, when it faces in the same direction as the direction of its day-by-day wander on the ecliptic.

In Spell 556, ꜥftt refers to a shrine instead of a coffer. Such shrines housed the statue of a god and written scrolls would be hidden under his feet. This semantic context helps to get a feeling for the statuary context in which ꜥfdt archive was imagined. It was an archive under a divine statue.

There are two more important texts, Spells 1116, and 1130. In CT 1116, Adriaan de Buck transcribed five caption-like textual elements he observed on a few coffins from Deir El-Bersheh. They belong to an illustration of the *Book of Two Ways*. He published these five lines as if they are one contiguous spell—but they are not, as Wael Sherbiny demonstrates.[154] I have reproduced Sherbiny's annotated illustration here to show the exact locations of these five captions (figure 53).

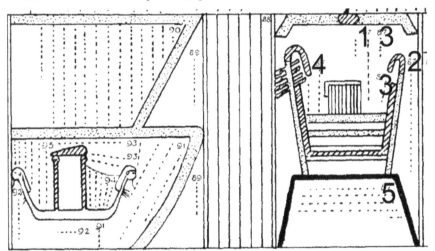

Figure 53: Illustration from the *Book of Two Ways* inscribed on the floorboard of Coffin B3C and annotated with five textual elements comprising Coffin Texts Spell 1116. From de Buck (1961); modified. Courtesy of the Oriental Institute of the University of Chicago.

You see a stylized barque on a trapezoid pedestal carrying a nine-striped, backless seat. Above hovers a canopy reminscent of the sky symbol *pt* [pet]. The caption inside the pedestal, textual element 5, puts the Vignette of *Rꜥ* and the ꜥfdt into the same scene. It reads [emphasis added]:[155]

This is the place of the **akh** *who is able to enter into the* **fire** *and open the* **darkness** *(but) who does not know how to ascend to this sky of Re-Horsemsu among the Suite of Re-Horsemsu with offerings in the Akhet of Re-Horsemsu. This is the true* '*ftt of* **Re**.

We are being told that the '*ftt* belongs to the Sun's akh spirit, "equipped" to "enter fire" and "open the gates" to the sky ruled by Horus the Elder, but not yet equipped to ascend. There seems to be a shell around the spirit made from fire and darkness and this shell of course are the nine elliptical bands in the Vignette of *R*ꜥ, [156] the orbits of planets as I have shown in Chapter IV.

Textual element 4 and 2 mark the place and caption the entire scene, respectively, where this immortal spirit is located:[157]

[4] The place of the equipped akh who exists as a god himself. [2] The place of the very truly equipped akh, who cannot die forever.

In textual element 3, we learn something about this spirit which is known to many travelers to Egypt: Almost no frontal views of Egyptian deities exist. Overwhelmingly, we only see their profiles:

There is no god who knows his front.

It is clear from this illustration that what is not being shown sitting on the seat inside this shrine-like bark was exceptionally holy—so sacred, or so bright, that it could not be faced. On another coffin, B1C, a feline figure is seen as a place holder, sitting on the seat with a cobra emerging from her back. The lion, of course, was a manifestation of an aspect of the Sun God.

Undoubtedly, it was the Sun's spirit in the Netherworld during its nightly sojourn to which this annotated illustration alludes. Unlike in this illustration, in the Vignette of *R*ꜥ the Sun God's face, in a highly unusual manner, is shown in full frontal view. I cannot emphasize enough how crucial this detail is. It proves that the Vignette of *R*ꜥ was forbidden knowledge, not to be seen by even those onto whose coffins the map and *Book of Two Ways* was painted and written. The only known exception was General Zepi. We may never know how or why he earned this extraordinary privilege.

Finally, we come to Textual Element 1, because it is, according to Wael Sherbiny, "one of the most enigmatic in the entire composition, and it has not yet been decoded."[158] Since there is no translation, I have reproduced—as does Sherbiny in his book—the transcription of all those El-Bersheh coffins on which it appears (figure 54).

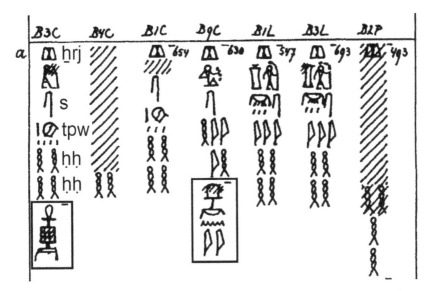

Figure 54: Enigmatic symbols (framed) used in hieroglyphic Textual Element 1/Spell 1116 from the illustration shown in Figure 53, found on various coffins from Deir El-Bersheh. From de Buck (1961); modified. Courtesy of the Oriental Institute of the University of Chicago.

Sherbiny hesitantly translates this line as:

The Ones who carry it (i.e. the sky), the First Ones (or: the chiefs), the pair of Heh-gods.

There they were again: The *ḥḥw* I was able to connect with The Nine mentioned in the text written around the Vignette of **Rˁ**.

Matching the strangeness of the vignette, this text is highly unusual. It uses Egyptian hieroglyphs, but they are not common in the Middle Kingdom. Rather they are written in the archaic style of early dynastic inscriptions that often used pictographic, not phonetic, symbols. These early inscriptions contained some symbols that disappeared from the canonical corpus of the later established hieroglyphic set. The last symbol on coffins B3C and B9C, for example, is an unknown ligature of three signs: Life, Seat, and Gold, *ˁnḫ-p-nbw*. Was this meant to be taken as a string of these three words, or a string of three sounds embedded in these three words when spoken? Unfortunately, there is no known way to reconcile all five preserved strings of hieroglyphs into one coherent meaning. However, I will note what I think it means: "Solar Seat of Immortal Life," *ˁnḫ-p-nbw*.

141

Could this be related to the Seat of the Sun of the Nine from the Roads of Mehen written around the Vignette of R^c I deciphered in Chapter IV and who I suspected to be one and the same with the eternal *ḥḥw*?

It seems as if not all of the original text was inscribed on all coffins. Either that, or the original was interpreted using different Egyptian hiero-glyphs. The location of the caption near the ceiling and the seat, and the Earth-Sky context of caption 5, led Sherbiny to favor cyclical eternity in the divine form of the *ḥḥw* [heh-hoo].[159]

This concept of eternity is also recorded on the Vignette of R^c. We are told that [emphasis added]:

> *The paths of fire go round about the seat of the Shining Sun, who guards the paths for the great bark of the Coiled One, who makes a circle for **myriad** after **myriad**.*

This idea of time lines instead of space orbits aligns well with what I think is the outcome of reinterpreting the image of heliocentricity as a celestial supercycle of time like precession, expressed in the picturesque language of a people who were describing a rare celestial concurrence of events. Then, *ꜥnḫ-p-nbw* might be understood as the coming alive of the Sun on its golden throne—as in appearing in a certain spot on the dawning horizon, for example the so-called vernal point due east on a spring equinox into a certain star constellation of the Zodiac hovering just above.

Regardless of the correct interpretation of Textual Element 1, like the Vignette of R^c, it falls completely out of place from the entire body of the already strange Coffin Texts. As if one could not top the uncanny strange-ness of it all, both appear together with a coffer full of the writings of Thoth, inside an underground archive, located under an arm, somewhere in the Netherworld: An *ꜥfdt*. And since the Vignette of R^c is a real painting inside a real coffin from the Middle Kingdom, it now became a compel-ling possibilty that so had been this *ꜥfdt*, a real coffer, inside a real archive, somewere under a real arm. *But whose?*

The context of Spell 1116 is the final stage in which the deceased approaches the Sun God within his sanctuary. Having been equipped with magical power to pass the guarded gates, the spirit of the mortal dead *N* now faces his destiny: The Sun's divine spirit[160] protected inside his, otherwise, impenetrable shield of fiery loops. The quest continues in that N now embarks with the Sun on a path across the sky.

The most important take-away lesson from this spell is how it unites two, to us, different concepts: one religious, the other scientific. On the one hand we behold a divine shrine, the shining spirit of the Sun inside, surrounded by a shield of flames and darkness. On the other hand, we have a deceased mortal who has passed a series of celestial, orbital gates that guard the normally discrete and separated tracks of the heavenly bodies in the sky.

The textual bridge that brings these two concepts together is the mention of gated walls of fire and darkness. These walls confine the orbits in the sky and shield the Sun God. This fusion of concepts, above all other discernable themes one may encounter in the Coffin Texts, appears strangest. In the cosmology of the ancient Egyptians, the gated paths of the ecliptic in the sky surround Earth, not the Sun. Yet it is the Sun that resides at the center of these very same paths in the way of the equipped deceased, which he must pass.

This is a glaring astronomical contradiction. It is an underappreciated paradox emerging from the main theme of the Coffin Texts and the so-called *Book of Two Ways* embedded within it. This paradox has been overlooked by Egyptologists. I can only speculate that few researchers have delved into the necessary depth of these texts to be afforded the opportunity to distill it from the obscurity generated by the ancient Egyptian reinterpretation of esoteric knowledge they must have inherited.

In CT 1130, a most powerful and awe-inspiring speech is given by the deceased having reached the solar sanctuary. He now slips into the role of the Sun God. He has reached the center inside the bands of fire and darkness, the center of the Coiled One, at the end of the Game Mehen, if you will. The speech he gives highlights *R*ꜥ's acts of creation, his laws, and mortals' sinning against them. He makes an apocalyptic prophecy of repeated destruction and creation. The text is awe-inspiring for it is an (imagined) account by a creator god who describes what he has done.[161]

This remarkable manifesto has indeed been mulled over many times but the one phrase which sticks out for me is this one:

... I will relate to you the two good deeds which my own heart did for me within the Coiled One [Mehen] in order that falsehood might be silenced ...

Sherbiny translates "two good deeds as one good deed after another."[162]

The speaker in this spell is N who assumes the role of the creator Sun God, and utters these words from within Mehen: He has made the air, the great flood, and equality between all and rules to preserve it; he has made a memory of the west, the place of dying and living again. These divine acts of creation are his legacy. He proclaims that he made gods and humans, the day and the night, and that he rules over the sky. He judges good and evil, possesses eternal life, and presides over creation and destruction. He is The Almighty, this much is clear.

But what is the significance of creation from within Mehen, the Coiled One? The coil and the snake were nearly identical symbols from early Egyptian history, as I showed in the previous chapter. Cobras, for example, were regarding as the protective and regenerative power ensnaring the Sun God. By contrast, the snake demon Apep was his arch enemy in the Netherworld. Yet, Spell 1116 also conveys the idea of a shield of fire and darkness. It relates to gates, portals, and guards in the Winding Waterways of the sky, the ecliptic paths of the Sun, Moon, and planets—in short the model of the universe shown in the Vignette of R^c.

Creation and the Heliocentric Solar System. Two ideas had become one.

This is a creation story. The creative act takes place where the Vignette of R^c tells us: where the archive is. To give you an idea of the magnitude of what all this means; it would be like finding a prehistoric cave with a box in it. Inside you would find the original story of the creation, destruction, and recreation of the world from an unkown author. *Can you imagine how you would feel?*

From coffins to coffers, I had come a long way. I had searched for a paradox. Now it stared at me like the Sun God in the painting. I knew that hiding behind the beautiful, lyrical language was an astronomical problem that once must have confronted and confounded the ancient Egyptians. From their own observations, they had learned about the sky. Yet, they came into possession of knowledge, in the form of a painted image like the Vignette of R^c, they could not explain. The idea depicted there did not make sense when held up against their own model of the world. And so they confronted

144

these contradictions in terms of what they knew: The Vignette of R^c was reinterpreted, the information reformulated in both familiar terms but also magical language to capture its complex essence. This is what led to the text around the painting called the *Roads of Mehen*. Meanwhile, images in the sky became symbols, and symbols became projections of power. Writing was invented, for to write meant to imitate creation.

This is how I have built a reasonable case to explain this paradox: once upon a time existed a real archive at Hermopolis that contained recorded information the ancient Egyptians did not discover on their own. But the earliest examples of symbols encoding this knowledge predate Narmer's unification of Upper and Lower Egypt. And so it must have come to the ancient Egyptians from another place and another time. It must have come to them before their land was ruled by kings and queens.

So profound, however, was its effect that it became the fundamental seed from which grew their vision of the universe, their symbols of power, their theology of creation, their cosmogony, and their vision of the afterlife.

An early hieroglyphic record suggested to me that an important archive had been opened and breached. The texts I presented here tell us that an equally important archive of paradoxical, anachronistic, astronomical knowledge incorporated into a story of creation existed in a library called the *House of Life* at Hermopolis. *Were these two archives connected?*

To find the answers, there was only one place to search. If there ever was a book in monumental form—a megalithic record of Egypt's story of creation—it stands in Upper Egypt. Even today, after more than two thousand years, it is as magnifiscent as haunting: The Temple of Horus at Edfu.

VII

Archive

H IGH UP, IN THE THIRD REGISTER, INSIDE OF THE EASTERN ENCLOSURE WALL
of the Edfu Temple is a back-and-forth dialog between one of Egypt's
Hellenic rulers from the House of Ptolemy and the gods. The king makes
various offerings and benedictions. The gods respond with blessings. Then,
the topic shifts to the creation and design of the temple to be made into the
primordial seat of *R⸱*. Various gods speak. Their utterances can be seen
carved next to their reliefs. This is a haunting place to visit. It feels like
you're passing by the acts of a stage play, animated from their frozen state
when you behold them, one after the other.

We learn something important about the content of two primordial
archives here, the *House of Scrolls* and the *House of Life*. The seven *ḏ3jsw*
[jai-soo]—materialized as baboons who represent the original words of
creation—are mentioned here by their names, not merely by their epithets.
They are flanked to the left and right by Seshat, the goddess of writing and
archiving, and Thoth (figure 55).

This scene sets the stage for *R⸱*'s entry into his monumental Edfu sanctuary, conceived and designed by Ptah and Thoth, and shaped into existence
by the *ḫnmw* [khe-ne-moo] potter spirits. With *R⸱* enter the Ennead, the
nine gods of the Heliopolitean pantheon, and the *ḫmnw* [khe-me-noo]
Chaos-Gods of the primordial eight. Together with Thoth, The Eight make
up the Hermopolitean pantheon. Thus, the Edfu Temple represents a physical model of the entire universe, according to the principle three spiritual
teachings of Egyptian religion: the school of Ptah in Memphis, the school
of *R⸱* in Heliopolis, and the school of Thoth in Hermopolis. In this epic
scene, all three are in attendance.

Archived Words of Creation

I highlight the setting of this scene because it is in this temple where we learn how creation became words, how words became writing, and how writing was archived. This, then, is the context to the following four utterances made by four of the seven *ḏ3jsw*.

Figure 55: Top, the seven *ḏ3jsw* creation words, and the seven potter spirits flanked by Seshat and Thoth. Bottom, the fourth through seventh *ḏ3jsw* with Thoth. Above the heads are their names. On their fronts are their utterances. From the third register of the inside, eastern enclosure wall of the Edfu Temple. ©, Émile Chassinat (1868-1948), Edfu Project. Public Domain.`

Their names are *qbḥ-snw.f*, *sḫpr-mw-smḫj-nww*, *b3q-b3q*, and ***mn-qb***. Since the substance of their material presence as baboons consists of the primordial flood waters, they personify these recorded utterances of creation, having taken shape from the sea of chaos. This is the moment when they are to be stored inside an archive.[163] If you will, we get to witness a recreation of the seven-sealing of the *Hall of Records*:

qbḥ-snw.f: Oh, great throne of *Rᶜ* since the Great Time, we

exalt you through the writings of *Rᶜ*.

sḫpr-mw-smḫj-nww: Oh, perfect mound which stood in the beginning, we praise your fame through the writings of the gods.

148

b3q-b3q: Oh, house which bears the strength of Horus the sky-traverser, we praise you in the *House of Scrolls.*

mn-qb: Oh, seat of the throne of Horus, splendid city, princess of cities, we provide the *House of Life* with glorifying words.

The chief translator into German of these texts, Dieter Kurth, is a world expert in Ptolemaic hieroglyphic texts. He justified his translation of the word *dsrw* with "glorifying words" with the overall liturgical context of the four statements cited here.[164] Basically, his argument, spelled out in note 4 to his translation, is that since the first three quotations deal with exaltation and praise, made in the form of public pronouncements of religious glorification, the fourth one must also be.

What Kurth may have missed here are two important elements. First, the first two quotations deal with words, while the third and fourth quotations deal with *the place* where the words are to be archived, the libraries, not the words themselves.

Second, the word *dsrw* [jese-roo] when separated into the two words *ds* and *rw,* literally means the *lion himself.* It also resembles *dšrw* [deshe-roo], which means "the red ones" or "flamingos." I wondered if this could have been another case of phonetic mimicry to accentuate the true meaning— but if so, what information was to be kept hidden from the casual reader?

Translating the statement by *mn-qb* with this other possible context in mind that implicates a library and not the words themselves, changes things quite a bit:

Oh, seat of the throne of Horus, splendid city, princess of cities, we provide the House of Life in the Lion himself [in the Red Ones].

The hieroglyphic preposition "*m*" can mean both *with* and *in,* and so this new translation is justified based on the possible lexical definition of that word.[165] But where is the *House of Life*—in the "lion itself" or in the "Red Ones"? I have more to say about this later, but for now the takeaway is that while the first interpretation speaks for itself, the second is an epithet related to lions. Therefore, by writing "the *House of Life* in the lion itself" or "in the Red Ones" means to place an archive inside, literally within a lion. This is the first clue connecting the *House of Life* to lions, an archive, and possibly a *House of Scrolls.*

Why did Kurth not consider this context and translation? Surely, a red lion serving as an archive would not have made sense to him. Instead, he pursued a context of the words per se, not the place to which they may have referred. No blame goes to this incredible scholar who has made sense of the mass of, often, strange texts.

Another example of the use of *ds-rw* can be found in an older inscription from the Middle Kingdom in the tomb of *jh3* [EE-ha]. *Jh3* was the overseer of the scribes in the *House of Life* at Hermopolis magna. The text states that "all *dsrw* are revealed to him" (figure 56).

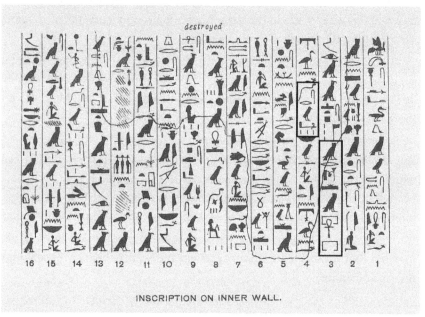

Figure 56: Titles of Middle Kingdom official *jh3* from his tomb at Deir El-Bersheh. Highlighted in in column 3 is the title Overseer of the Scribes in the House of Life. In column 5, the word *dsrw* is highlighted. From Griffith and Newberry, 1895, Plate XXI.

The word *dsrw* is contextualized with the arm symbol holding a coil. Here, the word is best translated as "sacred/secret things," certainly not glorifying words.

Back at Edfu, another hint in the name of the *d3jsw mn-qb*, which translates to "The Cool Endures." This refers to a place protected from heat, as in a chapel or, for example, an underground vault or cave. Thus alerted, we must also examine the names of the other three creation words:

qbḥ-snw.f, "He who cools his Brothers"; *sḫpr-mw-smḫj-nww*, "He who swells the Waters and raises Floods"; *b3q-b3q* relates to the moringa tree, an allusion to Osiris because "He Who Is in the Moringa Tree" is one of this god's epithets in the *Book of the Dead* where he also identifies himself with the Papyrus stalk.[166]

The House of Scrolls

Vaguely, the location of the archive of creation based on these veiled textual clues from the Edfu Temple began to take shape. They insinuated a cool place in an underground cave within a red lion. Sacred things inside related to Osiris. There was an allusion to flooding. The most compelling clue yet hid within the blandest of the names: *qbḥ-snw.f*. An unusually bland name in a set of epic utterances related to creation alerted me to the possibility of a Heka formula hiding within it. Indeed, what hides here is not only *qb-ḥnw*, an allusion to Osiris' grandfather *gb*/Geb and the god of *r-st3w*/Rostau, *skr*/Sokar, whose night boat is called the *ḥnw*/Hennu.

Also concealed in this *d3jsw*'s name is the *ḥn* chest, which is just another way to refer to the *'fdt* coffer (figure 57).

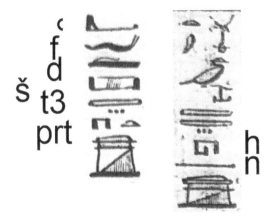

Figure 57: Two synonyms for the same pictogram showing an underground archival shrine. *'fdt* on the left and *ḥn* on the right. From pJumilhac, sheets XI column 14 and IV column 23, respectively. ©, François Olivier, modified.

You may wonder why the author of these texts did not unequivocally identify the archive explicitly and, instead, only left us cryptographic clues. The most likely explanation is that the archive was secret. Knowledge of its existence had to be passed along to only those who would be able to understand these clues. While I could not lean on anyone suspected Heka word in isolation to prove that an archive containing a creation story existed near the Great Sphinx, as a group, a string of Heka words spelled the beginnings of a connection between the *House of Life* in Hermopolis and another, more primordial archive elsewhere. This other archive had also stored the story of creation reenacted on the walls of the Edfu Temple. I even had a possible name for it: *The House of Scrolls.*

Was the content of this archive transferred to the House of Life?

This, still hazy, trace pointed to mythical Rostau, now Giza. The Edfu Temple is a textual gold mine, but to screen the massive volume of texts now translated into German by the Academy of Sciences of Göttingen's Edfu Project[167] is overwhelming. Weeks went by before I found other passages that revealed more clues. One such passage follows immediately after the utterances of the words of creation. It recites the words of Thoth after those exclaimed by ***mn-qb***. I have translated the Edfu Project's German interpretation of the originally hieroglyphic text into English:

*Words to be spoken by Thoth, the twice great, the Lord of Hermopolis: Oh **R𝒻**, the place has been fashioned inside of which you will endure for Millions and Millions of years.*

The place to which Thoth refers is the Edfu Temple itself where this inscription is located. However, this once Upper Egyptian sanctuary dedicated to the Sun God inside a megalithic book is not unlike the sacred center inside nine bands of fire and darkness painted onto a coffin board, we now known as the Vignette of **R𝒻** from Hermopolis in Middle Egypt. The parallels do not end here.

From Edfu, Thoth uttered his deeds of creation. Here is where we learned of a coffer of magical knowledge. Here is where we see illustrated a model of the universe that is not of ancient Egyptian origin. This universe, we were told, also has a size given in myriads and myriads, or millions and millions, of years.

The takeaway from this passage is that the fundamental idea of the Edfu Temple as a sanctuary of **R𝒻** from which creation is orchestrated is identical with that shown in the Vignette of **R𝒻**. It almost seems as if the painting inspired the theme of the temple. Like the nine orbits surrounding the seated Sun God in the vignette, the enclosure wall, on which the Edfu texts were recorded, surrounds the temple proper and its throne of R^c, as if it is the sky's imagined perimeter wall.

There are two other significant lines in the third register of the inner east wall of the Edfu Temple that solidify the connection between Edfu and Hermopolis, up the Nile to Memphis, and even Giza as to the location of the original archive. The first is about Seshat, Egypt's patron goddess of astronomy and archives.[168]

Words to be spoken by Seshat, the Great, the Mistress of the Script, great of Heka-Magic in the House of Scrolls.

This is a crucial piece of textual evidence because it can be connected to an exclusive, academic title inscribed on the funerary slab stele of a high ranked spiritualist, royal scribe, and archivist under King Cheops/Khufu: The shaman/*sm* priest Wepemnefret. He was entombed at Giza, west of the Great Pyramid. On the stele, the title symbolically relates to the protective lioness Mehit, and it is recorded immediately next to Wepemnefret's "Priest of Seshat foremost in the *House of Scrolls of Royal Knowledge*" title.

The Edfu inscription above told me that this archive contained records related to Heka magic in addition to astronomy confirming another connection I had already suspected: Difficult concepts related to the sky required descriptions which utilized Heka magic. In chapter V, I showed how the reptilian deities Heken and Hekaw conferred this power to the king who wielded it to control the timing of the universe.

Thanks to what was recorded on Wepemnefret's stele, I now knew that the *House of Scrolls* mentioned in Edfu was a real archive in ancient Egypt—but was this real library identical with the Netherworld House *pr-dw3t* that contained the magical *'fdt* coffer, mentioned in the Coffin Texts? The link, it turns out, was Mehit.

Lioness Guardian of the House of Scrolls

My ongoing challenge was to bridge the gap between myth and reality. As my research into the matter deepened, I saw this distinction become ever more artificial from the ancients' point of view. Mehit, the lioness, was to become the key to unlock this riddle to locate the *House of Scrolls*, quite literally. The following Edfu passage mentions Mehit who I now knew guarded this library:[169]

Words to be spoken by Mehit, the Eye of R^c, the one who dwells in Behedet,[170] the ruler of East-Behedet, Menet, the Great with painful flame, who protects the Prince of the White Crown in his sanctuary.

Who were Menet and the Prince of the White Crown? The German *Lexikon der ägyptischen Götter und Götterbezeichnungen Band III*, on page 286c and 287a identifies Menet and Menet the Great as a lioness goddess, appearing for example as Mehit, in a ritual function. I had Egyptological proof now that similar sounding names could refer to different aspects of the same entity, for example *mhj*, Mehen, and Mehit. Of great significance to me was also another lexical entry: Menet can designate a lion-shaped lock to secure a gate, i.e. the personification of the Egyptian word for lock *q3r.t* [gha-ret].

The Prince of the White Crown is an attribute of Osiris. In other words, this passage told me that Mehit was where Osiris was. Osiris' abode was *r-st3w*/Mouth of Caves/Giza not later than the Fifth Dynasty, also the realm of the even earlier *skr*/Sokar.

The connection was clear: Mehit was a lioness near Osiris in Giza and that too is, therefore, the place of the *House of Scrolls*.

I was also able to further narrow and define the manner in which Mehit protected Osiris. Osiris, like Sokar, was believed to dwell in the Underworld below the surface of the land, in the Netherworld of the caves riddling Geb, the Earth. From Wepemnefret's stele I knew that Mehit guarded Seshat's *House of Scrolls of the King's Knowledge*. Meanwhile, the Edfu inscription had told me that she guarded Osiris. Since he was below, she must have been above because that is how guards like jackals and lions are often shown in Egyptian art: They are couchant upon a shrine.

To corroborate this idea, I needed evidence to establish that the *House of Scrolls* was indeed below ground, as if it were an underground cave housing an *'fdt* portable archive into which had once descended a staircase or ramp. The word for ramp(s) is *st3(w)* and so *r-st3w*/Rostau was a good name for a place with underground caves and corridors (figure 58).

The Giza Plateau, as it is now called, sits on the Mokattam Limestone foundation. Seasonal Nile flooding has eroded it into a Karst over millions of years. The aquifers which have formed reach as high as five meters below the ground surface.[171] Needless to say, Giza is a world of caves.

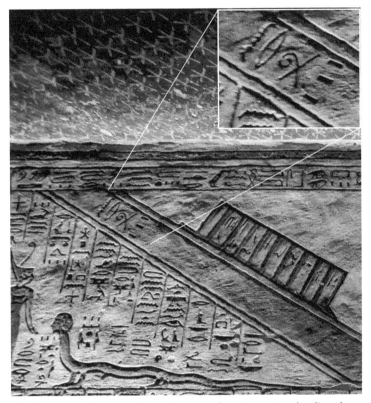

Figure 58: Illustration from the *Book of the Dead* showing a ramp leading down to the Netherworld of the afterlife towards the abode of Osiris. The inset in the right upper corner is a magnification of the inscription on the ramp. It spells *n r st3w*, To Rostau, or to the mouth or Gate above that leads into the Netherworld below. ©, John Lundwall, Valley of Kings, KV11, 2019; modified.

The sum of the textual evidence from Edfu and Giza's western cemetery pointed to an underground sanctuary of Osiris at Giza. In it was a real archive of Seshat housing Heka magic and astronomical knowledge recorded by Thoth. This sacred place was guarded by a lioness called Mehit. I now saw more clearly the lexical connection between a lock, a guardian who seals, and an archive which preserves *time*. I also understood the connection between the portable archive and the Netherworld House. It was underground at Giza, the real place associated with the gate to the Underworld.

Menet means "She who Endures." Its secret nature is captured in the name of its patron goddess: Seshat from *zš* [zesh]/write and *sšt3* [se-she-tah]/secret. Its name was the *House of Scrolls of the King's Knowledge*. The

Coffin Texts had made one thing crystal clear: From here, the Sun God created the world. From here had come what had leaked out of the *House of Life* into the tomb of General Zepi, the Vignette of *R^c*. This had all the bells and whistles of a real *Hall of Records*. I knew I had discovered its trail cryptically concealed in the vast compendium of hieroglyphic texts written over a time span of some three thousand years.

This *House of Scrolls* cannot have been a regular library of ancient Egypt, of which there must have been several. The descriptions of it in the theological and funerary writings peg this archive as a secret, sacred, ancient, and primordial facility, even by an already secretive, ancient Egyptian standard. It contained information from which the world was created and from which the kings obtained their power. It contained the necessary knowledge to become immortal in the afterlife. The likelihood that there was more than one such incredible place seems remote.

I was now in possession of another textual source that told me what I had only been able to vaguely discern from my Heka decryption of the utterances of the *ḏ3jsw*. I could put a name on the lion, or the lioness rather, in which the *House of Life*, now identified with the *House of Scrolls of Royal Knowledge*, was provided with sacrosanct knowledge: Her name was the same Mehit mentioned on Wepemnefret's stele. She was one of Egypt's oldest deities.

Her original function was to imbue mud sealings used to secure luxury items that were shipped to royal tombs during the early First Dynasty with a protective aura. Mehit, about whom I have a lot to say later, was the protective divine patron of Egypt's early royal administration established by Narmer. Even then, this aura imparted security and secrecy. *But what was the origin of these associations?* The answer to that ended up changing my life, but I am, once again, jumping ahead.

Here I must first explain an apparent paradox. How could Mehit have been at once in Behedet, one of the names for Edfu in the south of Egypt, and at Rostau/Giza in the north at the apex of the Nile Delta? This confusion arises, because there were two Behedet's, the original one in the Delta, located in the north of Egypt, and a later, second one, Behedet-South, so to speak, established sometime before the Third Dynasty.[172] Horus the Behedetite was originally a northern deity and, I argue, so was Mehit. Her name means The Northern One, or She who is in the North.

Sir Alan Gardiner identifies Behedet with *sm3-n-bḥdt* (his Sambehdet),[173] and locates it to the Island of Amun, Tell el-Balamun, where the Delta meets the Mediterranean Sea. According to him, the prehistoric north first conquered the south exporting the Horus myth while demonizing its Seth cult, centered in Ombos. Narmer's conquest of the north in 3000 BC, in Gardiner's reconstruction, was the counterstrike to that prior invasion. This theory explains how Mehit came to be part of the southern iconography found in the earliest known written records from Upper Egypt. She became associated with the southern animal shrine *pr-wr*, even though her prehistoric origins were really in the north.

I now had a good working model supported with textual evidence with a beginning and an end, though still in need of a bridge between. First Dynasty inscriptions recorded the opening of an archive as a year-defining event and a lioness guarding the early seat of the royal administration and symbolically locking the official seals of the king's accountants. An Old Kingdom tomb stele mentioned a physical, royal archive of Seshat guarded by this same lioness and spelled out her name, Mehit. The archive had a name: *The House of Scrolls of the King's Knowledge.*

From the Coffin Texts and the Edfu Texts, I had learned about the astronomical nature of an equally mysterious and magical archive of the words of creation, recorded by Thoth, which came into being when the world and universe around it were made by the Sun God. This archive's name was *'fdt.* According to records which had leaked from the Hermopolitean *House of Life*, and like Seshat's *House of Scrolls*, it textually mapped to Osiris, lions, the *dw3t*/Netherworld, and ultimately Rostau/Giza. The question to which all this pointed was: *Were these two archives one and the same?*

You might now rightly ask why this is still a question. Besides Mehit, I had one other potential pass across the perceived gap between myth and reality: The *House of Life*. It was mentioned at Edfu, but I wanted references to a physical place with that name for the skeptics who would not be willing to accept that myth and reality were artificial aspects created by an incorrect, reductive interpretation of Egyptian funerary texts. The first explicit, written mention of the *House of Life* does not occur until the Sixth Dynasty of the Old Kingdom during the reign of Pepi II Neferkare. (2278 BC to 2216-2184 BC).[174] At least, Sir Allen Gardiner, who compiled a list of more than sixty written reference throughout Egypt's long history, did not think so.

Three possibilities come to mind. First, there may not have been a *House Life* before Pepi II. Second, earlier written references to it are simply lost. We should never lose sight of this second possibility, as trivial as it may seem and as casual as it is sometimes dismissed only to be mentioned for completeness' sake.

I was acutely reminded that archaeology never sleeps when a Czech team headed by Miroslav Bárta recently published the titles of a high official from the mid Fifth Dynasty called Kairsu whose tomb, situated near the Abusir Pyramids of the Fifth Dynasty kings, they had excavated.[175] He was not only the foremost of the *House of Life* but also the keeper of secrets of the *pr-dw3t*, the *Morning House* as Egyptologists call it. This is, of course, the same *Morning House* which I knew from the Coffin Texts housed the *'fdt.* The secrets kept were therefore likely kept inside the *'fdt. The mythical 'fdt was a real archive!*

Bárta et al. make two important observations regarding Kairsu's title[176]: It appears first when the name of Osiris first appears in writing, and it is also strongly associated with the archaic creator god Khnum, a ram-headed deity, who, for example, is part of one name of Cheops/Khufu, i.e., Khnum-khuf, "Khnum protects him."

The aura emitted by these associations of the *House of Life* hints at Giza, the abode of Sokar and Osiris, at Osiris' protectress Mehit, at originalism and creation, and of course, at stored records related to these ideas. With the mid-Fifth Dynasty, we are less than half a century away from the events at Giza that led to the creation of the Great Sphinx from what may have preceded her. I began to wonder: *Was the House of Life created after the Great Sphinx was made because the original archive under her was moved to a new facility in, for example, Memphis?*

The third possibility is that the *House of Life* had another name. Surely, a facility by the name of "Life" existed long before Pepi II (figure 59). Here is the problem though: This mansion was probably a dining hall, not a library—at least that is what the titles suggest that were given to administer this part of the royal palace.

On the tomb stele of Fourth Dynasty Prince Netjeraperef, a son of Fourth Dynasty's founder king Sneferu, he can be seen to have carried the titles

Figure 59: The *Mansion of Life* from the tomb stele of Fourth Dynasty Prince Netjeraperef. The Museum of Egyptian Antiquities, Cairo, Egypt, 2018.

Priest of the Pyramid named Foremost Appearance of King Sneferu and Director of the *Mansion of Life*, literally He who is over the decree of the *Mansion of Life* (figure 60).

According to one of Germany's most influential Egyptologists of the late twentieth century Wolfgang Helck, this title, the *ḥrj-wḏb ḥwt-ꜥnḫ*, originally conferred onto the bearer the function of assigning or directing the king's guests to their seats in the royal dining hall.[177] This had to be a trusted individual, and so it makes sense that the task would fall on one of the king's sons. The identical title can be seen on a First Dynasty sealing found in Saqqara tomb S3505, where it is immediately next to other titles associated with the supply of grain to the royal house, likewise an important title evidently conferred to royal family members (figure 61).

This context is the principal basis for Helck's argument that the *Mansion of Life* was a dining hall inside the royal palace. His theory is further supported by two related titles conferring directorial positions to the same individual in the wine cellar *ḥrp-zḥ*, and the pantry magazines *ḥrp-jz-ꜥnḫ*.[178] It thus appears that the *Mansion of Life* was indeed a food-related facility. Is it possible that what once was the king's palatial dining hall was appropriated to serve as a library of secret scrolls? Yes, but I do not think so. Textual evidence argues for another chamber.

At first sight, the evidence does not look favorably on the *Mansion of Life* as the original *House of Life*. However, as these things usually go, it is

Figure 60: Titular column from the stele of Prince Netjeraperef showing the *ḫrj-wḏb ḥwt-ʿnḫ* title. The Museum of Egyptian Antiquities, Cairo, Egypt, 2018.

Figure 61: Sealing from the First Dynasty tomb S3505 at Saqqara showing a title sequence associated with the supply of grain including the *ḫrj-wḏb ḥwt-ʿnḫ* in the *Mansion of Life*. From Kaplony 1963, Tafel 94, 366.

more complicated than that. On the stele of Prince Netjeraperef, there are three other intriguing titles which complete the picture in an unexpected way (figure 62).

Figure 62: The Stele of Prince Netjeraperef. (a) marks the scribe symbol *zšw*. (b) marks the title *ḥrj-sšt3*, and (c) marks the title *zšw-mḏ3-nṯr*. The Museum of Egyptian Antiquities, Cairo, Egypt, 2018.

Not only was the Prince (a), the personal scribe of the king, but he was also (b), Director of Secrets, the *ḥrj-sšt3* [hery-se-she-tah], and most significantly (c), Scribe of the Divine Scroll, the *zšw-md3-nṯr* [zeshoo-mejah-neter].

Since Netjeraperef was buried in Dashur and probably lived during the time of Sneferu, he was older than Wepemnefret, who was buried in mastaba G1201 at Giza. Nevertheless, these two royal scribes likely overlapped as contemporaries. While there is a compelling context that Prince Netjeraperef was indeed a scribe with high level access to the most sensitive written records of the king, it appears that the archive in which they were stored was not the *Mansion of Life* because the symbol for it is in a different column as the three scribal titles.

Instead, the evidence suggests that Netjeraperef worked elsewhere, where Wepemnefret worked. And where was that? It was the Mehit-guarded Seshat *House of Scrolls of the King's Knowledge*. With Netjeraperef's active role in this archive is revealed a third type of written records kept there besides the astronomy and Heka magic: The Divine Scroll (figure 62 c).

The Real *Hall of Records* Has a Name

With this combination of astronomy, magic, and the divine, I was within reaching distance of a real physical *ʿfdt*. When I went to Egypt in 2018 with my cousin, Masood, I had a superb camera with me. On this trip, I had plenty of time to take detailed photos of the many hieroglyphic reliefs at the Cairo Museum. The funerary stele relief of Netjeraperef was one of many I photographed. The high-resolution photo ended up in a folder with a few hundred others. I would have forgotten about this exquisitely made piece of early Old Kingdom high relief if it hadn't been for Dr. Peter Der Manuelian who is the Barbara Bell Professor of Egyptology, Director of the Harvard Museum of the Ancient Near East, and a world expert on the Giza cemeteries.

I had contacted Dr. Manuelian with questions about his superb book *Slab Stelae of the Giza Necropolis*,[179] which includes the tomb stele of Wepemnefret. In answering one of my question about the different Old Kingdom styles of funerary stone plates, also known as steles or stelas (sing. stele/stela), he suggested I check out the stele found in the tomb of Prince Netjeraperef. Images of these steles and their translations are often difficult to find and access to publications about them is often closed, available only to institutional members, which I am not. I searched my Cairo Museum folder, and there it was, a high-resolution photograph of the tomb stele of Prince Netjeraperef.

It is thanks to this photo that I had the final break-through in this hunt for evidence for the real *ꜥfdt*. What I could not make out in my initial survey of the symbols on the stele to translate the titles was a small symbol squeezed between the arm symbol and the symbol of the scribe's palette. Initially, I thought this was a small animal. I had never seen this symbol before and skipped over it. This time, when I took a better look, I gasped: *There it was*!

Prince Netjeraperef was his father Sneferu's ***nsw-ḫrt-ꜥ***, the scribe of the "royal What is Under the Arm." On the stele, this cryptic title had been contextualized with the *ꜥfdt* coffer symbol (figure 63).

Figure 63: A segment from the third column of the stele of Netjeraperef showing the coffer symbol *ꜥfdt*. The Museum of Egyptian Antiquities, Cairo, Egypt, 2018.

The word *ḫrt* is a feminine gender adjective called a nisbe made from the preposition *ḫr*, which means below or beneath. In English, the idea of a nisbe can be explained by comparing "could you please get me the box which is under the shelf" with "could you please get me the below-the-shelf box." In the latter example, the preposition "under" in English becomes "below," used to characterize the box.

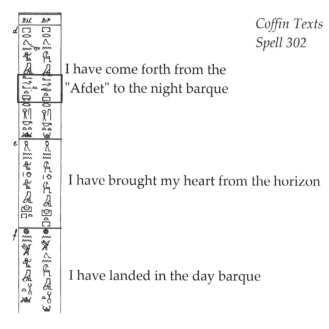

Coffin Texts
Spell 302

I have come forth from the "Afdet" to the night barque

I have brought my heart from the horizon

I have landed in the day barque

Figure 64: Coffin Text Spell 302 showing the coffer symbol and its spelling *ʿfdt*. From de Buck and Gardiner, 1951. Courtesy of the Oriental Institute of the University of Chicago.

In hieroglyphic, all adjectives, whether derived or not, function as nouns. Another way to translate *ḫrt* is with "the one below," or "the below-one." Consequently, *nsw-ḫrt-ʿ-zšw* translates into "The Scribe of the Royal One-Below-the-Arm" [Coffer]. That is how a nisbe was used in hieroglyphic.

There are two semantic uses of the nisbe *ḫrt*. It is used to figuratively indicate possession, in a sense of "this house is under my control," and to concretely relate the idea of a location underneath something else, as in "the land I own is under my feet." On Netjeraperef's stele, the coffer is identified with something which is either literally under an/the arm, or in the possession of someone, such as the king. The word arm is written with the arm word symbol. Its sound would have been something like "aw." The coffer symbol acts as a context marker to clarify what was meant by "that which is under the arm"—a coffer of documents, an *ꜥfdt*. This is the same symbol used in the Coffin Texts (figure 64).

At last, I had evidence of a real, physical archive of the king administered by a scribe who oversaw the divine scroll. The name of this archive was the same as the mythical archive mentioned in the Coffin Texts kept at the *House of Life*. The "under the arm" attribute suggested that this was an underground archive. And since I already knew that the guardian of this archive was Mehit, the logical conclusion was that the "arm" above *ꜥfdt* must have been one of the two forepaws of the lioness.

But this could be no real animal. It had to be a statue large enough to fit over an archive, and this would be in line with the idea that the ancient Egyptians kept secret documents under the shrine of a god or goddess. The style of naming something by describing an attribute of it, as in "under the arm," was also common in Egyptian texts and so this was not unusual.

The coffer symbol reminded me of the symbol for the prehistoric scribes' animal shrine **pr-wr** [per-wer] shown on some of the hieroglyph-inscribed bone tags found in Scorpion I's tomb UJ by the German Archaeological Institute under director Günter Dreyer (1942-2019).[180] This suggested to me that the coffer was a miniature model icon of this prehistoric shrine used by Egypt's oldest known scribes (figure 65).

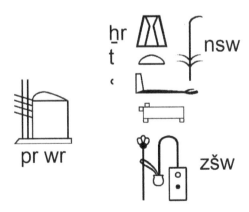

Figure 65: The title **nsw-ḥrt-ꜥ-zšw**, The scribe of the royal What is under the Arm. For comparison, the hieroglyph for the prehistoric animal shrine The Great Hall **pr-wr** is shown.

But there was an even more ancient angle to this animal-like coffer with respect to its being kept hidden underground. I could not help but remember a strange feature of the eight-thousand-year-old astronomical and spiritual meeting place of prehistoric cattle pastoralists in the southeastern Sahara: Nabta Playa, discovered in 1973 by a team of archaeologists under Fred Wendorf. Buried deeply under the main one of thirty so-called complex stone structures, ovals made from uprights and recumbent stone monoliths, the excavators found a massive rock apparently carved into the shape of a cow.[181] This, of course, is the now famous cow stone housed at the Aswan Museum.

From the complex structure above ground, called Complex Structure A, five megalithic stone lines (A1, A2, A3, B1, and B2) were shown to point to prominently bright stars in the night sky such as Sirius, Arcturus, and Alnilam in Orion.[182] The big surprise here is that the idea of an animal-shaped coffer hidden underground in association with astronomically aligned stone monuments, like the Great Sphinx, was nothing new in the ancient Egypt ruled by kings and queens. One must reach way back into prehistoric times to arrive at the concept's origin.

Finally, also, I had an explanation for the confusion in the later texts, in which the word *ʿfdt* could be anything from a chest, a chamber, a boat cabin, to an entire cave. The coffer was built to resemble the real, prehistoric *Hall of Records*, **pr-wr**. This was a concrete image of what the thus far elusive archive looked like. It was a probably portable chest, exactly as implied by Spell 225 from the Coffin Texts. I could picture a subterranean chamber carved out of the rock in which such a coffer was kept under guard, just exactly as I had pieced together from Spell 695: the **pr-dw3t**. Inside must have been symbolic records or images, what we might call writing, important enough to be guarded by people and gods. After all, these were the divine words for after the netherworld.

The image of a guarded box of written records also reminded me of the Ark of the Covenant. This wooden, gilded coffer contained the Ten Commandments, the Magical Rod of Aaron, and the food substance Mana. It was carried with staves and guarded by two angels, the cherubim. In *Exodus*, the Ark's Hebrew name is Aaron Ha-Edut, ‏תודעה וראן‎, meaning "Ark of the Testimony."[183] Was this name related to the Egyptian *ʿfdt*? It is

plausible, given that the Ark of the Testimony/Covenant would have originated in Egypt. However, I will have to leave this for others to investigate.

With a written hieroglyphic reference to a real *ꜥfdt-ḥrt-ꜥ* in the Old
Kingdom, odds were improving that this was identical with Seshat's *House
of Scrolls*. That meant Mehit was nearby. I knew I would eventually have to
prove that the arm was a forepaw of the lioness. For now, I could recapitulate how a portable archive could have been transferred from one secure
location to another, and how the *ꜥfdt* may have ended up in the *House of
Life* at Hermopolis, after its original location at Giza was for some reason
decomissioned.

Hall of Records, Breached

The next step in the investigation was to consult Jochem Kahl's catalog
of early Egyptian hieroglyphs to find the date of the earliest use of the coffer
symbol. To my great surprise, it dated to the reign of Horus-Djer, the third
king of Egypt after Horus-Narmer and Horus-Aha. Immediately, I scrolled
through Flinders Petrie's *Royal Tombs* to see the context of the first use of
the coffer under the arm symbol cataloged as Q15—and there it was carved
into an oil tag, an ancient Egyptian shipping label for precious goods
inscribed with significant events to commemorate a certain year (figure
66).

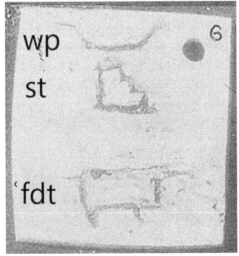

Figure 66: Ivory tag from the tomb of Horus-Djer (circa 3000-2900 BC). The three
symbols from top to bottom stand for *wp*, *st*, and the earliest example of *ꜥfdt-ḥrt-ꜥ*.
From Petrie (1901), Extra Plates, Pl, VA., 6; modified.

The three symbols shown are ***wp-st-ꜥfdt***. It means [clarification added]:

Opening of the Place of The Archive [Under-the-Arm].

I could not believe what I was seeing. This was a tag which identified a special event of significance, possibly, during the reign of Horus-Djer, but even earlier since there is no attribution to the reign of any king on this tag. Petrie discovered it in his tomb at Abydos, but as Wolfgang Helck reminds us, oil tags were reused in later years and the information they contained on the front had no relationship to their use.[184] He speculates that the tags were part of an inventory board listing various years on which other tags with numerical quantities of goods were hung. Eventually, the reverse side of these year tags were inscribed and attached to unrelated shipments.[185] Therefore, the opening of the archive under the arm need not have taken place during the time of Horus-Djer.

Whenever the event described by these three symbols took place, this event, and not another, was chosen to commemorate the particular year of its occurrence. The opening of the archive in which this coffer stood must have been momentous. But the tag does not indicate where the breach occurred. This puzzled me. Was the location secret and thus could not be revealed on this accounting record? It is, of course, tempting at this point to conclude that this had to be in Rostau/Giza, but the tag does not tell us directly. There is, however, one interesting connection, nevertheless.

Egyptologists tell us that no pyramids or a Great Sphinx existed on the Giza Plateau before the end of the Fourth Dynasty, some five centuries before the life of Horus-Djer. There is however a curious connection between Djer and Osiris, the Lord of Rostau/Giza, because the former's tomb was venerated as beloning to the latter beginning in the New Kingdom. The reason for this choice is unknown. This, I had to file away under "too circumstantial."

The Edfu Texts alluded to an archive near Osiris, but Egyptologist tell us that no record of this god exists until the Fifth Dynasty, until after 2500 BC. And so, linking the archive under the arm to Giza would require additional textual evidence which mentions Mehit and places her in that location.

One subtle clue on Horus-Djer's oil tag hints the archive was in Rostau. This clue, as usual, is hiding in plain sight: the staircase symbol. As an Upper Egyptian sound symbol, it reads as *st* [set], "place." In the corpus of early dynastic symbols were also logograms and pictograms whose images depicted what was meant.

As I showed earlier, on sheet IV, column 23 of pJumilhac, for example, the word *ḥn*, like the word *ꜥfdt* used elsewhere in this papyrus, means chest or coffer. The word is contextualized in the text with an icon of a shrine, into which descends a staircase (figure 67). The same iconography is more archaically expressed on Djer's oil tag with the staircase symbol *st* and the shrine-like *ꜥfdt* chest.

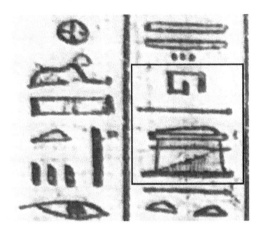

Figure 67: On the left, one of the words for coffer, *ḥn*, is shown. Its context symbol is a shrine into which a staircase leads. On the right, the same concept expressed by the two symbols for place, **st**, and coffer, *ḫrt-ꜥ*, from the oil tag found in the tomb of Horus-Djer.

As pJumilhac shows, the Egyptians of the Greco-Roman period had more than one word for an underground archival coffer in the shape of an animal shrine, containing esoteric, written records.

The word *ḥn* reminded me of the *ḥnw* bark of the hawk god Sokar, whose abode was also in Rostau, the mythical gate to the karstic underworld of natural ramps and caves.

On the Giza Plateau, archaeological evidence of a stair-like monumental structure cut out of the living rock exists. It must have existed before the Sphinx Temple was built. The idea of a megalithic staircase at Giza may at first seem ridiculous, given the orthodox narrative of when the pyramids, Sphinx, and temples were built. However, what is not immediately apparent to most, except a few archaeologists who have worked on the plateau, is that the Valley and Sphinx temples sit on a foundational terrace which is lower than the ground level of the ditch around the Sphinx, which, in turn, is lower than a terrace behind it (figure 68).

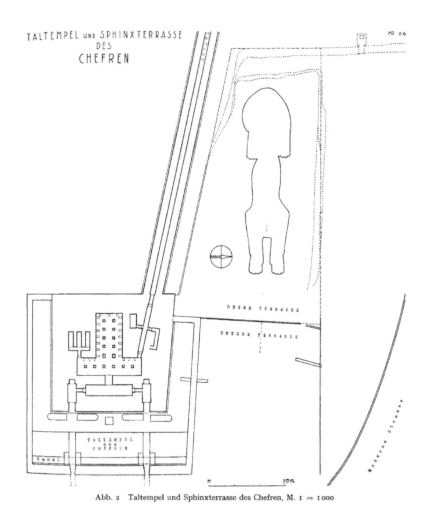

Abb. 2   Taltempel und Sphinxterrasse des Chefren, M. 1 = 1000

Figure 68: Terrace 1 and 2, before the erection of the Sphinx Temple, the Valley Temple, and its enclosure wall were built. From Ricke (1970), Figure 2. The position of two gutters are indicated.

The first thorough survey of the Sphinx Temple was conducted by a team from the Cairo branch of the Swiss Institute for Egyptian Building and Antiquity Research in 1965. They were Gerhard Haeny and Herbert Ricke. In Ricke's 1970 report,[186] he describes how the two-temple foundation was cut into the bedrock as a lower-lying terrace, relative to the higher Sphinx ditch, ending where the causeway enters through northwest corner of the Valley Temple and becomes incorporated into it.

The Sphinx Temple, therefore, sits on a step-like terrace, Terrace 1. At this level, it is circa two meters lower than the level of the ditch around the Sphinx, designated Terrace 2. Terrace 1 is not perfectly level, but gently slopes down towards the east and southeast.[187] This drop-off would have directed the flow of rainwater run-off away from the floor of the temple towards the basin in front of the pier. The border between Terrace 1 and 2, the step itself, does not run perpendicular with the due west-due east axis of the Great Sphinx, but rather with the north wall of the Valley Temple, which is not square to the other three walls. This is a key observation in Ricke's analysis because he interpreted it to mean that the blocks cut to carve out the temple foundation were used to first build the Pyramid Temple of Khafre, higher up on the plateau, and the Valley Temple by the Great Sphinx.

Then, the terrace was extended northwards, and the Sphinx was carved from the surrounding quarry, while the blocks hewn in the process were used to build the Sphinx Temple. The logic of this sequence depends on the fact that the step between Terrace 1 and 2 is perpendicular to the north wall of the Valley Temple. Ricke concluded, therefore, the Valley Temple's north wall served as the base for the perpendicular, northward extension of Terrace 1. In this scenario, the step came later, after the Valley Temple.

However, there are two logical problems with Ricke's building sequence: The first, he himself acknowledges. Two rain gutters were cut into the foundation of Terrace 1, one on the south side, and one on the north side. There is no obvious use for them. They direct the flow of water away from the overall southeastward slope of the terrace. More significantly, the south gutter was intentionally plugged with stone debris during construction of the Sphinx Temple, indicating that it was made for another prior purpose.[188]

The second problem is that the step could have served as the square reference for the Valley Temple; in other words, the sequence could have been opposite. The lower terrace in front of the Great Sphinx could have come first, serving as the base for the square corner it forms with the Valley Temple's north wall (figure 68).

Ricke himself speculates that a prior cultic shrine may have rested on Terrace 1, before the Sphinx Temple.[189] That means Terrace 1 could be older than any of the other structures, including the pyramids, and even the Sphinx and its precursor. The *st* symbol on the oil tag of Horus-Djer may, after all, not conceal the location of the archive with intent. It may have been an obvious megalithic structure at Giza identifying a monumental staircase up the plateau consisting of three steps, exactly as shown in the hieroglyph.

Elevations of the Mokattam Formation in profile published by Dr. Mark Lehner do in fact show another vertical drop-off of the bedrock fifty miles east of the Sphinx Temple. This marks the limit of Terrace 1.[190] A drill probe to the east of that underground vertical rock face unexpectedly revealed granite residue. Granite is not known to be part of the limestone formation that makes up the Giza Plateau (figure 69).

Lehner has explained this startling finding as a granite block that fell off the transport ship into the water basin in front of the temples. Others, who believe in the Edgar Cayce prophecy of the *Hall of Records*, have interpreted the presence of granite to indicate the existence of a, now deeply buried, façade which once formed the main gateway to the corridors and chambers system under the Sphinx.

Regardless, the physical evidence, left behind by man-made interventions to the limestone hill into which the Sphinx was carved, demonstrates a three-step rise, beginning some sixteen meters below current ground level, with the first step comprising Terrace 1, the second step comprising Terrace 2, the Sphinx ditch, and the third step made up by the uncut position of the western edge of the ditch, Terrace 3. It appears as if the three-step symbol on Horus-Djer's oil tag had a real counterpart in the foundations of the Sphinx complex.

Yet, this is not enough to make the case. Taken side-by-side with this geological evidence, however, is an inscription from the *Book of Two Ways* that corroborates it [clarifications added]:[191]

> *This N* [the deceased] *will get with them aboard the zšnt-boat towards the dockyard of the gods, that this N may hollow out a bark there two thousand cubits between its two heads, that N may*

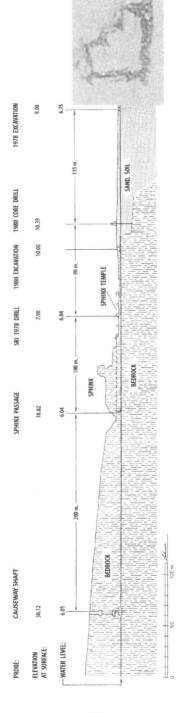

Figure 69: The step-like elevations of the bedrock into which the Great Sphinx was carved. To the right, for comparison, is the three-step hieroglyph for the word "Place", **st**. Modified Illustration from Mark Lehner (2017): "Drawing d-gen-040 from Egypt/Giza/East of Sphinx Temple". In *ARCE Sphinx Project 1979-1983 Archive*. ©, Mark Lehner, Megan Flowers, Rebekah Miracle (Eds.). Released: 2017-12-23. Open Context. <http://opencontext.org/media/554c2a1d-b690-46ee-b6c2-932b93b85c81> ARK (Archive): https://n2t.net/ark:/28722/k2vq35v7d.

go forth in it to the sky, that this N may sail in it together with Re, that this N may sail in it together with the One whose heart is monkeyish, and that this N may act as a pilot in it towards this district of Nut, towards this Staircase of the Mercury-bark ... [CT 1030]

... "Pass," says Horakhty, "that you may control the bark, the eye of your father!" [CT 1033]

The metaphoric allusions in these two segments of the same textual passage to the Eye of Horus, to the Sphinx[192] and its temple, Thoth-baboon,[193] with the dock[194] in front, and the stepped terrace on which they rest is further enhanced by the fact that the two westmost and two eastmost columns of the Sphinx Temple were possibly meant to represent the arms and legs of Nut.[195]

Linking the Archive to the Lioness

Everything was falling into place, but the last piece of the myth-to-reality link was missing, the association between the archive and the lioness. Geological and astronomical dating of the Great Sphinx pointed to a much older age for the monument, but the evidence has been dismissed by Egyptologists who insist there was no Sphinx before the Fourth Dynasty. Could it be that the mythical texts from Edfu and Hermopolis, along with the inscription on the stele of Wepemnefret, had gotten the archive right but not the lioness?

Textual evidence is powerful. It can corroborate—even trump— other archaeological evidence if it were not for the suspicion on behalf of modern scholars that ancient people did not describe their real observations when they composed religious texts. I hope by now I have dispelled this misunderstanding.

A few years ago, I could not shed some doubts about the theory proposed by John Anthony West, Robert Schoch, and Robert Bauval about an older Sphinx. Why was there no written reference to such a monument in the non-religious writings during the seven hundred years that had passed before the Fourth Dynasty, during which writing is known to have existed in Egypt? Why was there no record of a title, or function, or cult associated with the Great Sphinx, if it really towered over the gateway leading to Rostau from the Nile, long before Khufu's planners set foot on the plateau?

If an archive existed under the arm, and if that arm belonged to a lioness guardian, where was that lioness in the hieroglyphic record and what did it have to do with the Great Sphinx?

VIII

Mehit

IS THERE A WRITTEN RECORD THAT MENTIONS THE SPHINX BEFORE THE SPHINX was allegedly made? Answer that question in the affirmative, and you rewrite history.

But the Sphinx riddles any such effort immediately with perplexion: The most famous statue in the world, as far as written history is concerned, has no history, at least anything written, either before or long after Egyptologist say she came into being around 2500 BC. What the Great Sphinx was called even after the statue was allegedly made is still a mystery. But then suddenly, not one but two names appeared one thousand years after it stood grandly, but namelessly, over the Giza plateau. It's as if the Sphinx needed to make up for the gap.

To make history, you need a name. I started to wonder a couple of years back if there was a written record of something that would be related to the Sphinx, something that others may have missed under the influence of the over a century-old mainstream model— something that would prove, beyond a reasonable doubt, this monument was older than the Khafre-made-the-Sphinx narrative written in our current history books.

In the absence of a name, and a record to date it, I had to instead weigh what the geology, astronomy, and architecture said on one side and what the Egyptology said on the other. But I realized that this is comparing apples with oranges. There were arguments in each of these fields, pro and con an older Sphinx. I quickly came to learn that the debate about its age is a lot more complex than I thought because no one knew its name.

To tip the scale would thus require a name and a record before 2500 BC. What I didn't realize is that Egyptologists had long seen that name written but had not pinned it on the Sphinx. As usual, there was a paradox no one could explain. But the real mystery, I would find out, was this: No one could read the symbols it was written in because they belonged to a lost script. I had my Sphinx riddle.

In late April of 2017, I flew to Croatia to join a Heaven to Earth cruise organized by Bianca Childs, featuring Graham Hancock and Robert Bauval. For a week, we floated along the picturesque Croatian coast while listening to seminars. We had many great discussions in small groups over breakfast, lunch, and dinner. This is when I first met Robert Bauval and his wife Michele and Graham Hancock's wife Santha Faia. I only had one brief conversation about the number 43,200 and precession with Graham Hancock during this trip. I knew several of Bauval's books and had just published my first about how astronomy influences the architecture of the Great Pyramid, a topic of course Bauval had written about in his first book *The Orion Mystery* with Adrian Gilbert.

I was relatively fluent with the main other ideas he and his fellow heretics Graham Hancock, Robert Schoch, and John Anthony West had proposed over the previous quarter century that had upset the traditional narrative of history we learn in school. He had just published his first collaboration with Schoch, *Origins of the Sphinx*, and gave me a brand-new copy of the book one morning when my cabin mate Lee and I came back from a shore leave breakfast run, looking for a place that sells Burek. I immediately started reading the book. I must have finished it before the middle of May, after I had returned from Croatia.

I was familiar with most details about the thesis of the book. Bauval made the astronomical case for an older Sphinx, while Schoch recapitulated his geological findings. Both authors gave rebuttals to the accumulated criticisms over the years. There was one segment, however, which wouldn't leave me alone: the name of the Great Sphinx in the Old Kingdom. To my surprise at the time, this was not a settled issue. Bauval had proposed years earlier that Horakhty was the constellation Leo. This name, and Horemakhet, were mentioned on the New Kingdom Dream Stele placed between the Great Sphinx's forepaws. Horakhty is also mentioned in several passages of the Pyramid Texts. Bauval concluded this must have been the statue's original name and Horemakhet came later when New Kingdom pharaohs rekindled their interest in her.

That, however, was the extent of the evidence. This was profound, and profoundly paradoxical. The most iconic, lifelike monument in the world did not have its name plastered all over the thus far discovered records of ancient Egypt. Not one inscription from the Old Kingdom—the time when Egyptologists say the Great Sphinx was made—refers to her. *How could this be?*

To make matters worse, if Schoch and Bauval were correct that it is eight-thousand years older than we're taught, then why was there no mention of it, of Horakhty, or of Horemakhet, or of any other of the several much later names given to the Great Sphinx before the Old Kingdom?

During the seven centuries before the Fourth Dynasty,[196] the ancient Egyptians already wrote in early hieroglyphic. Even if they did not write about a gigantic stone statue at Giza, they would have had to at least draw it, paint it, or carve it into stone, ivory, or wood, would they not? Little did I know, I had already stared at the answer to this mystery but had put it on the back burner.

After Croatia, the riddle of the missing Sphinx's name began to nag at me again.

All three, Hancock, Bauval, and Schoch, were going to be at the 2017 UFO mega-conference Contact in the Desert, then still in Joshua Tree, California, scheduled for May 19-21. On the boat, Bauval and I had agreed to meet there again. I had about a week of time to think about this problem. A couple of days before the conference, I was scheduled to work in the High Desert community of San Bernardino County and spend the nights at my cousin Masood's house in Victorville. At the time, I was preoccupied with the mastaba tomb of Hemiunu, the alleged architect of the Great Pyramid and a relative of Khufu, the king who allegedly commissioned it.

Hemiunu's final resting place is a large, extending over little less than 102x52 Royal Egyptian Ells, rectangular mastaba called G 4000 in the West Field, one of three cemetery fields surrounding the Great Pyramid. I was looking for numerical evidence that might reveal what he may have had in mind when designing the Great Pyramid, and, if he designed the layout of the three Giza pyramids. Unfortunately, most of the reliefs once decorating this mastaba are lost, but in 1914, the German archaeologist Hermann Junker discovered one of the most magnificent pieces of Egyptian art from the Old Kingdom in a hidden niche at the north end of G4000: the famous statue of Khufu's vizier Prince Hemiunu. It now stands at the Pelizaeus Museum in Hildesheim, Germany. The life-size stone figure shows Hemiunu seated with his feet resting on a pedestal, inscribed with what must have once been a stunning color display of hieroglyphic writing. Hints of the colors are still visible today (figure 70).

Figure 70: Illustration of the pedestal inscriptions from the statue of Hemiunu. The tandem dual title with the lioness is framed. From *Giza I* by Hermann Junker (1929), Plate XXIII.

The inscriptions present the typical resume of titles and accolades one finds on Egyptian tomb walls. Among them is one that has mystified Egyptologists since Junker found the statue. This title is the second in a tandem set of two. All its known bearers, except the last one, Mery, carried both together as if they could not hold one without the other. Looking head-on at the right lower corner of the pedestal, the tandem title is carved in a short column, immediately next to Hemiunu's left foot. This is an interesting detail later noticed by Robert Schoch (figure 71). Was this a subtle hint?

Weeks earlier, when I originally saw the seven hieroglyphs that spell the two titles, the couchant lion among them did not jump out at me, strangely

Figure 71: Close-up of the same tandem title in front of the left foot of Hemiunu's statue. ©, KHM-Museumsverband; modified.

enough. I was not looking for a name of the Great Sphinx at that time. And so, as fate kept the upper hand for the time being, the lion symbol in front of Hemiunu's left foot had gone on the back burner. However, during the week between reading *Origins of the Sphinx* and Contact in the Desert, I remembered the mysterious symbol. This would end up changing my life.

Eureka, It's a Key!

The paradox of the missing name preoccupied me. I had been looking for an Old Kingdom name of a monumental, stony, lion-like statue. And now, here, on Hemiunu's pedestal, something like that stared back at me: a couchant lioness with rings around her neck, and with a strange, bent rod above as if it were coming out of her back. *How could this not be related to the Great Sphinx?* The pedestal came from the same era as this megalithic, likewise couchant, human-lion chimera.[197] Why had no one proposed the obvious before? What was I missing? Whenever one may think the Sphinx was made, here was proof of a lion cult from the same era.

What I had been missing was the translation of the tandem title. I visited the Pelizaeus Museum's website for information on the statue. There, the two titles were listed as:

Master of the scribes of the king, Master of [unknown title].

Was it possible that the museum had not updated its records and the second title had long been translated? An e-mail to the museum director confirmed that this was not the case. William Stevenson Smith, who had worked with George Reisner at Giza and then became curator at Boston's Museum of Fine Arts, wrote this about the dual title in a paper about the famous slab stele of Wepemnefret, also a carrier of the tandem title:[198]

As in the case of the false-door of a man named Mery (Smith, American Journal of Archaeology 46 [1942] 510), the order of the signs suggests that we might interpret the titles as Royal Architect and Scribe (or Building Supervisor, Royal Scribe), Craftsman of Mehit (the lioness goddess of the Thinite Nome). A similar form of the lioness appears on Early Dynastic seal designs, where she is obviously connected with the Upper Egyptian Sanctuary.

Peter Der Manuelian, one of the world's top experts on slab steles found in the West Field of the Great Pyramid, wrote this in 2003:[199]

"Commander of the king's scribes, 3 [translation uncertain] ... "

In a note to this translation, Der Manuelian added this:

Or possibly "overseer of the (cult image) of Mehyt"?

As I discovered later, no one, expert or lay person, had been able to read these two symbols of the lioness and the bent rod above. As to the latter, Petrie classified it among a list of signs some he thought were "not hieroglyphic."[200] Indeed, the ostensible fusion into a ligature of two symbols was not even something typical of Upper Egyptian hieroglyphic symbols but seemed to resemble in style the few known symbols from an otherwise lost script used in prehistoric, northern Egypt, in the Nile Delta region.

The people who lived there, near the twin cities *p* [pe] and *dp* [dep], also known as *pr-w3dt* [per-ooah-jet]/Buto/Tell El Fara'in, wrote in a different language than the people who lived in the main population centers of prehistoric Upper Egypt like Hierakonpolis, Abydos, Naqada and Thinis. This so-called Buto Script and language were largely lost when the Delta region was conquered. A possible relic of it remains in a sealing found by Karl Kromer, when he excavated south of the causeway of Menkaure.[201] Several other symbols from this script still appear in the earliest written records of the early dynastic state that formed after Upper and Lower Egypt were unified by Narmer. Most of them, however, disappear from the known hieroglyphic records by the time of Horus-Den, the fifth king of the First Dynasty after Horus-Narmer, Horus-Aha/Menes, Horus-Djer, and Horus-Djet.[202]

Not so was the case for the lioness symbol with the bent rod. It persisted for another five-hundred years, until the Fourth Dynasty, when it was carved into the pedestal under the statue of Prince Hemiunu in front of his left foot, as I noted above. Even though I had no idea how to translate the title with the lioness, and absent help from Egyptology, fortunately her name less the title had been spelled out elsewhere: on the stunning slab stele of another high official at the early court of Khufu buried in the West Field next to the Great Pyramid (figure 72).

Figure 72: The slab stele of Prince Wepemnefret from mastaba G1201. The tandem title is in the right top corner. ©, Phoebe A. Hearst Museum of Anthropology and the Regents of the University of California—catalog 6-19825.

It was found there hidden in mastaba G1201, the tomb of the *sm* shaman priest Wepemnefret,[203] by the Hearst Expedition under the now legendary American Egyptologist George Reisner in 1905, not far from Hemiunu's G4000. The stele reveals that both Wepemnefret and Hemiunu were bearers of this exclusive tandem title with the enigmatic lioness-bent rod fusion symbol. At the top, the name of the same lioness with neck rings is mentioned: She was Mehit. Literally, "She, the Northern One" (figure 73).

Figure 73: The topmost register from the stele of Prince Wepemnefret identifies the lioness from the tandem title as Mehit (framed). ©, Phoebe A. Hearst Museum of Anthropology and the Regents of the University of California—catalog 6-19825; modified.

It was Thursday night, May 18, 2017, when I went to bed thinking about what I had learned. My friend Alan Green had driven up to Victorville so that we could go to the conference together in the morning. Joshua Tree is about an hour's drive from Victorville through some serene, mountainous country on a sleepy Californian highway. The plan was to meet Robert and Michele Bauval at the conference sometime the next day. I still remember that night as vividly as if it were yesterday. I posted a choppy message on my Facebook page, more for myself than anyone else. It was a brainstorm. I wanted to pin it on my timeline. I felt it was important, more so than any other post I had made so far.

I could not sleep. My mind was racing. *What was the bent rod over the lioness? Was it a weapon, a tool, a surgical instrument?* My eyes were heavy, my head pounding. Exhausted I fell asleep. Then it came. The mental jolt tore me out of my restless sleep.

The red digits on the clock read minutes after five o'clock AM. *It is a key!* I was wide awake now.

If the bent rod was a key, then the lioness was not a lioness, but a statue guarding a door with a lock. Inside, had to be the royal archive called the *House of Scrolls of the King's Knowledge* on Wepemnefret's stele. I later learned how rare the title really was. In the five hundred years since Horus-Den, only five men are known to have carried it: Hesy-***R͑***, ***nfr-sšm-r͑/***

Neferseshem-*R͗*, alive during the Third Dynasty, and Wepemnefret, Hemiunu, and Mery alive during the Fourth (figure 74).

Figure 74: Wooden Panel from the tomb of Third Dynasty official Hesy-*R͗* showing the tandem title with Mehit on the bottom and the spelling of her name on the right. The Museum of Egyptian Antiquities, Cairo, Egypt, 2018.

Of great significance is that three of these five men were Heka magic masters of Mehit, intimately connecting the lioness with the skill to verbally animate and create (figure 75).

One title sequence inscribed on a wooden wall panel from Hesy-*R͗* 's Saqqara tomb proved that physicians, like Hesy-*R͗*, belonged to the ultra-select cadre of gods on the divine side, and spiritual ritualists in the mortal realm who used Heka. This explains why some of the elites from Deir El-Bersheh, like *gw3* for example, had been able to obtain unique spells for their coffins. They were practitioners of the craft in their function as healers.

At the end of *Hesy-R͗* 's Heka title, there is even a possible Heka allusion at play: The Elder of the Staff, *j3w mdw* [ay-ah-oo me-doo] contains an allusion to the Words of Thoth Moon, *mdw j3ḥ*. It appears as if Hesy-*R͗*

wr

jbḥ

swnw

ḥk3

mḥt

j3w mdw

Figure 75: Close-up of the same wooden panel as in the previous figure. The title sequence is transliterated on the right. It translates as Great Physician and Dentist, Heka of Mehit, Elder of the Staff.

was a student of both Mehit and Thoth, bringing these two into an alignment I did not yet appreciate then, in part, because I did not yet draw the connection from Mehit to the cow goddess Hathor and her lioness aspect.

This intimate association between Thoth, being a verbally equipped spell master, a so-called *3ḫw* [uh-khoo] spirit, and Mehit, is vividly illustrated in an even older inscription discovered on one of the many early dynastic mud sealings, about which I have a lot to say later. In this sealing, the Hieroglyphic words *3ḫw* and *3ḫtj* [uh-khe-tee], for "masterfully equipped," appear immediately next to Mehit with the bent rod. I think it is possible that the Herron Sign was later replaced with the Axe Sign meaning essentially the same thing, "master".

But hiding inside the word *3ḫtj* is the word *tḫj* [te-khee] for "plummet" and "architect", describing an aspect of Thoth, and also for "drunkenness", a likely pun linking the much later attested Middle Kingdom *Hathor* festival First of Drunkenness *tpj n tḫj* with Thoth-Moon (figure 76).[204] The significance is that the heart was the seat of the mind in ancient Egyptian belief and the Heart Sign, used to contextualize the word *tḫj* to denote Thoth, resembles the Jug Sign, which "transcends" the meaning towards drunkenness.

The Moon God Thoth represented reason opposing the occasional rage of the Sun God *Rˤ*, and that is why it is the power of nature to reason, imbued into Thoth, to whom the balancing of virtue and sin was delegated in the *Hall of Justice* inside the Netherworld, as vividly illustrated in the later imagery of the *Book of the Dead*. This was the deeper level of mastery implied by the Mehit title. The holders were "drunk" with special knowledge.

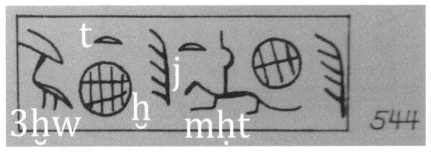

Figure 76: Sealings Number 544 from the early dynastic phase, Dynasties One and Two, circa 3000-2700 BC. Reading from left to right is the Herron Word Sign *3ḫw* followed by the three phonetically read hieroglyphs *t-ḫ-j*, and the Bent Rod-Mehit Sign. Photo from Kaplony, 1963.

There was obviously no more sleep in the cards for me that morning having been similarly "intoxicated" with this revelation. I turned on my computer and went to my Facebook page. Bauval and I had become social media friends a few weeks prior, and I wanted to alert him immediately about what I discovered. Every moment was like a heart-pounding, thundering wave in my ears. I was convinced that I had discovered something important.

I posted this to my Facebook page:

Just figured it out...I think it means "Key Master to the Sphinx Vault." In other words Hesy-Rˁ and Hemiunu held the key to the royal archives and the location of these archives were inside the Great Sphinx. It explains why in both reliefs both designations are found together. It means that the recumbent lion is not a phonogram ("ru") but a logogram....i.e., Royal Archives Vault.

It also provides proof positive that the Great Sphinx was originally a complete stone lion statue out of whose head a face was carved during the Fourth Dynasty and that this statue already existed in the Third Dynasty...corroborating Robert Bauval's, Robert Schoch's, and John Anthony West's contention.

Bauval saw the post and wanted to hear about it later that day. After breakfast, Alan and I drove to Contact in the Desert. There, we ran into Robert and Michele, but due to Robert's busy lecture and interview schedule, we did not have time to talk about Mehit. I briefly said to Robert, "I found the smoking gun." He must have heard this many times from many people.

It didn't matter. He wanted to hear about it. Another week passed before we would finally be able to talk about Mehit. It happened when he, Robert Schoch, and I were sitting at a breakfast table on a sunny morning in Sedona, Arizona, at the Cosmic Origins conference. I had driven for hours from my home in California to meet with Robert. I wanted to personally fill him in on what I had discovered about a monumental lioness called Mehit at Giza, who was created long before the Great Sphinx, and who guarded an archive of scrolls. At that time, I didn't think of the *Hall of Records*. It was all about textual proof for an older Sphinx.

To illustrate how the bent rod could functioned as a key, I had built a bolted lock and key model out of wood and copper[205] to demonstrate the locking mechanism. I had done some preliminary research on ancient locks and was prepared to make a short presentation. I knew it should not last more than a minute. Bauval had told me before that a good idea should not take more than thirty seconds to explain. I thought he was right. And so that was my goal. I had to get the story out as fast as possible, which really meant I had to just give the bottom line without the details. I figured it would be best to just show the idea in action instead of talking about it.

Driving to Arizona, I had no idea that Robert Schoch would also be sitting at the table. That was a good thing, or else nerves would have gotten the better of me presenting this in front of both. I was under high pressure, but I knew I would be able to deliver. I was in uncharted territory with Mehit, but so would be Schoch and Bauval, and all of Egyptology, for that matter. The excitement of a potentially major discovery about the Great Sphinx was incredible. I was caught up in the moment, but these moments are what explorers seek. It is a special feeling, alas much too short and rare.

Single Tumbler Bolt Lock

Figure 77: Screen shot from a video showing the mechanism of a hypothetical bolted lock that could be opened with a metal device resembling the Bent Rod-Mehit Sign.

With both Schoch and Bauval waiting, I set up my demonstration. I said only a few words about what I wanted to show. Bauval stood up and came around to stand behind me. I had their full attention. I showed how the mechanism might have worked and how the bent rod could have functioned as a key (figure 77). I explained how the idea of a key to an archive in the second half of the tandem title went well with the idea of a royal scribe in the first. Thanks to the way in which the titles were organized on Wepemnefret's stele, we were also able to place the titles into the context of an astronomical library of the king, whose patron goddess was Seshat. That, too, made the case for the key.

I quickly hit the key points: the key and the lioness had to do with writing, archiving, and the king's secrets, and we would be able to date all this to at least a century before Khafre, the king who supposedly ordered the sculpting of the Great Sphinx from the quarry rock.

My demonstration took less than a minute. Bauval returned to his chair at the far right of the breakfast table. At first, he did not say anything. We all looked at each other in complete silence for a few moments. It seemed like a long time. We were in a mild shock of disbelief.

Then Schoch said something like, "I think this is very important."

Bauval mumbled only a word: "interesting."

Building the Case

It took one minute and seven words from the three of us to begin a stretch of publishing[206] centered on the concept of Mehit as the primordial Sphinx guarding an archive underneath, presumably only very few humans have ever entered.

At the time, we thought the bent rod could have been a key just as I had imagined. It made sense, but the proof was still thin at that time. However, what we were proposing could be put to a test by probing Anomaly A to see if this seismically detected void was a man-made chamber with an entry. This was a testable prediction one could confirm or falsify. To bolster our case, we gave examples of ancient keys that vaguely looked like the bent rod.

Unfortunately, the archaeological records from the Old Kingdom are slim when it comes to locks and keys, though there are archaeological remnants of doorways and references to doors. I thought that proving this element in our proposal was crucial in making a stronger case for a drilling experiment. I also knew that proving the bent rod was a key would be difficult without an actual example of it in the archaeological record.

Since then, I have found more textual evidence. Now, I am even more convinced that this symbol represented a real object used either as a key, or a door bolt, or a door opener. Before I get into that, I want to mention an additional piece of physical evidence as well, of which I was not aware in 2017. This comes from the 1907 survey by the German Orient Society under Ludwig Borchardt of the pyramid complex of King Sahure at Abusir, a few kilometers south of Giza, where several Fifth Dynasty rulers and high officials were buried.

In Sahure's Valley Temple, a side entry connected the south pier to the main hall, leading east, and up the causeway to the pyramid temple and pyramid. This door had a jamb made from granite with drill holes for door guides made from basalt. The purpose of these holes and guides was to house the bolts that locked the door and when they were retracted to open it—two bolts at the top, and one at the bottom. To unlock the door, the wooden bolts were pushed into these fittings using a door handle. The handle, which in Borchardt's reconstruction of the mechanism connected the two upper bolts, looks like the object that hovers over Mehit's back (figure 78).

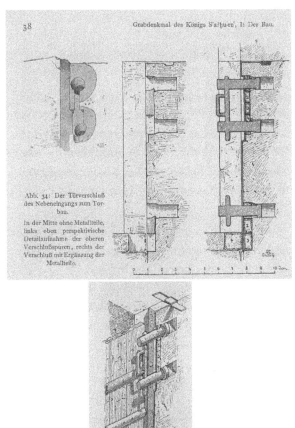

Figure 78: Side door entry to the Valley Temple of Sahure in Abusir, Egypt, reconstructed with the fittings of the locking mechanism. The door handle looks like the Bent Rod-Mehit Sign. From Borchardt (1910).

If not a key to a door, therefore, the bent rod could have depicted a door handle, whose design I could now date to the Old Kingdom.

The burden of proof to show that Mehit was a monument, and not merely an imagined, mythical lioness, depended on such physical evidence. It began with the notion that a physical, underground archive "under an arm" could not have been either an imaged or a real lioness but only a lioness statue. If there was a key, a bolt, or door handle leading "into" the lioness, then there must have been a door. If there was a door, the lioness must have been part of a structure one could enter.

Much depended on this because if we could prove that such a monumental lioness existed at Giza, then this would falsify the orthodox theory that the Great Sphinx is only as old as the Fourth Dynasty. And if this monumental lioness existed earlier than the Great Sphinx, then the textual trace I had uncovered, which pointed to esoteric knowledge inside an ancient archive older than historic Egypt, could refer to something real. But these were still a lot of ifs.

Also, there was one alternative interpretation of the bent rod sign given by Petrie that I could not ignore: He called the bent rod a yoke.[207] That made sense given the neck rings on the lioness. Mehit could have been an animation of the taming of nature, but only in the texts, not as a monumental animation. I ended up ruling this explanation out by happenstance, however, and in a way I could not have expected.

Mehit Semantics

In 2017, I did not yet know the name of the real archive, *ꜥfdt-ḫrt-ꜥ*. I was still missing that textual context then to understand the "under the arm" allusion in the name of Mehit; *mḥ* [meh] in Mehit is the hieroglyphic word for cubit. The Ancient Egyptian cubit measure was nearly the length of the posterior forearm and hand, what in English was called an "ell."

We also had not yet noticed the subtle clue about the placement of the tandem title with the bent rod-Mehit fusion symbol in front of the left foot of the statue of Hemiunu. Robert Schoch mentioned this in a seminar a couple of years later.

What had me still occupied then were the other semantic associations of the word Mehit. Not only did it relate to the cardinal direction north, also *mḥ* [meh], but also the related ideas of flooding and the cubit, used to

192

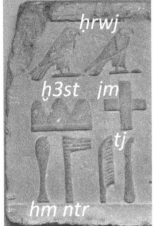

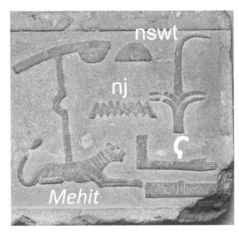

Figure 79: Above, lintel block from the false door of Mery's chapel from his Saqqara tomb, broken off on the right side. The Bent Rod-Mehit Sign is near the right end, here part of the new [*jmj r' zšw*] *nj nswt* ' title, which replaced the older *mdḥ zš nswt* (below right). Below left, the unique "Two Horuses of the Desert" title. ©, The Metropolitan Museum of Art, New York, NY. Public Domain; modified.

quantify the height of the Nile during annual inundations. I asked myself how this context, which had produced the word stem *mḥ*, related to the lioness Mehit, the goddess of the writers' guild, and protectress of an archive. Was the original lioness monument a flood measuring Nilometer when North Africa was still wet enough to raise the river to the elevation of the Sphinx ditch?

Now, in retrospect, all these clues are coming together to tell us something that crystallizes into a new model of the origin of the Great Sphinx: *mḥ*, as forearm, was the bridge between the archive's nisbe attribute *ḫrt-'*, "under the arm," and its guardian *mḥt* [meh-it]. Mehit's association with floods, in fact the Great Flood *wr-mḥt* [oor meh-it], and the Memphite creation myth can be found in the name of one of the seven *ḏ3jsw* creation words mentioned in the Edfu Temple that take shape from the chaos of the Great Flood during the order created by Ptah's utterance of his creation concept.

Its name is *shpr-mw-smhj-nww* [se-khe-per moo se-meh-ee noo-oo], S/he Who Swells the Waters and Raises Floods. Notice that this name carries the word stem *mh*.

As a lioness, Mehit was being alluded to in the Edfu Temple text utterance of *mn-qb* [men-gheb] (Chapter VII, "glorifying words") with the word *ds-rw* [jes-roo] "lion itself," or *dsr-rw* [je-ser-roo], "sanctum of the lion," or *dšrw* [de-sher-roo] "red ones."

All these subtle insinuations connect the lioness to the archive. It became obvious that whoever composed these texts had left many clues cryptically pointing to an archive under a lioness to preserve the memory, while at the same time keeping it a secret. But these clues would be, and have been, missed when viewed from the perspective of the current dogma of history.

Mery Under Khafre: The Mind Behind Remodeling Mehit?

The other interesting aspect of the Mehit story was that the title we reconstructed as *Guardian of the Royal Archives of Mehit*,[208] despite its importance and exclusivity, still disappeared after Hemiunu under Khufu, and the scribe Mery under Khufu's son Khafre.[209] With these two final bearers, any overt reference to Mehit in the context of royal scribing and the *House of Scrolls* vanished. *Why?*

This, too, was a clue that Mehit had something to do with the Great Sphinx, whose original construction historian commonly attribute to the time of Mery's king Khafre. But Mehit was much older than this king. Why did the exclusive title based on her likeness suddenly disappear from the historical record and *never reappear?* Here was yet another paradox, not resolved.

The correct explanation for this strange disappearance of something so prominent I think is that in the Fourth Dynasty, the Great Sphinx replaced Mehit. The new sphinx cult erased the older lioness cult. It is therefore possible that the cult of Mehit was no longer tolerated and systematically expunged from the public records of the Egyptian royal house. It only remained mentioned in privately held or secret royal records. But, if so, why? Religious dogma and secrecy come to mind.

If there was a hidden *ꜥfdt* portable archive under the arm of this original lioness monument, to keep it secret, any association with writing and storing of records had to be covered up. The silence of the Great Sphinx in Egypt's records may speak volumes about what was being hidden under her.

Another possibility is that this portable repository of arcane knowledge was moved to a different facility when Mehit became the Great Sphinx. This may explain why the first part of the tandem title went into obscurity. In fact, its original function was given a new title, and the second, "Master of Bent Rod-Mehit" part was eliminated, as I mentioned. Only veiled textual references during the centuries that followed kept the historical truth of the matter—but now covered up by a new dogma revolving around sphinxes—alive.

One of the best textual clues of this change- and make-over I speak of I discovered only recently. It can be seen on the lintel above the false door of the tomb of Mery (figure 79).

Instead of the old *mḏḥ zš nswt*, Royal Master Scribe, Mery was now the {*jmj rꜥ zšw*} *nj nswt ꜥ* [{ay-my raah ze-shoo} nay ne-soot aah] the Overseer of the Scribes belonging to the King's Arm." The beginning of the title at the right end of the lintel is missing but it is present on another stone block from Mery's tomb at the Louvre Museum in Paris, Stone A.[210] Apparently, the old *mḏḥ* axe symbol for "master" had been replaced with the much more common *jmj rꜥ* for "overseer," literally, "He in whom the mouth is" meaning "He who commands." The strange part is that *zš(w) nswt* for "royal scribe(s)" had been replaced with the more elaborate *zš(w) nj nswt ꜥ* for "scribe(s) of the king's arm" reminiscent of *ꜥfdt ḫrt ꜥ*, the "archive under the arm."

I think what happened here is that the Mehit-related aspect of the old title, which amounted to an archive under the lioness' forepaw, was pulled into the new scribe title, albeit cryptically, while the more overt Mehit part was let go. Let's now look at how this looks on the lintel above.

Literally "under the arm" is where the scroll symbol appears on this lintel (figure 79; lower right pane), the most prominent part and central piece of the entire false door. Not only that, the arm symbol hovers near Mehit's forepaw, as if a subtle clue, such that the scroll appears beneath the level on which Mehit is resting, both under and in front of Mehit, exactly where the archive is suspected.

Another, even more startling, clue that connects Mehit to the Great Sphinx is hiding on this lintel. I think this must be the very first mention, in anagrammatic form, of Horakhty and Horemakhet, the two names of the Great Sphinx in the New Kingdom based on what is written on Thutmose IV's Dream Stele between her forepaws (figure 80).

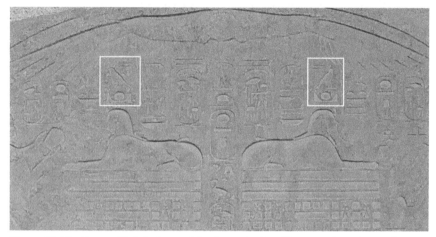

Figure 80: The Dream Stele in front of the Great Sphinx. The two mirror-imaged occurrences of Horemakhet are marked. This was one of two names for the Great Sphinx in the New Kingdom. The other was Horakhty. Giza, Egypt, May 2019.

At the left end of Mery's lintel are two falcon symbols (figure 79; lower left pane). They are part of a unique title, "not attested elsewhere"; the New York Metropolitan Museum has this title written as *ḥm ntr ḥrwj jmtj zmy.t* [hem ne-ter he-roo-ee aym-ty ze-meet] translated as "Priest of the two Horuses who are in the desert."[211] Besides Mery, no one else is known to have carried this title, as far as is currently known. Is it just me, or do you notice how a lot of peculiar occurrences related to both Mehit and the Great Sphinx cluster with Mery?

This just adds to the other mysteries of him, does it not? The two Horuses in combination with the double horizon symbol *ḫ3st* [khast] for "desert",[212] but read here by "The Met's" curator with the synonym *zmy.t*,[213] is really *ḥrwj jmtj ḫ3st* [he-roo-ee aym-ty khast].

Was this the name of the original cult of the Great Sphinx or a cryptographically rendered name for the new monument, and Mery was its priest? Either way, it can be anagrammatically read in reverse as *ḥrwj-3ḫ-tj-mj*, or *ḥrwj-mj-3ḫ-tj*. These two phonetic rearrangements come out to either Hor-akh-ty or Hor-em-akhet, the "Horus(es) of the (two) Horizon(s)" or "Horus(es) in the Horizon," the two confirmed names of the Great Sphinx: Horus at Rostau, the horizon on Earth, and Horus in the sky horizon.

The dot on the "i," proverbially speaking, is that *mj* sounds like *m3j*, "lion." What was Mery up to, you may rightfully ask?

From an artistic perspective, I like how he placed the Mehit title on one end, the right side where the text begins, and the Horuses title on the left side, where it ends. They are as far separated as possible, yet the balance of the ends connects them. Not only were lions and falcons both aspects of the Sun, but this is yet another clue that Mehit and the Great Sphinx are Origin and Destiny, if you will, connected in time at the body. The old name and statue had given way to a new monument with two names. The sphinx cult was born from the lion cult that came before and I think Mery was a key figure in this transformation.

This duality is also born out in the Earth-Sky relationship between the monument and a constellation, something that Robert Bauval discovered in *Origins of the Sphinx*, co-authored with Robert Schoch, which he had given to me in Croatia.

Silent Sphinx with No Name, then Two Names

In *Origins of the Sphinx*, Bauval discusses the enigma of the two names of the Great Sphinx in the New Kingdom.[214] He had asked himself why there were two names with almost identical meaning for the same sphinx, "Horus in the Horizon" and "Horus of the Horizon," but no name in the Old Kingdom when the Sphinx was supposedly made? Who was she before? Was there a second sphinx *in* the ground, or was there another one across the Nile?

This was something Flinders Petrie himself had wondered about and looked for. Bauval however resolves the paradox in another way: Horakhty was the celestial counterpart of the Great Sphinx on the ground named Horemakhet. In other words, the two sphinxes shown on the Dream Stele (figure 80) are the two Horuses, one on the ground, Horemakhet, and one in the sky, Horakhty. His textual interpretation of the Pyramid Texts leads him to conclude that the sphinx in the sky is none other than the constellation Leo.[215]

And since the constellation Leo has existed in the sky for much longer than even lions have existed on Earth, Horakhty must have been the name of the *male* lion statue he and Robert Schoch initially believed existed before the Great Sphinx. This, of course, was a few months before the three of us met and wrote the Mehit paper. With the new evidence at hand, however, I can now fill the textual gap we have been missing from before the Pyramid Texts, the earliest version of which date to two about 150 years after the reign of Khafre.

My conclusion from what I see on the lintel of Mery is that the origin of *both* names, and the birth of the Horakhty myth mentioned in the Pyramid Texts date to the time when the Mehit statue was remodeled into the Great Sphinx during the reign of Khafre.[216] In this way, the new Sun cult of a lion-man chimera replaced the old lioness cult. While the Great Sphinx remained silently nameless for a millennium, her lioness origins were erased from history. Mehit became an obscure goddess, her connection to the Great Sphinx having been purged from public records. It is even possible that Mery himself oversaw the remodeling project and became the first Priest of Horakhty, the long missing reference to a sphinx cult Egyptologist have searched for in vain.

Finally, the mystery of the nameless Sphinx began to unravel. The strange paucity of any mention of the Great Sphinx until the New Kingdom makes sense now. It was a new cult grafted over a much older one whose identity had been all-but-erased. In 2017, I did not know about the lintel from Mery's tomb. I searched for evidence that connected Mehit with Giza to be able to redate the Great Sphinx, but I did not then see the depth of it, as I see it now.

Lioness+East+Delta+Rostau+Archive =?

In the weeks following my breakfast in Sedona with Bauval and Schoch, I learned of the published drawing of a mud seal impression that generated three important elements in making this connection. This was a sealing, typically imprinted onto clay seals used to stopper jars (figure 81; figure 82), found by Flinders Petrie in the tomb of Horus-Djer at Abydos.[217]

It showed the figure of Mehit including a three-pronged bent rod emanating from her back, thus identifying her, if not by name, surely by her appearance (figure 83).

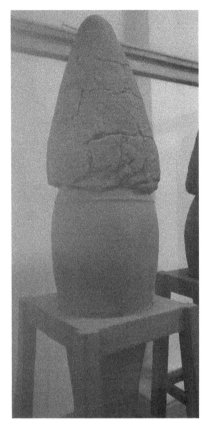

Figure 81: Cylindrical jar with conical mud cap. Seals were imprinted into the mud to prevent unwanted access. The Museum of Egyptian Antiquities, Cairo, Egypt, 2018.

Figure 82: Seal impressions on mud caps. The Museum of Egyptian Antiquities, Cairo, Egypt, 2018.

Figure 83: Sealing 116 from the tomb of Horus-Djer (circa 3000-2900 BC). (a) is the hieroglyph for east, *j3bt*. (b) is the hieroglyph for north, *mḥ(w/t)*. (c) is the lioness Mehit with a triple bent rod above. (d) is the scribes' tent in the shape of an animal shrine, the Great Hall *pr-wr*. (e) is the hieroglyph for the sound *st3w*, which means "caves" or "ramps". From Petrie (1901); modified.

The four key details on this sealing, which linked Mehit to Giza, were the hieroglyphic symbol for the cardinal direction east matching the due east orientation of the Great Sphinx, the location in Lower Egypt identified by the papyrus plant symbol *ḥ3* [ha], the *st3w* [sta-oo] symbol for "caves/ramps," relating to the ancient Egyptian name for Giza, *r-st3w* [ro-sta-oo], "Mouth of Caves," and the iconic animal shrine *pr-wr* [per-oor], "Great Hall," possibly iconized here as a tent, to represent the early, provisional, bureaucratic administration of dynastic Egypt. This transient facility persisted until a permanent royal palace called *p-ḥrw-msn*, Seat of Horus Striker, was built in the Delta at Buto.[218]

This sealing, Petrie's number 116, was our Exhibit A that Mehit was the name of a monumental statue at Giza and was associated with writing. Robert Schoch immediately drew a connection with the Dream Stele. On it, two sphinxes rest couchant on shrine-like buildings with doors and niches. They face opposite directions (figure 84).

We thus drew a connection with the writer's tent guarded by Mehit and the shrine under the Sphinx. If Mehit and the Sphinx are one and the same, so had to be the facility, basically a place where documents were written and stored: an archive. The icons had changed, but the idea was the same.

Figure 84: Great Sphinx and Dream Stele. The two Sphinxes rest couchant atop shrines with doors. Giza, Egypt, May 2019.

While any one clue may not suffice to make this case compelling, the sum of all the clues made the case that Mehit was a real entity, not merely a mythical lioness. We thought there was sufficient reason to suspect now that this lioness was a monumental statue that guarded a locked and secured underground facility located "under her arm," devoted to writing and archiving. This statue must have stood at Giza long before the Old Kingdom. All this evidence would be overlooked in a paradigm based on the foregone conclusion that nothing like it stood there before the Old Kingdom, let alone a lioness; hence, no one before me thought of it.

Based on the evidence we had then, we formulated our working model that what was being shown in the sealing was an early First Dynasty Mehit-guarded archive that constituted the provisional administration of the land Horus-Narmer (circa 3000 BC) had brought the two lands of Egypt under one rule, as documented on the Narmer Palette. After a hiatus in the archaeological record, during the second half of the First Dynasty and during the generally opaque Second Dynasty, the bent rod-Mehit title reappears in tandem with a royal scribe title conferred to only the highest officials at the royal court of the Third and Fourth Dynasties: Hesy-*Rˁ*, nfr-sšm-*Rˁ*/ Neferseshem-*Rˁ*, Wepemnefret, Hemiunu, and Mery.

Neck Rings

Even though the sealing was not mythical writing, but rather an example of a symbolically imbued lock used in the precious goods trade to secure shipments destined for the royal mansion and tombs, Mehit's link to Giza and the Great Sphinx needed a physical feature on the ground. This occurred to me while looking through my Egypt photos taken in 2017, when I first went there with Alan Green. On one of the photos I took of the Great Sphinx from the south side, standing on the causeway of Khafre's Pyramid, I noticed a ring-like erosion around the neck of the Sphinx, seen of course by millions of tourists before me. I mentioned this to Robert Schoch. He had in his collection old photos taken before repairs made to the Great Sphinx in the mid-1920s. We could see at least one, if not two, rings partly encircling the neck of the monument (figure 85).

The lioness figurines used to play Mehen also had neck collars. Naturally, we wondered if a weathered monument eroded around the neck had inspired this ornamental feature on game pieces and symbols used in writing. We all agreed that this was sufficient evidence to petition for a revision in Sphinx history pending verification of a testable prediction our model made.

For Schoch, Bauval, and West, this was a new development. They had speculated that the original, prehistoric monument, from which the Great Sphinx was remodeled, might have been a male lion.[219] What had influenced their thinking was that the celestial lion, the constellation Leo, which they believed Old Kingdom Egyptians had recognized as such, may have been imagined a male. This is because a lion's mane indeed appears to be traced by the arc of four stars in Leo, sweeping towards the east from γ *Leonis Algieba*. As a side note, I think it is possible that the hook-like shape of

Figure 85: Older photo of the Great Sphinx prior to restoration work in the 1920's. The neck appears ornamented with rings. Gilman Collection, Purchase, William Talbott Hillman Foundation Gift (2005). ©, The Metropolitan Museum of Art, New York, NY. Public Domain.

this asterism may have also inspired comparison with a falcon beak thus explaining why a lioness monument had two names related to Horus.

In fact, supporting their theory of a male lion were these two very names on the Dream Stele. *She* was identified in terms of Horus, a male god, as both Horakhty and Horemakhet. Egyptologists had long added their weight into the Sphinx gender identification guessing game. They attributed *her* face to that of Khafre, despite evidence found by Frank Domingo in 1993[220] that the facial features of the monument and the king were not the same. Add to this confusing picture that the ancient Egyptians, at various times and places, worshiped at least nine different female lion and feline goddesses: Mehit, Sekhmet, Tefnut, Pakhet, Seret, Shesmetet, Bastet, Mekhit and Menhyt and at least six males Apedamak, Mahes, Aker, Ruty, and Tutu.[221]

While our new model proposed that the Great Sphinx originated from a monumental lioness by the name of Mehit, we could not conclude whether she had been at Giza five hundred or seventy-five hundred years prior to the time of Khafre. Regardless, we could now finally offer up textual proof from the Egyptians themselves that the Great Sphinx was only a remodeled statue. This proof counters the conventional narrative taught in schools, textbooks, and on TV. It says that most of the Great Sphinx is older than 2500 BC.

We published our findings in the journal *Archaeological Discovery* in August of 2017.[222] Later, Robert Schoch published a less technical, more lay person-oriented article in *Atlantis Rising*, which he also reproduced on his personal website.[223] To honor the life and work of John Anthony West, who was still alive in 2017, we named the bent rod symbol after West's initials: J.A.W. The combination of the JAW Sign and Mehit, I will henceforth call the JAW-Mehit ligature since that is the term used to designate two letters fused into one symbol.

Lions in Egypt Before the Great Sphinx

Three further pieces of evidence point to a monumental lioness at Giza before the Great Sphinx. The first are two similarly shaped lion statues made from terracotta and clay (figure 86).

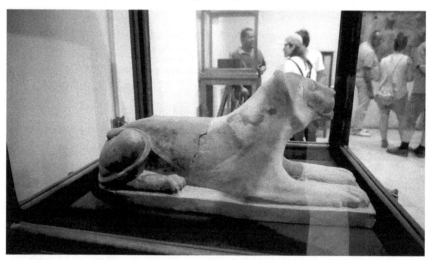

Figure 86: Recreated terracotta-clay composite lioness statue, pieces of which were discovered in northwest Saqqara, dated to the Middle Kingdom. The Museum of Egyptian Antiquities, Cairo, Egypt, 2018.

While they are dated to the Middle Kingdom, one bears a clear mark of the Old Kingdom, suggesting it was a copy of an older model. They were both found together in a T-shaped, rock-cut shaft on a hillside in northwest

Saqqara.[224] This hill is west of the ridge on which the archaic-style First Dynasty mastabas were built, separated from it by a Wadi, 1.5 km northwest of the Serapeum, and southwest of the Abusir Pyramids.

Between the forepaws of the terracotta version remains the miniaturized left foot of a human being. In front of the foot is something uncanny: the cartouche of Khufu, *nswt bjt* [ne-soot bit], King of Upper and Lower Egypt (figure 87).

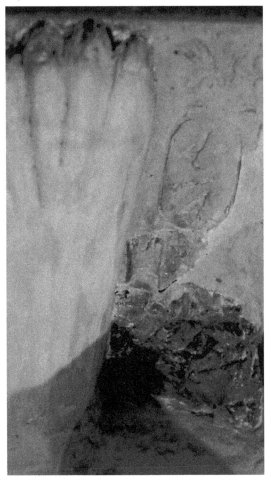

Figure 87: The cartouche of Khufu and his left foot between the forepaws of the Saqqara lioness. The Museum of Egyptian Antiquities, Cairo, Egypt, 2018.

Even though the head of this statue is missing, it is preserved in its clay counterpart. Unmistakably, she was a lioness. This reconstructed statue, approximately two feet long, with the Khufu cartouche is housed at the Cairo Museum, immediately next to the famous statuette attributed to him. The closest we may ever come to know what a stony Mehit at Giza may have looked like before she became the Great Sphinx is this lioness from "Lion Hill" at Saqqara.

The second piece of evidence was discovered in 2011 during excavations of an Old Kingdom harbor on the Red Sea coast of Egypt by a French-Egyptian-American team headed by Pierre Tallet, El Sayed Mahfouz, Damien Laisney, and Gregory Marouard.[225] Among several important finds from the early Fourth Dynasty[226] were potsherds decorated with ink markings. These drawings depict a sitting, statue-like, female lioness (figure 88).

Figure 88: Ostracon from the Wadi El-Jarf. Painted image of a couchant lioness. ©, Pierre Tallet.

Together with the symbol for "great," *wr*, written above the lioness, the inscription was interpreted by Tallet's team to mean "Great Lion," *wr-m3j* (figure 89).

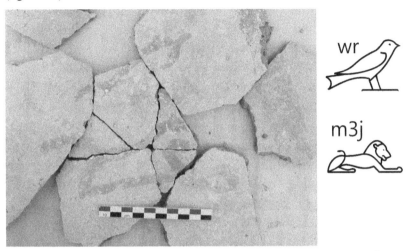

Figure 89: Pottery marks from cave G15 at the Wadi El-Jarf spelling out *wr-m3j* [oor-my], Great Lion. ©, Pierre Tallet.

They demonstrated that this was part of the name of a worker gang called Great are the Followers of the Lion, *wr-m3j-smsw-ʿprw* [oor my sem-soo aah-proo] (figure 90).

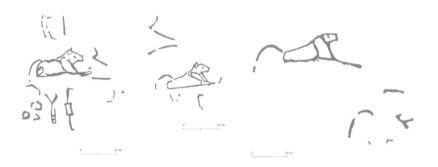

Figure 90: Tracings of painted stone blocks showing the couchant lioness hieroglyph as part of the worker gang's name Great are the Followers of the Lion(ess). From Khufu's Harbor at the Wadi El-Jarf: ©, Pierre Tallet.

I see a possible bridge between the name of this "Great Lion" here and the word for "Great Flood," *wr-mḥt*, I mentioned above. This name comes from the much later Edfu Temple. The papyrus fragments found by the French archaeologists also bear inscriptions which log stone shipments from the Turah[227] quarry to Giza in association with several mentions of Khufu and his late vizier Ankhaf, buried in the East Field next to the Great Pyramid. There is an unmistakable link between this harbor and Giza. Just as unmistakable is the prominent lion cult, clearly dated to a time before Khafre.

In fact, imagine walking up to the Step Pyramid of Djoser when it had just been completed. This was between one and two centuries before Khafre. You would have walked through a most unusual, apparently ceremonial gate, lined by winding snakes in relief, and alternating stacks of couchant jackals and lionesses. Evidence of one such gate was found by a Saqqara archaeological team led by Yahia Eid and Zahi Hawass.[228]

These three examples highlight something important, maybe not often appreciated: The Great Sphinx did not come out of a vacuum. It was born into the context of a long-standing worship of lions.

As deeply cultural this old lion cult appears in a time before Khafre, also, as puzzling, it seems that it was suddenly supplanted by the sphinx cult during his reign. This is not to say that lions completely disappeared in art and text. However, a new sculptural theme was born, that of a lion chimera, half-lion, half-human. In parallel with this theme, other seismic shifts took place in religion,[229] in the royal cult, and in its expression in architecture.[230] The most important shift was a more intense focus on the Sun God *R*[f] (Chapter V).

These shifts explain how lions suddenly became sphinxes, not how sphinxes appeared from nowhere. It only seems that the sphinx had no prior origin because that origin was expunged. To make the claim that the Great Sphinx was a late, whimsical idea in the masterplan of Khafre's Pyramid Complex is to ignore the entire lion context I just described. This makes no sense. On the other hand, what does make sense is a remodeling of a prior female lion statue into a sphinx. This goes hand-in-hand with the shifting religious theme toward the Sun God.

Sphinx Debate Fatigue

At this point, it seems Egyptologists would begin to take notice that something about the orthodox Great Sphinx creation theory is off—but they have not. The Khafre-Sphinx Theory, promoted over the last century by thought leaders in the field such as George Reisner, Selim Hassan, Herbert Ricke, Mark Lehner, and Zahi Hawass has become gospel. From within this paradigm, any evidence to the contrary appears flawed. And since it appears flawed, it is—in their minds. No further scrutiny must be given to investigate paradoxical findings that make no sense in the mainstream theory that has now become history.

Let us examine briefly on which pillars the orthodox theory rests. This debate has been well covered by Mark Lehner, John Anthony West, Robert Schoch, Robert Bauval, and Graham Hancock in their various publications over the years. I will just summarize it here and add a few of my own observations.

On what the feuding camps seem to agree is that the Sphinx, Sphinx Temple, Valley Temple, causeway and Pyramid Temple next to Khafre's Pyramid were all part of the same building project. They disagree on when this project was conducted. While the building sequence and architecture may tie these five megalithic structures together[231], it does not date them, unless any one of them can be independently dated. The rationale is therefore if you can date one, you date them all.

Mark Lehner's most direct evidence for a date besides ^{14}C-dating of one charcoal sample collected from a wall recess in the Sphinx Temple,[232] is Old Kingdom debris *under* one of the huge blocks in the northeast corner of the Sphinx ditch, presumed to have been destined for the Sphinx Temple but apparently abandoned when construction abruptly stopped. Implicitly, the inference drawn from this evidence is that since the debris is under the block, the block must be younger than the debris. Lehner's team also found Old Kingdom items embedded in sediment inside quarried depressions on the north wall of the ditch. To him, this meant that the last people to extract stone blocks from that wall were Old Kingdom workers, and this evidence dates the whole project.

Robert Schoch's most direct key evidence is the subsurface decay of the limestone floor of the Sphinx ditch. This underground stone weathering process begins as soon as the surface rock is exposed to air. The data he and

209

Thomas Dobecki collected corroborated the impression he gleaned from the water-eroded appearance of the enclosure wall around the Sphinx not seen elsewhere on the Giza Plateau—for example, on the rock-cut tombs of Debehen near Khafre's pyramid, G8090, and on the tomb of Kai further east and lower in the central field, G8720. When interpreted as water damage, this damage and decay of the Great Sphinx complex could only have occurred when North Africa received much more rain than it has in the last five thousand years.

Robert Bauval's most direct key evidence is the orientation and symbolism of the Great Sphinx as an equinoctial marker and the implication this has for rewinding the precessional clock to a remote time before the Old Kingdom. This part of his theory depends on an awareness of the lionlike shape of the constellation Leo, the precessional reference point in the sky. The orientation of the three pyramids relative to the Orion belt stars corroborate Bauval's model.

The chief reason why the two camps are at odds is this: Each side believes that their type of evidence is more compelling and weighs more heavily than that of the other. The other camp's theory thus carries less weight. Lehner and Gauri believe Schoch's interpretation of the geological data are flawed. Archaeoastronomers like Edwin Krupp, Giulio Magli, and Juan Antonio Belmonte believe that the astronomical knowledge attributed to the layout of the monuments by Bauval is anachronistic to the Old Kingdom.

Schoch and Bauval, like Hancock and West, have for long charged that Egyptologists have succumbed to insular thinking having placed too much faith in their archaeological methods and not enough in the ability of other sciences to contribute. Schoch and Bauval also criticized the chief dogma of history that cultural and material progress has always proceeded linearly as opposed to cycles of high culture and industry followed by periods of decline and climatic resets. This dogma generates the very bias that an older Sphinx is implausible and therefore impossible. This is a slippery slope argument that defies scientific logic, of course.

Babu: Seat of the Soul (Hieroglyphic), Opener (Sumerian)

There are no winners in this debate because it is still too short on evidence and too big on ideas. The balance is off, and that's why it is the ideas that are clashing. The fervor behind the opinions on both sides has created an impasse, no one has interest to bridge any longer. What should happen to move forward out of the impasse is to continue with research and let new evidence speak, not ideas about what is likely and what is not.

Unfortunately, the flow of evidence is limited by chance discoveries. You can hardly conduct controlled experiments in Egyptology and getting a research permit is a process dominated by academic institutions and stacked heavily against outsiders. Nevertheless, academic Egyptologists, historians, and anthropologists accuse the alternative history camp of this very same "sin," theories based on little evidence.

When Bauval, Schoch, and I proposed the Mehit theory, we stepped into the lion's den. We presented Egyptological evidence of the topmost category, writing, the crown jewel of all the types of proof in archaeology. Writing best reveals intent, and images best reflect physical reality, provided we can correctly read the signs. So why is it not yet enough to tip the scale? Let me play devil's advocate. Let me find potential flaws in our own theory.

One of the more controversial assumptions, besides the conclusion, of our theory was what had come to me in that leap of imagination: The idea that the bent rod above Mehit was meant to represent a key. What if it depicted a different object and not a key or door handle? I already alluded to Petrie's idea that it may be a yoke.

What if the meaning had nothing to do with the image shown but with a sound related to the image? In other words, what if the lioness and bent rod above represented the sound of a word instead of the image of it? This is, after all, the fundamental design of hieroglyphic. I really had no basis for assuming or concluding that the JAW Sign part of the JAW-Mehit liga-ture was even a distinct symbol, used separately from the similar Mooring Post Symbol representing the sound *qd* [qed] with which the comprehen-sive Unicode.org catalog of over seven thousand known hieroglyphs had co-mingled it.[233]

You could even say that I was biased, looking for a meaning related to writing. I was thus guided by my own hand to arrive at the idea of a locked archive that needed a key to be opened. As with any scientific model, one puts it to a test by confirming or falsifying its predictions. My prediction was that the JAW Sign was a key. This can be tested, at least theoretically, with a drill probe and visualization of Anomaly A in front of the Great Sphinx. We do not have a problem with scientific logic here; we have a problem of logistics imposed by the Egyptian Ministry of Antiquities. I do not blame them. They want to preserve their monuments for the future.

But bear with me. There are two pieces of circumstantial evidence in support of our translation of the JAW-Mehit ligature. First, this combination of symbols was not used anywhere else in a written hieroglyphic document discovered to date. The renowned German Egyptologist Wolfgang Helck proposed that these two symbols, and several others, were part of a foreign script used by the people from Buto in the north of Egypt, comprising the Nile Delta.[234] Helck also speculated that this script was pictographic. What you see is what it meant, unlike hieroglyphic, which is used phonetically—what you see are mostly sound symbols. Given the vividly picturesque Egyptian hieroglyphs, it is understandable that they were not deciphered for centuries. Western scholars were too bedazzled by what they saw when they should have opened their ears and listened instead to how the Copts and Arabs spoke.

Second, votive steles dedicated to a deceased person were often contextually organized. The various titles of Egyptian officials were spatially sorted on stone plates into thematic groups. Wolfgang Helck, an expert on ancient Egyptian bureaucracy, cataloged the numerous titles and categorized them by their association with official rank, academic guild (i.e., scribes), provisions (production of food, clothing, luxury goods), and royal court rank. When we look to the slab stele of Wepemnefret to know the context into which the tandem title including the JAW-Mehit ligature was placed, we find it in a demarcated, vertical column on its right edge housing his academic titles (figure 91).

And what was written in that column [emphasis added; footnote markers omitted]?

> *"Commander of the king's **scribes**, [translation uncertain], priest of Seshat, foremost of **the archive(s)** of the keeper of the king's property ..."*[235]

I am using one official translation here, not my own, to emphasize the fact that this comes from Egyptologists themselves. My own translation is in the figure legend. Before the Mehit title is listed a scribal title, after it is listed an archivist title. Context is almost everything in this business of interpreting ancient texts. The frame around this set of titles classifies them as academic.

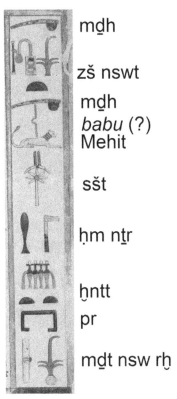

mdh

zš nswt

mdh
babu (?)
Mehit

sšt

ḥm ntr

ḥntt

pr

mdt nsw rḫ

Figure 91: The rightmost column from the stele of Prince Wepemnefret. The inscription literally reads: Overseer royal Scribes, Overseer Opener [Babu] of Mehit, Seshat Priest, Foremost of the *House of Scrolls* of the King's Knowledge. ©, Phoebe A. Hearst Museum of Anthropology and the Regents of the University of California—catalog 6-19825; modified.

We can therefore conclude that the JAW-Mehit ligature was flanked on both sides, above and below, by titles which conferred functions related to document handling: writing and archiving.

In fact, the patron goddess Seshat, under whose divine auspice Wepemnefret served as priest, was ancient Egypt's foremost patron goddess archivist and astronomer, just as the title sequence states. One of Egypt's oldest goddesses, she is first mentioned on the Palermo Stone in a register dated to the reign of First Dynasty's Horus-Djer. The evidence from the stele of Wepemnefret puts the official function embedded in the JAW-Mehit title squarely at the doorstep of an archive.

The JAW-Mehit ligature occurred on royal and private seals used to secure containers of precious goods from the very beginning of Egypt's provisional tent administration. This imparts the idea of security. Merge these two ideas, a lioness guard to secure an archive, and the idea that the bent rod was meant to represent a key, an opener, or a bolt to a door to this secured, royal facility is no longer farfetched; it is now rather probable. Yes, I am making a case based on probability for all those who want to say it is improbable.

But I do not stop here. Let me play devil's advocate again. The stakes here are high. The best possible, direct evidence to be procured that JAW-Mehit was either key, a door handle, or a bolt inserted into a lioness statue would be a direct translation. This seems impossible since the script from where those symbols came is extinct. In the absence of this gold standard, I had already resigned myself to the idea that the only other way was a direct probe of Anomaly A, the Dobecki-Schoch Chamber, to look inside and see if there is a locked door.

However, I have recently discovered something rather startling. It surpassed my wildest expectations. I had joined Robert Schoch's May 2019 Zep Tepi Tour to Egypt. This was also the time that Mark Lehner's Ph.D. thesis and supporting documentation had been made available on the internet. Out of this trip came a long paper Robert and I co-authored, about which I have much to say later.

One piece of it, however, becomes relevant to the mystery surrounding the JAW Sign. In thumbing through drawn reproductions of decorated pottery pieces in Petrie's Royal Tombs of the First Dynasty, Extra Plates, I found the JAW Sign among pages of many pot shard marks Petrie had reproduced (figure 92). It was a stroke of luck that I would find these four instances of JAW.[236]

Unmistakably, there it was, only not written together with a lioness symbol on these pots, but with a symbol reminiscent of a winged disk, Gardiner W8. This was exciting. At this point, I had doubts if my idea that JAW was a key could still be correct. I searched for W8 in Vygus' hieroglyphic dictionary. I found this symbol in four categories of words. The common theme is "strong bond." This includes granite, family, taxes—undoubtedly a form of economic bondage—and oil used as currency to pay tributes/taxes. There was no money in those times. The context of the jars in a royal tomb

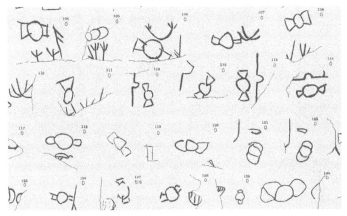

Figure 92: Pottery marks on jars from First Dynasty royal tombs at Abydos. The Bent Rod symbol can be seen in four examples next to the Winged Disk symbol Gardiner W8. From Petrie (1901), Extra Plates, Plate LV a.

helped to narrow the possibilities; I ruled out family and granite as having anything to do with these pots. I focused on taxes payable in precious oil from the occupied region in the Delta and shipped as grave goods for the burial of the Thinite kings at Abydos where Petrie had found these shards.

If W8 meant taxes in the form of oil quotas, then I reasoned that the JAW Sign had to designate the origin of the shipment. Oil production in the Delta came from *b3-st* [ba-set], "Seat of the Soul," also known as Bubastis.[237] Another Egyptian word for *st* "place" was *bu*.[238] *ba-bu* or *bu-ba* in hieroglyphic means the "Place of the Soul" or the "Soul of the Place."

According to Helck the predynastic people in Lower Egypt's Delta may have used a pictographic script just like early Sumerian language. Could these two foreign tongues be related? I put this idea to a test. I scoured the online Akkadian Dictionary kept at the University of Chicago's website for "babu" and "buba." Then came the big surprise. Mind you, this was tossing a wide net, a long shot. The odds, the probability, to find something valuable was low. Let my experience be a lesson to all those afraid to explore longshots, especially when someone else tells you it is.

Babu, in Sumerian, means "opening" or "opener"![239] I could not believe it. I had found direct evidence that my key prediction was correct. I had a tangible bridge from the mysterious JAW Sign to the idea of a key or door opener (figure 93).

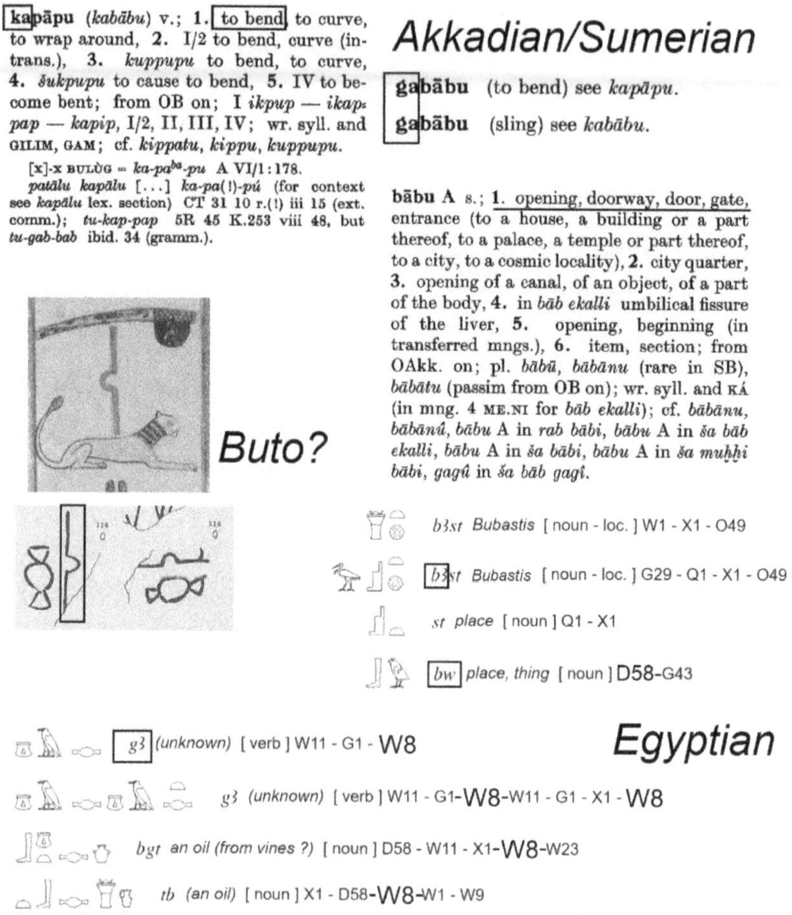

kapāpu (*kabābu*) v.; **1.** to bend, to curve, to wrap around, **2.** I/2 to bend, curve (intrans.), **3.** *kuppupu* to bend, to curve, **4.** *šukpupu* to cause to bend, **5.** IV to become bent; from OB on; I *ikpup — ikap-pap — kapip*, I/2, II, III, IV; wr. syll. and GILIM, GAM; cf. *kippatu, kippu, kuppupu.*

[x]-x BULÙG = *ka-pa^{ba}-pu* A VI/1:178.
paṭālu kapālu [...] *ka-pa*(!)-*pú* (for context see *kapālu* lex. section) CT 31 10 r.(!) iii 15 (ext. comm.); *tu-kap-pap* 5R 45 K.253 viii 48, but *tu-gab-bab* ibid. 34 (gramm.).

Akkadian/Sumerian

gabābu (to bend) see *kapāpu.*

gabābu (sling) see *kabābu.*

bābu A s.; **1.** opening, doorway, door, gate, entrance (to a house, a building or a part thereof, to a palace, a temple or part thereof, to a city, to a cosmic locality), **2.** city quarter, **3.** opening of a canal, of an object, of a part of the body, **4.** in *bāb ekalli* umbilical fissure of the liver, **5.** opening, beginning (in transferred mngs.), **6.** item, section; from OAkk. on; pl. *bābū, bābānu* (rare in SB), *bābātu* (passim from OB on); wr. syll. and KÁ (in mng. 4 ME.NI for *bāb ekalli*); cf. *bābānu, bābānû, bābu* A in *rab bābi, bābu* A in *ša bāb ekalli, bābu* A in *ša bābi, bābu* A in *ša muḫḫi bābi, gagû* in *ša bāb gagî.*

Buto?

b3st Bubastis [noun - loc.] W1 - X1 - O49

b3st Bubastis [noun - loc.] G29 - Q1 - X1 - O49

st place [noun] Q1 - X1

bw place, thing [noun] D58-G43

g3 (unknown) [verb] W11 - G1 - W8

Egyptian

g3 (unknown) [verb] W11 - G1-W8-W11 - G1 - X1 - W8

bgt an oil (from vines ?) [noun] D58 - W11 - X1-W8-W23

tb (an oil) [noun] X1 - D58-W8-W1 - W9

Figure 93: The JAW Sign is the Sumerian word babu and means "Opening/Opener". Together with W8, it means Oil Taxes from Baset in the language of Upper Egyptian. In Sumerian, it means "bend". ©, Seyfzadeh and Schoch, 2019.

I knew I was onto the right track, when I looked up ga-babu, the combination of Gardiner W8 and my preliminary reading of the JAW Sign. Indeed, this was also a Sumerian word which meant "to bend"![240]

A bent opener, as in *bent rod*. Imagine my disbelief as to what I had just discovered. You would think it does not get better than this, but it did. There is an Egyptian word which is almost identical to Sumerian ga-babu, and this word gives a similar meaning: *q3bw* for "winding." This word is used within the context of Pyramid Text 684 of Pepi II to describe where the deceased and resurrected king will spend some of his time in the sky: in the meandering coils of the Winding Waterway with the Beautiful Star maiden *sb3t nfrt* [seb-at nef-er-et], probably a name for Venus.

Thus, *q3bw* are the bends and curves of the water canal in the sky, the ecliptic, the same bends taken by the planets when it looks as if they go back and forth in space and time (figure 94).

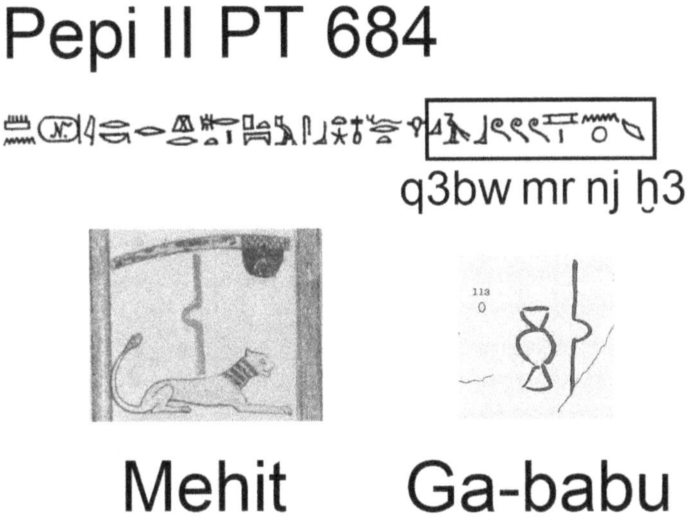

Pepi II PT 684

q3bw mr nj ḫ3

Mehit   Ga-babu

Figure 94: The hieroglyphic word *q3bw* [gha-boo] for "winding", in the context of the Winding Waterway, Pyramid Text 684 of Pepi II. For comparison, the JAW-Mehit Sign from the Stele of Wepemnefret and the bent rod next to Gardiner W8, reconstructed here as Ga-Babu, meaning "bend". From Petrie (1901), Extra Plates LV A.

I now had an example of a word that would have sounded nearly identical in Sumerian and Egyptian and meant the same. The symbol which is part of the word to express the concept of bending, the JAW Sign, is itself bent proving that it was, in fact, a pictograph, not a phonograph.

With this one example, I was able to prove that a language bridge may have existed between the Egyptian Delta and Sumer, and that the symbols used in writing were pictograms, not phonograms. I can now present the pronunciation and translation of JAW: Babu-Mehit, "Opener of Mehit."

Quite literally, the JAW Sign had opened a door to a wide new field of pursuit onto which no one has ever stepped: the lost language of the

Buto-Maadi culture. A cultural bridge between Sumer and Lower Egypt has long been debated, but to my knowledge, no one has shown a linguistic link. The archaic language of the Delta is now lost, except for a few symbols that survived in hieroglyphic, like the JAW Sign.

I concluded that the JAW Sign depicted a real, concrete, bent object used to open a doorway into a void under the lioness statue. Neither a mythical lioness nor a real lioness makes sense, given this translation of the symbol. The textual evidence for a monumental lioness that once guarded an underground archive at Giza is overwhelming at this point. Where was this Mehit-secured archive on the Giza Plateau? There is only one logical answer: Where now stands the Great Sphinx.

Resurrecting the Lost Language of the Egyptian Delta

These linguistic insights gained open multiple avenues for other researchers to pursue. For example, based on the research template I now have at hand, I predict that the occupied people of the Delta—after Narmer sacked their territory at the start of the dynastic state of Egypt—used their script phonetically to let the occupiers from the south know what they were sending as tributes. In other words, while ga-babu meant bent in their own tongue, it sounded like something the southerners would recognize as "oil taxes from Baset."

This explains why there are symbols in hieroglyphic which have different sound values. One may have come from the north and one from the south. It may, then, be possible to resurrect the lost language of the Buto-Maadi starting with a set of such equivocal symbols and then scanning the Sumerian dictionary for words whose sounds resemble those of their Egyptian counterparts. Such words might then be like those once spoken in the Delta. As excavations proceed and long-buried relics of the Delta's prehistoric culture are recovered from thick layers of alluvial mud, evidence of the missing link may one day surface. The context I have establishing here aids in their decipherment.

The phonetic play on written words, of course, is known in two other contexts, one well known, the other one not so well. It is well known that the Egyptians used group-writing, initially individual hieroglyphic letters, later syllables, to mimic the sound of foreign words for which they had no

Egyptian equivalent.[241] It is not so well known that this phonetic play was also the basis for Heka, language of the spiritualists.

In our 2018 paper *The Inventory Stele: More Fact than Fiction*, Robert Schoch and I show in detail, based on an initial insight by Wolfgang Helck, how the prehistoric statuette-making ritual was phonetically embedded inside the text of the famous *Mouth-Opening Ceremony*. This ritual is written on the north wall of the sarcophagus chamber of the last king of the Fifth Dynasty, Unas,[242] and later kings and queens of the Sixth Dynasty.

Here, as with some titles, a concrete rite made way for a ceremonial, merely symbolic ritual enactment, hence stylized from its primordial roots.

Mehit's Neck Discovered

But back to Mehit and the Great Sphinx. Is there any other physical evidence that the Great Sphinx was remodeled from a monumental lioness? Recently, an attendee at a conference who was sitting next to me listening to a seminar by Robert Schoch performed a sculptural analysis of the Great Sphinx. He published his findings in *Archaeological Discovery Journal*. His name is Robert Neyland, and he discovered what he interprets to be the still present remnant base of the original lioness' neck on the back of the Great Sphinx.[243] In other words, the older monument is literally peeking out from the "new."

This layer of rock had been described before, but Robert Neyland realized that this must be the residual stump of the original neck. The rest of the rock layer eroded away or was carved off during remodeling, while making the Great Sphinx's head from that of the lioness. Neyland speculates that the neck and back area of the lioness monument were converted *into a nemes* tail. This ornamental feature was the "ponytail" visible on many sphinxes which rested on the back, immediately behind the neck. He also concluded that the current Sphinx head, including missing pieces, would fit inside the larger head of a lioness proportional with the rest of the body of the Great Sphinx. Its neck projects to the rocky stump on the back. Hence, an even larger male lion head with mane need not have preexisted from which the head of the Great Sphinx was carved. Neyland also ruled out other animal heads, for example, a jackal.

The initial proposal made by Schoch and West, and then separately by Bauval, was that the head of the Great Sphinx is too small for the body.

The view from the orthodox side, represented by Mark Lehner and Edwin Krupp, to which Schoch and Bauval have separately responded, was that the Sphinx was meant to be seen from the front, where it is nearly proportional.[244] They claim that there is no proof that the ancient Egyptians recognized Leo before the Greco-Roman period.

I do not need to recapitulate this dispute because the new textual and physical evidence, more decisively than ever, points to a female lion by the named of Mehit was present at Giza for at least five hundred years prior. However, I want to add this: In his Ph.D. thesis, Lehner reasoned that the body of the Sphinx was artificially lengthened because of a wide defect in the rock, called the Major Fissure.[245] This, according to Lehner, had to be done to avoid a square cut-off in the back through the hip. If this is true, then it means the monument was not only meant to be seen from the front.

The Critics May Ask...

In a scientific pursuit, you cannot afford to suspend objectivity too long. Even if you think you've had a breakthrough, another finding throws you a curve ball. This is why you cannot only lean on the pro of your argument; you have to weigh in on the contra and probe the pro. Here are a few potential questions the critics may have, and how I would answer them.

1) Mehit was a southern symbol from Upper Egypt. How can she have been a monument in the north at Giza?

Mehit literally means "she who is north," or "the northern one," *(fem.)*. Even though Mehit is commonly associated with Thinis, the Upper Egyptian early, First and Second Dynasty royal capital of the unified kingdom in Upper Egypt, I think the preponderance of the evidence points to her original location in the north, at Rostau, the seat of Aker, as the sealings suggest.

A great textual piece of evidence that the hieroglyphic word for north in the feminine gender, *mḥ(w/t)*, was synonymous with the couchant lioness *mḥt*/Mehit can be seen in the Sokar chapel of the New Kingdom Temple of Seti in Abydos.[246] Here, Mehit is the deity associated with the northern Heb Sed concourse corner stone, the so-called *mḏnbw mḥtj* [me-den-boo me-hetee], whose southern, also deified, counterpart is called the *mḏnbw rsw*. *mḏnbw* can be translated as "turning point."

These stone markers were placed inside the jubilee court of the Egyptian king to mark the northern and southern extremes of the concourse of his symbolic run around his Earthly and Heavenly realms.[247] Remnants of such marking stones can be seen in the courtyard of the Step Pyramid of Djoser, and they are shown as hieroglyphic symbols in various inscriptions recording the thirty-year Heb Sed jubilee festivals of several Egyptian kings, as early as the First Dynasty.

On a wall of this chapel dedicated to Sokar, the couchant lioness hieroglyph is inscribed next to the northern *mḏnbw*. Mehit was not just the name of a lioness goddess that also happened to be the word for north; she was, by her very name, one and the same with this part of Egypt. She was not thought of as a southern goddess.

One day, when Thinis will be found and excavated, new evidence will come to light clarifying Mehit's true origin, but for now I am convinced she was originally from Lower Egypt, specifically from Rostau. The scale tip heavier towards the north than the south if you look at all the evidence.

2) If Mehit was a prehistoric, monumental lioness statue, why does she not appear in text or image before Narmer?

She may, only without the JAW Sign, and there is a good reason for that.

Among the symbol-inscribed bone tags found by Dreyer in Tomb UJ, which is not far from the tombs of the Thinite kings in Abydos, were nine that depicted an animal-shaped shrine and various standing or couchant animals in front (figure 95).

Figure 95: Bone tags from Tomb UJ. One these nine of the larger set, the Great Hall animal shrine is depicted, guarded by a couchant animal. Number 69 looks vaguely like a lion. Photo taken July 2019 from Dreyer 1999, Tafel 30.

These tags are in Egypt's oldest known set of written records. Three types can be made out: Possibly a standing elephant on six of nine tags,[248] a couchant animal with pointed ears or horns like a rhinoceros,[249] and a couchant animal without them.[250] The latter one looks only vaguely like a lion,[251] but this is in doubt.[252] Regardless, there is no bent rod, no JAW Sign above any of the animals on the bone tags found. The JAW Sign above a lioness guarding an animal shrine first appears less than two centuries later, on sealings dated to Narmer.[253]

Hence, even from predynastic times there was a preexisting, Upper Egyptian iconography revolving around animal-shaped halls, dedicated to a regional, administrative function. Its prototype was the Great Hall *pr-wr*.[254] That there were several of these halls is suggested by the clan-like identification with at least two different wild animals, although they could still all be the same animals in different poses, for example an elephant.[255]

If any of these images is, in fact, a lioness, then why was the JAW Sign later added to make her into JAW-Mehit? If none of these animals depicts a lion, then where did she and the JAW Sign come from? Surely not the south. To answer these questions, we must consider both scenarios.

The more straight-forward case is that none of the animals shown on the tags from tomb UJ are lions. In that case, the JAW-Mehit sealings came with Narmer's conquest of the north. This means the lioness iconography—as her name "Northern One" indicates—came from there as well, together with the JAW Sign from Buto. The reason why, in this case, a lioness replaced elephants, rhinoceroses, or jackals, is that Mehit was a northern icon. This substitution is, of course, consistent with the idea that a monumental lion statue stood at ancient Giza and explains the paradox of a northern lioness in front of a southern animal shrine.

It is exactly the imposing appearance of a giant stony lion that would prompt the king's seal makers to replace the southern *pr wr* animal guards with the lioness while still using the *pr wr* icon to refer to an archival facility discovered beneath. The JAW Sign was added to indicate that this facility had been opened, gated, and secured with a keyed lock, accessible only by the king's scribes.

Only they were the original, skilled, and masterful ones, the *3ḫw*, who knew how to write. They could create and capture shadowy outline images of things on papyrus, just like their prehistoric *sm* shaman ancestors who captured the shadows of the deceased in trance to bring them back to life inside of statuettes made for their grieving family members.

They were Egypt's first "civilized" animators, the *ḥk3w*, and that gave them immense power because they knew the secret of renewed life in the afterlife, the ultimate desire of the royals who yearned for immortality. That is why they were the Masters of the Opener to Mehit. They knew the secret of symbolic creation based on the intellectual facilities of the creator god Ptah. They had been inside the archive under.

In the scenario I describe here, it was Horus-Narmer who breached the *Hall of Records*, the archive under Mehit, and the oil tag found by Petrie in the tomb of Narmer's grandson Horus-Djer recorded this Opening of the Place of the Archive. This event was momentous because 3,000 years of high culture emerged after it.

The more complicated case is, if indeed the lioness sits in front of at least some, or only one, of the *pr wr* shrines inscribed on the Tomb UJ tags. In this case, Narmer invaded Lower Egypt bringing with him a home-grown iconography depicting his provisional administrative facility complete with lioness but without the JAW Sign. This makes only sense because the JAW Sign came from the people who used it, the conquered Lower Egyptians from Buto.

But why the couchant lioness, when the common animal of choice at home was an elephant, rhinoceros, or jackal?

The best answer to this I can give is that the choice of a lioness in either of these two cases is still peculiar. I am trying not to use hindsight to argue here because there is, of course, things you haven't seen in the remaining chapters of this book. Suffice it to say, I think it is better to define, instead, what we need to falsify my theory that Mehit was a stony lioness at Giza when Narmer invaded Lower Egypt, and that this is the reason why the icon of her appeared in the written records after that.

Logically, I would propose that this requires a monumental lioness statue with something on her back, still undiscovered under the sands near archaeological remnants of a large building, somewhere near today's Girga, Egypt, where ancient Thinis is believed to have been (Chapter IV, figure 15).

3) Just because Mehit appears in the texts as a couchant lioness does not mean she was a physical statue. Why could Mehit not have been a symbolic patroness deity dedicated to the writers' guild?

This is what German Egyptologist Wolfgang Helck (1914-1993) might have argued. He is no longer alive. But he wrote about this topic at length, more than anyone else. This is the most compelling argument against a Mehit statue at Giza because, as Helck proposed, there is a context for purely symbolic patron deities: numina,[256] sanctified guilds, if you will.

Helck interpreted the various deities and their symbolic inaugurations documented in the records of the Thinite era as numinous, meaning spiritually imbuing, protective patrons, uniquely chosen for each branch of the economy.[257] Let me call this Helck's Numina Model. It is a contextual argument. Based on the Numina context it proposes, we would interpret the deity concept of Mehit as the numen whose spirit imbued the craft of writing as a protective power. The icon of the lioness is therefore to be taken as cultic and symbolic, not concretely as if it were a depiction of a physical entity, such as a lioness statue.

My rebuttal to applying Helck's Numina Model to Mehit is two-fold. First, real, physical entities and functions like statues, facilities, and professional guilds were behind the numina. The House of Scrolls of Royal Knowledge, for example, in which Wepemnefret served, was sanctified by Seshat and guarded by Mehit. What argues for a physical Mehit and against an imagined, ethereal lioness spirit is the real physical object hovering above her, the JAW Sign. In the reconstruction I outlined earlier in this chapter JAW means Opener and is pronounced "babu."

Second, as per Helck's own analysis, the JAW-Mehit ligature is not a phonetic Egyptian hieroglyph, but a pictographic construct from the language once spoken and written around Buto in the Delta and Lower Egypt. As Helck reconstructs this now lost script[258], its basic unit of coding, nowadays called a "morpheme," appeared to be used syllabically to spell out Egyptian words, rather than consonantally, as does hieroglyphic. Said another way, the image shown in symbols used in Buto each had a name, and that name formed the basis for a syllable used to make words in the Egyptian language. But how did these Buto symbols work to spell the words of the language spoken in Buto?

In their language the images related to the meaning of the words they spell. Call it a picture script: The symbol images tell the story, symbol by symbol, word by word.

Let me use the same example that Helck used to illustrate this idea: The name of Horus-Narmer, the Upper Egyptian ruler who conquered Lower Egypt around 3000 BC and established Dynastic Egypt. "Narmer" was spelled with two symbols: *mr* "chisel" and nʿr "catfish".

Helck points out that the *Egyptian* translation of these symbols as the words *nʿr* and *mr* when combined to make *nʿr-mr* would have been "*Schlimmer Wels,*" in German, "Bad/Sick Catfish" in English.[259] Of course, as he points out, this would be nonsensical since too irreverent a way to spell the name of the ruler of Egypt.[260]

The better explanation is that these Buto symbols were only used as syllables in Egyptian, not as words. The only reason why they were chosen to spell the king's name is that the Buto words for catfish and chisel must have sounded like the syllables of, or rather words forming the king's name in Egyptian. Thanks to the phonetic value of Hieroglyphic, we have an idea what they must have sounded like, i.e., [~Naar-~mer]. One possibility that makes a lot of sense is the combination of the words *nrw* [Ne-roo] for "bull" or "Feared One" and *mry* for "fighting bull." Narmer is shown in bull form on the verso of the Narmer Palette, for example, and one of the meanings of the word *mr*, written with the Hoe Sign, was used in predynastic times in a battle context besides, ironically, meaning "love."

I think the true name of Egypt's first king was something like Feared Fighting Bull. That is why the JAW Sign must have not only referred to a real object in Buto but was also used to spell that word there. In combination with Mehit, it had to have meant Opener Mehit in Buto, in a real physical sense, exactly as shown in the image of the lioness with the bent rod entering her back. Ancient Giza, of course, was near Buto, and, as I proved earlier, so was the northerner Mehit.

Third, the concept of numina stands in contradistinction to the immanent character of Egyptian deities, referring to James Allen's quote in Chapter 1. They were the real forces of nature. They did not animate object from a distance by imbuing them with spiritual power. A statue of stone was not alive by virtue of a distant power separate from the monument. The monument was immanently alive, in a divine sense. It lived. What that means is that when the ancient Egyptians referred to a divine entity, they had a physical reality in mind. Even though they could not see Shu, they could feel the air on their skin. Even though they could not see some of the gods, they could smell them in the scents of nature. By the same token, the guardian Mehit was as real to them as the seal imprinted with her likeness and used to secure a jar of precious oil. The power of that seal was based on a real physical threat of punishment from a real, physical, stony, fear-instilling, giant lioness.

4) Many titles in ancient Egypt were only ceremonial and did not describe a concrete function. Why couldn't the JAW-Mehit title be such an honorific badge?

This could also be a concern Wolfgang Helck might raise, based on his writings. He might argue that, regardless of the initial function for which it was conferred, the dual title with JAW-Mehit had no longer a concrete but more of a ceremonial character during the Old Kingdom. It imparted an aura reverend to the earlier Thinite era of the First and Second Dynasty, when scribes worked first inside of a provisional animal shrine and later inside the royal palace both symbolically, not physically, protected by the lioness Mehit.

In Helck's reconstruction of how title functions evolved over time— let's call this his title conversion model or Helck's Rule in his honor—the general trend was that materially significant tasks during the early phase of the kingdom that related to the procurement for and allocation of food for the royal household became subspecialized. That led to an explosion of titles. Many of these titles were carried forward and awarded symbolically as temple titles. They officiated the royal funerary provisions mandate once the bureaucratic state apparatus was fully developed.

I am with Helck and Helck's Rule when it comes to most ancient Egyptian titles. One way you could explain the motivation behind not retiring defunct titles is to keep the growing number of state officials loyal to the king. Various hollow titles could be conferred merely as a token of royal benevolence. That this worked is indicated by the fact that the recipients proudly listed their titles in their tombs.

Helck might thus be justified, if he were to, hypothetically speaking, argue that the Overseer of JAW-Mehit title was conferred onto top state officials like Hesy-*R*ꜥ, Nefersešem-*R*ꜥ, [261] Wepemnefret, Hemiunu, and

Mery to decorate them with honors, rather than handing them the key to a secret royal archive.

However, the *mdh*-JAW-*mht*/Overseer of JAW-Mehit may be an exception to Helck's Rule. For starters, the *mdh*-JAW-*mht* bearers were top officials to begin with. They did not need ceremonial titles.

More importantly, there is another title whose fate serves as an example of an alternative title conversion model to the Helck Rule. This title was as archaic as *mdh*-JAW-*mht*. Over centuries time it converted to the topmost office in charge of the Heliopolitean priesthood. But was this merely a ceremonial title whose beginnings were material? Does Helck's Rule always apply? Let's examine how this title conversion happened.

This title designated the *m33w wr* [ma'-aoo mor] function: He sees the Great One. The Great One was Horus. It was exclusive, held by princes. *m33w wr* first appears during the reign of Horus-Den, the fifth king of the First Dynasty.[262] From then on, its use continued through the Fourth Dynasty and even after. The most famous holder was Third Dynasty *jm-htp*/Imhotep under Djoser, who must have been a contemporary of Hesy-*R⸢*, bearer of *mdh*-JAW-*mht*. Was this a merely ceremonial title by then?

To reconstruct the function behind Egyptian titles, Egyptologists must develop the context of other, known titles within which the unknown title appears. For *m33w wr*, this original context was the supervision of construction, what we would call a project manager. This can be gleaned, according to Helck, from other, related functions that co-aggregated with *m33w wr*, and dealt with construction supply and supply storage. At inception, this title, therefore, designated a concrete, practical, supervisory function at the highest level; it was not initially ceremonial. But was it ever?

Interestingly, its name hints at an astronomical, observatory origin related to any one of the Horus forms in the sky, for example the star Sirius. There is more to this title conversion than one that went from true to trivial. This is where title analysis becomes interesting.

Applying his title conversion model, Helck makes a connection between stone quarries at Heliopolis and the famous Temple of the Sun there, *jwnw* [ay-oo-noo] a.k.a. ⸢*n*. He concludes that the physical proximity of the two led to the later title transfer from supervising construction to supervising priest-astronomers at the spiritual center of the state during the early Third Dynasty. This sounds reasonable at first sight, does it not?

But I think what Helck overlooked here is the close relationship between Egyptian astronomy and Egyptian monuments. The real bridge, I argue, is that the building code was astronomical and so it makes perfect sense that the chief contractor of the king also had to know astronomy. This dual responsibility is amply demonstrated at Saqqara, where Imhotep is implicated as the builder of the Step-Pyramid complex[263] as Djoser's *m33w-wr*. And so, I would counter here with the argument that The One who see the Great One was not ceremonial at all. This was the chief astronomer, who defined the ancient building code, so to speak.

By the same token, I would claim an exception from Helck's Rule as it pertains to the *mdḥ*-JAW-*mḥt* title. As I indicated at the outset, I think the exception to the rule is carved out when high officials are concerned. They had no need to polish their resumes because they were at the top already.

5) The First Dynasty sealings with JAW-Mehit show the lioness next to the Upper Egyptian *pr-wr* shrine. Was that building not in Upper Egypt as opposed to Lower Egypt, or ancient Giza for that matter?

The original building in the shape of a monumental animal shrine, the so-called "Great House" or "Great Hall," *pr-wr* was once thought to have stood in Hierakonpolis in Upper Egypt, identified with the ceremonial center HK29A used for ritual animal sacrifice. However, the lead excavator Renee Friedman has since put this identification into doubt.[264]

Wherever the shrine depicted in the sealings originally stood, however—and it may have been in the first capital of the kingdom at Upper Egypt's Thinis—what is shown in the sealing with JAW-Mehit was only a transient, off-site facility, modeled after the permanently installed original elsewhere. It is that recreation of the original, not the original itself, depicted in the sealings.

The proof for this, besides the location identifiers on Petrie's sealing number 116 I explained above, is that there were three, not one, such transient facilities in the early phase of the kingdom. All three served as temporary scribal bureaus representing the long arm of the king in the conquered land, so to speak. Their purpose was to administer tributes from Lower Egypt to Thinis, where the early kings still lived and needed provisions in life and death.

These make-shift "bureaus" can be identified by their different sealings. Written mentions of them eventually disappeared from the archaeological record in the first half of the First Dynasty, within about a century after Narmer. They were replaced by a permanent scribal installment inside a new palace built for the kings in the Delta. Here are some of the details of the evidence for what I state.

From Horus-Narmer onwards, *pr-wr* appears with JAW-Mehit on sealings attached to both royal, and private shipments of Goods. There are at least twenty-five such sealings listed in Peter Kaplony's published catalog (figure 96).[265]

Figure 96: Above, First Dynasty sealings (number 138) showing the JAW-Mehit ligature in front of the animal shrine *pr-wr*. The fish- or swallow tail symbol is not an Egyptian hieroglyph. Wolfgang Helck referred to these lower Egyptian symbols as written "noch in Butischer Schrift und Sprache," meaning "still in the script and tongue of Buto in the Delta. Below, sealing number 27 B, is the royal seal of Horus-Aha with which the Mehit seal was cross-signed on shipments to royal tombs. Photos from Kaplony, 1963.

Initially, the Mehit seal disappeared only from royal shipments, but its use continued for private—meaning high officials and members of the royal house—shipments until Horus-Djet.

Under the reign of his successor Horus-Den, the fourth king after Horus-Narmer, it disappeared completely.[266] In one late example from the niched mastaba tomb 3506 in Saqqara, JAW-Mehit, in front of *pr-wr*, appears with a conjoined, double lion, later identified as Ruty and Aker.[267] Besides sealing 116, this one further corroborates that what is shown in the sealing was in ancient Giza. Aker was believed to be the entry to, and exit from, the *dw3t* Netherworld in Rostau (figure 97).

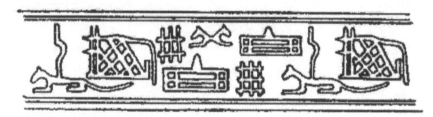

Figure 97: Aker with Mehit guarding the animal shrine. Photo from Kaplony, 1963.

The disappearance of the Mehit seal, and the temporary facility it represented, correlates with the establishment of a textually and archaeologically documented royal building in Buto called "Seat of Horus Striker." In parallel, on one sealing (figure 98), Mehit reappears, now within the confines of a palace installation called a *ḥwt* [hoot].[268] This could be equated to an administrative office building or space within a palace.

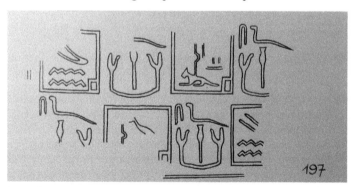

Figure 98: Sealings Number 197 from the reign of Horus-Den. The JAW-Mehit ligature can now be seen inside a *ḥwt*, a part of the royal palace. The name of the royal seal-bearer is *sḏk3* Sedjka. Photo from Kaplony, 1963.

The existence, and disappearance, of two other, temporary, offsite bureaus during the early First Dynasty, can be dated to a period from the reign of Horus-Aha until Horus-Djer.[269] These seals display rows of animals with animal traps and a tandem set of royal seals, respectively. Both were phased out by the reign of Horus-Djer.

My interpretation of these records is that the early state required the quick assembly of regional administrative posts controlling and enforcing the flow of goods, in the form of tributes or taxes, to the king. These provisional posts became superfluous once regional palaces were built, and the king established permanent residences in the occupied land. One of these outposts, the most prominent one, was the one shown in the JAW-Mehit sealings. The evidence from these sealings located this facility to ancient Giza.

How Far Can Texts Take Us?

This book is about the hieroglyphic evidence for an archive under the Great Sphinx. Tracing the evidence for it backwards in history, backwards in time, I cannot take the argument with me further back than the earliest known written records found in Egypt, about 3200 BC. This does not mean, of course, that I cannot falsify the Khafre-Sphinx Theory with the evidence I have uncovered. Any proof for a monumental sphinx or lion *any time* before Khafre would do that.

But in 2019, I thought I had exhausted the hieroglyphic angle for an older Sphinx. I had no way to pursue Anomaly A to prove there is a real *Hall of Records* under the Sphinx, whatever it may have looked like. At the time, I presumed that this archive would still be sealed, if it ever existed at all. There was no proof to be had of its existence.

Then came new information and new insights. Besides the sealings of the First Dynasty, there were labels made from bone, inscribed with information needed to ship oil from the province in the north to the kings in the south. These shipping labels used an interesting set of symbols: half a lion, the front, or the back.

This opened a new line of investigation for me because Robert Schoch and I had earlier explored the power of recorded, megalithic symbols to seed a civilization at Göbekli Tepe. I asked myself if that is what we might be looking at with the Great Sphinx. Perhaps, the archive was the Sphinx itself, a monolithic, megalithic symbol that sparked high culture by the Nile.

The break-through came when Mark Lehner's Ph.D. thesis became public because the information he published helped to bridge a lost link between statue and symbol and, ultimately, a solution to an epic theme of human history—the link between symbol and civilization.

This chapter in my search for the *Hall of Records* begins with a crack.

IX

Fissure

W HOEVER FIRST THOUGHT OF INVENTING WRITING MUST HAVE HAD SOMETHING on the mind that could not be said and heard. No. It had to be recorded and read. But why?

It depends on who you ask. There are those who think that the history of human civilization, for example, cultural and ideological advances in architecture, art, faith, and science, rode on the back of materialistic advances in the methods used to produce and store food and make shelters. To them, writing was invented out of material necessity. It made life easier.

But there are others who think it's the other way around. They say that material progress only happens when people cooperate. To them, writing, the recording and display of symbols to communicate ideas, inspired people to come together in peace and celebrate a higher cause. That, after all, was the spark that fueled the forge of civilization. To them, writing made life meaningful.

Believe it or not, even political ideology has become mixed up in this standoff between two opposing paradigms that have variously influenced how discoveries in anthropology and archaeology are interpreted to write our history. But which is right? The Great Sphinx has something to tell us about that for the strangest of reasons: The rock from which it was made has a crack.

Among the over 5,000-year-old, earliest known hieroglyphs in ancient Egypt are two that seem even stranger: You see only half a lion, either the front or the back. The original idea that led to their invention must have been profound because they were used in most fundamentally material and primordially spiritual hieroglyphic writings. This chapter is about that original idea.

Clash Over the Age of the Great Sphinx

In late August 2019, I was excited to meet Mark Lehner, one of the most influential and iconic Egyptologists in the world. He made a name for himself researching the Giza Plateau and literally putting it on the map with detailed surveys.

Lehner's perceptive observations form an important element in the orthodox, main-stream narrative of who built the pyramids, Sphinx, and temples out of the limestone layers which make up the Mokattam Hills—and when. But he did not begin his career in the orthodox camp. On the contrary. Ironically, Mark Lehner first went to visit Egypt in the early 1970s because of none other than Edgar Cayce and his foundation, the Association for Research and Enlightenment (A.R.E.).

The mission of his American Research Center in Egypt (ARCE)-funded project at Giza in the late 1970s and early 1980s was to survey and map the Great Sphinx. This work would eventually become the basis of his Yale University Ph.D. thesis *Archaeology of an Image: The Great Sphinx of Giza*. But the bulk of Lehner's notes, photos, drawings, and the thesis itself did not become widely available to the public until 2018 when ARCE digitized these files and placed them into an online archive.[270]

I have been an ARCE member for a couple of years. Until the COVID-19 pandemic, I regularly attended seminars held at the Bowers Museum in Santa Ana, the meeting place of the local ARCE chapter in Southern California. I had sponsored two seminars for 2019. One of the speakers for whom I had ear-marked the money was Mark Lehner, the other James P. Allen, who directed Lehner's ARCE project and is now a world-renowned expert in hieroglyphic. When you sponsor a speaker for ARCE, you meet them for lunch. And so, on a hot last day of August, I was anxiously driving to the Bowers to meet Lehner about whom I had heard, read, and seen so much. He is one of the perceived thought leaders of the field in general and the leading authority on the Giza Plateau; anyone interested in the Sphinx and pyramids has likely read something written by him.[271] I was looking forward to meeting a legend of Egyptology in such a personal setting over lunch.

However, I had reasons to be nervous. In my hand I was holding a folder. It contained a paper Robert Schoch and I were to publish within a couple of days. We were presenting hieroglyphic evidence for an older Great Sphinx contradicting the model Lehner had proposed in his thesis, including the age of the Sphinx that most consider to still be correct.

If you have ever written a thesis, you know what I mean: It is a personal matter. Years of your formative life go into producing it. Since the Great Sphinx is as near to Lehner as it is to Schoch and me, I wanted him to be the first to see it. Lehner and Schoch go back many years, but their first encounter was anything but friendly. Their tense meeting set the tone for the years that followed. I did not want to have our first meeting to go that way.

When Schoch and West released their findings to the world at the 1991 Geological Society of America Meeting in San Diego, California, Egyptologists did not take to them kindly. Mark Lehner—then already the de facto expert on the Great Sphinx having just published his thesis on the matter—stepped into the public arena. He was pitted against a young geologist, Robert Milton Schoch, seven years his junior, also from Yale University. The meeting would escalate into a clash of titans that made news around the world. Months later, at the 1992 A.A.A.S.[272] meeting, Lehner and Schoch met face to face. They were accompanied by geologist Lal Gauri and geophysicist Thomas Dobecki on the podium in front of an audience of the curious and the media. Before Schoch and Dobecki got involved, it had only been the Egyptological establishment versus the outsider West, armed with a book by French alchemist René Adolphe Schwaller "de Lubicz" (1891-1962), in which the author thought that the damage of the Sphinx complex was different from that on other monuments at Giza and suggested it had to be caused by water.

The foundations on which orthodox Egyptology was based were shaken to their core when Schoch and Dobecki put a scientific basis under Schwaller's idea. To make matters worse for Egyptologists, the two geologists concluded after a few weeks of seismic experiments that the Great Sphinx must be thousands of years older than archaeology had pieced together in a hundred years. It was not only Yale versus Yale, but also geology versus Egyptology, and a short stint at Giza versus years of studying for and preparing a Ph.D. thesis. The outsiders West, Schoch, and Dobecki had turned up the heat on the establishment with hard scientific data.

The dispute about the age of the Sphinx was further dramatized on TV with the widely watched 1993 NBC documentary *Mystery of the Sphinx*[273] presented by none other than "Taylor" from the original 1968 film *Planet of the Apes*. Charlton Heston had branded "epic" in the movies. He was the perfect choice to narrate to an audience of millions this epic drama about what history we are to believe. What began as a scientific controversy now became a major fissure between two academic disciplines represented by two opposite personalities from the same Ivy League School: the flamboyant, eloquent Mark Lehner and the mild-mannered, steady Robert Schoch. At least this is how it was billed in the media which had a field day with it.

Schoch's evidence, the Water Erosion Hypothesis, and the seismic refraction data which corroborated it, threatened to wipe away, in a single swath, years of pain-staking, archaeological work conducted by Lehner and the ARCE team. But Lehner, assisted by counter arguments from geologists Lal Gauri, Thomas Aigner, and James A. Harrell fired back with ammunition from both sides, geology and Egyptology. His concluding remarks in a Kmt Magazine interview sum up to something like this—I only paraphrase here because he did not respond to my request to quote him: Rather than the crux of the debate being a clash of the disciplines, as in Egyptology versus geology, he questioned the quality of the geological evidence put behind the Water Erosion Hypothesis and contrasted that perceived quality to the size of the claim in opposition of what Egyptologists have offered as evidence for their version of how old the Great Sphinx is. Reading this last part from his interview, you can also tell an undercurrent of his disenchantment with how he may have felt that West and Schoch had come across as dismissive of the body of evidence constituting the Egyptologists' point of view.[274]

I was aware of this complicated history between Lehner and Schoch. I knew there could be tension.

But the meeting with Lehner was spectacular, as far as I was concerned at least. We discussed his current projects at Giza. He invited me to visit with some of his team members to review some sealings they had discovered reexamining Karl Kromer's dig in the early 1970s. I did not give Lehner my paper with Schoch until the end of the lunch. I slid the folder over to his side with the words, "I would like to give this to you Dr. Lehner. This is a challenge." He nodded with interest at first.

When he saw the title page with our names, he became silent. I almost wished I had not given it to him because I did not want to give him a bad feeling and ruin a great first meeting; on the contrary, I wanted to make his day. As we left the restaurant with Mrs. Lehner to proceed to the lecture hall, I wondered if he was a bit shaken up by this surprise. But later, during his superb and masterful lecture, he greatly impressed me with his discipline, respectful restraint, and attempt at even-handedness even in front of an audience mostly composed of like-minded peers. Perhaps he still feels connected with his own esoteric roots, even though he has long buried them on his path elsewhere.

Whatever the case, I was impressed. He came across as someone who respects his history and growth as a scholar as something personal and unique, no matter its beginnings.

Mark Lehner originally came to Egypt in 1973 hoping to find evidence that would bear out Edgar Cayce's prophesies about the *Hall of Records*. But even back then, he harbored early doubts based on anthropology courses he had taken at the University of North Dakota.[275] Be that as it may, he published *The Egyptian Heritage-Based on the Edgar Cayce Readings* a year later.[276] But this same time, in 1974, must also have been seminal because the tide of his convictions turned. After reading a book[277] about how beliefs can clash with evidence and still prevail, he began to question the physical reality of the *Hall of Records* more systematically, and how it contrasted with the archaeological evidence he had begun to learn about.

My understanding of how he resolved his own conflicting views on the matter is that he eventually concluded that the Cayce prophecies ought not be interpreted literally but more in terms of a symbolic, mythical truth not unlike how academic scholars view Plato's Atlantis story: There was no real Atlantis. It's only a parable, a didactic device to teach another, more profound truth.

His sharpest critique of Cayce believers, "dilettantes and New Agers," is that they, unlike his own coming to terms, want to focus on the supernatural and not look at the real people who actually made Egypt's monuments, even *When Prophecy Fails*.[278] To know them and their achievements, he argues, means you have to have studied at least some of what Egyptology has discovered. That, however, is often lacking in the esoteric camp.

This criticism of course flows in the same vein as that he directed against John Anthony West and Robert Schoch in the last paragraph of his 1994 Kmt rebuttal I quoted above.

I am paraphrasing only the few tidbits I was able to find about this subject written by Lehner himself in response to questions asked to him by Graham Hancock and Robert Bauval. Personally, what interests me about Lehner's Edgar Cayce and Egyptian history is that it is not unlike mine as it relates to writing this book. I, too, wanted to know if there is real physical evidence for a *Hall of Records*, but, unlike Lehner, I was *not* a believer before or even now.

I do not think that Edgar Cayce told us anything we could not have known from the writings of the ancient Egyptians, even in the 1930s. However, Edgar Cayce affected many people in positive ways. How could I know what he knew, or how he came to understand it? I respect his legacy and those who believe in him.

That something like a chamber, treasure, or tomb may lurk under the Great Sphinx had already long been rumored, prompting several attempts to look beneath her, even in the 1800's.[279] Iconic explorers like Giovanni Caviglia, and the early Egyptologists Auguste Mariette, Gaston Maspero, George Reisner, and Selim Hassan had already spread the mystique of the Sphinx around the world. Remember, mystery sells. Money was needed to fund the enormous excavations at Giza required to move mountains of sand and rubble. Even a hundred years ago—and more—the Sphinx, like today, was likely in the news for more than one reason. If you combine what was known from the texts with the idea of a chamber pursued by Egyptologists themselves, the truth is that the *Hall of Records* was not such a new idea in the 1930s.

In contrast to Lehner's final take on Edgar Cayce's *Hall of Records*, I am presenting Egyptological evidence, the kind that turned Lehner away from the prophecy, that argues the exact opposite of what he concluded: There was a real archive under Mehit according to the textual trace I have investigated, and there is enough evidence for it to warrant another probe of the area Dobecki and Schoch called Anomaly A. The ancient Egyptian writers could have told us the truth, in a real physical, not mythical sense, no matter what anyone wants to make of the prophecies of Edgar Cayce.

I also want to emphasize that the narratives presented by Egyptologists, even when based on physical evidence, may still reflect some deeply held beliefs. I have found that belief-based bias does not leave its mantle on the coat hanger outside the doors of academic offices.

I am looking forward to Lehner's own, more complete account of his early beginnings in Egypt.[280] He announced he would write about it during his talk on that day in August of 2019. I, his sponsor that day, sat in the audience and watched a legend speak about his work, just as I have watched my friend Robert Schoch, a legend himself, when he speaks about his. Only one of these two legends can be correct about the age of the Sphinx, but this is the least important part of the confrontation. Tragically, the lasting effect of it is the impasse which divides them. Poetically speaking, they are two legends symbolically separated by a major fissure.

Sphinx Split in Two

The irony is that one way to bridge this impasse may be a real fissure that exists in the form of a still not well-studied geological defect running right through the Sphinx and enclosure (figure 99).

It is a gash in the rock from which the Great Sphinx was made (figure 100).

In his thesis, Mark Lehner named it the "Major Fissure" to distinguish it from other, similar, but smaller defects running through the monument.[281] This was the same fissure Auguste Mariette had described in 1857 (see Chapter II)—except that when Lehner examined it, it had been converted into an artificially walled shaft made by a restoration team under French Egyptologist Émile Baraize who repaired the Great Sphinx from 1925 until 1936 under the auspices of the Egyptian Antiquities Service. To enter henceforth, one had to open a hatch at the top of the waist of the Sphinx and rope down or stare down at a safer distance from above.

Whichever way Lehner did it, he, unlike Mariette, did not see a chamber at the bottom of the now modified fissure, only a narrow crack into the, to date, still unknown:[282]

> *The interior sides of the shaft show the unweathered bedrock surface and sporadic patches of Baraize's stone-cement blocking. The bedrock might have been squared artificially; however, no chamber, as such, is cut at the bottom, which is about 11.50 m*

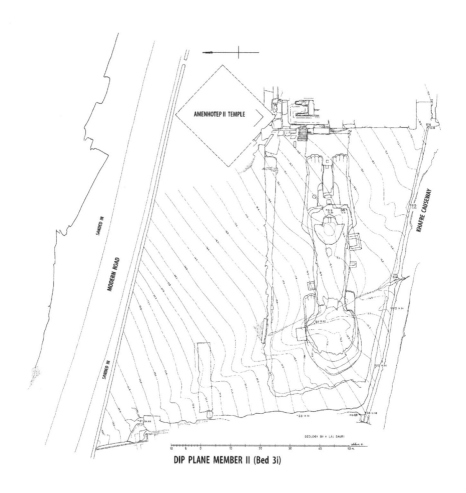

DIP PLANE MEMBER II (Bed 3i)

Figure 99: The course of the Major Fissure through the elevations of the Middle Member of the Mokattam limestone formation. It cuts through the causeway, the ditch, and the Great Sphinx. Illustration courtesy of Mark Lehner (2017): "Drawing d-sa-005 from Egypt/Giza/Khafre Causeway." In ARCE Sphinx Project 1979-1983 Archive. ©, Mark Lehner, Megan Flowers, Rebekah Miracle (Eds.) Released: 2017-12-23. Open Context. URL: https://n2t.net/ark:/28722/k29s2043b

Figure 100: Dated photo of the Great Sphinx before restorations under Émile Baraize in the 1920's. The Major Fissure splits the monument at the waist. Photo courtesy of Archives Lacau, Centre Golenischeff, EPHE, PSL. "Black and White Photo 02440 from Egypt/Giza/Unspecified Sphinx Area 7." (2017). In ARCE Sphinx Project 1979-1983 Archive. ©, Mark Lehner, Megan Flowers, Rebekah Miracle (Eds.). Released: 2017-12-23. Open Context. URL: https://n2t.net/ark:/28722/k2bp09n39

Figure 101: The repair work by Émile Baraize filled in the Major Fissure through the waist of the Great Sphinx. Giza, Egypt. May 2019.

*from the top of the back, or about 1.0 m short of the outside floor
level of the Sphinx sanctuary. The bottom is irregular bedrock
with a much narrower crack continuing deeper, although the
situation is obscured by grey cement spilled during the Baraize
operation.*

What stands out in these observations is that the still original part of the
interior of the fissure appeared squared and that there is an unexplored crack
through its base. Lehner could not survey the entire fissure floor because of
the modern time debris left by the Baraize' repair (figure 101). Taking the
sum of Mariette's and Lehner's observations, I conclude that the bottom of
this fissure must be cleaned and reexamined in situ before one can know
whether there is, after all, a hidden chamber made by ancient builders.

It would help to know when this fissure cracked the rock and why it
happened. Did it happen before the monument was carved, or after? Was
it caused by an earthquake, or some other force of nature? In his thesis,
Lehner describes entering the Major Fissure in one other place, besides the
one I just mentioned: the ditch to the north of the Sphinx.

According to Lehner, the crack in the ditch caused by the Major Fissure
north of the Sphinx narrows to a slit approximately five meters below ground
level. He observed evidence of a water table just above that level.[283] The
question "What came first, Sphinx or fissure," must thus be expanded to
"Sphinx complex or fissure."

The takeaway, for now at least, is that the weight of the evidence leans
on the latter. The fissure came first, then came the Sphinx. The walls of
the interior of the fissure inside the Sphinx appear worked (squared). This
suggests the builders wanted to smoothen a natural surface created by the
force which had already split the rock. Based on this assumption, Lehner
speculates that the unusual width of the Major Fissure prompted the builders
to lengthen the body of the Sphinx to avoid an artificially square rear.[284]

Apparently, Lehner believed that the fissure existed before the monument. Part of his reasoning was based on the Sphinx's disproportionately
long body compared to the small head. In the Mehit model proposed by
Bauval, Schoch, and me, the original monument was a proportionate lioness
made disproportionate only when an Old Kingdom ruler, possibly Khafre,
re-carved the bigger head of the lioness into the smaller head of a pharaoh
with the royal nemes headdress.

In the last chapter, I mentioned sculptural evidence from an artistic perspective for an originally proportionate monument provided by Robert Neyland who believes he found the remnant of the base of the lioness' original neck.[285] Also potentially arguing for an older Major Fissure is that Lehner found a cultural deposit in the debris filling the crack in the ditch I mentioned above. If this deposit can be dated to the Old Kingdom, then the fissure must be older yet.[286] The type and origin of these items have not yet been published.

When I asked Lehner about the items found in this deposit during our lunch, he told me the analysis was still in process. While we will have to wait for final confirmation, indications for now are that the geological event which caused the fissure occurred more than 4,500 years ago, before the time in which Lehner believes the Sphinx was made.

Split Lion Hieroglyphs

The age of the fissure, you may wonder, is crucial to the argument Robert Schoch and I made in the paper to which I earlier alluded.[287] In this paper, we argue that its presence created the megalithic image of a split lion(ess), with front, middle, and hind parts. This tripartite appearance of the revered, albeit damaged, statue, we argue, inspired some of Egypt's oldest written symbols, which are much older than the commonly cited age of the Great Sphinx (figure 102).

Figure 102. Examples of split lion symbols, written in ink onto jars. Circa 2900 BC. Photos from Emery (1954).[288]

We proposed that the unusual iconography of these symbols, which irreverently show a truncated animal known to have been revered by the ancient Egyptians, is evidence of an unnaturally appearing, real-life model that inspired them. This model was a monumental stony lion carved out of rock through which the Major Fissure coursed. Since we knew that the symbols are older than the Great Sphinx, so also had to be the lion statue they depict, including the crack that split it open at the waist.

Why the inventor of these symbols incorporated the truncation and split features into their design instead of ignoring them as imperfections of a magnificent statue is an important aspect in our model. We proposed that the symbol creator viewed them not as accidental imperfections but rather believed them to be of divine cause. Thus, the appearance of the statue, no matter its imperfections, was not to be embellished in its symbolic representations.

While the symbol with the frontal half of the lion is dated to as early as Horus-Narmer and Horus-Aha, circa 3000 BC,[289] the first known use of a symbol showing the hind part dates to predynastic ruler Jrj-Hor,[290] circa 3100 BC. (figure 103)

Figure 103: Frontal half of a lion used as a symbol on First Dynasty oil tags. The Museum of Egyptian Antiquities, Cairo, Egypt, 2018.

The first known use of the fissure-like symbol dates to a grave, sixty meters north of Scorpion I's Tomb UJ, where Dreyer found Egypt's oldest written records,[291] dated to circa 3150 BC.[292] Since the older graves of Cemetery U are situated further north, the fissure-like symbol dates to, as far back as, 3200 BC, or earlier (figure 104).

Figure 104: Predynastic jar from grave U-546 with the fissure symbol. The Museum of Egyptian Antiquities, Cairo, Egypt, 2018.

Schoch and I concluded that if the split-lion iconography on symbols used in writing is at least 5,200 years old, then so must be the idea that inspired it. That idea, we argue in the paper, was the monumental lioness Mehit at Giza which, already then, would have had a major fissure cutting through her waist to create the idea of a split lion in the minds of prehistoric observers. This evidence further strengthens the theory that there was a lion-like monument at Giza long before the Great Sphinx.

It adds to the geological evidence observed by John Anthony West, Robert Schoch, and Thomas Dobecki in the early 1990s, and the astronomical evidence put forth by Robert Bauval and Graham Hancock in the mid-1990s.

We now, in 2021, also have textual, classic Egyptological evidence in writing, the subject of the previous chapter, that the Sphinx is much older than most Egyptologists would like us to believe. Robert Schoch and I have since expanded the scope of our theory. We believe that the dramatic and imposing appearance of the split lioness inspired writing in the first place. Her symbolic impact sowed the seed of civilization—writing, congregation and settled life, megalithic architecture, domesticated food production, the arts and science.

Writing at Göbekli Tepe

This idea came to us from what we earlier discovered at another, pre-historic megalithic site, still unexplored in 1992, Göbekli Tepe, the oldest known structures of which date to the tenth millennium BC. There is no shortage of ideas as to what the mysterious reliefs carved into several of the T-shaped pillars were meant to mean, but I think we had a fortuitous edge. As is the case with the monumental lioness in Egypt that we think seeded a civilization through her sheer symbolic power, we think another version of the same process happened in Göbekli Tepe.

The question I then still asked myself was this: Was the archive the statue herself, and what was in it was really the idea it planted in prehistoric people to use symbols to unite, write, and create?

You can certainly record a story with pictures, but it only becomes writing when the pictures are used as words and eventually as the basic sounds, we string together to say those words. To give an example, we think that the JAW-Mehit ligature symbol literally meant opener of Mehit and more abstractly Guardian of the Mehit archive. Therefore, JAW-Mehit was used as a picture word phrase, probably by people who lived in Lower Egypt who used this more primordial form of pictographic word writing.

In the hieroglyphic script of Upper Egypt, however, phonographic sym-bols stood for the sounds making up these words. This is a more advanced way to write because you can use fewer symbols to spell most of the words you need. You do not have to find an image for each word in the language. This may explain, in part at least, why foreign picture words from Lower Egypt disappeared from Upper Egyptian hieroglyphic soon after unifi-cation of the two lands by Horus-Narmer. The words they represented could now be spelled with a smaller set of sound symbols. Picture words made a big come-back in hieroglyphic, however, in the New Kingdom, Late Period, and during Ptolemaic rule. The initial set of seven hundred hieroglyphs used in old Egypt became a very confusing repertoire of over seven thousand symbols used to add visual nuances to phonetic spellings and to cryptographically enhance the more abstract meanings.

In the summer of 2018, Schoch was interested in the potential that the animals and abstract symbols on some of the T-shaped pillars were an early form of writing. The discoverer of Göbekli Tepe, Klaus Schmidt himself, had hinted in one of his lectures that they may tell a story. He published a paper with Ludwig Morenz in 2009, sketching out a blueprint of how one might go about to prove an early form of symbolic writing there.[293]

The other way to look the symbols on these T-shaped pillars is, of course, that they could have just been non-symbolic images combined in an act of artistic expression, without a deeper meaning, let alone written text. The question was, of course, how could one tell? Help came unexpectedly from the script of another, much later culture, you might say "lost" until just few decades ago due to lack of interest more than anything else.

Lost Trojans

I had never been to the Göbekli Tepe site.[294] I felt apprehensive about this and expressed my concern to Schoch about not having the visual context and feel for this magnificent, ancient place. Still, I began to fish for something that could help us. In the beginning of a project, I usually toss a wide net. I may branch out into only vaguely related areas and sometimes even into areas that may not have any obvious connection with the question at hand. Often, this is when I find the most interesting things.

This time the net fell on two interesting internet lectures: One given by Eberhard Zangger at the Swiss Mountain Resort of Klosters in 2015[295] entitled *The Luwians: A Lost Civilization Comes Back to Life*, and the other presented by Petra Goedegebuure at the Oriental Institute in Chicago in 2016 on Luwian hieroglyphs. I had never heard of the Luwians. It turns out that many historians, archaeologists, and the public at large today have not either. The reason is that the culture of the Luwians has not been adequately studied until recently. Politics are to blame to no small degree.

When initial evidence of the major Bronze Age civilizations across the Levant and the Mediterranean coasts surfaced in the late 1800s and early 1900s, thought leaders in the field began to literally rewrite history to accommodate the new findings, but they were not always guided by evidence. One, outspoken and influential alike, was the English archaeologist Sir Arthur John Evans (1851–1941). He had excavated the Minoan palace at Knossos on the Greek island of Crete in the early 1900s. Evans painted a lop-sided picture of history by amplifying the importance of the three main Greek cultures, Minoan, Cycladic, and Mycenean, but initially neglected the Hittites and Trojans in Asia Minor and ancient Armenia that make up part of today's country of Turkey. This left a big void of Bronze

Age history creating paradoxes few have wanted to investigate, even in this century. Evans deserves some blame for that.

He loved Greek culture. On the other hand, he was offended by what he considered the barbaric Turks who were at war with the Greeks in the Greco-Turkish War (1919-1922). Evans did not mince his words expressing his disdain. This anti-Turkish bias by such a giant of archaeology squelched efforts by others to research the cultures of Asia Minor for decades and fill the gaps in history.

For example, Zangger points out a paradox begging to be investigated: Most of the celebrated Greek scientists, philosophers, and poets before Socrates came from the western coastal area of Asia Minor. But this was far east and away from the major Greek economic centers on Arthur Evans' map of the Bronze Age, i.e., not mainland Greece or its islands to the south. What nearby economic infrastructure in western Asia Minor had supported such a high culture in this region? There was none, or rather, none had yet been discovered. This, even though nineteenth century travelers to Anatolia had long found numerous rock reliefs with symbolic inscriptions *not* written in cuneiform, the lingua franca of ancient Mesopotamia and beyond.

The break-through came in 1946 with a relief at Karatepe in southern Anatolia. This bilingual inscription, the equivalent of what the Rosetta Stone did for Champollion, helped German archaeologist Helmuth Bossert and his Turkish student from Istanbul University, Halet Çambel, translate the unknown Luwian language into the already translatable Phoenician language.

The solution to the paradox of high culture at the western coast of Asia Minor with no economic infrastructure to fuel it is now known: This lost civilization were the Luwians, who for example built the legendary city of Troy. The Luwians existed long before, and long after the Hittite Empire, had their own system of writing using Luwian hieroglyphs, and were probably the mysterious, marauding sea peoples who attacked Egypt during her nineteenth and twentieth dynasties. It is a confederation of Luwian city states that may have brought the Hittite empires to its knees, or at least that is what Eberhard Zangger thinks.

God Symbol

From Petra Goedegebuure's lecture at the O.I., I learned that Luwian hieroglyphs, not unlike Egyptian hieroglyphs, encoded a combination of partial and whole words. The main differences are that Luwian sound symbols derive from the initial sound of a spoken word whose image is shown in the symbol, the so-called acrophonic principle, and that they included vowels.

Egyptian sound symbols, on the other hand, typically encode dominant consonants from within the words, which may or may not be the first few sounds. In addition, except weak, vowel-like consonants like "3" [uh], "j" [aye], and "w" [ooah], there are no pure vowel symbols in hieroglyphic, even though they were undoubtedly spoken based on what Coptic sounds like. Another difference is that the basic sound unit to make words in Luwian is a syllable and in hieroglyphic it is a consonant.

However, both languages occasionally use symbols that encode an entire word—both Luwian and Egyptian, at times, use logograms. Word symbols represent the whole spoken word, not merely a partial sound of a such word. One often used Luwian word symbol is the word for God.

At 17:00 into Petra Goedegebuure's lecture, I had to hit pause. There it was: the Luwian symbol for God. I knew immediately I had seen it before. *But where?*

Uncannily, I had seen it on photos of the carved belt worn by a T-shaped stone monolith in Enclosure D at Göbekli Tepe (figure 105). *Could this really be the same symbol?* I was looking for proof of writing, but I had not expected *this*.

The earliest known Luwian records date to circa 2000 BC, but pillar 18 of Enclosure D was at least 7,500 years older. Could it be that humans invented abstract symbol writing much earlier than commonly believed, before they lived in stable settlements, before they planted and raised food?

Luwian symbols have been found from all four corners of Asia Minor including the region of Göbekli Tepe. This somewhat raised the odds to my thinking that there could be a connection, no matter how far-fetched. One problem with the idea was that the megalithic circles, ovals, and squares at Göbekli Tepe were deliberately buried by the same culture that built, worshiped, and feasted there. The site was discovered in a pristine state by

Figure 105: Top, the Luwian symbol for God. ©, T. Bilgin; modified. Bottom, the symbol carved on Pillar 18 inside Enclosure D at Göbekli Tepe, recreated at Şanlıurfa Museum, Şanlıurfa, Turkey. Photo taken January 2020.

Klaus Schmidt and the German Archaeological Institute in the mid-1990s, after more than nine thousand years. However, I had to consider one scenario Schoch and I had envisioned: that megalithic structures from a lost civilization discovered by ancient people could seed new civilizations by their perceived symbolism. In this case, I had to consider that much later cultures in the region including the Luwians could have stumbled over T-shaped pillars marked with non-symbolic images, and simply invented a system of writing because they believed the pillars to be of divine origin, not because they saw word symbols they could read, or shared a common linguistic origin and its symbols.

Nevertheless, I was struck by the fact that the Luwian God symbol look-alike made sense in the context of an ornamental belt on an abstract statue of a supernatural being in Enclosure D at Göbekli Tepe. This is a context the Luwians would likely not have known from an accidental surface find since these statues were deep under the ground hidden for most of the Neolithic through the Bronze Age until the mid-1990s when Klaus Schmidt discovered them.

Therefore, what made the most sense to me was the tradition of the original script must have stayed alive above ground. This cultural link across a millennia-long gap between the indigenous Luwian people of Anatolia and Armenia in the Bronze Age and the people who built Göbekli Tepe during the Neolithic age of Mesopotamia implies a deeply engrained habit to record and store ideas.

Would it be possible, then, to crack the code of the images on the T-shaped pillars? Would it be possible to translate the story Klaus Schmidt had divined they tell, using the hieroglyphs of the Luwians? A lofty goal, but all it takes sometimes is one tiny crack in the door to a mystery and it opens itself for you. The Luwian God Symbol was a good opener.

In his earlier publications, Schmidt, for example with Joris Peters, had searched for clues in the composition of dead animal remains at Göbekli Tepe. By identifying animals either killed for food, or perished from other causes, they hoped to find the reason why certain animals were carved onto only some of the T-shaped pillars.[296] Without strongly favoring any one explanation and only tentatively falsifying one of them,[297] the authors tended towards totemism or shamanism. About the T-shaped pillars themselves they asked:[298]

> *Do they represent anthropomorphic gods, shamans, ancestors, stone spirits or even demons?*

Interestingly, they restricted their interpretations of the megalithic stone decorations at Göbekli Tepe to the realm of pre-civilized Earthly rituals, such as rituals for the afterlife, shamanic rituals to promote spiritualism, hunting rituals, totem-like identification of various regional tribes, and rites of passage. They largely ignored any potential preoccupation with the sky with respect to interpreting the imaged carved into the pillars or the pillars themselves.

Alternative history researchers and archaeoastronomers quickly filled this niche left by the archaeologists. They focused on the sky over Göbekli Tepe. Researchers like Burra G. Sidharth,[299] Robert Schoch,[300] Giulio Magli,[301] Andrew Collins,[302] Martin B. Sweatman,[303] and Dimitrios Tsikritsis, for example, believe that the pillars and animals are imagined shapes prehistoric people saw in prominent groups of stars, like our constellations. These researchers have proposed, for example, that the carvings represent monumentalized records of precession, or a pictorial narration recounting a catastrophic event worthy of remembrance, as well as a warning to future people.

The third possibility, that animal and abstract symbols were used to record and store ideas has not been further investigated. In the absence of a code breaker like the Rosetta Stone in Egypt, or the Phoenician-Luwian bilingual Kara Tepe stone plate, this would be a difficult undertaking. Without anything in the archaeological record that resembles writing for an almost eight-thousand-year long timespan between the oldest pillars of Göbekli Tepe and Luwian seals with hieroglyphs, this possibility seems far-fetched.

Yet, animals prominently feature in the pictographic alphabets of ancient people like the Luwians and the Egyptians. The proportion of animals and animal parts making up symbols in the almost six hundred different Luwian hieroglyphs is more than ten percent. In the earliest known set of Egyptian hieroglyphs, animals accounted for almost half of all symbols. Göbekli Tepe, of course, is littered with animal images, with a few abstract shapes among them. If the site were from the Bronze Age, would other archaeologists be more inclined to consider that they are a form of writing?

Ask yourself why they might not think it is. Is it *only* for lack of sufficient evidence, or is there *also* a dose of probability bias confounding the judgment? That deeply ingrained bias comes from our linear, materialistic model of history, doesn't it?

"Animal Spirits" versus Marx

As unlikely as it may seem, it is possible, regardless of our paradigmatic probability bias, that snakes, foxes, bores, cranes, aurochs, wild sheep, wild ass, gazelles, leopards, bears, and scorpions along with H-shaped, C-shaped, U-shaped, and half-moon shaped-images carved in high relief onto T-shaped megalithic pillars were words or syllables lined up to make words and to tell a story. This, unlike images used to imitate the real world without intent to communicate a worded message would indeed be writing.

Ludwig Morenz, Klaus Schmidt,[304] and Robert Schoch[305] had asked themselves this very question years earlier on the heels of an idea first floated by renowned CNRS[306] archaeologist Jacques Cauvin at the turn of this century. Cauvin suggested that Pre-pottery Neolithic writing, symbolism and religion came *before* a settled lifestyle and domesticated food production. If it can be proven that spiritualism, symbolism, and writing came before a settled lifestyle, then the dogma widely accepted by many archaeologists, historians, and economists that material progress was needed to make ethereal pursuits possible will fall.

With the Luwian word for God in hand, I briefly met with Schoch and his wife Catherine "Katie" Ulissey at the Portal to Ascension Conference in Irvine, California, in October of 2018. Out of this meeting came my, thus far, favorite publication. We co-authored an article for *Archaeological Discovery Journal*: "World's First Known Written Word at Göbekli Tepe on T-Shaped Pillar 18 Means God."

In this February 2019 paper, Schoch and I lay out the evidence that ties the Luwian hieroglyphic language to the stone images of Göbekli Tepe. We concluded that written language was not only invented by prehistoric human beings before they grew and raised food but also that the power of written symbols was the organizing principal that catapulted human existence from living in small bands of hunters and gatherers to larger groups of people unifying under a non-material, higher-order, spiritual idea.

This congregational effect—modern economists call it agglomeration—set the stage for innovation and implementation, the engine of human progress. God and ethereal culture in the form of symbolic writing came *before* material evolution. The spiritual aspect of living together, we argued, is what made the material possible, the exact opposite of the prevailing paradigm. Therefore, *God before symbols*; *symbols before food*.

That is the far-reaching dogma buster we confirmed in the paper. We concluded that Jacques Cauvin had been correct. There was writing at Göbekli Tepe. That, to us, was the seed of civilization; forgotten knowledge in the form of an idea preserved in symbolic writing passed to another time to relaunch civilized living in large groups after a wave of destruction. That was the seed: The power of symbols to congregate scattered people. When people united, they conquered adversity best. Do we not do that now?

This mechanism of cultural evolution is in stark contrast to the prevailing archaeological dogma of the twentieth century that cultural evolution only rides on the back of material and methodical evolution unrelated to outside influence by other cultures, either older or intruding. Materialism dictates that progress is a largely linear, one-way climb up the ladder of progress. This assumption is really the core reason why cultural evolution is likewise believed to be linear since only materialism drives culture in this paradigm. This is how this model of Marxist archaeology works: from originally primitive and egalitarian, through ever more advanced, yet inequitable, slavery, feudalistic, and capitalistic intermediate phases, to eventually reaching the final stages of socialism and purely egalitarian communism.

In other words, this school of thought, Marxist archaeology, wants to interpret the past in a way to predict what will, but really what it thinks *should*, happen in the future. It is the subjective, normative bias creeping into efforts to make sense of archaeological finds that is unscientific, since it corrupts the needed objectivity with ideas about what ought to be, rather than what the evidence suggests. If you wish, you can put a name on one of the consequences of normative bias: political correctness.

The materialistic model of cultural progress developed in the early to mid-Twentieth Century has biased archaeologists and historians in their interpretation of material remains from people alive in remote times. Like Arthur Evans, Australian archaeologist Vere Gordon Childes was instrumental in propagating Marxist scholarly bias in a generation of western archaeologists who followed him. This bias, though challenged since by processual archaeologists,[307] still reverberates today as post-processual archaeology, characterized by its insistence that subjectivity is justified when interpreting archaeological material.

If you thought archaeology has nothing to do with politics and only science, think again. The materialistic angle to reading the past originally came from the fundamental economic principles of state and family thought of and formulated by Karl Marx and Friedrich Engels in the late nineteenth century. Based on Marxism, Soviet archaeologists like Vladislav Iosifovich Ravdonikas (1884-1976) proposed a state-approved theory of cultural human evolution. This theory was based exclusively on material progress. The

Soviet state wanted to hit back against culture-historical archaeology it associated with elitism and inequality, because this interpretative approach to reading the past had likewise been abused to create a biased angle in the furtherance of authoritarian and dictatorial ideologies, based on differences between people and populations.

Childes became a principal proponent of Marxist archaeology in the west. The irony is that Ravdonikas studied Neolithic petroglyphs at Lake Onega, east of Finland, where the swan is a prominent supernatural symbol carved into the rock many times as a spiritual aid to help prehistoric humans overcome material hardship due to floods caused by climate change.[308]

This ideological bias—the theory by Ravdonikas that there can be no cultural progress without first a step forward in the technological level of materialism and needs met—turned into blinders afflicting the discipline of archaeology even today. It means that the tacitly preferred interpretation of an archaeological find is a material, pragmatic explanation. But why is it preferred?

Because the wide-spread bias generated by a paradigm that teaches materialistically driven culture, or any paradigm I should add, makes the interpretation appear more plausible, and hence more acceptable, even though it is nothing but a normative bias disguised, in this particular case of Marxism-influenced archaeology, as a materialistic context standard.

In other words higher culture, due to intrusion, is shunned as an explanation for a material find if the level of materialism discovered does not support it. The shunning is then justified based on a lack of context. Hence the argument is dismissed as implausible. Since archaeologists profess they must use context to divine the meaning of their unearthed relics, the bias they, wittingly or unwittingly, employ to generate that context can create the illusion that their interpretations are based on reasonable, and therefore plausible, standards when these standards could in fact be based on subjective ideas influenced by unscientific, normative doctrines.

To be clear, any plausibility bias, whether based on biased ideas about what the context should be or not, has nothing to do with science. In science, anything possible, *no matter how improbable*, could be the right explanation for an observation unless it is falsified by proof. My point is simply that plausibility is no substitute for evidence. Yet, plausibility arguments seem to, at times, creep into a scholar's rationale, and it happens across all disciplines, especially archaeology and history.

In contradistinction to the material model of history, a non-material, primarily idea-based organizing principle could have just as much of an evolutionary advantage as a material one. This force would be in the ball-park of what John Maynard Keynes called "Animal Spirits."[309] Material progress depends on time-consuming skill and method development, which requires risk-taking and a supply surplus. Cultural progress can, in fact, be much faster.

If there ever was a selective advantage for human beings to gather in larger crowds to exchange ideas and help each other to make them into methods, as opposed to roam in small bands, then a unifying idea could spark, and rapidly so, a leap in progress. And to create such a spark, sym-bols and writing were the flint and tinder. Schoch and I call this spark the seed of civilization.

As I continued to learn about Luwian, I was struck by the simplicity of the acrophonic principle employed to make the symbols. Learning to read would simply require recognizing the image shown and pronouncing its first two sound elements, for example "el" in "elements." The leap from artistic drawings to symbols used to write, as I see it, begins when drawn images are used to name things. This is what I think some of the groups of animals represent carved from the T-shaped pillars. I think they are names. I agree with Morenz and Schmidt who considered the same.[310]

Yet, when it comes to representing higher ideals, abstract symbols do better than concrete ones. Different people will identify with different concrete images, but they may be willing to unify and share ideas and things under the same abstract symbol that favors no one group's identity to be claimed. It is this context, within which the more abstract T-, H-, U-, and C-like symbols at Göbekli Tepe could be viewed. Interestingly, while Schoch and I came to the conclusion that the word for God on Pillar 18 was a congregational, group-unifying symbol, Bruce Fenton made the connection between this symbol and a similar Aboriginal sign that means "two people sitting to share knowledge."[311] Whether or not there is a causal link, as Fenton proposed, this parallel is still remarkable in terms of the universality of the association between two completely different cultures and times.

Symbolic versus Concrete Archive

When I look at the Great Sphinx through this prism of symbols and writing, naturally I ask myself the same question. Was she really an outgrowth of Egyptian High Culture during the Pyramid Age or did an earlier statue in her place, by sheer virtue of its magnificence, launch, or rather relaunch, a deeply cultured civilization by the Nile? Did its mere symbolism of divine creative forces on Earth spark the invention of writing as an inspiration to reenact creation on rock, wood, bone, and papyrus? Let me show you what I have in mind when I ask this question.

The symbol of Heka is one of the oldest Egyptian hieroglyphs known: It is made from the lion's hind paws, haunch, and tail. And how did the Major Fissure split the Great Sphinx (figure 106)?

Figure 106: The Heka divine force of nature, symbolized by the lion's hind section, and placed on a standard. Compare the iconography to the hind section of the Great Sphinx split off by the Great Fissure (now repaired), and the iconography of JAW-Mehit. From one of the Lebanese Cedar panels originally decorating wall niches in the Saqqara mastaba tomb of Hesy-*Rᶜ*. The Museum of Egyptian Antiquities, Cairo, Egypt, 2018, and Giza, Egypt, 2019.

This was my initial, more modest, more ethereal working hypothesis before I began to write this book in December of 2019. I thought that a prehistoric lioness statue could have been the civilization-seeding equivalent of the Luwian God symbol on Pillar 18, and that the three symbols of a split lion in Egypt had their origin in the appearance of this fissured and split stony Mehit at Giza who then became the Great Sphinx.

I remember one evening in Torremolinos, Spain after dinner with Robert and Michele Bauval and his brother, the architect Jean-Paul, with his wife Pauline Bauval. We were strolling down the promenade when Robert asked me if I had plans for a book. I told him that I had thought about it, but that I did not have a good idea for a topic. I thought that I had told my contribution to the Sphinx story as best as I could have done. But I could not get Robert's question out of my mind. Did he sense something over dinner I said could grow into that idea?

During that summer and fall, I tossed my net wide and far. I started reading about libraries and archives. I ended up with the word *ʿfdt*, the coffin texts, the *Book of Two Ways*, and finally the Vignette of *Rʿ*. Robert's harmless question made me look for a new question and that is exactly what I found.

With the new evidence I found, I was forced to fearlessly ask a much more concrete question about the Great Sphinx. It went beyond my original, modest model of seeding civilization. I now had to consider, no matter how implausible, that a real archive was once under her, an archive of prehistoric symbols, symbols such as the ones carved on the T-shaped pillars of Göbekli Tepe, which triggered a leap in the quality of life and led to the development of the ancient Egyptian culture. And I would then have to consider from where these symbols came.

My research had put me where I did not want to be: in front of Plato's Atlantis story and Edgar Cayce's prophecy of the *Hall of Records*. This quest is the holy grail of alternative history researchers who believe that ancient cultures across the world have too much in common to not have had a common origin of knowledge to seed their civilizations. This is the core thesis the hunt for evidence of which Graham Hancock has made his life's work to pursue and has chronicled in the books he has written over the years. Up to this point, I had looked at the *after*, the power of symbolic seeds sown once inherited to jump start a new cycle of civilization. Now I was confronted with the *before*. Who first made them, and how were they passed on?

In our "Fissure," paper, Robert Schoch and I wanted to explain the profound effect symbols had on the people who lived by the Nile, as we had proposed in Mesopotamia. The prophecy of the *Hall of Records* is about an archive of exceptional knowledge yet to be unsealed by humanity. But we had collected evidence of the footprints of a strange infusion of esoteric culture pervading the ancient Egyptians, as if an Atlantean archive had long been opened.

The split lion iconography suggested by the fissured lioness was used in two completely different contexts involving writing, one economic and the other spiritual. Could material and cultural evolution both be fueled by the same idea of a split lion? For an idea so pervasive, it must have been there from the beginning of civilization.

Snapshot of Giza before the Sphinx

That is what we observed: The idea of a split lion appeared on shipping labels used in ancient Egypt's oil trade *and* in her most intellectual cosmogony, that of Memphis describing how the world was created. It boils down to oil and creation words.

Oil was a precious commodity to the ancient Egyptians, even before unification. The production, filling, sealing, shipping, and storage of oil across Egypt was therefore an important aspect of the economy of the king's land and its trade with foreign people. It is this economic context in which we see some of Egypt's earliest known written documents in the form of painted marks, sealings, and shipping tags (figure 107); the latter used in Egypt's precious oil deliveries.

Oil tags, as they are called for short, were squared bone pieces. Carved from wood or ivory, they contained three basic pieces of information: They identified the reigning king of the time and his vizier; they identified the significant events of the year of this king's reign in which the given tag was made; they identified information about the oil's quality, quantity, and shipping destination.

The reason why archaeologists were able to discover many of these written economic records is that they were attached not only to shipments sent to the living but also to the tombs of the dead. Kings, queens, and high

Figure 107: Oil shipping tag from the reign of Horus-Djet, First Dynasty, dated to circa 2900 BC. From the Saqqara mastaba S3504. The Museum of Egyptian Antiquities, Cairo, Egypt, 2018.

officials believed that they needed these supplies in the afterlife. In their tombs, these economic records remained preserved for thousands of years.

In the example above, we are informed that the era is the reign of Horus-Djet and his vizier *Swḏk3*. The year is that in which the symbols of the ibis and the double lotus were born, in which a basement facility was planned, and in which the king stayed at the palace of the two mistresses—make of it what you will. The association between ibis and basement is an intriguing combination suggesting the planning of an underground facility used for writing and archiving.

The oil mentioned in this tag is of an intermediate press effluent quality, the quantity is 1100 (1000+100) fruit branches, and the destination is the south. Notice the symbol resembling a leg, or fissure, which indicates intermediate grade. I should clarify at this point that the standard interpretation of the symbol is an animal leg encoding the word for repeat, *wḥm* [oo-hem]. Schoch and I thought that it must be a symbol for a better grade than a repeat press since it was attached to a container inside of a private, high official tomb at Saqqara. We concluded that this must be an intermediate, middle grade between best first and worst last, symbolized by frontal and caudal lion parts.

This symbol is the same, so we argue, as the one on the predynastic jar from tomb U-546 (figure 104). Instead of representing *wḥm*, it means intermediate grade, symbolized by a fissure or crack-like symbol splitting front and back. This interpretation is supported by ivory tags Dreyer and the D.A.I. discovered at Tomb UJ (figure 108).

Figure 108: Three of the ivory tags found by the German Archaeological Institute at *Rᶜ- pqr*/Umm El-Qa'ab at Abydos. ©, Günter Dreyer. Public Domain.

Among these earliest known examples of writing, the official start of history if you will, is one tag which shows the same symbol under the crescent sign next to what looks like a cobra symbol for the sound "*ḏ*" [jeh] and the mountain sign *ḏw* [joo] demonstrating the practice of phonetic complementation even at this early stage of the language (see Appendix). This combination could be read as "Mountain of Darkness" or "Dark Mountain." Darkness is deepest between evening and morning, and so this imagery makes good sense. The fissure sign denoted the middle of the night when darkness peaks between sunset and sunrise. I should add that one other way to read the crescent sign is *ḥwᶜ* [hoo-aah], "tiger nut." Thus the combination of crescent-fissure by itself as seen on the jar from Tomb U-546 may indicate "tiger nut oil, intermediate press." On balance, therefore, interpreting the fissure sign to mean "middle/intermediate" makes a lot more sense than to read it as "repeat/recurrent."

In our reconstruction, which agrees with that of Wolfgang Helck, the frontal lion symbol designated the first liquid fraction of the oil press. This was the best quality oil and is the most common symbol seen on jars found in royal tombs. The fissure-like symbol, we argued however, denoted intermediate quality, and did not represent a repeat run of the already once-extracted wet paste through the oil press. A repeat press would yield an inferior oil quality than what the caudal half of the lion indicated. The latter, we concluded, was used to label the last fluid fraction of the oil press, the most inferior effluent after the first, and intermediate. Records of this inferior cut were only found among private persons' grave goods.

The significance of these symbols in the overall context of writing in Egypt cannot be overstated. The split lion iconography had captivated and prompted Egypt's original scribes to assimilate it into the language as word symbols for first, between, and last. This, I emphasize, even though the lion was a revered animal, as can be gleaned from predynastic palettes where it is always shown whole as a symbol of strength and power.[313]

Why did the king permit to depict such a majestic beast in pieces and use the parts to designate front and back, first, and last? My explanation for this is that the ancients must have witnessed a real, physical example of this impressionable iconography, including the split. This physical model of the symbols must have been so profoundly influential that it was believed to have been made by the gods, including the otherwise irreverent crack in the middle.

At this point everything was pointing to the stony lioness Mehit, but what I was missing was an actual image to prove it. And this image, surprisingly, exists in the form of an ebony plate Egyptologists have interpreted to be another oil tag (figure 109).

This wooden tablet, like the sealing from the Abydos tomb of Horus-Djer showing Mehit at Rostau, was found there by Flinders Petrie. On it, and unmistakably so, is a lion and a square building, the two comparing roughly in size. Inside the building are three ape-like figures. When I first saw this, I thought this is as good an ancient snapshot, as a tourist today would take standing south of the Great Sphinx with a view of the monument and the Sphinx Temple in front. There even is another subtle feature which identifies this image with the Sphinx ditch: the vertical drop-off from terrace 2 to terrace 1 on which the Sphinx Temple rests. In ancient Egyptian art, three-dimensional depth was depicted vertically and so the walls on this relief are not vertical but were meant to show depth.

The problem for the orthodox model of the age of the Great Sphinx is this: This tablet is five centuries older. It shows not a Sphinx, but a lion. I say it is Mehit. This is as close to a falsification of the main-stream model as you could devise: an actual image of a lion statue at Giza before the Old Kingdom.

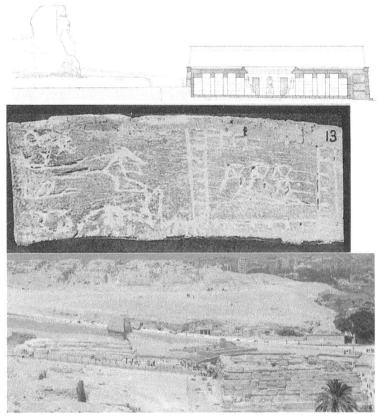

Figure 109: Top, graphic recreation of the Great Sphinx and Sphinx temple, simulated view from the south looking north; Ricke (1970), Plan 4, mirrored. Middle, Ebony Wood tablet found in the tomb of Horus-Djer by Petrie (1901), extra plates. Bottom, photo of the same view. ©, Digital Giza, Harvard University.

I did not dig up this tablet. Petrie did over a century ago. Why did Egyptologists miss the significance of this? Because they have been led by the prevailing historical narrative to reject the idea of a monument at Giza before the Great Sphinx in the Old Kingdom. This wooden tablet is much older than Khafre, the alleged maker of the Great Sphinx, alive around 2500 BC.

The only reason why the conventional interpretation entices is that one's reason must tolerate the lesser paradox: that this is an oil tag which designates a quality of oil, *at once superior and inferior*, in the same jar. Does this seem more acceptable because it relieves one of the obligations

263

to accept a lion older than the Sphinx the size of an entire building, and the likes of it can only be seen at Giza?

Could I be accused of succumbing to my own confirmation bias in expecting a lion monument before the Old Kingdom only to find it here? Of course.

However, the strangeness of this tablet does not go away, no matter through which prism you view it, orthodox, or alternative. None of the usual symbols typically seen on oil tags are unequivocally visible, not that this matters to what we are seeing on this tablet. There is no sign of the king or his vizier, there is no year symbol (*rnpt*), there are no events recorded to identify which year is meant, there are no symbols designating the quantity of oil or its destiny, and there is no hole to affix it, if this were a shipping label.

Even if the front and back of the lion here are oil quality identifiers, we are still left with the paradox I already mentioned: Why would anyone label oil quality as both superior and inferior? I think, we must come to terms with what we are concretely looking at here. We must consider a different model of history. I think what we are looking at here is what the other evidence I have cited so far is already telling us: This is the wood-carved image of Mehit, the stony lioness.

We must consider that what is shown on this tablet is what inspired Egypt's first scribes to invent three symbols for the purpose of writing in the economic context of oil shipping. To her front was a temple connected with three monkeys, not three prisoners as Flinders Petrie suggested. The figures shown do not look human to me. They look like seated baboons. There is good evidence that baboons featured prominently in at least one of the two temples in front of the Great Sphinx and symbolically in the other. *But what is the meaning of this strange image? Is it a real scene or is it mythical?*

Three Monkeys, Moon, and Creation

Eventually one must pull all the evidence together that has been scattered around into one place to see the larger proof. That time has now come. We have three written records from the same grave, the tomb of Horus-Djer, the third king who reigned over the two lands of Egypt: A sealing which shows Mehit in front of the *pr-wr* shrine looking east at Rostau (Chapter VIII).

A bone tag that records the opening of the place of the archive (Chapter II). And now, a monumental lioness statue next to the temple with three baboons inside.

But there is one more crucial piece of evidence I must mention here. During the reign of Horus-Djer, a new goddess appears on the scene, by inauguration so to speak. She was none other than Seshat, the patroness of astronomy and archiving (figure 110).

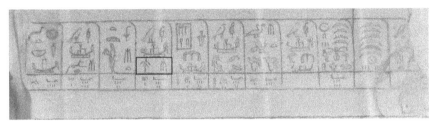

Figure 110: Royal Annals of the Old Kingdom of Ancient Egypt, Palermo Stone fragment. This row from the recto shows the yearly entries during the reign of Horus-Djer (circa 2900 BC). The frame highlights the year of the inauguration of the Seshat symbol as a numen, *ms-sšt*. Copy of the Palermo Stone original. The Museum of Egyptian Antiquities, Cairo, Egypt, 2017.

Her name[314] is recorded on one of the fragments left of a stone plate called the Royal Annals of the Old Kingdom of Ancient Egypt, the Palermo Stone. Even though this stone plate was prepared in the Fifth Dynasty, the entrees believably chronicle the year-defining events attributed to the kings of Egypt's first four dynasties, and the first three kings of the Fifth. Even a few archaic, predynastic rulers are mentioned. On the Palermo stone, a copy of which can be viewed at the Cairo Museum, an entry identifies a particular year of the reign of Horus-Djer, when the king travelled his land by ship at the occasion of the biennial Horus-Escort[315]; the Nile level during this year's inundation was five cubits. In the same year, the Seshat symbol was born.

Let me be blunt here, if I may: The inauguration of the ancient Egyptian goddess of archives during the reign of a king when an archive was opened while an east-facing lioness at Rostau guarded a writer's shrine sitting next to a temple with three creation words in the shape of baboons sums up to a lot of footprints leading to the real *Hall of Records*.

These are the pieces of a story that recounts the opening of a hidden archive under the Sphinx and what was found inside: a symbolic record of creation. The image you are looking at carved into ebony is an image of creation, but we don't have the whole story. The tablet is broken.

What I will do now, and in the next chapter is to reconstruct the origin of this creation story for you with the evidence I have discovered. I will take you to the real *Hall of Records* and what was inside.

Like the ibis and the lion, it turns out, the baboon and the lion go far back in the records of ancient Egypt. For example, in the burial chamber of the once magnificent, First Dynasty mastaba 3507[316] atop the northeast ridge of the Saqqara necropolis. This is where high officials like princes, princesses, and viziers of the early royal court were buried. British Egyptologist Walter Bryan Emery (1903-1971) found reliefs of lions and baboons in S3507. It helps to visualize the exact architectural context of these reliefs to appreciate their significance.

The tomb likely belonged to an old woman, queen Her-Neith, the wife of Horus-Djer, who was the grandfather of Horus-Den during whose time the tomb was probably built. Yes this is the same Horus-Djer who left us with more than one perplexing record Petrie discovered in this tomb at Abydos. The next piece of the puzzle is the burial chamber of his wife Her-Neith at S3507. This was the lowest point of the niched mastaba dug deep into the bedrock.

Inside the chamber, Emery found reliefs of lions and baboons near the place where the deceased queen rested. The motives shown in these images were not from the physical world of the living. They were images of the Netherworld. The chamber was meant to be in the *dw3t*. What was above, however, also mattered.

The above-ground roof of the burial chamber was a sloped mound of rubble resting on a flat timber ceiling covered with bricks in a shape resembling a pyramid, Egypt's first known use of this geometric design. The mud brick pyramid was then embedded inside the large rectangular, niched mastaba also built with mud bricks (figure 111).

Under this pyramid ceiling was another, deeper roof covering the south side of the burial chamber that was made from sculpted stonework. This stone roof protected the jars and pots carrying the grave goods, while the wooden roof over the northern part protected the sarcophagus of the queen. The lion and baboon reliefs belonged to the stone roof in the chamber. The latter was probably removed by tomb robbers in the process of breaking

Figure 111: Reconstruction of Saqqara mastaba 3507 by Walter Emery. Shown here is the burial shaft. The southern part was roofed with stone slabs and the position of the lintel with the lion relief is indicated by the pointer.

into the burial shaft. It was later reused to case a Third Dynasty shaft, cut into the rubble fill of one of the magazines of S3507.[318]

The important context of the couchant lion motive was its position in a protective roof inside a subterranean chamber covered by a pyramid-like mound. The lions symbolically protected the jars of precious goods underneath the roof and whatever else the queen took with her on her journey beyond. The big, sitting baboon in the other relief faces the approaching figures of the ancestral kings of Egypt, the manifestations of the Sun on Earth (figure 112).

Figure 112: Stone reliefs from the burial chamber of S3507. The upper pane shows couchant lions, and the lower pane shows The Great White Ape of the Ancestor kings, seen here approaching. Photos of Emery (1958), Plates 96 b. and 97 a.

He is the Great White (Baboon) of the Great Ones/Ancestor Kings, the *ʿ3 ḥḏ wrw* [aah-uh-hej-ooroo]. He was a symbol of divine, and royal ancestry, related to the Moon. The meaning of these features in the tomb of Her-Neith is that of a queen who expects to meet her royal forefathers in the afterlife once she resurrects. That resurrection happens in her coffin chamber, guarded by lions above, under the roof of a pyramid, the mound of original creation where order defeated chaos. In other words, the coffin chamber of Her-Neith is a recreation of the original archive under the Sphinx. What is missing is the portable archive.

268

How did her tomb designer know how to build this chamber unless he was inside the real chamber under the real lioness statue, where baboons stare from megalithic posts out at the rising Sun God?

Seated baboons in general were symbolic of the divine voices who greet the rising Sun in the east. And so I think what we are looking at in the wood-carved relief Petrie found in the tomb of Horus-Djer shown in figure 109 is the original, east-facing lioness statue, her temple, and three Sun-greeting baboons. The baboon was a manifestation of Thoth, the thinking heart-mind of the Sun *R͑*, and it was the animated being representing the first seven words of creation (figure 113), the *ḏ3jsw*, uttered by the creator god Ptah in the Memphite cosmogony of ancient Egypt.

Figure 113: Relief of the inner, western enclosure wall of the Edfu Temple showing Thoth, the seven *ḏ3jsw* baboons, and the two *šbtjw*. Edfu Temple, Egypt, May 2019.

Remember these words (see chapter VII)?

mn-qb: Oh, seat of the throne of Horus, splendid city, princess of cities, we provide the House of Life with glorifying words.

I interpret the symbolism as that of a union between the Sun and the Moon, creation as a thought first, then an utterance, the record of it created and stored in an archive for posterity, so that it may be consulted if ever needed again.

In the tablet, these creation words literally sit in the Sphinx Temple. This is where the original *House of Life* must be. This is the *House of Scrolls under the Arm*. This is the Netherworld House that contained the *ʿfdt* coffer of secret documents, the ones recited in the moment of divine creation of the universe and everything in it. But how can we be sure there ever were baboons there?

Indeed baboons were no strangers to the Valley Temple next to the Sphinx Temple. When German Architect Uvo Adolf Hölscher (1878-1963) excavated the portal and area in front of the Valley Temple[319]—the interior of which had already been cleared by Auguste Mariette between 1853 and 1860—he found the broken pieces of a giant granite statue of a baboon which once stood in a niche high above the southern Hathor gate to the temple.[320] This niche, like its northern gate counterpart, is still visible today.

With this context in mind, an association between a monumental lion and three baboons inside a temple, as shown on Horus-Djer's ebony wooden tablet, is made. Three stone pillars line the south and north edge of the central court of the Sphinx Temple. In our most recent 2019 paper, *Major Geological Fissure through Prehistoric Lion Monument at Giza Inspired Split Lion hieroglyphs and Ancient Egypt's Creation Myth*,[321] Schoch and I propose that these six pillars, three on the north end and three on the south end, symbolized three baboons. They have strange but now familiar names.

The fact that there are three baboons in the temple is not a coincidence. These three baboons can only be the same ones mentioned in the Edfu Temple where they represent three of the seven creation words. Their names are: The Beautiful Front, The Equipped Behind, and the Lord of the Red Ones. Three symbols to show a split lion and three baboons. Was there a connection?

In early 2019, I began to scour the Edfu texts that had recently been published and made available online by the Edfu Project.[322] The Edfu Temple proper is surrounded by a massive enclosure wall inscribed both inside and outside. It is within these texts that one finds numerous references to Thoth and baboons.

The texts in one place state, for example, that Thoth is the Heart of *Rʿ*, the Lord of Hermopolis, and the Master Scribe of the library. In another place, Thoth is identified in the form of an epithet as the *s3 wr ḫnt st-Rʿ* [sa-ur-khntj-set-rah], the great protective baboon on the seat of *Rʿ*.[323]

Yet in another inscription it is said that Thoth records the words of the seven baboons, the *ḏ3jsw* who come from the Great Mehit, the personification of the Great Flood, *wr-mḥt*. Elsewhere, we are told that the seven baboons are the words of creation at the beginning of the making of the world by Egypt's ultimate creator god Ptah in the Memphite cosmogony. Appropriately they are shown on the temple walls as scribes holding reeds and scrolls in their hands (figure 114). The association between these baboons, writing, and Thoth is unmistakable; so is Thoth's association with a library.

The most relevant inscription here, however, is the epithets given to three of seven baboon creation words to whom I earlier introduced you: Beautiful Front, Equipped Behind, and the Lord of the Red Ones (figure 114). Here they were.

Figure 114: Below, three of the *ḏ3jsw*. Above, their epithets: Beautiful Front, Equipped Behind, and the Lord of the Red Ones. Edfu Temple, Egypt, 2019.

The symbol used to write "front" on this segment of the Edfu wall, the frontal half of a baboon or even a lion, and the symbol used to write "behind" is the hind portion of a couchant lion or baboon. The third epithet, the Lord of the Red Ones, *nb dšrw* [neb-dje-se-roo] is a clever allusion to the red-faced, blood-tinged lions during a feast. In addition, *dš rw*, when read as two words, means *separated lion*.[324] By itself this word play may be insignificant, but in the context of symbols which show an animal split in two, one must begin to pay attention to such insinuations.

The evidently pervasive use of three symbols related to a split animal, whether lion or baboon, does not confine itself to a side story at Edfu, but is rather central to the Egyptian creation story recorded on the frieze immediately above the relief of the seven *ḏ3jsw* in the most inaccessible part of the temple. In the Memphite Cosmogony, creation is an act of thought and utterance. The medium through which Ptah utters the words of creation is *mḥt wrt* the Great Mehit, from whom they manifest as baboons. The gods of Egypt were the forces of nature. Baboons are not symbolic of but are one and the same as Ptah's creation words.[325] As such they are intimately connected with the origin of the world, with Egyptian Genesis. The "Great Lion(ess)" is even mentioned by name in the archaeological record of Khufu's Harbor at Wadi El-Jarf, discovered by a team of archaeologists led by Pierre Tallet: *wr-mj* [oor-my].

When viewed with this context of the creation story at Edfu, an ebony plate showing a couchant lioness next to a temple with three baboons makes a lot of sense. Are we still not ready to accept that what is being depicted there is the wood-carved "photo" of a real, primeval temple and stony lioness meant to symbolize Ptah's completed act of creation? Are the three baboons not the manifest creation words housed in the primordial archive of this temple? Are we here not looking at the First Moment of the First Time, *zp tpj*, and the original temple of Thoth?

Such profound effects on material and cultural expression in writing did the iconography of a split lion have on Egyptian civilization that the inspiration for it must have been triggered by something truly awesome. I think this awesome something was what we see on this piece of ebony: a monumental statue split by a force of nature standing magnificently at the foot of a hill formed by the Mokattam formation which courses through the Giza Plateau.

Thus far, the trail of written evidence that began in the *House of Life* at Hermopolis had taken me from a strange record of heliocentricity to an archive under an arm at Giza. That arm was the arm of Mehit, who symbolically protected the words of creation manifested as an aspect of Thoth, the baboon. Whoever made this archive laid into the ground the seeds of

Egypt's civilization, symbolic writing and the model of the universe that puts the Sun in its center.

But this gives rise to another question. If Mehit the lioness was a symbol of the Sun, then what was the role of the Moon in all this? What was the role of Thoth? The answer to this question I could not possibly have foreseen. It ended up taking me closer to the answers to the fundamental questions of my quest: When was Mehit made, and who made the archive under Mehit?

X

Thoth

IMAGINE YOU WERE AN ANT SITTING ON THE TIP OF A TINY BRANCH ENTANGLED inside the canopy of a tree. You can't see the tree for the twigs. But what happens when you simply crawl down the branch and just keep crawling? You end up finding the trunk of the tree and even the roots if you end up underground.

This trip down the tree begins with *Who was Thoth*? Was he ibis, baboon, the Moon, architect, judge, spell master, scribe, or scientist—or even all these? How did one god come to mean so many things?

To learn what Thoth had left under Mehit, I had to discover what united Mehit and Thoth in the first place. I had to meet Thoth at his origins. I had to walk back the lore of antiquity, through the myths of ancient Egypt, all the way back to the dawn of shaman culture. That is where I found Thoth. But Thoth is not who you and I may have thought He is.

While the evidence marries Mehit with the early beginnings of writing in ancient Egypt and likewise attributes it to the Egyptian Moon god Thoth, strangely, nothing brings together Mehit and Thoth. An archive under Mehit with three of Thoth's *ḏ3jsw* is difficult to think of without a mention of his name. Thoth, after all, is the author of the book in the mythical Archive under the Arm, the funerary texts tell us. The problem is, while lion and ibis appear together in predynastic art, none of the First Dynasty sealings with Mehit also show an emblem of Thoth the ibis. This, even though the ibis was already venerated as an image of a god before the creation of the dynastic state and before the first use of the Mehit seal by Narmer's administrative scribes (figure 115).

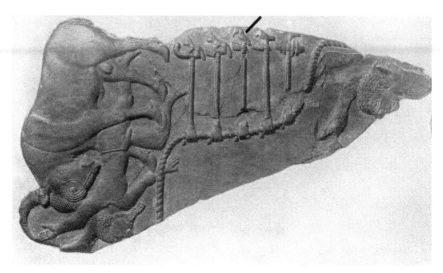

Figure 115: Bull Palette, dated to the Naqada III period, circa 3300-3100 BC An ibis on a standard is marked, next to the falcon god. Louvre Museum, Paris, France. Image from Petrie (1953), Plate G; modified.

Certainly, birds occur in some Mehit-sealings, but none of them are ibises.[326] Further complicating matters is that the iconographic prominence of Thoth only begins during the Old Kingdom, when that of Mehit already comes to its end (figure 116).

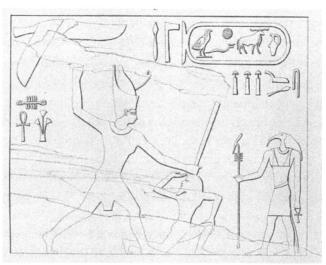

Figure 116: Illustration of a rock-relief showing Thoth presiding over Khufu as the king smites an enemy. Wadi Maghara, Sinai Peninsula. ©, Lepsius Tafelwerke, Old Kingdom. Lepsius-Project, Sachsen-Anhalt.

Looking for Thoth lore after the Greco-Roman era, you will not be hard-pressed to find plenty of vague associations between sacred books, Hermetic knowledge, the Emerald Tablet, secret archives, and hidden books. Invariably, the Great Sphinx gets mixed up with these tales, and a colorful carpet is woven from threads of few facts and lots of fiction.

The task laid out here in this chapter is to filter out the layers of hearsay and innuendos centuries of storytelling might have added to the core of physical reality on the ground. Its purpose is to investigate if the ancient Egyptians themselves gave us written clues about a direct link between a lioness guarding an archive of secret records and the Moon God of science and writing. By now I'm sure you suspect the encrypted nature of the information would make it difficult to be found. That's what I suspected too, and I wasn't disappointed.

Ultimately the bridge from Thoth to Mehit spans the gap between the astronomy of the Pyramid and Coffin Texts and symbolic writing. Without help from Egyptology, I could not have uncovered it. I am grateful, especially, to the great works of German Egyptologist and Astronomer Rolf Krauss[327] and Belgium-trained Egyptologist Wael Sherbiny.[328] The key to solving the puzzle began for me, however, when I found a sealing from the First Dynasty with Mehit in a context I had missed before. To resume the path of my investigation, I therefore take you now to a sealing with not one, but three lions (figure 117).

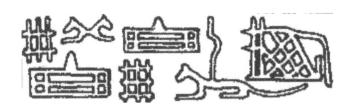

Figure 117: Sealing of Mehit from circa 2900-2800 BC showing the double lion Aker, commonly associated with ancient Giza, Rostau. From the Saqqara mastaba S3506, discovered by Walter Emery. From Kaplony, 1963, Tafel 43, Figure 151.

Conjoined Crescent

On this sealing, Mehit guards the administrative facility of the early kingdom in the familiar manner. The two repeated symbols phonetically spell the royal scribes' name, in this case *ḥtp* [hetep]. But what about the double lion symbol? That was later known as Aker. He was the god in Rostau who personified the netherwordly passage on whose back the shadow spirits of the royals and elite floated in their boats on their way to resurrection and ascension. We can draw a connection between this arrangement of symbols from the Early Dynastic Period, and a small illustration with captions[330] found on the floorboard of a Middle Kingdom coffin (figure 118). Cataloged as B3C from Deir El-Bersheh, it was discovered in a non-royal, private tomb. The illustration is from the *Book of Two Ways* I introduced in chapter IV and is unique to this cemetery.[331]

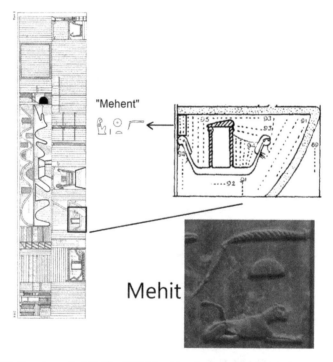

Figure 118: Floorboard of Coffin B3C. The Aker barque illustration is magnified and rotated. Embedded textual elements are shown as dotted lines. Textual Element 10 mentioning "Mehent" is framed. For comparison, the spelling of Mehit as seen on wood panels from the Saqqara tomb of the Third Dynasty official Hesy-*Rᶜ*. From de Buck (1961); modified.

You see a crescent-shaped boat resembling a double-headed humanoid, conjoined being. The braided beard indicates it is a god. On it is an enclosed shrine in familiar shape: An *ꜥfdt*, but here in boat-cabin form. One of the captions informs us that Osiris is inside the shrine hidden from Set, his archenemy.

In the Vignette of $R^ꜥ$, it is the Sun God who is shielded by the orbits of The Nine *ḥḥw*, or the nine elliptical bands called the Roads of Mehen in the text surrounding the vignette. The clue in the vignette connecting $R^ꜥ$ and Osiris is the Sun God's headdress. There you see an Osirian barque, a double-headed conjoined snake atop a pair of corkscrew ram horns. Two ostrich feathers and the White Crown of Egypt fuse into Osiris' Atef crown atop this barque (figure 119).

Figure 119: The crown of $R^ꜥ$ in the vignette. ©, Werner Forman Archive; agefotostock® HEZ-2571859.

You may think that the motives shown in two later examples from the Middle Kingdom came from the earlier in the Early Dynastic Period, but this is not so. All three have a much more ancient, prehistoric origin. We can see them in their primordial from painted onto predynastic pottery, some 5,400 hundred years ago (figure 120).

Instead of ostrich feathers, we see the whole bird. Instead of a double headed fantasy being, we see a crescent-shaped barque. Instead of the *ꜥfdt* boat cabin, we see two cabin-like boxes.

What did these haunting images mean in their original form? The Vignette of $R^ꜥ$ helps us to confirm what Egyptologists tell us about the

Figure 120: Predynastic Upper Egyptian Decorated Ware from circa 3450–3350 BC Rogers Fund, 1907. Photo courtesy of The Metropolitan Museum of Art, New York, NY. Public Domain.

ostrich and its feathers. They are symbols central to Egypt's concept of rebirth, cosmic order, justice, and truth,[332] all wrapped into the concept of Ma'at, embodied by Osiris, and administered by Thoth. This context of cosmic and righteous order is also conveyed by the vignette. The Roads of Mehen envelop the Sun God in a protective egg-like shell and grant him eternal life for myriads of recurrent time. The presence of the *ꜥfdt* on the boat and the boxes before indicate the stored, secret knowledge of this cosmic time order. The substitution of the ostrich and its feathers with Osiris indicated that this god personified the same regenerative power encapsulated by the bird before.

In sum, what we see on the predynastic pot is a cosmic scene related to resurrection just like the more stylized iconography derived in later times.

Let's review the sequence over time: The crescent boat from predynastic times becomes a double lion during the Early Dynastic Period associated

280

with Mehit. The double-headed snake in the vignette is replaced by a conjoined humanoid barque in the Middle Kingdom.

The reason why these different versions of the same motive were always difficult to associate is that, over time, animal symbols became replaced with other animals, then stylized, and eventually humanized. But once you see different symbols representing same ideas from different eras, the original meaning can be distilled. The later versions with text help to reverse interpret the earlier ones without written annotations.

Lions and the Moon

This is exactly what I want to do now because the captions in the illustration from the *Book of Two Ways* give us a rare glimpse into the details of what this boat was all about. The context of the scene is that *N* has become Thoth Moon to ritually heal the mortally wounded Osiris aboard this barque, about to succumb to Seth's treachery. In exchange, *N* receives eternal life. The caption written over the stern of the bark proclaims:[333]

> *This N is Thoth, the Lord of the rites for Osiris, and the Lord of rites for this N. These belong to this N's father, Osiris, who is in the hill, to Aker, and to Mehent.*

At last an inscription that mentions Thoth, Aker, and Mehit together. We learn that the barque is Aker, except here, in the later, humanized sphinx form, not as the earlier double lion barque. We are also told that *N* as Thoth is using magical rites belonging to the Rostau trio Osiris, Aker, and Mehent to save Osiris. The key take-away is that Thoth is not the owner of the rituals he administers, but the Rostau trio is.

Mehent, of course, is just another way to invoke Mehit. The hieroglyphic spelling confirms this conclusion (figure 118). The textual element immediately before the above tells us what the healing substance is: The Horus eye, an immanent manifestation of the waxing Moon.

> *... Give the Eye of Horus to Osiris! Your eye is pure. Rise up that you may live after this N has pleased you and after he has given the Eye of Horus.*

"Giving the Horus Eye" however is just a ritual umbrella term for the actual magical remedy administered, which is a spell not casually to be invoked unless done using Heka. What I think this spell is really meant to activate is the name of the lioness Mehit using the word Mehent. Basically, N, as Thoth, administers the magical remedy Mehit, the Eye of Horus, to Osiris to heal him.

This was an eye-opener for me. I wondered now if Mehit might not have started out as a solar goddess. The solar association comes from one of the Horus-Djer sealings.[334] There, she faces due east, *st3w*/Rostau behind her in the west.

But if she was a Moon-fixated lioness staring due east, then this could have been an *equinoctial* Full Moon. A rare astronomical event, indeed.

To test this idea, we can look to any possible Moon connection with Aker. But I must briefly review something about the Moon that will help to find the answer.

Each day the Moon drifts on its orbit by approximately 13° from west to east on the ecliptic. It completes a full orbit in 27.3216 days and repeats its phase in 29.53 days. The earliest visible sign of its reappearance after New Moon is an up-facing crescent just above the horizon at sunset in the west. Then, from one evening to the next, the Moon appears to climb up the ecliptic such that its "face" looks east, in *the same* direction in which it wanders (figure 121).

This west-to-east movement is opposite to the apparent movement caused by our own rotation past the Moon. We see the Moon becomes visible somewhat higher over the horizon each day, but then slowly, over the course of hours, falls back again to eventually sink in the west as we rotate east. We rotate faster than the Moon orbits. Therefore, in this waxing phase of the Moon, the face of the crescent moves in the same direction as the true motion of the Moon on the ecliptic and opposite the apparent, retrograde movement caused by our own rotation.

Said another way, if you compare the waxing Moon to the horizon, it wanders backwards and opposite its crescent face. If you compare it to the stars of the ecliptic, the Moon moves forwards in the same direction as its crescent face.

In the second half of the lunar cycle, after full Moon, the Moon wanes from the west because the Sun is to its East. Now the Moon's wander is with its face towards the west when looking at the horizon and opposite its face to the east when looking at the map of the stars.

Figure 121: Waxing Crescent Moon over the evening horizon in the west. Venus above. Southern California, December 2019.

The takeaway is that to the ancient Egyptians who saw a face on the crescent side of the Moon, the movement looked to be "eyes forward" or "eyes in the back." This duality concept is the same as that coming to us from the Pyramid Texts, according to Rolf Krauss.[335]

On the illustrated Coffin map, Aker appears in the form of a bark with a shrine-like cabin. Not surprisingly, the Pyramid Texts contain passages about ferries and ferrymen. What we are looking for is a ferryman on the ecliptic, the Winding Waterway according to Krauss.[336] I now show you Pyramid Text 569, also known as Recitation 508, from the Pyramid of Sixth Dynasty King Pepi I, who reigned over Egypt circa 2331–2287 BC. The passage reads (figure 122):

> *His-Face-Behind-Him, ferryman of the Winding Water Lotus Canal has docked for him [Pepi].*

This is an explicit textual reference which clarifies two things about the ferryman: He has his face behind him, opposite his floating direction, and

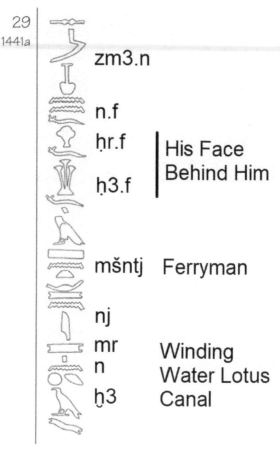

Figure 122: PT 569, verse 1441a from the Pyramid of Pepi I. Transliterated and translated into English.

he is on the ecliptic. Krauss further proves that this His-Face-Behind-Him is the same ferryman as the one who transports the sky goddess ***nwt*** [nut]. He is the ferryman of the gods. He is the door guard of Osiris.

Finally Krauss identifies His-Face-Behind-Him and his counterpart His-Face-In-Front with the waning and waxing, respectively, crescent Moons. In other words the Pyramid Texts can be demonstrated to codify a real astronomical phenomenon, the Moon's orbital motion vis-à-vis the ecliptic and horizon. This scientific observation was put it terms of the metaphor of a barque with two faces sailing forward or backward, ferrying around the gods across the night sky. Given this insight, we can now explain Aker.

This two-prow bark representing the crescent phases of the Moon, as the Pyramid Texts tell us, is identical with Aker, the bark shown to ferry Osiris, Thoth, and Mehent/Mehit, and the Eye of Horus. Since Aker is the double lion, we now have direct proof that the ancient Egyptians originally viewed Mehit and Aker as manifestations of the different phases of the Moon, not the Sun.

This was a big surprise to me. I had always assumed that the Giza lion was a solar animal. I began to understand why the archaic Moon cult of Mehit was suppressed and replaced with the solar-oriented Sphinx cult in the Old Kingdom. Perhaps it only survived in cryptic references because of the secrecy of the priestly scribes who preserved this legacy in concealed form. The name Mehit had to be hidden in secret Heka formulations. I understood why there was no reference to the Great Sphinx in the Old Kingdom except Horakhty and its precursor name The Two Horuses *ḥrwj*. The Great Sphinx and the Sun cult of Horakhty had only recently been grafted over a much more ancient and richer Moon cult. It is even possible that the worship of Mehit was forbidden, explaining why the name disappeared into obscurity.

So far so good, but if Mehit was an aspect of the Moon on the ground, then I was still unclear how that related to Thoth, the Moon himself. The more pressing question was how any Mehit-Moon-Thoth bridge translated into divine writings by Thoth, his book and the *ꜥfdt-ḥrt-ꜥ* under the arm of Mehit. The Edfu Texts tell us that the divine writings were the creation words of Ptah whose consort was Sekhmet, also a lioness. Air-Shu's consort was Moisture-Tefnut, also a lioness deity in the Heliopolitean cosmogony. Together, they were *rwtj*/[roo-te], a double lion.

Shadow Catcher

On the trail of the origin of Thoth himself, and his association with the Moon, with the ibis, with the baboon, with astronomy, with writing, and with judging in the Hall of Ma'at, I returned to textual element number 10 in Wael Sherbiny's Part 17 of the so-called *Book of Two Ways*. It told me one other, crucial piece of information about Thoth I had missed [emphasis added]:

> *This N is Thoth, the **Lord of the rites** for Osiris, and the Lord of rites for this N. These belong to this N's father, Osiris, who is in the hill, to Aker, and to Mehent.*

The Lord of Rites is the ritualist, the Heka magic master, whose utterances activate certain written symbols and summon their hidden meanings, employed here to help Osiris by uttering Mehent to activate Mehit. At the royal court of Egypt, the chief ritualist was the Scroll Master. He bore the title *ḥrj ḥb* [che-ry-heb], He Who Possesses the Ceremonial Scroll. Note how the word *ḥb* relates to the word for ibis, *ḥbj* [heb-ay]. The origin of this title was traced by Wolfgang Helck.[337] The *ḥrj ḥb*'s function split off the powers held by the primordial, prehistoric shaman, who was the *ṯt* [thet] in the First Dynasty, as the royal administrative apparatus grew. This was an act of, what we might consider, separation of powers (figure 123).

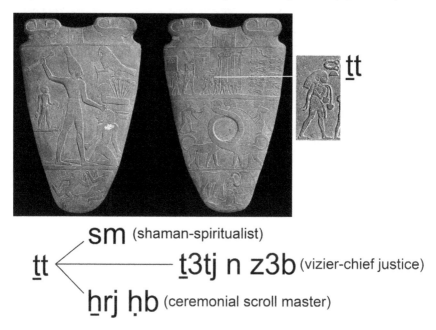

sm (shaman-spiritualist)

ṯt ⟵———— ṯ3tj n z3b (vizier-chief justice)

ḥrj ḥb (ceremonial scroll master)

Figure 123: The Narmer Palette from circa 3000 BC. A figure can be seen walking in front of the king—marked and magnified on the right—who is given the title *ṯt* [Thet]. By the end of the First Dynasty, this title was replaced by three new functions, separating the original powers held by the prehistoric chieftains' shaman priests.

Helck interprets the reason for the split as a need for a more civilized function, guided by the written word, as opposed to guidance based on internal voices and messages received in trance to advise the prehistoric chieftain. This more archaic function was relegated to the now less powerful *sm* shaman after the split. The third power, held by the chief justice and officer of the royal court, fell to the *ṯ3tj* [tha-ty]. Thoth incorporates these three secular aspects: The Spiritualist, The Ritualist, and the Justice. That is why he was the Thrice Great. But which of these invented writing?

All three of these leader roles in ancient Egypt were typically conferred to members of the king's family, usually, but not always, his sons. In two of these secular powers, it is easy to recognize their divine counterparts held by Thoth: Ritualist and Judge. But what about the power of the *sm*? Here again, Wolfgang Helck, in a fascinating analysis, textually reverse engineers an archaic ritual called the *Statuette Making Ritual* from the *Mouth Opening Ritual*, the latter a key rite recorded in the Pyramid Texts.

The relevant segment in this ritual occurs at the beginning when a protected zone is created in which the *sm* falls into trance donning a leopard-skin robe.[338] During this hypnotic state, animal spirits are activated with Heka spells to help the *sm* catch the shadow of a deceased in the Underworld, the place to where shadows escape once detached and released from the dead. The ancient Egyptians believed that the shadow was an essential aspect of being alive. The most important attribute of a shadow is that it is an outline of a shape but is solidly dark within that outline, just like symbol traced in black ink with a reed.

It is from the *sm*'s archaic role as a shadow catcher that we can see the origin of writing and why it was placed at the feet of Thoth, who incorporated aspects of the *sm* together with the other two executive arms of the royal house.

Hieroglyphs, after all, are just that, shadow-like outlines on papyrus, and shadow-casting contours in raised or sunken relief. They are, if you will, the shadows of ideas, captured in medium during the act of writing. Since the shadow contained an aspect of being alive, so did hieroglyphs, and so did the later letters of our own alphabets. These outlines can be viewed as the ghosts of real things, animate and inanimate. They become alive in our dreams, stories, and imagination. In ancient Egypt that meant they had to be activated phonetically through utterance and invocation, through Heka. They could be captured as written symbols. What archaic Thoth the shaman did in trance to revive a statuette, he now did with black ink and his reed. He had become a writer.

The model at hand explains the various roles of Thoth as the god of writing in his power as a shaman, as the god of ritual ceremony in his power as a Heka master, and as the god of justice in his power as reciting divine laws and applying them to the souls petitioning him to join the realm of the gods. It appears as if the primordial title of the _tt_ inspired the idea of Thoth, or it was the other way around. Regardless, just as Thoth was a celestial companion of the Sun God, his human counterpart, the _tt_, was the right arm of the Egyptian king.

The Narmer Palette contains another, fascinating clue to a possible primordial origin of Thoth's later attributes. On Egyptian reliefs, the king is often shown larger than life. Common people appear comparatively small. The appearance of the _tt_ on the palette, however, suggests that he may have been a dwarf.

Indeed, excavations at HK6—an elite prehistoric, Upper Egyptian cemetery in Hierakonpolis—in 2012 unearthed the grave[339] of a dwarf buried with various wild animals, including a leopard and baboons.[340] The interpretation is that dwarves were skilled animal handlers, especially of baboons. That may explain the basis for the connection between the later Shaman _sm_-priest and animal spirits since animal handlers would be able to read and communicate with the animals to be able to calm their wild nature and tame them.

The ultimate beasts to tame were animals dangerous to people, like hippopotamuses and lions. On the Narmer Palette, the idea of taming is taken to the fantastic on the obverse where two fabled beasts with long necks and lion-like bodies are being restrained by people. Stan Hendrickx has interpreted this to mean that the taming of wild animals was like the conquest and subjugation of human enemies and their territories.[341] Capturing and taming animals to keep them alive instead of hunting them for food, therefore, could have been practice for warfare—or just a sport.

Dwarves enjoyed high status in Egyptian society and at the royal court.[342] This prestige may have its prehistoric origins in the status they had earned as animal handlers. Given this context, it makes sense why Thoth was the mind of _R_, and why it was the _tt_ who alone was permitted to walk in front of the king. He was the one who would first inspect the captured enemies to advise him. He knew to communicate with animals and tame them, and that means he was entrusted to communicate with foreign enemies. He was the world's first diplomat. The way the Narmer Palette's victory scene is staged suggests that, from its beginnings, the kingdom projected a good cop/bad cop image to the people: a fierce warrior king tempered by a diplomatic *ṯt* whose functions would later separate into distinct positions filled by a vizier, a ritualist, and a spiritualist.

In *The Inventory Stele: More Fact than Fiction*,[343] Robert Schoch and I propose that the role of the lioness in writing came about because she is the master huntress in the wild. It would be her spirit, above all others, the *sm* might recruit to capture run-away shadows from the underworld. As a fierce protectress, prehistoric people may have thought of her likeness as the perfect image to guard the literary shadow catchers and outliners. I refer, of course, to the scribes.

Moon Phase Hieroglyphic

However, in order to tie Thoth to both the Moon and Mehit at Rostau, and to make the case that it is Thoth's written records which lie dormant in an archive beneath, we have to revisit the Moon in the texts; though not the crescent Moon Aker, the double lion Earth god. Instead, we must look for the Full Moon, the Eye of Horus, to which the inscription from the boat illustration in the Book of the Two Ways I mentioned above led us.

A good place to begin is to examine the word for full Moon in hieroglyphic, *(tpj) smdt* [te-pee sem-det] (figure 124).[344]

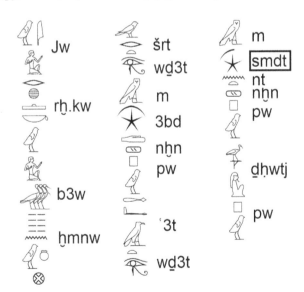

Figure 124: Hieroglyphic Spell 156 from the Coffin Text of Deir El-Bersheh Coffin B4L. The word for "Full Moon" is framed. Adapted from de Buck and Gardiner (1938).

Immediately, two words jump at us here: *sm* and *dt*, phonetic bridges to the *sm* and the *ṯt*, both secular aspects of Thoth. This segment from Spell 156 of the Coffin Texts helps us with a clue [emphasis mine]:

> *Oh, you souls of Hermopolis, I know you. The small Eye of Horus on **Crescent Moon Day**, the Big Eye of Horus on **Jasper Full Moon Day**, this is Thoth.*

Unlike de Buck and Gardiner, I translated the oval bead symbol Gardiner O47 *nḥn* [ne-khen] in the second instance, instead of reading it as a context symbol, because it is preceded by *nt*—either meaning "of," or acting as a phonetic complement and aid prompting the reader to pronounce O47. There are two possible meanings:[345] *of nḥn*/Hierakonpolis, or *ḥnt, ḥnmt, or mḥnmt*/Jasper, a red-brown precious stone, like red-orange Carnelian. Jasper and Carnelian were used to make jewelry. Since Hierakonpolis made less sense here, I asked myself if Spell 156 used the word Jasper to allude to the Full Moon in the Coffin Texts?

I speculated that Jasper beads may have been cut into various shapes to imitate the phases of the Moon. However, better support for reading *smdt nt nḥn* as Full Moon of Jasper, or Jasper Full Moon comes from one other possible meaning of *smdt*, "bead necklace."[346] A phonetic link between *smd* and Mehit appears in one member of the *smd* star decan family, called *smd mḥtj* [sem-ed-mehetee].[347] Despite the intriguing possibility of a jasper-colored Full Moon, the Moon is not red but silver, isn't it? I could not yet see the color connection.

Uncannily, the word *smdt* was also used in the context of cryptographic writing (see Appendix). This is pointed out by Andrés Diego Espinel citing an intriguing hieroglyphic passage by the New Kingdom high official and architect Senenmut who wrote that he invented new cryptographic royal insignia using his own "*smt*" instead of resorting to examples used in his ancestor's creations.[348] Espinel explains *smt* as being derived from *smdt* meaning scheme or rule in this context.

Something was still missing, but all these connections began to resonate in my mind: Hierakonpolis, the *ṯt*, Thoth, the Full Moon, Jasper, and cryptographic writing.

Spell 156 clarified to me that both crescent and Full Moon were aspects of Thoth, small and big, in his manifestation as the *wḏ3t* [weh-jat] Eye of Horus. The word *smdt*, if it is a contraction of *sm* and *dw3t*, also suggested to me that the Full Moon might have been a prehistoric kind of shaman day. In the Full Moonlight, shadows can be seen at night. Since the *sm*'s function was to capture shadows from the underworld, the shadows were needed to animate statuettes made in memory of the dead. I wondered if such rituals took place at night when the full Moon was up. A nighttime ritual may also explain why the full Moon aspect of Thoth was associated with writing. Writing was, after all, capturing outlines of humans, animals, and things on ivory, wood, papyrus, and stone. The act of writing is really a symbolic form of the shamanic shadow hunting ritual. This is one way you could construct a syncretic link between Earth and the sky, between the *tt* and Thoth.

This is how the cryptographer's scheme, the *smdt*, may have originated in prehistory: It was the *sm*'s journey into the subconscious, into the twilight world of the shadows, the *dw3t*. The experience must have been so profound that standard symbols just did not suffice to *capture* the experience. A special form of hieroglyphic writing was needed, one which conveyed the experience of the other senses besides the sights like, for example, the sounds of the *dw3t*.

What felt like nothing more than a step away from the this far elusive link between Mehit and Thoth, I still could not put my finger on it. Like the Great Sphinx, Mehit was oriented due east. Only the head and neck of the lioness were remodeled into a human king or queen from the Fourth Dynasty, not the couchant body. Before considering the rare case of a Full Moon on the day of an equinox, I had to first review the more general case of new and full Moon, as it occurs each month on any day of the year.

Equinox Lunar Eclipse

On new Moon day, the Moon rises and sets with the Sun. But we cannot see it because it is in a zone between us and the Sun in which no sunlight can hit the Moon's surface and then bounce back at us. But there is a rare exception: a solar eclipse, a special kind of New Moon, if you will, in a particular area of that zone. In an eclipse, the Moon looks like a shadow over the Sun, more often a partial shade than a total cover. If this isn't already spectacular enough, there is an even rarer eclipse: the Ring of Fire. This happens when New Moon falls into this special area between Sun and Earth on a day when the Moon is also at its furthest orbital distance from Earth. That is when the Moon cover over the Sun is a slight bit smaller than the sunny disk beneath it. Depending on your mood, it is either an awesome or a terrifying sight. In connection with this real celestial spectacle, I want to mention something from the Coffin Texts. In Spell 80, the mortal spirit of *N*, the deceased, speaks to the gods. He mentions the Island of Fire, a place mentioned often in the Coffin Texts:[349]

> *I am the living one who is on his neck and my throat is made to flourish, (even I) whom Atum made into the Grain-god when he caused me to go down into this land, to the - Island of Fire, when I became Osiris the son of Geb.*

The Island of Fire is a place of the gods in the Netherworld. I would like you to keep this in mind for later.

On full Moon day, the Moon rises east when the Sun sets west, and sets west when the Sun rises east (figure 125) The Earth is between the Sun and the Moon.

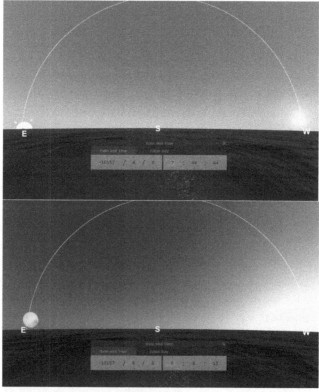

Figure 125: An eclipsed Full Moon rise due east on an equinox. The date is 10158 BC. Graphic made using Stellarium 0.14.3.

In the same way that the Moon can eclipse the Sun at new Moon, the Earth can eclipse the Moon in its full Moon phase. But we do not get a lunar eclipse every month at full Moon. As is the case for solar eclipses, the reason for this is that the Moon's orbit is slightly (5.15°) tilted relative to the plane of our orbit, the ecliptic (figure 126).

Figure 126: The Moon's orbital tilt shown as a wheel of time, relative to the orbital plane of Earth. The two orbits can be seen here to cross in the foreground at the interorbital node. Graphic by Anthony Sturmas, Asturmas Studios.`

For a solar or lunar eclipse to happen, new Moon or full Moon must fall on a day when the Moon happens to cross as close as possible to the nodal intersection between these two orbital planes. This crossing of the ecliptic plane by the Moon defines the name of the astronomical phenomenon we see: eclipse. If the new or full Moon is slightly above or below Earth's orbital plane, even only by a couple of degrees, there is at best a partial or penumbral eclipse, or as is the much more common case, no eclipse. Eclipses are rare and that's why the ancients might have thought of them as special, as we do now.

The chance of an eclipsed full Moon *near* due east on the evening of a spring or fall equinox is a truly rare event, much rarer even than an eclipse on just any day, because, of course, an equinox only happens twice a year. Such a day, when night and day are equally long, would be special indeed, because like any eclipsed full Moon, the equinoctial lunar eclipse creates not a silver white Moon, but a bloody red one, mixed with brown and green. Four events must coincide for this to happen: an equinox, a Full Moon, an orbital nodal transit to produce an eclipse, and an observer watching it all in the right spot on Earth. And what would this look like? A Jasper-red Blood Moon (figure 127).

Figure 127: A total lunar eclipse from the Saros 127 family. Southern California, on October 8, 2014 at 3:29 a.m.

Could this be it? A full, red-faced Moon to match a due east-focused, red-faced lioness (figure 128)?[350]

Figure 128: Blood-faced Lioness during a meal. ©, Karim Iliya.

Was Mehit made to commemorate a truly rare, astronomical event, the day when the left, lunar Eye of Horus looked injured and bleeding (figure 129)?

Figure 129: A Blood Moon rise in the east in front of a recreated, prehistoric monumental, red-faced lioness statue along with temples and causeway. Graphic by Anthony Sturmas, Asturmas Studios.

Was this the day when Egyptian stories tell us Seth/Mercury gouged the eye of the son Horus avenging Seth's murder of Horus' father Osiris? Was this day in an era when the equinoctial sun rose into the constellation Leo, the mythological era of the First Time, Zep Tepi, as Hancock and Bauval have proposed?[351]

In the past, I had wondered why an advanced, prehistoric culture able to build a monumental lion with knowledge of astronomy and precession would not monumentalize the exact date of its groundbreaking. Was an epoch—such as the centuries of time when Leo rested on the horizon in the spring during a part of the Younger Dryas, a post-ice age cold spell on Earth dated to a period extending from circa 12,900 to 11,700 years ago (10900 – 9700 BC)—the entire message of the Sphinx left to posterity to enshrine precession as a vast cycle of time?[352] Or was there a foundation stone, so to speak, an exact date I mean, so that the monument would leave no doubt as to the moment in eternity that inspired its creation? What could be better than to make that stone the monument itself?

With this new astronomical model of the idea behind Mehit, several things made more sense to me. I better understood its role as a distinct, commemorative time marker. It enshrined the rare intersection of three celestial cycles: the cycle of the Sun, the cycle of the Moon, and the cycle of a star in Leo. Mehit marked one day of Millions that passed, a day during the epoch of Leo, during the Younger Dryas.

If the Sphinx and pyramids are a precessional clock with an accuracy in the centuries, then this clock using Mehit would sharpen the resolution of that clock to a single day. When Mehit became the Great Sphinx, this more finely tuned time indicator marked by the Moon gave way to the hazier pointer represented by the Sun. No wonder the master architect of ancient Egypt's pantheon is Thoth, not R^ς.

Whoever conceived the original statue of the lioness, Mehit, had a brilliant mind: a red lion face, staring due east at an eclipsed Moon rising into the lion in the sky. This monumental design is better than a date carved into the rock. Rather, the rock itself, the lioness, became the written symbol of that date. In stoic silence, the message she embodied lasted longer than what could be erased by the hammers and chisels of time and people.

Scanning a three-hundred-year sample of lunar eclipses compiled by NASA, I only found five total eclipses which coincided to within two days with an equinox, either spring or fall.[353] This exercise confirmed the rarity of such a concurrence. It means that during any precessional epoch that, on average, lasts circa 2,160 years,[354] there could be no more than forty equinoctial lunar eclipses and no more than twenty on the spring equinox. Only few of these would have been visible from any particular place on Earth.

With this new model of Mehit's message, I understood why the Egyptians chose the word *j3bt* [aya-bet] for east/left.[355] It contains the word *j3* for Moon.[356] Interestingly, *bt3* [be-tah] means crime and sin and *bt3t* means injury.[357] These words resonate, too. The equinoctial blood Moon symbolizes the crime of Seth, the injuring of the Eye of Horus on the day of R^ς 's passage from winter to spring.

Why Due East?

This refined astronomical model of the prehistoric design of Mehit predates ancient Egypt by thousands of years. It explains an anachronism represented by a well-known aspect of the Great Sphinx I have been at a loss to explain for some time: Why would this statue have been made in the Old Kingdom to face due east when there is no aspect of Egypt's culture that emphasizes the spring equinox? The first of spring did not coincide with the inundation of the Nile. That happened around the summer solstice, three months later. Why not make the Sphinx face the summer sunrise, north of due east?

Instead I now think that the spring, or fall, equinox mattered to the prehistoric culture that built the original statue Mehit, Old Kingdom Egyptians long afterwards remodeled into the Great Sphinx without changing her due east orientation. Perhaps this, much more ancient, culture existed during times when the northeast African climate was different, for example colder. Perhaps this culture celebrated the beginning of spring and the end of winter.

The chief argument against any significance the ancient Egyptians may have attributed to the due east position on the horizon has to do with the very contentious and complicated subject of Egyptian calendrics. Without throwing myself into this bloody arena, the central issue argued over for over a hundred years now is when the civil calendar of 365 days was first inaugurated, what was its astronomical basis if any, and how was time being tracked before? To an ancient observer, an equinox was a station on the horizon, midway between the heights of summer and winter. A more sophisticated definition occurred when accurate time measurements showed that the length of day and night were the same, within the error of the method used, for example, a water clock.

However knowing the two days each year when this occurred had no practical significance to the people who lived up and down the Nile. They were concerned with the yearly flood. This life-or-death event happened near the summer solstice when heavy rains in the Ethiopian Highlands caused the waters of the river to swell and flood down its gradient for over four thousand miles to the Delta and the Mediterranean Sea. If the exact timing of the flood had been confined to a small window of days each year, simply counting the days from one flood to the next would have sufficed as the kind of count we would call a year.

Alas, the yearly inundation of the Nile was an unpredictable event. It varied by as much as seventy days from year to year.[358] The "Nile Year" could be less than three hundred, or more than four hundred days long. While this may have been tolerable by the smaller communities of predynastic

Nile dwellers, once Egypt became a unified kingdom, predictability was key for the collection of taxes in the form of agricultural and crafted goods. This then became the pretext for the civil year, but the method of its design remains contested to date.

What mattered to me, however, is an insight by Rolf Krauss related to the Palermo Stone, recounted by archaeoastronomer Juan Antonio Belmonte.[359] Remember this is a fragment of a stone stele which once contained the entire Royal Annals of the Kingdom of Ancient Egypt, from archaic times to the first few kings of the Fifth Dynasty. Krauss noticed that one of the yearly registers recorded for the First Dynasty was only ten lunar months and twenty days long. This is too short to have any logical relationship with an astronomical cycle. This entry, however, makes sense if what was being tracked was the time interval between two inundations, circa three hundred and twenty days in this case.

In other words, during the early phase of Egyptian civilization, evidence suggests, not the Sun, but the Moon and the Nile were the measure of time. There was no practical reason to focus on the day of an equinox or solstice.

Archaeoastronomers have noticed that the focus on due east presents a problem with no good explanation. To try to explain it, they have proposed that the due east orientation of a number of Egyptian monuments may be incidental to its right-angle relation with the actually intended target located due north. Juan Antonio Belmonte, Mosalam Shaltout, and Magdi Fekri studied the orientation of three-hundred thirty ancient Egyptian temples and found that the equinoctial orientation was the most frequent one employed by the architects.[360] However, the authors argue that Egyptian surveyors were primarily aiming for the northern sky where the imperishable stars dwelled. As a result, the due east orientation of many monuments, including the Great Sphinx and its temples, may be of no importance. It may be incidental to the due north orientation.[361] In other words, according to the authors due east did not matter. But there is a problem with this.

As independent Egyptologist Alexander Puchkov has shown, Old Kingdom pyramids were, in fact, not orientated with due north in mind.[362] What only looks like a due north focus are several stars near due north. Consequently due east cannot be an incidental right-angle orientation relative to something that is not due north.

While I agree that the ancient Egyptians were not focused on due east, I disagree that the due east orientation was incidental to a focus on due north. Due east did not matter to the dynastic Egyptians, that much is clear. This part is, in fact, confirmed by Egyptologists and archaeoastronomers themselves. In the paradigm of history in which they reside, they cannot properly explain this paradox. The best they can do it to say due east was incidental.

In the paradigm of history proposed by alternative researchers, however, the due east orientation can be explained as an anachronism from another time. The due east focus may have mattered to people who came to the Nile before the ancient Egyptians. It is these earlier people who could have left their cultural imprint on the ancient Egyptians. One of those imprints, the lioness statue, could have inspired the focus on due east. I think this yet another example of what I mentioned in Chapter I: Paradigms can create unresolved paradoxes that persist until the paradigm is revised. This is what I think we must consider here.

A due east facing lioness is anachronistic to ancient Egypt. This supports her prehistoric origin. The cultural association between her and the Moon suggests that she stared due east at a lunar astronomical event, coinciding with the solar rise into her celestial counterpart. Can we now put a date on the creation of Mehit and the archive under? In principle, this has already been answered by Robert Bauval, but I would like to introduce a slight, but crucial modification to more accurately time it.

Dating the Lioness

In Bauval's reconstruction the Giza pyramids and the Great Sphinx are a key on the ground to another time in the sky. They are oriented in such a way as to prompt the observer to precess the sky back in time, until the three stars of Orion's belt align with the three pyramids, and the Great Sphinx's stare points to Leo over the horizon on the first day of spring. Bauval reconstructs the epoch when this ground-sky match occurred to 10500 BC, the mythical First Time Zep Tepi, when Osiris ruled the world with a pantheon of fellow gods and goddesses.[363]

In the Pyramid Texts, this journey back in time plays out in the sky along the ecliptic on the map of the Zodiacal constellations, interpreted to be the path of the Followers of Horus.[364] Bauval sees this movement ritually recreated with a ceremonial procession in honor of the dead Horus king. The goal was to resurrect him as an immortalized spirit with the regenerative power of his father Osiris represented by the three pyramids on the ground and by the constellation Orion in the sky. That power drew nearest when Orion reached its lowest point over the horizon during the precessional cycle, such that the king could unite with the Osirian stars. That era was Zep Tepi.

Bauval assumed that the vernal point mattered to the builders of this precessional time machine at Giza. The vernal point is where the Sun crosses the horizon due east at an azimuth of 90° on the morning of an equinox.

Here is the modification I propose to Bauval's model of dating the monument and Zep Tepi. The idea is illustrated in figure 130.

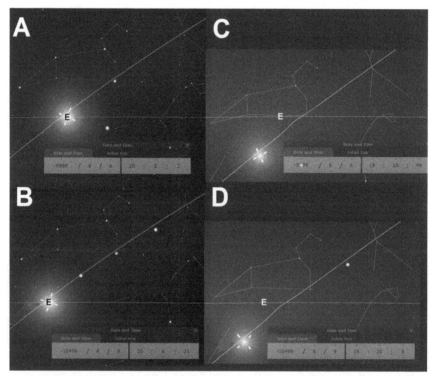

Figure 130: Horizontal position of Leo on the vernal equinox in 10,000 and 10,500 BC A and B show the star constellation relative to the vernal point at the moment of sunrise due east; C and D show Leo's position with the Sun at -10° elevation. Graphic made with Stellarium 0.14.3.

First off, I want to make a trivial observation which has more to do with nomenclature than with observational significance. The precessional epoch and astrological age in 10,500 BC was defined by a vernal point[365] observable somewhat half-way between Virgo in the east and Leo in the west. Bauval refers to this as "near the beginning of the Age of Leo." This makes sense because you can see the constellation at dawn above the horizon.[366] Depending on how one defines an astrological age or epoch however, some may construe this to still be during the Age of Virgo, not yet the Age of Leo, even though you would never actually observe the age-defining constellation according to this definition. The Sun blocks it from our view because the Sun is between it and us.[367]

More importantly, the constellation Leo would have appeared on the horizon before the Sun at dawn, not with the sunrise. This is really what likely mattered to an observer, ancient or modern. With this caveat in mind, I repeated Bauval's reconstruction using Stellarium. I compared the sky elevation of Leo on the spring equinox of 10,000 BC and 10,500 BC (figure 130), panels A and C versus B and D, respectively), shortly before and at sunrise.

Accordingly, Leo hovers still high over the horizon in 10,500 BC. Bauval's own data, using a different program, show the Sphinx closer to the horizon at 10,500 BC, though he also placed the Sun somewhat lower at -12°.[368] Before sunrise with the Sun at an elevation of -10°, for example, the center of the constellation was somewhat south of due east but already well separated from, and above, the horizon (figure 130, panel D).

Five centuries later, however, around 10,000 BC, Leo appears couchant immediately on, and parallel to, the horizon at dawn, before sunrise (figure 130, panel C). The center of its starry torso coincides with due east. This image of the near-horizontal constellation best fits the couchant Sphinx—and Mehit. What this means is that the 10,000 BC elevation of the constellation, visually in immediate contact with the horizon, created the pre-sunrise image of a horizontal, lion-like, equinoctial Sun marker, in agreement with Bauval's larger point that that it served as a model for the statue in this space and time.

One could imagine how prehistoric observers might have anticipated "Leo touchdown," so to speak, for several centuries before 10,000 BC, witnessing a gradual approach towards the horizon as the vernal point precessed westward along the ecliptic from Virgo to Leo. The completion of the carving of the monument from the limestone hill at the foot of the Mokattam formation could have occurred in that century when Leo reached the horizon just before sunrise.

The accuracy of computer-simulated reconstructions of the night sky over such vast time spans depends on the software but, regardless, is subject to accumulated errors the further back in time one projects. What I want to do here is not to pinpoint a specific year or date in the past yet, but rather a time span within which the sky appeared in the way I reconstructed here. The main take-away is that there was a period, sometime between 10,500 and 10,000 BC, during which the constellation Leo appeared couchant on the horizon before sunrise. This position placed the vernal point of the spring equinox at the constellation's center. The five centuries during which this beautiful horizontal image could be seen on the first day of spring overlapped with the last half of the Younger Dryas.

To appreciate the uniqueness of Leo's couchant horizontal orientation in 10,000 BC, it helps to reconstruct the sky at other times when the constellation heliacally rises after a period of absence (figure 131).

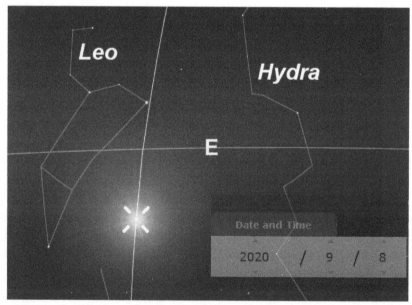

Figure 131: The rising of Leo above the horizon in the year 2020. Stellarium Version 0.14.3.

In 2020, for example, Leo rose in September. Instead of assuming a couchant position on the horizon, as it did in 10,000 BC, it now appears tilted upwards. That is why Leo's emergence above the morning horizon during the late eleventh millennium BC was visually so unique, so stunning, so impressionable.

Given this narrowed time frame for Zep Tepi, 10,500 – 10,000 BC, we may now attempt to define an exact date: the image of a starry lion sitting on the horizon in the morning before sunrise, and a fully eclipsed red Moon during the night before or after. The odds of this concurrence, as I had convinced myself, are miniscule given the fact that a full precessional cycle lasts close to twenty-six thousand years and total lunar eclipses on any given calendar day are likewise exceedingly rare events. Yet, such an unusual day can be reconstructed (with caveats such as the effect of ΔT[369]) to have occurred in 10,120 BC. This is an example of a candidate year when the idea to build a lion monument at Giza may have been born (figure 132). In this example, the Moon near Pisces.

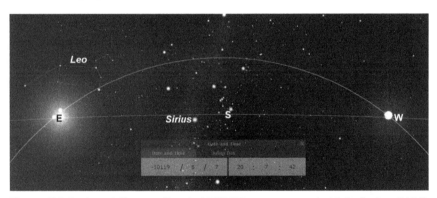

Figure 132: Equinoctial lunar eclipse in 10120 BC, reconstructed with Stellarium 0.14.3. The vernal point is at an azimuth of 89°49' with the Moonset at 267°14'. The location is Giza, Cairo (UTC+2) and the time is Julian Day -1974748. The lunar magnitude diminishes during the preceding evening at 10:22 (UTC-12, 8:22 pm local time) and recovers at 13:24 (UTC-12, 11:24 p.m. local time). Earth rotational Time correction based on Algorithm by Espenak and Meeus.[370] Stellarium Version 0.14.3.

In 10,120 BC, observers would have witnessed a blood-red Full Moon in the East on the eve of spring. Leo appeared on the horizon at dawn. The monument created was aimed at the center of the constellation and that center was due east, thus uniquely marked with a time stamp not duplicated since.

According to Herodotus, the Athenian stateman Solon met the Egyptian pharaoh Amassis II before he met with Croesus in Sardis.[371] This meeting narrows Solon's visit to Egypt to a time frame ranging from 570 to 560 BC because Solon died before Amassis. The proposed date of the construction of Mehit to Solon's learning of the Atlantis story sums to a time span of 9,550–9,560 Julian years of 365.25 days, or 9,556–9,567 Egyptian years of 365 days.

Eclipse in Hieroglyphic

If a lunar eclipse mattered so greatly, influencing the creation of the original lioness monument by a prehistoric culture thriving during the Younger Dryas in northeast Africa, then why did the later dynastic Egyptians throughout their long history of keeping records remain silent on such uncanny Moon events? No doubt, both solar and lunar eclipses occurred during the many centuries of Egyptian civilization, as they have for nearly all of Earth's existence. Yet there seems to be no word for the phenomenon and no description of it in any texts. The strangeness of this omission is only underscored by the fact that eclipses are unions of Egypt's most prominent deities, Sun R^ς and Moon Thoth. It seems inconceivable that no words were written about such drama unfolding in the sky, yet this is what most Egyptologist will tell you, including Zahi Hawass whom I once asked about this in an e-mail.

Why the scholars may have overlooked eclipses in the writings of the ancient Egyptians is the immanent character of Egyptian metaphorical science. Ancient astronomers visualized the forces of nature, likely including eclipses, as gods, or their aspects, and not as the dry descriptions, devoid of colorful content to which we are accustomed. Here is an example.

NASA's Five Millennium Catalog of Lunar Eclipses website lists an event on September 25 in the year 52 BC. The Moon fell under the cover of Earth's shadow thirty-seven minutes before midnight and became a Blood Moon for fifty-three minutes. This happened when the full Moon had entered the region of the ecliptic occupied by the stars that make up the constellation Pisces, between Taurus and Aquarius (figure 133).

Astronomically, there is no doubt that this eclipse occurred. The only question is whether it was observed in Cairo. September 52 BC was a time when Cleopatra's grandfather, Ptolemy XII, had used Roman military help

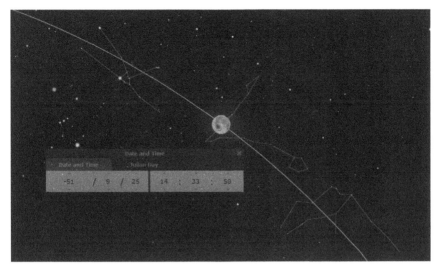

Figure 133: Known lunar eclipse visible in Cairo, Egypt in the year 52 BC The Moon was in the constellation Pisces flanked by Taurus to the east and Aquarius to the west. Graphic made with Stellarium 0.14.3.

to regain power over Egypt after he had been exiled a few years earlier. He died within six months of this eclipse leaving the throne to Cleopatra, the last of the Ptolemies.[372] It is during this final phase of Hellenic control over Egypt that a chapel dedicated to Osiris was built on the Temple of Hathor at Dendera in Upper Egypt. A portico was later added to during the reign of Tiberius (14-37 AD). Into the ceiling of this columned entry, a domed bass relief was installed depicting a combination of Egyptian and Mesopotamian constellations, planets, and decans, illustrated and annotated. This is the famous Dendera Zodiac.

On one of my Egypt trips, our touring host had taken us[373] to a papyrus shop in Cairo. I could not resist the beautifully colored creation by one of the artists there. In fine detail, he had painted his version of the Dendera Zodiac onto a sheet of papyrus (figure 134).

I did not have to think twice about buying it. Since then, I have certainly glanced at it as I have passed its new home in a bowl on my dining table—but I did not realize how important it was to become. Among the many details, there is one small icon M. Gamal took great pains to exquisitely detail: the Eye of Horus symbol. But there is another crucial detail. It hovers directly above what is a clear depiction of the constellation Pisces (figure 135).

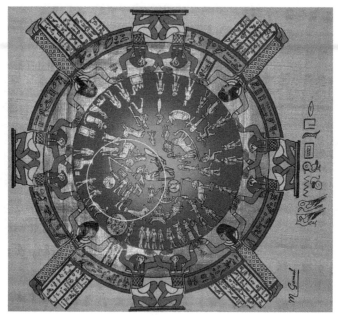

Figure 134: Dendera Zodiac painted onto papyrus by a certain M. Gamal. The white circle highlights a section showing evidence of both solar and lunar eclipses.

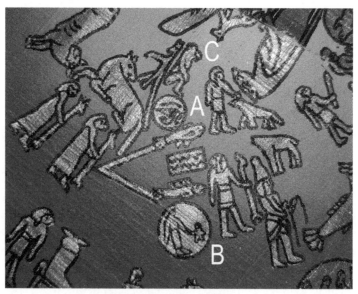

Figure 135: Highlighted area from the Dendera Zodiac papyrus shown in Figure 134. (A) shows the Eye of Horus symbol inside a circle. (B) shows a circle with a woman holding a baboon by its tail. (C) shows a baboon leaning against a jackass symbolic of Seth.

The first to point out this striking detail of Egyptian astronomy were French astrophysicist Eric Aubourg and French Institute for Oriental Archaeology researcher Sylvie Cauville.[374] I think that these two scholars are correct and are in bewilderment about the otherwise and likewise excellent Juan Antonio Belmonte's untypically dogmatic dismissal of it.

There has, for a long time, been a general aversion and resistance to accept evidence generated by other disciplines, especially astronomy. The blame for this goes around, but I think the chief reason is that the early efforts, for example by Piazzi Smyth, were somewhat tainted by linking them with a religious agenda, possibly contrary to that of the nation which hosts and guards Egypt's monuments. This experience likely generated a barrier today's scholars of astronomy may feel compelled to overcome by displaying a hypercritical stance even at the risk of dismissing a real discovery. That is the unfortunate outcome of dogmatism in any field in which researchers from other disciplines seek to gain and fear to lose approval and recognition.

What makes Aubourg's and Cauville's insight so compelling is the fact that the Eye of Horus symbol above Pisces is immediately below an image of a baboon leaning, back-to-back, against a long-eared jackass (figure 135, A). That is a symbol for the also long-eared Seth, the archenemy of the Osirian Triad, Osiris, Isis, and Horus (figure 135, C).

In the stories, it is Seth who gouges out the left eye of Horus, making it the bloody piece of mess hiding behind the mysterious symbolism of the Eye of Horus. There is the lunar context hiding next to the unidentified symbol of a Moon disk housing the Eye of Horus. It could hardly be more obvious that this was hieroglyphic code for an eclipse, at least during the late period of Egypt. However, there is yet more evidence.

The baboon of this pair atop the now suspected Red Moon Eclipse sign proves that the Eye of Horus disk is the hieroglyphic symbol of a lunar eclipse. The baboon's iconic, ischial callosities on its rear are red. That explains why the ancient Egyptians associated this animal with lunar eclipses. They also drew a link to the rising Sun from this animal, as they did from the image of a couchant lion, because of its distinct "wa-hoo," or "ra-hoo" sound.[375]

Lion and Baboon, Sun, and Moon

The baboon, in other words, makes perfect sense as a symbol of an equinoctial eclipse in the sign of Leo. This explains the primordial origin of the *ḏ3jsw* words of creation. It explains why they were shown split into front and back halves, imitating the fissured stony lioness. It explains why they personified the recorded words of creation. It explains why they, the manifest records of creation, were archived inside a red-faced lioness to mark the time when they were uttered and recorded.

This time, I argue, was a day when a lunar eclipse occurred at dawn in the sign of the lion, exactly on that part of the horizon at which the lioness was built to stare. The last time this happened was at the end of the eleventh millennium BC. What was, at first, an unlikely marriage between Thoth-Moon in the sky and Mehit-lioness on the ground, suddenly made sense to me. I had identified the primeval source of this Sky-Earth union as a rare astronomical phenomenon which had brought them together. *A marriage in the sky.*

The Significance of the Blood-Red Moon

I now had two possible connections between the eclipsed equinoctial Full Moon and the lioness Mehit: One is the link proposed by Hancock and Bauval, which places the constellation Leo into the star zone above the due east horizon during the Zep Tepi epoch. This connection required knowledge of the solar cycle and its relationship, via an equinoctial marker, to the precessional wander of the map of stars lining the ecliptic.

The other is the link I am proposing here as a commemoration of the Original Sin. An unknown culture had monumentalized the metaphor of an equinoctial lunar eclipse in the form of a feasting huntress—a blood-tinged, red-faced lioness, to imitate the Blood Moon in the sky, above her celestial likeness on the eastern horizon. This link intertwines two astronomical paths: the precessing path of the Sun on the ecliptic, codified as the Path of Horus,[376] and the path of the Moon codified as the Eye of Horus.

As rich as these connections may appear, they do not yet consummate the marriage I began to see between the Blood Moon and Mehit. I discovered that it got even better, even more profound. While the former's message was the precessional link back in time to Zep Tepi and the dominion of Osiris, the latter dated the reason for the creation of the lioness monument. The lioness symbolized astronomical order in the form of cyclical time eternity, *nḥḥ* [ne-heh], personified by the *ḥḥw*.

The astronomical knowledge sealed under the lioness—the Heliocentric Solar System—was yet another message of universal order. That order was the structure of the sky as it must have been then known by a people we no longer know. The heavenly bodies navigated on ring-like paths encircling the life-giving Sun. Myth enveloped the science and explained it like a shield of snakes protecting the creator god from the chaos looming outside his sphere of influence.

This order, the one we once again think is correct, was illustrated in the Vignette of *Rᶜ*. The ancient Egyptians reinterpreted this prehistoric model of the sky in terms of their own, geocentric perspective. Concentric elliptical paths around the Sun, thus, became a spiraling journey of the soul to the universal solar center to reach immortality. To leap from ellipse to ellipse, the gates which held the rings in order had to be breached, *passed* in other words, with the help of Zunthu, the ferryman of The Nine. Only the gates could explain the otherwise inexplicable: how the planets could go backwards and forwards on the Winding Waterway, almost as if they could go forwards and backwards in time eternally. To move freely unleashed from the flow of time is the best way to understand the primordial, pre-creation, chaotic force of nature embodied by the *ḥḥw*. That chaotic and free motion unhinged from time is captured well by this phrase: *The gates are confused.*

Astronomer-priests equated the coiled movement towards a spiritual center with the circumpolar rotation, where they placed the motor of the universe. To control this sky motor was a power the kings of Egypt aspired to master. To symbolize its possession, it was represented as a coil, mounted on the starry handle of the northern sky, the constellation Ursa Minor, the sheepfold in some ancient interpretations.

The colors of the Blood Moon were also that of the Earth, of Geb. The lioness thus also became a symbol of the vessel, the crescent ferry in the shape of the double lion Aker, which could be witnessed at night in the two faces floating across the sky, forward sometimes, backward at other times. Inside it carried the Sun on its journey through the underworld.

Thoth was the Moon, and his animals were the lioness, the baboon, and the ibis with the crescent beak. As a huntress and protectress of her off-spring, the lioness' spirit, above that of all animals, would be best harnessed to chase after the fleeting shadows of the dead, for ancient people surely saw that long shadows stretch away from the living when the night nears.

The shamans knew the language of wild animals and learned to tame them. With their help and while in trance, they captured the shadows of the dead to imbue them within something tangible and lasting, a statue first, and much later an upright mummy made from the limp and lifeless corpse of the dead. This very act became symbolized as writing, the capturing of shadowy outlines on medium to bring alive that which once was, the memory of a story, the memory of the living, just like a statuette standing in a niche inside a votive chapel. And this is how the Moon God became the god of writing, as the shaman became a scribe. Writing had been invented. Creation had been imitated.

Aker: A Tale of Two Tails

As I neared the end of writing this book, I remembered a loose end I had to tie together. What I thought would be a minor detail ended up opening a wide gate into the past. It all began with the origin of Aker, the double lion in the underworld on whom the night barque of the Sun God travels by night (figure 136).

Figure 136: Akerw and the night bark. KV9, tomb of Ramses V/VI. ©, Manna Nader, Gabana Studios Cairo, Egypt.

This is the same barque from the map of the *Book of Two Ways* that carries the ailing Osiris, Thoth, the Eye of Horus, and Mehen. On it, the Heka-equipped ritualist becomes Thoth to save Osiris and receives favorable treatment in the afterlife. On the map, this barque is in the shape of a double-headed, human, chimeric being. The Pyramid Texts inform us that this duo of His-Face-Behind-Him and His-Face-In-Front was the ferry which travels the Winding Waterway. As I mentioned before, Rolf Krauss astronomically identified this boat as the waxing and waning crescent Moon.

However, in New Kingdom tomb paintings of scenes from the related Book of Amduat/Within the Netherworld, the barque is shown as a double-headed snake (figure 137).

Figure 137: The Night Barque with the protective shrine encircling the Sun God's spiritual essence while journeying the Netherworld. The prow and stern are shaped like snake heads. From KV9, tomb of Ramses V/VI. ©, Manna Nader, Gabana Studios Cairo, Egypt.

What is the exact relationship between the barque and the double lion? Is the barque a part of Aker's back curvature, or is he the personified waterway on which the barque travelled? The break-through came when I recognized the same sickle-shaped bark and shrine-like cabin on decorated pottery, one example of which I showed earlier featuring an ostrich (figure 120). But there are other, similar pots and jars made in Egypt's predynastic time. They tell an eye-opening story (figure 138).

The crescent boat motive was common not only on this style of prehistoric Upper Egyptian pottery but can also be seen on the famous painting

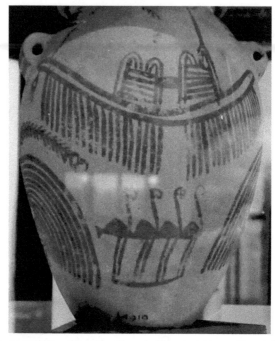

Figure 138: Decorated Vase from the Naqada II period, Upper Egypt. The Museum of Egyptian Antiquities, Cairo, Egypt, September 2018.

inside Tomb 100 discovered at Hierakonpolis. This was a large predynastic settlement in the south of Egypt active for centuries before the Narmer,[377] only matched in importance by the Lower Egyptian city of Buto. According to Belgian Egyptologists Stan Hendrickx and Mercer Eyckerman, both world experts in ancient Egyptian and predynastic iconography, the boat theme relates to the afterlife.[378] I had taken a photo of such a jar in the Cairo Museum. There are two cabins prominently displayed. Could these two cabins be the earlier equivalent of the two Sphinx shrines on the much later Dream Stele (figure 139)?

I also noticed the flamingos, *dšrw* [desh-roo], which reminded me of the red ones from the Edfu Temple insinuated by the glorifying words, *ḏsrw* [jes-roo], to be placed into the House of Life. I knew I was in hot pursuit of the original record referring to an archive under the Sphinx now. Everything happened fast. All the pieces fell into place.

The incredible solution to this problem has always been staring at us from a familiar site in plain sight. The night barque of the Sun god was the transfigured and fused two tails of the conjoined Sphinxes forming Aker.

Figure 139: The two Sphinxes on the Dream Stele between the forepaws of the Great Sphinx. Giza, May 2019.

That explained why a double lion had morphed into a two-headed snake. In the Dream Stele, the cartouche of Thutmose IV is nestled between the two haunches of the east and west-looking Sphinxes (figure 139).

I remembered how Robert Bauval had thought these were not mere mirror images in a symmetric display of artistry but distinct entities.[379] He had been right after all. The two Sphinxes were not the same, they were His-Face-Behind-Him and His-Face-In-Front, yesterday-west, and tomorrow-east, the entry to, and exit from, the *dw3t*. Their tails, fused in the center between them, became the night barque. They morphed themselves into *Rˁ*'s crescent boat, once in the Netherworld of Rostau, the mythical realm believed to end beneath the spot where the Dream Stele stands today. From here are released the resurrected souls back into the sky from the spirit-incubator called the *3ḥt*, the sub-horizontal realm beneath the sky zone. As if an intended clue to the oldest mystery of the world, the name of Thutmose inside his cartouche, *ḏḥwty-ms* [je-hoo-tee-mes], written with the symbol of Thoth was placed beneath the two sphinxes.

There it was: *the sign of Thoth under the Sphinx.*

If there is still a lingering doubt whether in place of the Great Sphinx, there once stood a monumental lioness, then an unequivocal version of the Mehit sealing from the First Dynasty found by Walter Emery at North Saqqara in 1953 should put it to rest (figure 140).

Figure 140: Mehit sealing from the Saqqara tomb S3504. From Emery (1954).

In this sealing, the same shrine known as *pr-wr* can now be identified with the cobra-guarded solar sanctum in the form of the boat cabin of *R*ꜥ 's night barque as well as the *ꜥfdt* archive.

And what is below the shrine: a double-headed snake. This proves not only that Mehit was at Rostau, but that she guarded an archive for the afterlife. This is confirmed by a Mehit sealing recovered from the grave of a court servant, dated to the reigns of Horus-Djer.[380] In this unique example, the JAW Sign is replaced by an upright registry of papyrus scrolls (figure 141, below).[381]

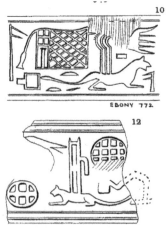

Figure 141: Mehit sealings from Abydos. Above, Mehit with the JAW Sign. Below, the JAW sign is replaced by an upright papyrus scroll symbol *mḏ3t* [Me-jat]. From Petrie (1925).

314

There is even a suggestion here of a square, underground chamber with an access ramp.

Under the Moon Goddess

Once you are on fire, you cannot stop. I kept scouring the records of ancient Egypt for more revelations I knew I could now see in the light of the prior discoveries. I have learned that with Egyptian hieroglyphic, the deeper layers of possible connections seem to be largely unexplored. Might there be something else in predynastic ceramic art to tell us about the origins of these symbols? Can we step closer to the content of this mysterious library presented to us on a celestial platter made up of Thoth's spreading arms? Is it possible to imagine this crescent boat who's on-the-ground equal was a female lion statue called Mehit? Can we look beneath her to open the door to the archive under? *The answer is yes.* It comes in the form of a paradox.

The clue of something possibly paradoxical was that Stan Hendrickx and Mercer Eyckerman puzzled over two symbols found on pots and jars, decorated with the crescent, two-cabin boat: strange appearing female figures and the so-called Naqada plant.[382] The authors suggest that one of the female figures and the plant appear to be one and the same entity, as if she were a transfigured, supernatural being. These wide-hipped, cone-bottomed, humanoid figures have oversized, disc-shaped heads. The Nekhenee[383] potters variously painted them on, or around the crescent boat, and within an *'fdt*-like shrine, like Osiris and R^f. There, she stands next to a smaller, human, apparently male figure. (figure 142)

Nearby are two rows of six, and eight sickle-shaped symbols on small pedestals. Next to the shrine is an emblem composed of a ring on a pole. (figure 143)

This is one of several, so-called standards that look like clan- or boat-identifying banners. The ring banner also marks the ostrich/*njw* [nah-yoo] boat (figure 144).

The female figurine appears to have an alter apparition. A tree takes her place above the boat in one example (figure 145). This duality explains the strange pose of the raised arms with the contorted wrist flexion forming a ring, as if to imitate the canopy of a tree and the ring standard.

Identical in pose is the famous bird-headed terracotta figurine found at El Ma'mariya, Egypt dated to the same era,[384] which Hendrickx and Eyckerman

Figure 142: Decorated predynastic pottery discovered at Hierakonpolis dated to circa 3500–3300 BC. Rogers Fund (1936). ©, The Metropolitan Museum of Art, New York, NY. Public Domain.

Figure 143: Close-up of the female figurine and male under a canopy with ring banner. Rogers Fund (1936). ©, The Metropolitan Museum of Art, New York, NY. Public Domain.

Figure 144: Predynastic, Upper Egyptian, Decorated Ware from circa 3450–3350 BC. Same jar as in Figure 120. Rogers Fund (1907). ©, The Metropolitan Museum of Art, New York, NY. Public Domain.

Figure 145: Decorated, predynastic pottery discovered at Hierakonpolis, dated to circa 3500–3300 BC. Rogers Fund (1936). ©, The Metropolitan Museum of Art, New York, NY. Public Domain.

have likened to a bovine bucranium. The evidence for this interpretation is a cosmetic palette with the image of a cow head adorned with star symbols, and with horns shaped like the raised arms.[385] This archaeological context from the Fayum area of Egypt identifies her as a stylized, personified icon of a cattle cult.[386]

The head of the female boat figure here, however, is not bird shaped. That suggested to me she was another, though related, goddess worshiped in Upper Egypt. My overall impression was that I might be looking at one of two predynastic precursor deities later syncretized as Hathor the Mistress of the Sycamore, and Iusaaset the Acacia goddess, one based on the sky and trees, and the other based on fowl and cattle. The association with the Sycamore Fig Tree reminded me of a comment made by the famous Egyptian archaeologist, Selim Hassan. In his excavation reports on the Great Sphinx, he mentions an ancient, still-alive Sycamore grove at the south end of Giza, near the old lioness. I also remembered the Sycamore mentioned in the Inventory Stele, struck by lightning, and inspected by king Khufu.[387]

Shown beneath one of the mysterious goddess' boats is a box under an arc-shaped cover in place of the ostrich (figure 146).

Figure 146: Decorated, predynastic pottery discovered at Hierakonpolis, dated to circa 3500–3300 BC. Rogers Fund (1936). ©, The Metropolitan Museum of Art, New York, NY. Public Domain.

The barque, the box under the arc, Flamingos

The distant memory of a jubilant chant began to echo in my ears: "… we provide the *House of Life* with *glorifying words.*" Was I looking at a predynastic image of the archive under the Sphinx? There they were next to it, the cone goddesses, the Flamingos—*the red ones, the ḏsrw creation words, Flamingos, ḏšrw, lions!* Was this the prehistoric book of Thoth inside the box, the throne of *R*ꜥ, the cabin of Osiris? This possibility exceeded my wildest expectations—but things got even stranger.

The Naqada plant emerges from a box just like it. Here, it is surrounded by strands, radiating from a ring immediately above it, shaped like the boat emblem (figure 147).

Figure 147: Predynastic, Upper Egyptian, Decorated Ware, circa 3450–3350 BC. Rogers Fund (1907). ©, The Metropolitan Museum of Art, New York, NY. Public Domain.

The box looks like the throne in the Vignette of *R*ꜥ. *I was looking at its prehistoric origin.*

I could not believe it. I had found it—proof positive that the ideas painted into Vignette of *R*ꜥ on the coffin of General Zepi, the Sun God creator of the universe sitting on a box-like throne, surrounded by the ḥḥw orbits of cosmic eternity; all these elements had come from a far more ancient, predynastic original in the shape of a plant. Adding to the excitement was a similar example kept at the Robert and Frances Fullerton Museum of Art on the campus of the California State University at San Bernardino whose director Eva Kirsch I know well since she is also the director of the local chapter of the American Research Center Egypt. I remembered seeing one of these vividly decorated boat jars a couple of years prior, at Eva's museum. I asked her if she had photos; she did. On one of the two, I was greeted with two surprises: Instead of the box there was a cone (figure 148).

Figure 148: The Naqada Plant, cone version; circa 3500 BC. Object on extended loan from Dr. W. Benson Harer. ©, the Robert and Frances Fullerton Museum of Art at California State University, San Bernardino.

Onto the bottom of the jar had been painted a coil, the royal symbol of the power to turning of the sky and create cosmic order. And next to it was something, a tree, an animal skin, perhaps the symbol for the sound *st*? Was it an African Sycamore or an Acacia?

I'm surprised no one else heard the bells ringing in my head at this point. So many different avenues which had opened themselves during the many months of research suddenly all converged to one point. The bottom of this jar spoke volumes (figure 149).

Figure 149: The coil on the bottom; same jar as Figure 148. Object on extended loan from Dr. W. Benson Harer. ©, the Robert and Frances Fullerton Museum of Art (RAFFMA) at California State University, San Bernardino.

Here were the symbols of a forgotten cosmology, the cone-shaped seed of something fundamental to the worldview of our distant ancestors from our forgotten past. They left it for another time, another people, a new cycle of civilization. The symbolic depth is incredible.

The branch and fruiting body growing from the Naqada plant likely prompted Egyptologists to think of it as a plant. But for my part, I could not get around the striking similarities between it and the Vignette of R^c. The painting is as a fusion of the ideas embodied by the Naqada plant and the crescent boat. The boat became the crown of the Sun God. It represented his higher powers and consciousness. I no longer saw a plant but the throne of R^c. Above it hovers the ring or a disk, the symbol of the Sun. From it, orbital rays radiate from it on the jars, and encircle it in the vignette.

And that, after all, explained to me the box. It was the prehistoric version of the *ꜥfdt*. In the vignette, the Sun God *sits on it. Of course! How could I have missed it?* The archive under the Sphinx symbolized a solar concept. The Sun is in the center. The heliocentric universe painted on the spheroid body of a predynastic Egyptian jar. How could this be? *The jar itself was a model of the universe!* This was the final proof: I was in shock. The archive under the Sphinx had been opened a long time *before* Narmer set his foot on Rostau.

What had "come out" of this primordial archive was symbolized by the Nekhenee pot painters as a ring surrounded by the strands. This ring grew into a fruiting branch, or was it an ostrich feather (figure 150)?

Figure 150: Decorated, predynastic, pottery showing the Naqada Plant, ten (left), and nine (right) concentric elliptical rings. Discovered at Hierakonpolis, dated to circa 3450–3300 BC. Egypt Exploration Fund (1899). ©, The Metropolitan Museum of Art, New York, NY. Public Domain.

A symbol of regrowth and new life, regardless. Plaster fragments depicting this plant-like image were found by an elite tomb at Hierakonpolis' cemetery HK6. It was meant to be an image for the afterlife, like at the cemetery of Deir El-Bersheh where the vignette was found on the coffin in the tomb of General Zepi.[388]

But if the Naqada plant was indeed identical with the coffin painting that had started my investigation, then what became of the tree goddess with the cone-shaped legs? There was only one logical answer: she had been replaced with a male god in the Vignette of R^{ς}. Her raised arms pose compares to a victory pose seen in another, earlier-dated context of hunting enemies and animals painted on White Cross-lined pottery from the Naqada I period, dated to 4000-3500 BC. As Hendrickx explains, this raised-arm gesture was a triumphant pose celebrating the subduing of the wild, chaotic forces

322

threatening hunter societies.[389] On these older pots and jars, the figures were male warriors. They can be seen wearing a headdress with branches or feathers and a foxtail-like belt accessory.

In the later boat context seen on Decorated Ware from Naqada II, dated to 3500-3200 BC, the raised arm pose of the tree goddess could be a triumphant or a votive and worshiping gesture. Given the funerary context of these pots, it must be the latter. If her arms shaped themselves into the canopy of a tree, then what did her disk-like head represent? And what about her cone-shaped legs? The cone reminded me of the seven Sumerian Abgal fish sages or Ummanu oxen[390] from the myths of Mesopotamia. They were the knowledge keeping spirits, not unlike the seven Egyptian *ḏ3jsw*, the flood-born, baboon-like creation words mentioned in the Edfu Texts. They carried reeds to write. These sages carried cones and fertilized trees. There it was again: *The seed of civilization, symbols.*

I remembered the Assyrian reliefs of these Apkallu I had seen at the Egyptian Museum in Munich. They can be seen using cones to fertilize trees from seed buckets. The cone-shaped legs of the boat goddess reminded me of the tree cone they were holding in the hand. In one instance cited by Hendrickx and Eyckerman, the Naqada plant's base is cone-shaped in place of the box as if the two were interchangeable in their meaning. There it was again: *The symbol of recorded knowledge.*[391]

According to one interpretation, the strands of the Naqada plant wrapped protectively around the box could represent the hair strands of the tree goddess.[392] This raised the fascinating possibility that all this was merely an imagination, created inside the disc-shaped head of the goddess. It suggested that she had conceived the whole universe inside her head in symbolic form. Was this a feminine creator who intellectually forged the universe with nothing but pure thought? Is this not the same idea as that in the much later Memphite cosmogony centered on the male creator god Ptah?

The single known example of the Vignette of *Rˤ* had been painted onto the coffin interior near the head of the mummy of General Zepi. He was not only a member of the Hermopolitean elite but someone who had enjoyed special access to the House of Life. Likewise he would have had special access to the deepest secrets there. He would have known the secret of divine creation. This matched the elite tomb context of the Naqada plant at Hierakonpolis' cemetery HK6. This elite, funerary connection across a time span of more than one thousand five hundred years underscores the fundamental nature of the knowledge these symbols represented. Undoubtedly it dealt with an afterlife concept only few of ancient Egyptian society could know.

If the images on these pots were an imagination of the tree goddess, then it makes sense why the elite of Hierakonpolis wanted them nearby. Their desire to be imbued by divine knowledge for the afterlife rhymes perfectly with the idea of a Heka-equipped ritualist who navigates the Netherworld to reach the seat of resurrection to reach immortality. The knowledge to attain this ultimate state all of us wish for had been sealed inside of the box, the boat pedestal, the throne of R^c, and the animal shrine *pr-wr*. In the end, all these were but different images of the same idea: an archive of astronomical knowledge interpreted as something spiritually divine. For the first time, I understood why the general wanted this painting near his mummified head. He wanted *to know*.

Prehistoric Codex Universi

One piece missing to tip the balance towards astronomy and divine knowledge, and away from a concrete image of a plant—the current consensus reading of this image by academic scholars—were the elliptical rings, the orbits. Painted on all these jars are wavy elliptical rings in a concentric pattern. Their number vary between seven and ten. They are connected to a set of rings around the mouth of the jar (figure 151).

These bands looked like the ecliptic water channels from the vignette, but what if they were ropes or ornamental jewelry chains? It dawned on me that the key to the puzzle was the branch which seemed to grow out of the Naqada plant. It is the same branch as that which is attached to the boats at the prow, the standard, and the pedestal inside the boat cabin on which the goddess stands.

Could what I first thought was an ostrich feather be, instead, a palm-like branch growing from the ring over the box seen in the Naqada plant? Its curved shape reminded me of the later Egyptian hieroglyph for the word year, *rnpt* on which Thoth and Seshat recorded the years of the kings and queens of Egypt. Three of these symbols and three raised-arm figure symbols for million/myriad can be seen on the throne of R^c in the vignette. It means "myriads of years" (figure 152). You already know them: the *ḥḥw*!

Figure 151: Decorated, predynastic, pottery discovered at Hierakonpolis, dated to circa 3500–3300 BC. Rogers Fund (1936). ©, The Metropolitan Museum of Art, New York, NY. Public Domain.

Figure 152: The throne from the Vignette of *Rᶜ*. On it, are three hieroglyphs for year *rnpt*, and below, three *ḥḥw* signs for "myriads" or "Millions." ©, Werner Forman/ Universal Images Group and Werner Foreman Archive/ Heritage Image, respectively; agefotostock®; modified.

That was the missing piece: the fourteen symbols, the small crescents on pedestals (figure 153).

Figure 153: Small crescent symbols on pedestals next to a boat floating through the afterlife. Rogers Fund (1936). ©, The Metropolitan Museum of Art, New York, NY. Public Domain.

They stood for eternity, for time before time, for the chaos into which creation created order. These were the eons of time measured in millions, billions of years, fourteen of them, recorded on the palm branch on the tree-goddess' celestial bark. Could there be a better set of symbols to represent an archive of astronomical time records in the form of a notched palm branch growing out of a box, from a ring, sending out elliptical bands like the fireworks of cosmic creation? If this is what was once meant to be painted on these almost six-thousand-year-old jars, the symbolic design to convey the concept would be ingenious by any standard then or now.

What had been missing to read this symbolic code was the right context. It had been erased by the implausibility brush of modern, dogmatic thinking about our history. In the right context of astronomy, these artistic objects tell us not only a great deal about how prehistoric people visualized the afterlife, but it also tells us how they viewed their place in the vastness of space and time. The depth of symbolism captured with such masterful strokes of red paint on clay was so profound that it influenced the formation of the main power symbols of Egypt: The cartouche, the snake coil, the ring, the ouroboros, the Osirian crown, the royal throne, the coffer symbol, the animal shrine, the night bark, and the sun disk ensnared by the cobra. All these power symbols of three thousand years of Egyptian history we admire on monuments, study, photograph, display, and wear ultimately came from the Naqada plant, the symbol of the mind of a prehistoric creator goddess, whose name we may never know.

Or may we? If I learned anything in my search for answers about the Great Sphinx and the Vignette of R^{ς}, it's this: Lost civilizations are never lost. They will always leave a trace. You can find those traces if only you know where—and how—to look.

The Creator Goddess Celebrates

All this was so overwhelming to process at first that I found no pause to ask the ultimate question of my entire quest: Where had this idea originated? Who was *she*?

I had begun my quest with the story of the *Hall of Records*, a tale of recorded and preserved knowledge from a time and place of which Plato wrote. From where I was now, these ideas seemed so far removed and remote.

Edgar Cayce created the brand of the legend of the *Hall of Records* of Atlantis, but I now knew that this idea was so much older than Cayce, older than even Plato, much older, yet, than I initially imagined. I had traced the origin of this archive to the fourth millennium BC, three thousand years before Plato. I had textually dated the place where it had been hidden under the monumental lioness Mehit. *I had astronomically dated Mehit* to the eleventh millennium BC corroborating previous geological and astronomical data by John Anthony West, Robert Schoch, and Robert Bauval. I had refined this date to the celestial marriage of the Sun, Leo, and the Moon which had narrowed it to less than a handful of candidate dates for the creation of the archive and the stony lioness made to guard it.

In *Magicians of the Gods*, Graham Hancock draws a connection between the Sumerian flood myth, inscriptions on the walls of the Edfu Temple, the Atlantis story, and the Middle Egyptian story of the *Shipwrecked Sailor* who is stranded on a mystical island.[393] The common thread Hancock recognizes is the story of a fall, and then the rise of an age of beings whose few survivors set out on water to recreate the world and spawn civilizations anew. These messengers of a lost past are the seven sages, magical water spirits called Apkallu. Next to them, Hancock implicates the *šbtjw* [shebti-oo] mentioned at Edfu to have been among them.[394]

My own search had led me to a female tree-goddess who had intellectually conceived the solar universe within her mind, symbolized by a ring around a disk. From my own studies of the Edfu Texts, I knew that the *šbtjw* were two titanic forces who had feuded on a primordial island. They were water and land symbolizing chaos and order. This battle was the story of the Great Flood, personified in the texts as the Great Mehit, **wr**-Mehit. When the battle subsided and the mud settled, these two spiritual beings now became the creative facilities of Ptah. They were the *distant* idea and the *near* force of focused thought. And so, they were called The Far, as in small, and The Great, as in big.[395] We know these facilities as in-the-back-of-the-mind and front-and-center. They are with us all the time.

I would like to ask you now to take a second look at this couple (figure 143). Were these two concepts, creative idea and focused thought, the male and female aspects of the creation of the world? Does this jar show us an image of the First Couple of the First Time whose symbol of union was a ring made up of two halves? Does this jar show us an image of the two *šbtjw*?

To answer this question, I had to look up the Egyptian word for ring. I knew that the word for arm was ꜥ [aah], and the word for two arms was ꜥwy [aahooee]. I also knew the hieroglyphic names of the *šbtjw*, **w3j** [uaee], The Far, and **ꜥ3** [aahuh], The Great. To my immense surprise, the word for ring is ꜥwꜥw [aahoo-aahoo]. It is the same word as saying "arm-arm," i.e., "two arms."[396]

Also written at Edfu in the same place on the western half of the north wall, in the third register, where the creation scene with the *šbtjw* unfolds, is the introduction to this epic saga given by Thoth. He is the one who records this story from the seven uttered words of creation. They are the *ḏ3jsw,* whose substance, we are told, is the great floodwaters of *wr-mḥt* [oor-mehit].[397]

Like the Sumerian Apkallu, they were water spirits. The parallels are unmistakable. Graham Hancock was right.

No doubt in my mind, the original, post-diluvian, Egyptian creation story unfolds according to a script written by the Moon. I came to realize that the disk above the boat-faring tree goddess was not the Sun, but *it*, the Moon. She was *The Great*, the goddess of the Moon. Is that not Thoth's epithet: *the twice/thrice great*? The Moon personified the creative intellect of the Sun, the *Mind of R͑*. We call it Logos.

In the Vignette of *R͑*, the disk forming the tree-goddess' head became an image of the Sun God. The text tells us that this is so. It is the Sun God who creates the world in the Coffin Texts. But what had taken me to this image of a tree-goddess painted on predynastic pottery was not the Sun, but the crescent Moon-barque and Aker.

The conclusion is inescapable: Six thousand years ago, the symbol of the heliocentric universe was not a male Sun God but a female Moon Goddess who triumphantly outstretched her arms and celebrated something wonderful—the creation of the universe. This jubilant pose celebrated the seasonal growth of a cosmic tree and the union of the cosmic masculine with the cosmic feminine. It symbolized a celestial marriage in the shape of a ring. Was this the symbol of a real event in the sky? Was it an annular solar eclipse when the Moon covers the center of the Sun, but not its rim? *A Ring of Fire. The Island of Fire!*

During a solar eclipse, ancient observers would learn that the Moon is closer than the Sun. This is something impossible to know otherwise since the dome of the sky appears flat. Our depth perception fails when we try to gauge depth at a distance. An eclipse could have clued in prehistoric sky watchers that the Sun, Moon, planets, and stars travel on dedicated tracks and that *the sky has depth*. Perhaps then, the Great and the Far were just the primordial names for the Moon and the Sun. Perhaps, a solar eclipse appeared like a union between them, symbolized by the ring that formed from the rim of unblanched light (figure 154).

Figure 154: Annular solar eclipse showing the spectrum of shapes, including crescent and ring. Placer County, California; May 20, 2012. Composite time lapse. ©, Tony Hallas.

The words *šbt* and *šbn*, from which the word *šbtjw*[398] comes, after all, can mean a tree, the coil on Lower Egypt's Red *ḏsrt* Crown, and to mingle, mix, exchange, and consort.[399] In a solar eclipse, the Moon consorts with the Sun. Since solar eclipses cluster in time with lunar eclipses, the *šbtjw* may have been the symbol of the equinoctial solar eclipse that occurred at the same time as the Younger Dryas equinoctial lunar eclipse, enshrined by Mehit. Both may have occurred in a specific month sometime near the end of the eleventh millennium BC, when conditions on Earth began to recover from high floods caused by some cosmic, climatic calamity. These real events were captured in this Egyptian story of creation. Myths are not just stories. They tell us about real events imagined and remembered through stories. Just like we imagine our existence through story, does that make it any less real?

The insight that the sky has depth must have logically predated any idea about the three-dimensional structure of the known universe and its center.

Could the original astronomical discovery of human beings be any more fundamental than the idea of sky depth and space symbolized by a ring?

The original number of nine ellipses seen in the vignette did not seem to matter in the cultural context of the Naqada people because the number did not make sense to them. They worshiped the Moon and counted the months between inundations of the Nile. These "years" ranged from seven to ten months.[400] That explains why the number of rings varies on the different jars. I think these jars, like the oil tags later, could have been made to commemorate a two-inundations period. That was the time after which the regional rulers would begin the cattle count to levy taxes on the farmers. With that cattle count came the fear of punishment and death, which explains the related themes of seasonal growth and the afterlife. The king or queen, after all, came on a boat to collect taxes. In this way, the waterway circuits in the sky became the months of the year. That explains why the rings are wavy. The orbits became the circuits on the winding waterway, completed by the Moon before the next flood of the Nile.

The imagery of the Naqada plant suggests that the ellipses came from the ring in the center. Rings came out of the box. This is the ring on the standard which identifies the boats of the ostrich and the tree-goddess. The symbol of the ring pervades predynastic Egyptian art, such as the cosmetic palettes and the Mehen game. Eventually, it morphed into concentric rings, spirals, coils, and snakes. A solar eclipse, even today, is a celestial spectacle of such profound cultural impact that it is easy to see how it may have inspired the ring. The Vignette of *Rˁ* helps us to recreate the context we missed. It has always been about astronomy. Within that context, we can now understand these misunderstood symbols of the past.

It is time now to restore something important. I think that before Egypt became a unified land, Thoth was not a god but a goddess. In the beginning was not he, Thoth, *ḏḥwty*, the Thrice Great. In the beginning was Mehit, maybe Mehen, the Great, the *wr*-Mehit, the harbinger of floods, one of the *šbtjw,* one of the original cosmic Two of creation. *mḥ*, after all, is not just an ell to measure, it is also the forearm itself. It is what makes us so human.

In raising her arms, the Moon Goddess signaled that she was one with time, the unit of that which measures the order of the universe. The word *mḥn*, to this day, hides in our own word for *month*. May the first name of the Moon, from the First Time, not be forgotten.

I think what you are looking at in figure 146 is an image of the original *Book of Thoth*—the Osirian Box guarded by Mehit, lioness goddess of the Moon, she who marks, counts, and records the myriads of years, the eons travelled on the cosmic highway of the stars. Allow me to guide your attention once more back to figure 64, Coffin Text Spell 302, to point out the connection between archive and boat:

I have come forth from the ʿfdt to the Night Barque.

This takes us all the way back to the beginning in an eternal cycle of cosmic order. The lioness was a marker of time. She protected recorded knowledge about the structure of the universe. Time and space, the quintessential elements of our existence in the vastness of what is around us to infinity.

And if you wondered what this Moon goddess with arms raised has to do with a crescent snake boat and a lion, then you are wondering what I was wondering until the very end of writing this book when it finally dawned on me: Around the time the Younger Dryas ended,[401] the ecliptic angle was such that it made several instances of a rare Full Moon possible: Rising into the "outstretched arms" of what we call Virgo, the constellation just east of Leo on the ecliptic and in the Zodiac (figure 155)![402]

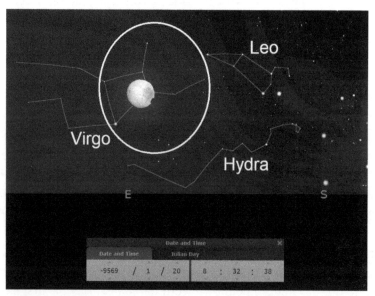

Figure 155: The eastern sky after sunset in 9570 BC The Full Moon rises into Virgo. Graphic made with Stellarium 0.14.3.

I finally understood the origin of the much later myths of the Heavenly Cow,[403] the Drunkenness Festival, and the Legend of the Wandering Goddess myth.[404] The common theme of all these is that of the vengeful and raging aspect of the Sun God, variously represented by the lionesses Tefnut, Mehit, or Sekhmet. In one theme, for example, he sends his emissary eye into catastrophic battle against rebellious man. He only relents after an epic frenzy of destruction. His eye is none other than the otherwise docile and loving cow goddess Hathor, now suddenly enraged, and, in some versions, transfigured into an unhinged lioness. He pacifies her with a drink to look like the blood for which she thirsts. But I think in its original meaning this was drinking the mind-opening wisdom of Thoth, the power to learn about nature we call reason. This is related to the trance-like state entered by the prehistoric *sm* shamans enabling them to chase after the lost shadows of the dead in the Underworld and to animate the memory of a deceased with their likeness in the form of a statuette, and, ultimately, a mummy.

It made sense now. The cattle horn and lion images were neighboring star signs in the sky. The conventional interpretation based on astronomy is the Sun recurring to its summer solstice sunrise position on the horizon as a harbinger of the yearly inundation putting a relieving end to the dry months of drought that precede it. But what if this myth was originally based on a distant memory, or an archived record later retrieved, of a real catastrophe that befell Earth and ended the Younger Dryas cold spell? What if the cow goddess' transfiguration into a lioness marked the timing of events due to precession that occurred when the vernal equinox completed its shift from rising into the constellation Virgo to an astronomical epoch coinciding with the rise of Leo appearing couchant above the predawn horizon in 10,000 B.C.?

Knowledge of the sky, its Sun-centered, orbital structure, and its periodic workings was the secret to understanding the cyclical nature of events, both good and bad. If you could know the sky in this way, you were masterfully equipped, drunk and intoxicated, if you will, with deep wisdom. You would know of cosmic and Earthly chaos, but also of order: as above so below. Knowing this eternal order of cyclical time, you would understand the fundamental secret of creation, death, and rebirth, and that there cannot be order without the chaos from which it is born.

I think this is the wisdom one might have learned from what was once kept in the real *Hall of Records* under the lioness, under Mehit. With this wisdom came solace and reason over rage, power over the crippling fear of relentless, never ending chaos of nature. With reason and order came civilization. This was Thoth's legacy, *her* legacy.

Thinking of Plato's *The Critias*, I wonder now if an Egyptian priest from the Temple of Neith at Sais told Solon the story of a demigod, born to the god of the sea and an Earthly mother, who raised his arms to carry not the Moon, but planet Earth? But that is really for you to imagine, and for me to leave at your disposal.

And this, my fellow explorers, travelers, and seekers, this is as close to the original content under the Sphinx as I can take you. That is until someone can drill a small hole into Anomaly A, the Dobecki-Schoch Chamber under the left forepaw of the Great Sphinx. I would make that hole where Mark Lehner left his tiny signature, barely visible and unlikely known by anyone other than He, I, and now you, on one of his high-resolution maps.

Postscript

S OMETHING STRUCK ME ABOUT BJÖRN BILLSON'S IMPRESSIONS INTERPRETING the Vignette of R^ς and the inscription mentioning the Roads of Mehen. I had forgotten about it until writing the end of this book.

He wondered if a transfer of knowledge from an aspect of ancient Egyptian life may have occurred to become part of the body of magical spells written for the afterlife. Billson, like I, must have sensed the strangeness of the vignette within the funerary context. He tried to explain it from within the conventional historical paradigm. He reasoned that the Roads of Mehen could have been a secret initiation ritual in life, for example, adapted for the dead. Essentially he reasoned the transfer came from *within*, from *inside* the culture and knowledge of the ancient Egyptians.

I am neither a credentialled historian, astronomer, nor Egyptologist. I am a practicing physician, diversely trained, and credentialled in the physical and social sciences as they apply to health and illness of people. I am trained as a scientist. My skill set is scanning, filtering, distilling, and learning from a vast volume of knowledge available to the public and applying it to solve a problem. This skill set was my chief asset while investigating the hieroglyphic evidence for an archive under the Sphinx. Given a lot of time and work, I knew I might acquire what I needed to know to solve a mystery in need of a multi-disciplinary approach. I had to be a team of experts, all combined into one person. My publisher calls me a true *amateur*. Centuries ago, we were the polymaths, the ones who asked questions others did not want to ask, and used, what Hermann Hesse might have called, *Das Glasperlenspiel* to answer them.

Does this somehow make me unable to compete with a group of Egyptologists, language experts, astronomers, and historians, trained and credentialed from within the paradigm we call history? You get to decide that. My only edge is this: I am an outsider. I can pierce a dogma from the *outside*, put it into doubt by a paradox the insiders cannot explain. I am a heretic. As an independent researcher of prehistory, this is my sole credential. Yes, there is an element of heresy in each and every good scientist, the willingness to imagine explanations no one else imagines to explain what defies explanation.

But could it really be that a culture unknown to us observed the sky like Galileo Galilei more than twelve thousand years ago? Could it be that these people figured out the heliocentric nature of our solar system, as much later did Aristarchus, Copernicus, and Kepler? Could it really be that the people of this culture we do not know left their astronomical records inside a coffer, secured it inside an underground vault, and carved a stony lioness out of the living rock above to alert us and tell us when they did this?

This is the thesis of *Under the Sphinx*; this, I argue, is exactly what happened. A transfer of knowledge occurred, just like Björn Billson says. Yet, unlike he, I argue it came from the *outside*. It came from another place and another time because this knowledge cannot have come from the ancient Egyptians, and if it did not come from them, our model of history is wrong. A better model means that what we call the ladder of progress is really a wheel, that some knowledge and know-how was inherited, and history is not a one-way street, but a cycle. The importance of this new model of history cannot be overstated. Our unknown ancestors felt compelled to immortalize a message to us, a message not too different from a broken Lady Liberty half-buried in the sand on the shore of a lost world that once stood proud and tall. As it ended, so could we. How could the ancient Egyptians have passed this message forward to us in a way we might one day decipher?

We should consider that it was not Plato who invented Atlantis, but the Saite priest who told a fanciful story to Solon. Perhaps that priest knew of the secret knowledge of the Vignette of R^c and weaved it into a tale for the Greek.

Or we should consider the Vignette of R^c was nothing but a scribe's musing in the House of Life, with a Sun encircled by road- or waterways on Earth. Or was it an ostrich egg with nine shells?

But what if there were some things in ancient Egyptian art which could help us with clues that a transfer of knowledge occurred, and that a hidden archive of it was discovered and breached, releasing these records, such as the Vignette of $R^ʿ$ into the hands of prehistoric people who lived by the Nile?

For these things, we must travel back in time to Hierakonpolis, the City of the Falcon, *nḫn* [ne-khen]. It is a hot sunny day in 1899. The place: an area east of the fort at Hierakonpolis, an area then called the Predynastic Cemetery. There and then, Frederick W. Green had taken over supervision from James E. Quibell (1867-1935) during the second season of excavations. He was about to make a great discovery. Here is the pretext.

In the first season during 1897-1898, Quibell and Green had found, among other incredible relics, the Narmer Palette under the Temple of Horus. To give you an idea of its importance to Egyptology, when you walk into the Museum of Egyptian Antiquities in Cairo, Egypt, and head straight, for no more than a few steps after the main entry, you walk up to a glass display. In it is the Narmer Palette (figure 156).

Figure 156: Recto and verso of the Narmer Palette. The king's name "Catfish-Chisel," *nʿr-mr*, is framed. The rectangular structure is marked. ©, Public Domain.

Millions of people have looked at it. So have I. But just a couple of months ago, I recognized a familiar shape on its verso, the backside. It shows Narmer wearing the Red Crown. This, and other elements shown, suggest that the verso is about Lower Egypt. To the far left, above Narmer's sandal carrier is a strange rectangle inscribed into the top part of which is a hieroglyph: It is the sign for **ḏb3**, [Je-ba], and means "finger" in hieroglyphic but is also the ancient name for Edfu. *Where had I seen this?*

According to an elegant rationale by E. A. E. Reymond, however, **ḏb3** originally referred to the primordial perch made by the **šbtjw**, on which a falcon landed, and thus becomes Horus divine.[405] This perch was the very first, the very original seat of Horus, woven together from the reeds on the banks of an island surrounded by the chaotic, cosmic waters, as told by the Edfu Texts.

And then I remembered. It reminded me of the arc above the box under the crescent ship of the Moon Goddess (figure 157).

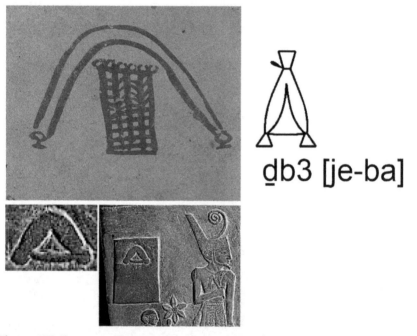

ḏb3 [je-ba]

Figure 157: Top, magnification of the arc and box elements in Figure 145. Bottom, magnified view of the rectangular structure and **ḏb3** sign from the verso of the Narmer Palette. Right, the **ḏb3** hieroglyph illustrated.

Whatever this rectangle on Narmer's Palette is, an enclosure, a chamber like the "Robing Room," [406]—mentioned in Coffin Text Spell 155 (Chapter VI) and possibly the same as the Netherworld House in which the **ꜥfdt** archive was stored—or a stylized primordial island of creation, it must have been holy because in it we see Egypt's oldest hieroglyph yet: The Perch of Horus woven for him by the First Couple of creation, the finger of God, if you will, on which his emissary majestically lands to symbolically seed a new civilization: *ḏb3*.

Where did this seed come from? Do civilizations arise here and there like primordial perches from chaos, or do they travel the sky and seas and spread their wings? Maybe, there is some of both in our path from where we began. But what were the ancient Egyptians telling us about where they came from?

Let me show you one other relic from Narmer's time. This is the head of a ceremonial mace found by Quibell and Green steps away from the Narmer Palette. The scene carved into the stony orb is that of the king's jubilee festival. He is wearing the Red Crown sitting in a raised pavilion being presented with war loot like animals and slaves. The idea is that a king, once he and his reign reached a certain age, had to reaffirm his abilities and then be symbolically reborn. He had to symbolically resurrect.

What drew my attention in this regard were two icons, a half oval shrine with a mummy-like person inside, a so-called naos in Greek and *ḏb3*[407] in hieroglyphic, and *ḥḥw*, used here to indicate a million (figure 158).

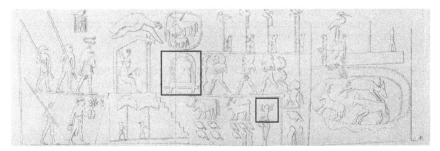

Figure 158: Sketch of Narmer's Great Mace Head inscription. The sedan chair with half oval ceiling housing a statue-like figure, and the *ḥḥw* symbol are framed to highlight them. From Quibell (1900), Plate XXVIB; modified.

Regardless of how these symbols became part of this scene and ceremony, they are key elements in the Vignette of *R ͨ*, the idea of eternity and eternal life embodied by the Sun and the planets reinterpreted as a path to immortality.

What you are looking at in this sketch from the original may be as close as we will ever come to know the original form of the information stored in the archive under Mehit.

When I first suspected that the archive under Mehit was first breached by Narmer, I had arrived there indirectly, by circumstantial evidence such as what can be gleaned from his palette and mace head. But the better evidence is always of the direct kind. I had come to accept that finding something like that would be next to impossible. But not so.

Petrie found one sealing of Mehit in Abydos that shows the lioness, in her unmistakable form with the JAW Sign, and one of two chisel signs above her neck (figure 159).[408] This sign was also used to spell the name of the king, *nˁr-mr* (Chapter VIII).

16

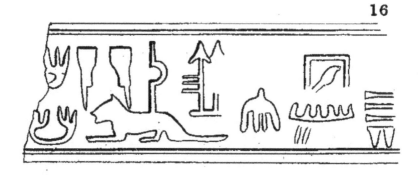

Figure 159: Mehit Sealing from Abydos found by Petrie. Two *mr* chisels can be seen above the lioness, one directly over her neck. From Petrie (1925).

These dual chisels could be part of a name, or one is part of a name, and the other indicates an action, like chiseling or carving. It is even possible that one chisel refers to the king, as in other examples in which the catfish alone refers to him.[409] And if so, does this sealing hint that he opened the Mehit archive, or repaired her statue, or made it in the first place?

These incredible finds from Abydos and Hierakonpolis chronicle Narmer's history-making life. The Narmer Palette and mace head discovered by Quibell and Green in their first excavation season are among the earliest written records in the world, at the cradle of our current cycle of civilization. This is the context into which I now want to put Frederick Green's discovery in the summer of 1899. Green was a man with many interests.[410]

He made telescopes, tinkered with engine motors, made maps, and taught himself hieroglyphic. He took one course in Egyptology and trained with Flinders Petrie. In his later years, he was a medic who converted a laundry truck into an ambulance during World War II.

Green was a modern-day polymath, in the best sense of the word. He was an outsider. In a symbolic sense, I cannot think of a better person to have discovered the famous Tomb 100 painting dated to circa 3500-3200 BC, [411] several centuries before Narmer! It was made during the same predynastic times, when the incredible decorated jars were made painted with crescent boats, the Moon Goddess, and Naqada plant I have shown you earlier.

Tomb 100 was an unusual grave on the easternmost part of town. A worker alerted Green that he had spotted painted walls inside.[412] The scene was that of boats, people, and animals very much like the themes on the predynastic pots and jars I had marveled at (figure 160).

Figure 160: Original Reproduction of the painted south wall of Tomb 100 at Hierakonpolis. From Quibell and Green, 1902; Plate LXXV

Some people have since interpreted these images as an invasion,[413] some as a story,[414] and some as a depiction of the afterlife.[415] But there is one tiny detail that I almost missed, even though I have stared at this painting many times. This is an oval, egg-shaped object on the one boat which looks different from all the other (figure 161).

The colors of the three stripes of this cabin-like object are two red and one black on white, like those of the nine bands shown in the Vignette R^c. Next to it is the box-like pedestal with handle. I cannot be certain that what is shown here is the predynastic precursor to the vignette of R^c next to the

Figure 161: The black boat with the oval cabin on the wall painting of Tomb 100; magnified in the inset, right lower corner. From Quibell and Green, 1902; Plate LXXVII.

ʿfdt coffer. However, of what I can be certain is that like the vignette, this object was special, for it took a special boat to ship it from here to there, wherever here and there were in this image of the real or the imagined.

Near Tomb 100, Green discovered marked pots and on one of them was painted the symbol of a ring-like wheel (figure 162).

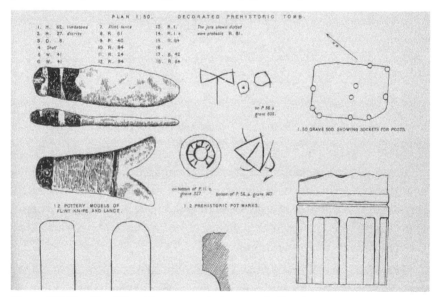

Figure 162: The Ring Wheel Pottery mark. From Quibell and Green, 1902; Plate LXVII.

I cannot be certain that this is the same ring shown atop the standard of the tree goddess, but of what I can be certain is that it, like the coil symbol, was painted on the bottom of a jar.

Did our ancient ancestors try to tell us that esoteric, astronomical knowledge came to them on a boat travelling on a real waterway or one imagined in the sky? Did the painter of this mural leave us with an illustration of the celestial highway on which the planets float along their dedicated waterways? If the archive under Mehit was still sealed at this time, how did the ideas enshrined in the Naqada plant and the Moon Goddess make their way into prehistoric Hierakonpolis, a bustling city by the Nile, long before history declares the onset of civilization in Egypt began?

I raise a new question with no answer to give you, but what more does scientific inquiry really do? We can shine light on parts of the unknown with new discoveries, though without the whole, the parts raise new questions, and new paradoxes. And so, we never reach it, the end of the unknown, do we? So be it, for now, until new discoveries lead the way again.

Not too long ago, we believed that we were the outcome of a one-shot universe that began with a bang from nothing and will grow to infinity. But nowadays, physicists are talking about a sea of universes arising out of lonely quantum fluctuations, some stable some not, all floating down a cosmic river as fractal flow and spiraling inwards like turbulent vortices. These coils explain the flow of time from temporary order to inevitable chaos down a spiral on which we cannot flow back.

Each of these universes are supposed to be inside of that which is inside of them to infinity, black holes within black holes, on which the information is archived on the rim, while the experience we call life happens in the center. If this is true, then what we think is substance is no more material than a hologram. Yet, it could be worse, since we are nothing more than virtual minds in a simulated computer program made to study the past.

These ideas are so mind-boggling, yet most of us go about our normal ways, and for good reason: It makes no difference in our daily lives. Our world is what we know on Earth. What happens up there in the sky, let alone beyond, only matters when it affects our weather, or when we watch in awe the occasional spectacles of nature as they play out above our heads. And so why does it really matter, if once stood a lioness over an archive that concealed something precious enough that a culture, which, like us, loved to look up at the sky in wonderment and wanted to preserve what they saw in some way? Why does it matter that our ancestors, who we no longer know until we can simulate them, had insights into how time flowed and how there can be order in a sea of glimmering lights and shiny discs?

I think that the answers to these questions lie within each one of us. We, like our ancestors, struggle to survive, but when we figure that out, we want to pass something on, as if it is our next most important calling. That something, if nothing else, we hope is true for only that which is as true as possible in our time can last the longest.

That was the message left for me. I found it under the Sphinx.

A Description of the City of Atlantis
Based on *The Critias* by Plato—
Scene Two

S OLON LISTENED IN SILENCE WHILE THE PRIEST DESCRIBED THE CITY OF ATLAN-
tis. When he was finished, he hesitated for a moment.

"Her name ... what did you say was her name?"

and the priest of Saite replied:

"You Greeks have a word, do you not, it is κλείω for **close**. And this word gives you also κλείω for celebrate."

"Yes, this is so," spoke Solon.

"Then, the best way for me to say her name is Cleito."

Figure 163: The Night Barque of the Horus king, ruler over Upper and Lower Egypt. From *Amduat for Amenophis, priest of Amun*. Egypt, Thebes, 21st dynasty (1070-946 BC). ©, bpk Bildagentur / Aegyptisches Museum und Papyrussammlung, Staatliche Museen, Berlin, Germany/ Sandra Steiss/Art Resource, NY.

APPENDIX:

Hieroglyphic

THE MOST IMPORTANT FEATURE OF *MDW NṬR* [MEDOO-NETER], WORDS OF GOD/ Nature, as the Egyptians called their own language, is that it was largely written with symbols to record the sounds of words, not the images they depicted. This seemingly simple concept is what kept hieroglyphic shrouded in mystery for centuries after it had died out. The bedazzling images of its symbols seduced many a scholar to look for meaning in what they saw instead of the sounds they encoded. When you see the hieroglyph image of an owl, it is the sound of our letter "m," not the hieroglyphic word for owl, *jmw*. When you see the symbol of a winding, horned viper, it means the sound of our letter "f," not the word "snake," which is rather *ḥf3* [he-fa]. These examples illustrate a common way how sound symbols were chosen. The dominant sound in *jmw* is the consonant "m," explaining why the owl symbol was chosen to represent that part of the sound of the word. The dominant consonant sound in *ḥf3* is "f," which is likely why the snake was chosen to codify this sound.

Besides monoliteral hieroglyphs such as these, there are those which encode combinations of two or three consonant sounds like *mḥ* [meh], a biliteral, or *st3* [stah], a triliteral. Hieroglyphic uses two other classes of hieroglyphs which were not used to encode sounds: context symbols, also called determinatives, added to clarify the meaning of a word spelled-out phonetically with sound symbols, and word symbols, or logograms like *zšw* [ze-shoo] for example, which encoded an entire word, "writer/scribe" in this example.

Indeed there are symbols which mean what they show, for example, the symbol of a striding lion *m3j* [mah-ee]. It means lion. Or the symbol of a

347

chest on legs that stands for coffer *ʿfdt* [ahf-det]. Another example is the hieroglyph which means scribe. It depicts a color palette and stylus.

The oldest evidence of this system of writing was discovered in the south of Egypt in the tomb of Scorpion I at Abydos by Günter Dreyer and his team of archaeologists from the German Archaeological Institute (DAI). The inscribed bone tags they found date to circa 3200 BC.[416] However, there was another, possibly even older, system of writing in Lower Egypt in the Delta region. This system was probably chiefly based on pictographs, not phonographs, as the one used in Upper Egypt. After Narmer sacked the north of Egypt, and the Delta became part of the unified land under his rule, some symbols of this script were adopted by the dominant language of the conquerors, but most are now lost to us. Apparently, these symbols were not read as individual and elemental sounds, or combinations of sounds, but as syllables.[417]

They bore a direct pictographic connection with the syllable they encoded. For example, the symbolic image of a man diving into water apparently meant just that or something close to the idea of diving.[418] When Karl Kromer excavated an ancient dumpster site south of the Giza Pyramids, he found one clay sealing with, as yet, unknown symbols among other debris that suggested to him the dynastic pyramid builders of Egypt had razed a preexisting culture to the ground and then built their own monuments over it.[419] If this is true, this prior culture could be called a "lost civilization" of whose existence we no longer know and which barely left us remnants of its presence in prehistory.

Like English and many other languages, *mdw nṯr* has a lexicon and grammatical rules that define how words are connected to make sentences. There are no upper and lower cases, no commas, no quotation marks, or colons, and no full stops to guide the reader how to separate the words from each other. The script can be written in vertical columns and in rows, from left to right, or right to left. The direction of reading is towards the faces of the figures shown in the hieroglyphs, whichever way written. There are several phases of the language: Old Egyptian, Middle Egyptian, Late Egyptian, Demotic, and Coptic, the final phase before it became extinct.[420] The knowledge of hieroglyphic was likely passed from Egyptian Copts to Arabs during the early centuries of the Roman empire, but then it became lost. Later Arab scholars began to recover parts of it during Medieval times,[421] and it is this literature which probably helped Jean-Paul Champollion with his own research to decipher hieroglyphic.

The chief hurdle, however, in recreating the experience of what it must have been like to speak and write in *mdw ntr* and hieroglyphic is the absence of written vowels—encoding resonant sounds like ah, eh, eeh, oh, and ooh—we use to connect the non-resonating consonants. The language of the ancient Egyptians died with the last people who spoke and wrote it, and so there is no way any longer to know for sure what it sounded like. The two "e's" in the word neter, for example, are only a reading aid supplied by modern convention of language experts, who sometimes also insert an "o." In hieroglyphic, neter was written as *ntr* and medu as *mdw*. Therefore, we do not know how the words *mdw* and *ntr* were pronounced. In this book, you will see transliterations of hieroglyphic words which follow the official, international rules of Egyptology. For ease of pronunciation, however, I have, at times, added the "e's," especially for names. This process is called the transcription of hieroglyphic. Its aim is to allow us to pronounce.

For example, the name *wp-m-nfr.t* is a string of consonants we obtain from the transliteration of an ancient Egyptian name, written in hiero-glyphic. This string is impossible to deal with in English. By adding a few "e's" in between, it becomes manageable for a western audience, used to vowels in written text: Wep-em-ne-fret, or Wepemnofret, a son of Khufu and one of his early officials. He was one of the very few in history to have carried the distinguished tandem title Master Scribe of the King, Master of the Mehit [Archive].

The bridge back in time to resurrect the sound of spoken Egyptian is Coptic. Coptic was written using a modified Greek Alphabet. Its vowels helped Egyptologists to reconstruct the sound of *mdw ntr*. In Coptic, for example, *ntr* is pronounced *nátur* [nat-hoor] identical to the German word *Natur* for nature.

What it misses in vowels, hieroglyphic makes up in consonants. A few had to be marked with special characters generating the extended Latin consonant set used to transliterate hieroglyphic:

3: As the "uh" in umbrella

ꜥ: As the "aw" in awning

b: Boat

d: Day

ḏ: Jim

f: Firmament

g: Gate

ḥ: Hot

ḫ: Try to say "shoe" while making a smile.

ẖ: A snoring sound

j: Substitutes for any vowel, though usually pronounced "eye"

k: Calendar

m: Moon

n: Night

p: Pendulum

q: Try to say "go" with your mouth wider open.

r: Ray

s: Solar

š: Shine

t: Tilt

ṭ: Thunder

w: Woo

y: Yonder

z: Zodiac with a lisp

Here is an example (figure 164). This is a relief of a scribe called Mery, alive during the reign of Khafre and probably entombed at Saqqara. This beautifully executed hieroglyphic text in raised relief gives me an opportunity to show you how the script is translated into English. The text is written both in a row from the right upper corner to the left upper corner (facing the faces), and from the right upper corner to the right lower corner. In figure 165, I have transliterated the hieroglyphs into the standard European system, conventionally used in Egyptology as listed above. Transliteration is the process of converting hieroglyphs into characters we can pronounce. There are a handful of special characters I listed above. This example gives us the opportunity to review them. The best way to demonstrate what the

Figure 164: Lowermost pane of Block B from the wall of the chapel of Mery. Louvre, Paris. With permission, Image #: DAE-99000478 ©, DEA / G DAGLI ORTI / De Agostini Editore; agefotostock®.

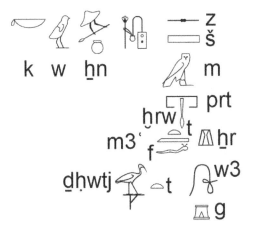

Figure 165: Transcription of the hieroglyphic text from Block B, Relief of Mery.

letter ẖ stands for is for you to make the sound "sh" and then smile at the same time. This is not a sound used in English, but in German, for example, it is how "ch" is pronounced in the word *Milch* (milk). The letter š sounds like "sh" in English.

The letter ḫ is the sound you make when you snore. The letter "3" is a short "uh". The letter ꜥ is a sound like "aw," but with your mouth half-way to say "oh". The letter ḏ is the like the sound of "J" in the name Jim. And the letter ḥ sound just like our "h". Of note, a "j" stands for the sound "ay" and a "y" stands for "ee". There are a couple of other sounds used in hieroglyphic with special Latin characters, but they are not important here. The inscription in the column is transliterated:

zš m prt ḫrw ḫrt m3ꜥ.f u3g ḏḥwty

Using only the common Latin letters with "e" vowels added as a pro-nunciation aid, this would be transcribed as:

zesh em peret ḫeru ḫeret ma'ah w3g deḥwty

Translating this transcription of Hieroglyphic into English:

The writing is an invocation [while] in possession of truth, Wag Festival, Thoth festival.

The inscription in the row which is read from right to left cleverly repeats the context or word symbol zš/scribe, also phonetically spelled out in the corner common to the row and the column. The inscription is transliterated as:

zš ḫnw.k, transcribed to the more readable zesh ḫenw.k

The dot before the "k" separates the word *ḫnw* from its ending "k". One way to read this is using a common verb construction called the stative[422] for actions expressing motion is:

He who writes: "I have sailed."

One way to interpret this line of text is that Mery has died but still writes from the afterlife. Interestingly, he invokes the *w3g* and Thoth festivals dedicated to Osiris and the Moon, both gods of the night, yet this scribe lived at the time of Khafre, when the Sun had become the principal god of the state under Khafre's father Khufu.

You may have noticed that a few symbols are redundant. This is called phonetic complementation. The name of Thoth, *ḏḥwty*, for example, has

352

an added bread loaf symbol which stands for the consonant "t". This is a pronunciation aid scribes added to help the reader interpreting the word from a list of choices, or simply to guide the reader as to the meaning of the word symbol written—in this case, the symbol of an ibis on a standard. The "t" helps the reader realize that the ibis shown does not stand for the Egyptian word for ibis *ḥbj*, but the sacred ibis *ḏḥwty*.

This phonetic hint is a good segue for me to introduce you to a fascinating topic within Hieroglyphic writing: enigmatic writing and what we might nowadays call cryptography. For example, suppose the scribe had used an owl on a standard instead of the ibis. Would we still recognize the written word for *ḏḥwty*? Probably not. And that would have been the point. However, an initiated reader would know that both ibis and owl are birds and thus recognize that the owl is code for the ibis in this context. This is just one of several ways that enigmatic writing was composed by the time of the New Kingdom, when it really took off as far as is known.[423]

My purpose here is not to delve into the details of ancient Egyptian cryptography, but only to mention that it existed and that this is an actively pursued subject in Egyptology. Enigmatic writing was used in three main contexts: Royal monument, private tombs, and in the books which dealt with the afterlife.[424] In the tomb of Thutmose III in the Valley of the Kings, for example, enigmatic writing is used extenisvely (60 percent of the text) in the fourth and fifth hour of the Amduat painted on the oval wall of the sarcophagus chamber.[425]

But why encrypt texts at all? Why make it difficult for the intended audience to read the texts? The answer may surprise you. The purpose was actually not to conceal meaning. On the contrary. The likely purpose was to codify, using new symbols or new ways to use symbols, difficult concepts like regeneration, resurrection, and transits from one realm into another, and to attach a special transformative character to regenerated spirits by spelling their names enigmatically.[426] The most important proof that the scribes meant to express difficult ideas more freely with more contextual resonances, and not to conceal meaning, is the fact that several enigmatically written passages in the Netherworld books are accompanied, side by side, by the standard spelling. Therefore, cryptography is really not a good way to describe engimatically written texts. Illuminated and visually inspired writing is a better way to describe it.

I want to give you just a taste here to get the idea, but also to demon-strate that anagrams were deliberately used to encode divine names. I have adapted a couple of examples given by University of Chicago Egyptologist François Gaudard in his chapter contribution to the book *Visible Language*: Ptolemaic Hieroglyphs.[427]

These are two examples are how the names of Ptah and Amun were cryptographically, and enigmatically encoded (Figure 166).

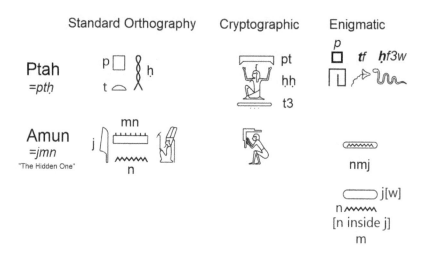

Figure 166: Anagrams of the spellings of Ptah and Amun by cryptographic and enig-matic transformation of the names. The examples are adapted from Gaudard (2010).

I using enigmatic here as a more extreme version of cryptographic only to illustrate the spectrum along which the codification process can far remove the spelling from the plain original, orthographic way, even though a logical bridge persists, as you will see. Ptah, for example, is ana-grammatically spelled in the cryptographic version as "Sky-*ḥḥw* -Earth", *pt-ḥḥw-t3*, with the consonantially extracted *ḥ* falling in the middle for decorative reasons in that the symbol of the god *ḥḥw* is holding up the sky while standing on Earth.

Consonantal extraction is based on a principle originally defined by British Egyptologist Herbert W. Fairman (1907-1982) that lays out the rules by which the composite sound values, for example *ḥḥw*, of multi-literal hieroglyphs were distilled down to only one consonant, in this case *ḥ*.[428]

In the more extreme, enigmatic example, the symbol for "p", the Square Box Sign, is imitated by one Hieroglyphic symbol for the sound of our letter "h", for the sole reason that the shapes are similar. The sounds *t* and *ḥ* are consonants extracted from the Hieroglyphic words for "spit", *tf*, and "snake," *ḥf3w*.

In the case of the personification of invisibility *jmn*, Amun—the chief deity of the Theban theology in the New Kingdom—the extremely, enigmatic way is to spell the name backwards, i.e., anagrammatically, as *m-n-j*. In the example given, this is cleverly done by placing the Water Line Symbol for the sound "n" into the oval Island Symbol for the sound "*jw*" [Ay-oo]. The sound "j", again, is consonantly extraced here from *jw*. The hidden aspect of Amun is thus encoded in two ways, pictographically as the water hiding inside the island, and logically, via an anagram. In the cryptographic version, the idea of being hidden is more decoratively expressed with an image of a kneeling man hiding behind a corner (figure 166).

Finally a few words about phonetic insinnuations or Heka Magic. I cover this in Chapter III, but I want to briefly touch on one aspect of it here: how to prove that it was intentionally done, as opposed to being a coincidental, non-intended resemblence of the sounds of two words.

The closest way to describe what Heka was is a pun although this does not quite do it justice. The purpose of using Heka was not to joke but to imitate creation by verbally animating, and thus activating, the inaminate or dormant without directly naming it. Heka, defined in terms of how the ancient Egyptians thought of it, was beautiful, skillful, and effective speech.[429]

Barbara Richter analyzed the occurrence of word plays in the *pr wr* sanctuary of the Temple of Hathor at Dendera, Egypt and found that true puns made up 8 percent of all confirmable insinuations.[430] Most of these puns were homophones, meaning, same word but different meaning. Heka however goes beyond true puns because both heterophones and even anagrams could serve as punning utterances. Richter's litmus test to distinguish intentional from coincidental puns is that there should be a relationship between the pun and the scene, or image, or idea that is being textually enhanced in this way.[431]

In the case of enigmatic writing, the proof of its intentional use can be ascertained when the scribes supplied the standard orthography of a text next to the enigmatically written form. In the case of phonetic innsinuations, proof of intent is similar, but not always given, as is the case in enigmatic writing.

Let me give you an example of a phonetic word play where we can be virtually sure that it was intended to show you that it existed. In the Pyramid Texts of Pepi II, PT 600, Recitation 359, we find the following passage:

jšš.nk m šw tfn.k m tfnt [Ay-shesh-en-nek m Shoo, tef-en-ek m Tefnoot].

This sentence is part of an inscription addressed to the creator god Atum in Heliopolis, who has made, in an act of emitting his bodily fluids, the first two of his children. James P. Allen translates this as "You sneezed Shu and spat Tefnut" and points out in his notes that the verbs *jšš* for "sneeze" and *tfn* for "spit" are world plays on the actual names of the two deities, who are mentioned by name immediately next, Shu and Tefnut.[432]

With this brief introduction, I hope to have diffused the first layer of intimidation that we may confront when we behold this beautiful language. For the purpose of this book, this is all you will need, but I hope that it will inspire you can launch your own explorations, as has been the case for me.

About the Author

MANU SEYFZADEH IS OF GERMAN AND persian descent. He grew up in Germany and Iran during his early years and emigrated to the United States at age twenty to study medicine. After four years of premedical college education and eight years of medical and science training at the University of California, Irvine, he earned his M.D. and Ph.D. degrees and went to Baylor School of Medicine in Houston, Texas, for his internship. From 1996 to 2001, he specialized in dermatology and participated in the UCLA S.T.A.R. program to train as a medical scientist researching in the field of molecular immunology and targeted anti-cancer drug design.

Since 2002, he has worked as a clinical dermatologist in private practice and at various clinics in California, Arizona, Texas, Idaho, and Wisconsin. He led the Medical Global Brigades on three charity missions to Nicaragua and Honduras and co-founded a charity called Esperanza 4 U with Elia Favela Gutierrez to serve orphans and the poor in Tijuana, Mexico.

His entry into Egyptology and ancient civilizations came with reading a book, *The Orion Mystery*, by Robert Bauval and Adrian Gilbert, and watching a documentary film, *The Pyramid Code* by Carmen Bolter. These impressions inspired his studies of archeoastronomy, relearning geometry and architecture, and eventually self-teaching the hieroglyphic language of the ancient Egyptians with the book *Middle Egyptian* by James Peter Allen.

Since 2016, Manu has authored a book about the architecture of the Great Pyramid and published several papers with Robert Schoch and Robert

Bauval about the Great Sphinx, pyramid architecture, the Inventory Stele, and the symbols on the T-shaped pillars at Göbekli Tepe. With *Under the Sphinx*, he is making his findings available to a wider audience with the goal of bringing the public at large closer to the magic and meaning of numbers and words in ancient Egypt and to help advance the progress of knowledge about how they seeded the origin of ancient civilizations.

Bibliography

Al-Din Al-Suyuti, J., Nemoy, Leon (1939). The Treatise on the Egyptian Pyramids. *Isis*, Vol. 30, No. 1, pp. 17-37. English translation from original Arabic.

Allen, J. P. (2005). *The Ancient Egyptian Pyramid Texts*. Atlanta, GA: Society of Biblical Literature.

Allen, J. P. (2006). *The Egyptian Coffin Texts, Volume 8. Middle Kingdom Copies of Pyramid Texts*. Chicago: Oriental Institute Publications. URL: https://oi.uchicago.edu/research/publications/oip/egyptian-coffin-texts-volume-8-middle-kingdom-copies-pyramid-texts, last accessed March 8, 2021.

Allen, J. P. (2013). A New Concordance of the Pyramid Texts. Vol. IV PT 422-538. Providence, RI: Brown University.

Allen, J. P. (2013). A New Concordance of the Pyramid Texts. Vol. VI PT 673-*806. Providence, RI: Brown University.

Allen, J. P. (2014). *Middle Egyptian. An Introduction to the Language and Culture of Hieroglyphs*. Third Edition. Cambridge University Press.

Attia, V. I. (2018). Ostriches in Ancient Egypt (Pharaonic& Coptic epochs). URL: https://www.researchgate.net/publication/323016775_Ostriches_in_Ancient_Egypt_Pharaonic_Coptic_epochs, last accessed March 8, 2021.

Bárta, M., Jirásková, L., Krejčí, J., Odler, M., Brůna, V. Brukner Havelková, P., Sůvová, Z. (2020). Tomb of Kairsu discovered in Abusir (AC 33) In *Prague Egyptological Studies* XXV/2020, pp. 35-58.

Batygin, K. and Brown, M. E. (2016). Evidence for a distant giant Planet in the Solar System. *The Astronomical Journal*, Vol. 151, pp. 1-12.

Bauval, R. and Gilbert, A. (1994). *The Orion Mystery*. New York, NY: Three Rivers Press.

Bauval, R. and Brophy, T. (2011). *Black Genesis*. Rochester, VT: Bear & Company.

Bauval, R. (2014). *Secret Chamber Revised*. Rochester: Bear & Company.

Belmonte, J. A., Shaltout, M., Fekri, M. Astronomy and landscape in Ancient Egypt: Challenging the enigma of the minor step pyramids. Papers on Ancient Egypt: *Trabajos de Egiptologia*, *4*, pp. 7-18.

Belmonte, J. A., Shaltout, M. (2009). *In Search of Cosmic Order*. Cairo: Supreme Council of Antiquities Press.

Billson, B. (2010). *Two Aspects of Middle Kingdom Funerary Culture from two different Middle Egyptian Nomes*. Master of Philosophy Thesis. Institute of Archaeology and Antiquity College of Arts and Law. The University of Birmingham.

Boehmer, R., Dreyer, G., Kromer, B. (1993). Einige Frühzeitliche ^{14}C-Datierungen aus Abydos und Uruk. *MDAIK,* 49, pp. 63-68

Bonani, G., Haas, H., Hawass, Z., Lehner, M., Nakhla, S., Nolan, J., Wenke, R., Wölfli, W. (2001). Radiocarbon Dates of Old and Middle Kingdom Monuments in Egypt. Near East Chronology: Archaeology and Environment. *RADIOCARBON*, *43*, pp. 1297–1320.

Borchardt, L. (1910). *Das Grabdenkmal des Königs S'aȝḥu-Reʿ. Band I: Der Bau*. Leipzig: J. C. Hinrichs'sche Buchhandlung.

Brandl, B. (2016). *The Sealings and the pr-wr Labels from Tomb U-j at Umm el-Qa'ab, Abydos Reconsidered*. In *Egypt at its Origins 4*, Matthew Douglas Adams, Béatrix Midant-Reynes, Ellen M. Ryan and Yann Tristant (eds.). Leuven, Paris, Bristol CT: Peeters.

Budde, D., Dils, P., Goldbrunner, L., Leitz, C., Mendel, D. (2002). *Lexikon der ägyptischen Götter und Götterbezeichnungen Band III*. Leuven: Peeters.

Budge, Sir E. A. W. (1978). An Egyptian Hieroglyphic Dictionary. Volume II. New York, NY: Dover Publications, Inc.

Budge, Sir E. A. W. (2018). *The Literature of Ancient Egypt: Including Original Sources: The Book of the Dead, Papyrus of Ani, Hymn to the Nile, Great Hymn to Aten and Hymn to Osiris-Sokar*. Publisher: e-artnow.

Case, H., Payne, J. C. (1962). Tomb 100: The Decorated Tomb at Hierakonpolis. *The Journal of Egyptian Archaeology, 48*, pp. 5-18.

Collins, A. (2017). Göbekli Tepe's Vulture Stone: A Warning Across Time or Signpost to the Land of the Dead? Putting into Perspective the carved Imagery on Göbekli Tepe's Pillar 43 in Enclosure D. URL: http://www.andrewcollins. com/page/articles/sagittarius.htm, last accessed March 8, 2021.

Creighton, S., Osborn, G. (2012). The Giza Prophecy: The Orion Code and the Secret Teachings of the Pyramids. Rochester, VT: Bear & Company.

De Buck, A. (1935). *The Egyptian Coffin Texts I. Texts of Spells 1-75.* James Henry Breasted, Thomas George Allen, Adriaan de Buck and Sir Alan H. Gardiner (eds.). Chicago, IL: The University of Chicago Press.

de Buck, A. and Gardiner, A. H. (1938). *The Egyptian Coffin Texts II. Texts of Spells 76-163.* John Albert Wilson and Thomas George Allen (eds.). Chicago, IL: The University of Chicago Press.

de Buck, A., Gardiner, A. H. (1947). *The Egyptian Coffin Texts, Volume III.: Texts of Spells 164–267.* John Albert Wilson, Thomas George Allen, and Elizabeth Blaisdell Hauser (eds.). Chicago, IL: The University of Chicago Press.

de Buck, A., Gardiner, A. H. (1951). *The Egyptian Coffin Texts, Volume IV.: Texts of Spells 268–354.* Adriaan de Buck and Sir Alan H. Gardiner (eds.). Chicago, IL: The University of Chicago Press.

de Buck, A. (1956). *The Egyptian Coffin Texts, Volume VI.: Texts of Spells 472–787.* Adriaan de Buck and Sir Alan H. Gardiner (eds.). Chicago, IL: The University of Chicago Press.

de Buck, A. (1961). *The Egyptian Coffin Texts. VII. Texts of Spells 787-1185.* Adriaan de Buck and Sir Alan H. Gardiner (eds.). Chicago, IL: The University of Chicago Press.

Der Manuelian, P. (2003). *Slab Stelae of the Giza Necropolis.* William Kelly Simpson and David b. O'Connor (eds.). New Haven and Philadelphia: Publications of the Pennsylvania–Yale Expedition to Egypt.

Dobecki, T. L., Schoch, R. M. (1992). Seismic investigations in the vicinity of the great Sphinx of Giza, Egypt. Geoarchaeology: An International Journal, Vol. 7, No. 6, pp. 527-544.

Drake, S., Kowal, C. T. (1980). Galileo's Sighting of Neptune. *Scientific American*, Vol. 243, 6, pp. 74-81.

Dreyer, G. (1999). *Umm el-Qaab I: Das prädynastische Königs-grab U-j und seine frühen Schriftzeugnisse.* Deutsches Archäologisches Institut, Abteilung

Kairo, Archäologische Veröffentlichungen 86. Mainz: Verlag Philipp von Zabern.

Edgar Cayce Foundation (1971). *ARCHAEOLOGY: EGYPT & GOBI 10500 BC Research Potential. A compilation of Extracts from the Edgar Cayce Readings.* Virginia Beach, VA: E.C.F.

El-Daly, O. (2005). *The Missing Millennium: Ancient Egypt in Medieval Arabic Writings.* Portland: Cavendish Publishing.

Elshamy, M. (2019). Deciphering Hierakonpolis Tomb 100.

Emery, W. B. (1954). *Great Tombs of the First Dynasty.* Vol. II. Egypt Exploration Society. London: Oxford University Press.

Emery, W. B. (1958). *Great Tombs of the First Dynasty. Vol. III.* Egypt Exploration Society. London: Oxford University Press.

Fairman, H. W. (1945). An Introduction to the Study of Ptolemaic Signs and their Values. *Bulletin de l'Institut Français d'Archéologie Orientale*, 43, pp. 51-138.

Faulkner, R. O. (2004). *The Ancient Egyptian Coffin Texts (Aris and Phillips Classical Texts) (v. 1-3).* Liverpool, UK: Liverpool University Press.

Faulkner, R. O. (2003). The Literature of Ancient Egypt. William Kelly Simpson (eds.). New Haven/London: Yale University Press.

Fenton, B. (2017). A Global Aboriginal Australian Culture? The Proof at Göbekli Tepe. *New Dawn Magazine*, 2017, July-August (163).

Friedman, R. (1996). *The Ceremonial Centre at Hierakonpolis Locality HK 29A.* In J. Spencer (ed.), *Aspects of Early Egypt*, pp. 16–35. London: British Museum Press.

Pieri, A. (2011). A Special Person in a Special Place: the Dwarf of HK6. *Nekhen News*, 23, pp. 7-8.

Gardiner, Sir A. H. (1927). Egyptian Grammar. London: Oxford University Press.

Gardiner, Sir A. H. (1938). The House of Life. *The Journal of Egyptian Archaeology,* Vol. 24, pp. 157-179.

Gardiner, Sir A. H. (1944). Horus the Beḥdetite. *The Journal of Egyptian Archaeology,* Vol. 30, pp. 23-60

Gaudard, F. (2010). *Ptolemaic Hieroglyphs*. In *Visible Language: Inventions of Writing in the Ancient Middle East and Beyond*. Christopher Woods, Geoff Emberling, and Emily Teeter (eds.). Chicago: Oriental Institute Museum Publications, pp. 173-188.

Green, J. C. (1998). F. W. Green (1869–1949): A Family Profile. *Nekhen News*, *10*, pp. 15-16.

Griffith, F. L., Newberry, P. E. (1895). El Bersheh. Part II. London: Office of the Egypt Exploration Fund.

Haklay, G, Gopher, A. (2020). Geometry and Architectural Planning at Göbekli Tepe, Turkey. *Cambridge Archaeological Journal, 30*(2), pp. 343-357.

Hancock, G., Bauval, R. (1996). Message of the Sphinx. New York: Three Rivers Press.

Hancock, G. (2015). Magicians of the Gods. London: Hodder & Stoughton Ltd.

Hassan, S. (1949). The Sphinx: Its History in the Light of recent Excavations. Government Press, Cairo.

Hassan, S. (1953). The Great Sphinx and its Secrets. Historical Studies in the Light of Recent Excavations. Government Press, Cairo.

Hawass, Z. A. (1987). *The Funerary Establishments of Khufu, Khafra and Menkaura during the Old Kingdom. A Dissertation in Oriental Studies.* Ph.D. Thesis, University of Pennsylvania.

Hawass, Z. A. (1994). A Fragmentary Monument of Djoser from Saqqara. *The Journal of Egyptian Archaeology*, 80, pp. 45-56.

Hawass, Z. A. (1996). *The Discovery of the Satellite Pyramid of Khufu (GI–d)*. In Studies in Honor of William Kelly Simpson, edited by Peter Der Manuelian (Museum of Fine Arts, Boston: 1996), pp. 379-98.

Hawass, Z. A. (1997). Zahi Hawass talks to KMT about matters on the Giza Plateau. KMT, 8, 2, pp. 16-25.

Helck, W. (1987). *Untersuchungen zur Thinitenzeit*. Wiesbaden: Otto Harrassowitz Verlag.

Hendrickx, S., Huyge, D., Wendrich, W. (2010). *Worship Without Writing*. In *Egyptian Archaeology. Blackwell Studies in Global Archaeology*. Wendrich, W., editor. Chichester: Wiley-Blackwell. Pp. 15-35.

Hendrickx, S., Eyckerman, M. (2012). Visual representation and state development in Egypt. *Archéo-Nil*, 22, pp. 23-72.

Hölscher, U., Borchardt, L., Steindorff, G. (1912). *Das Grabdenkmal des Königs Chephren*. Leipzig: J. C. Hinrichs'sche Buchhandlung.

Ivanov, K. (2017). Pr-dw3t - The House of Morning Adoration. *Academia.edu*.

URL: https://www.academia.edu/36901641/Pr_dw3t_The_House_of_Morning_ Adoration, last accessed March 8, 2021.

Junker, H. (1929). *Giza I*. Wien und Leipzig: Hölder-Pichler-Tempsky A.-G.

Kahl, J. (1994). *Das System der ägyptischen Hieroglyphenschrift in der 0.-3. Dynastie*. In Göttinger Orientforschung, IV. Reihe Ägypten, Band 29. Wiesbaden: Otto Harrassowitz Verlag.

Kaplony, P. (1963*). Die Innenschriften Ägyptischer Frühzeit*. III. Band. Wiesbaden: Harrassowitz Verlag.

Kendall, T. (2007). Mehen: The Ancient Egyptian Game of the Serpent. Ancient Board Games in Perspective. British Museum Press, London (2007): 33-45, last accessed March 8, 2021.

Kitchen, K. A. (1975). *Ramesside Inscriptions: Historical and Biographical*. Oxford: B H. Blackwell LTD.

Klotz, D., Stauder, A. (2020). *Enigmatic Writing in the Egyptian New Kingdom*. Berlin/Boston: Walter de Gruyter Gmbh.

Krauss, R. (1997). *Astronomische Konzepte und Jenseitsvorstellungen in the den Pyramidentexten*. Wiesbaden: Harrassowitz Verlag.

Kromer, K. (1972). *Österreichische Ausgrabungen in Giseh: Vorbericht über die Frühjahrskampagne 1971*. Wien: Kommissionsverlag der Österreichischen Akademie der Wissenschaften.

Kurth, D., Behrmann, A., Block, A., Brech, R., Budde, D., Effland, A., von Falck, M., Felber, H., Graeff, J.-P., Koepke, S., Martinssen-von Falck, S., Pardey, E., Rüter, St., Waitkus, W., Woodhouse, S. (2014). *Die Inschriften des Tempels von Edfu. Abteilung I Übersetzungen; Band 3. Edfou VI*. Gladbeck: PeWe-Verlag.

Layard, A. H. (1853). *Discoveries in the ruins of Nineveh and Babylon*. New York: G. P. Putnam and Co.

Lehner, M. E. (1991). *Archaeology of an Image: The Great Sphinx of Giza.* Ph.D. Thesis, Volume 1 (Text). New Haven, Connecticut: Graduate School of Yale University.

Lehner, M. E. (1994). Notes and Photographs on the West-Schoch Sphinx Hypothesis by Mark Lehner. *KMT*, 5, pp. 40-48.

Lehner, M. (2002). Unfinished Business: The Great Sphinx. Why it is most probable that Khafre created the Sphinx. *AERAGRAM*, 5-2, pp. 10-15.

Lehner, M., Hawass, Z. A. (2017). *Giza and the Pyramids. The Definitive History.* Chicago: University of Chicago Press.

Lepsius, C. H. (1849-1859). *Denkmäler Aus Ägypten Und Äthiopien.* Richter, Text und Tafelwerke. Berlin: Druck Von Gebr. Unger.

Magli, G., Belmonte, J. A. (2009). *Pyramids and stars, facts, conjectures, and starry tales.* In *In Search of Cosmic Order* (eds. Belmonte, J. A. and Shaltout, M.). Cairo: Supreme Council of Antiquities Press.

Magli, G. (2013). Sirius and the project of the megalithic enclosures at Göbekli Tepe. *Nexus Network Journal*, 17, 2016, pp. 1-11.

Malville, J. McK, Schild, R., Wendorf, F., and Brenmer, R. (2007). Astronomy of Nabta Playa. *AFRICAN SKIES/CIEUX AFRICAINS*, No. 11, pp. 2-7.

Mariette, A. (1857). *Le Serapeum de Memphis.* Paris: Gide.

URL: https://digi.ub.uni-heidelberg.de/diglit/mariette1882bd1/0101/text_ocr, last accessed March 8, 2021.

Morenz, L. D., Schmidt, K. (2009). *Große Reliefpfeiler und kleine Zeichentäfelchen. Ein frühneolithisches Zeichensystem in Obermesopotamien.* In: Petra Andrássy – Julia Budka – Frank Kammerzell (eds.), *Non-Textual Marking Systems, Writing and Pseudo Script from Prehistory to Modern Times.* Lingua Aegyptia – Studia monographica 8, Göttingen, pp. 13-31.

NBC [National Broadcasting Company]. 1993. *The Mystery of the Sphinx* (television documentary). Hosted by Charlton Heston, featuring John Anthony West and Robert M. Schoch. First aired in the United States, 10 November 1993, 9–10 p.m. Eastern Standard Time. (Note: The version of the show that is currently generally available on DVD, YouTube, and other outlets, is not the original show; it was re-edited and expanded with supplementary and extraneous material. Robert Schoch had no control over this re-editing and he objects to some of the material included in the expanded version.)

Neyland, R. (2019). Mehit's Stump: Unmasking the Great Sphinx of Giza. *Archaeological Discovery*, Vol. 8, pp. 1-25.

Nour, M. Z., Iskander, Z., Osman, M.S., Moustafa, A. Y. (1960). The Cheops Boats. Part I. Cairo: General Organization for Government Printing Offices.

Oppenheim, L., Editor-in-Chief (1965/1998). *The Assyrian Dictionary*. Fourth Printing. Volume 2 B. URL: https://oi.uchicago.edu/sites/oi.uchicago.edu/files/uploads/shared/docs/cad_b.pdf, last accessed March 8, 2021.

Oppenheim, L., Editor-in-Chief (1956/1995). *The Assyrian Dictionary*. Fifth Printing. Volume 5 G. URL: https://oi.uchicago.edu/sites/oi.uchicago.edu/files/uploads/shared/docs/cad_g.pdf, last accessed March 8, 2021.

Payne, J. C. Tomb 100 (1973): The Decorated Tomb at Hierakonpolis Confirmed. *The Journal of Egyptian Archaeology, 59*, pp. 31-35.

Peters, J., Schmidt, K. (2004). Animals in the symbolic world of Pre-Pottery Neolithic Göbekli Tepe, south-eastern Turkey: a preliminary assessment. *ANTHROPOZOOLOGICA*, Vol. 39, pp. 179-218.

Petrie, W.M.F. (1901). *The Royal Tombs of the Earliest Dynasties*. Part II. London: Offices of the Egypt Exploration Fund.

Petrie, W.M.F. (1901). *The Royal Tombs of the Earliest Dynasties*. Part II. Extra Plates. London: Offices of the Egypt Exploration Fund.

Petrie, W.M.F. (1925). Tombs of the Courtiers and Oxyrhynkhos. London: British School of Archaeology in Egypt University College, and Bernard Quaritch.

Petrie, W.M.F. (1953). Ceremonial Slate Palettes. Corpus of Predynastic Pottery. London: British School of Egyptian Archaeology; Bernard Quaritch.

Quibell, J. E. (1900). *Hierakonpolis. Part I*. London: Bernard Quaritch.

Quibell, J. E., Green, F. W. (1902). *Hierakonpolis. Part II*. London: Bernard Quaritch.

Reisner, G.A. (1912). Solving the Riddle of the Sphinx. *Cosmopolitan* 53, pp. 4-13.

Reymond E. A. E. (1962). The Primeval Djeba. *The Journal of Egyptian Archaeology*, 48, pp. 81-88.

Richter, B. A. (2008). The Amduat and Its Relationship to the Architecture of Early 18th Dynasty Royal Burial Chambers. *JARCE* 44, pp. 73-104.

Richter, B. A. (2012). The Theology of Hathor of Dendera: Aural and Visual Scribing Techniques in the Per-Wer Sanctuary. Ph.D. Thesis. University of California, Berkeley.

Ricke, H. (1970). *Der Harmarchistempel des Chefren in Giseh.* Beiträge BF 10. Mainz: Rheingold Druckerei.

Robinson, Peter (2006). Ritual Landscapes in the Coffin Texts. A Cognitive Mapping Approach. In: Rachael J. Dann (eds.), Current Research in Egyptology 2004. Proceedings of the Fifth Annual Symposium, University of Durham 2004. Oxford: pp. 118-132.

Schoch, R. (1992). "Redating the Great Sphinx of Giza." *KMT, A Modern Journal of Ancient Egypt*, Vol. 3, No. 2 (Summer 1992), pp. 52–59, 66–70.

Schoch, R. (2012). *Forgotten Civilization: The Role of Solar Outbursts in Our Past and Future.* Rochester, VT: Inner Traditions.

Schoch, R. M., Bauval, R. (2017). *Origins of the Sphinx: Celestial Guardian of Pre-Pharaonic Civilization.* Rochester, VT: Inner Traditions.

Seyfzadeh, M., Schoch, R. M., Bauval, R. (2017). A New Interpretation of a Rare Old Kingdom Dual Title: The King's Chief Librarian and Guardian of the Royal Archives of Mehit. *Archaeological Discovery*, Vol. 5, pp. 163-177.

Seyfzadeh, M., Schoch, R. M. (2018). The Inventory Stele: More Fact than Fiction. *Archaeological Discovery*, Vol. 6, pp. 103-161.

Seyfzadeh, M. and Schoch, R. M. (2019). Major Geological Fissure through Prehistoric Lion Monument at Giza Inspired Split Lion Hieroglyphs and Ancient Egypt's Creation Myth. *Archaeological Discovery*, 7, 211-256.

Seyfzadeh, M. and Schoch, R. M. (2019). World's First Known Written Word at Göbekli Tepe on T-Shaped Pillar 18 Means God. *Archaeological Discovery*, 7, pp. 31-53.

Sharafeldin, M. S., Essa, K.S., Youssef, M. A. S., Karsli, H., Diab, Z. E., Sayil, N. (2019). Shallow geophysical techniques to investigate the ground water table at the Great Pyramids of Giza, Egypt. *Geoscientific Instruments Methods and Data Systems*, 8, pp. 29–43.

Sherbiny, W. (2017). *Through Hermopolitean Lenses: Studies on the so-called Book of Two Ways in Ancient Egypt*. Leiden: Brill.

Shockley, V., Aleff, P. (2013). The Phaistos Disk: A New Approach: Part 3: The race between the light and dark sides of the moon on the Phaistos gameboard. Popular Archaeology, June Issue: pp. 1-13.

Sidharth, B.G. (2010). Precession of the Equinoxes and Calibration of Astronomical Epochs. URL: https://arxiv.org/pdf/1001.2393.pdf, last accessed March 8, 2021.

Smith, W. S. (1942). The Origin of Some Unidentified Old Kingdom Reliefs. *American Journal of Archaeology*, 46, 4, pp. 509-531.

Smith, W. S. (1963). The Stela of Prince Wepemnofret. *Archaeology*, 16, 1, pp. 2-13.

Smith, W. S. (1942). The Origin of some Unidentified Old Kingdom Reliefs. *American Journal of Archaeology*, XLVI, 4, pp. 509-531.

Spencer, A. J. (1978). Two Enigmatic Hieroglyphs and Their Relation to the Sed-Festival. *The Journal of Egyptian Archaeology*, Vol. 64, pp. 52-55.

Stephenson, F. R., Morrison, L. V., Hohenkerk, C. Y. (2016). Measurement of the Earth's rotation: 720 BC to AD 2015. *Proceedings of the Royal Society A*, 472, pp.: 1-26.

Strudwick, N (1985). *The Administration of Egypt in the Old Kingdom. The Highest Titles and their Holders*. London: KPI, Ltd.

Sweatman, M. B., Tsikritsis, D. (2017). Decoding Göbekli Tepe with Archaeoastronomy: What does the Fox say? *Mediterranean Archaeology and Archaeometry*, 17(1):233-250.

Tallet, P., Marouard, G. (2014). THE HARBOR OF KHUFU on the Red Sea Coast at Wadi al-Jarf, Egypt. *Near Eastern Archaeology*, 77, pp. 4-14.

Temple, R. and Temple, O (2009). *The Sphinx Mystery: The Forgotten Origins of the Sanctuary of Anubis*. Rochester, VT: Inner Traditions/Bear & Company.

Vygus, M. (2015). Vygus Egyptian Dictionary. URL: https://www.pyramidtextsonline.com/documents/VygusDictionaryApril2015.pdf, last accessed March 8, 2021.

Yoshimura, S., Kawai, N., Kashiwagi, H. (2005). A Sacred Hillside at Northwest Saqqara: A preliminary Report on the Excavations 2001-2003. *MDAIK* 61, pp. 361-402. Mainz am Rhein: Philipp von Zabern.

Wickramasinghe, C., Bauval, R. (2017). Cosmic Womb. The Seeding of Planet Earth. Rochester, VT.: Bear & Company.

Wilkinson, R. H. (2003). *The Complete Gods and Goddesses of Ancient Egypt*. London: Thames & Hudson.

Witsell, A. (2018). Kromer 2018: Basket by Basket 2. *Aeragram*, 19, 1, pp. 2-9.

Endnotes

CHAPTER I: PARADOX

1 Layard 1853, pp. 197-198.

2 Drake and Kowal 1980.

3 Batygin and Brown 2016.

4 With permission.

5 With Permission.

6 Zecharia Sitchin (1920–2010) based on his interpretation of Sumerian texts proposed in his Earth Chronicles Volumes as early as 1976 that there was a hidden planet called *Nibiru* on an extreme orbit past Neptune, populated by the *Annunaki* who visited Earth in the distant past and influenced its evolution.

7 Robinson 2006.

8 Billson 2010, University of Birmingham Master's Thesis, pp. 28-30.

CHAPTER II: BREACH

9 Kahl 1994, p. 676, q 15.

10 Edgar Cayce Foundation 1971. Mentioned in whole or partly for example in readings 378-12, 378-13, 378-16, 519-1, 1486-1, 2012-1, 2329-3, 2402-2, 2462-2, 5748-5, 5748-6.

11 Bauval 2014, pp. 234-250.

12 Allen 2014, p. 54. With permission.

13 Budge 2018

14 Mariette 1857

15 From the original French by Mariette (1857*): "Un autre trou existe dans le dos et vers la naissance des cuisses. Le P.Vansleben parle ainsi:*

«... elle a par derrière une cave sous terre, d'une largeur proportionnée à la hauteur de la teste, dans laquelle j'ay regardé par une ouverture qui »y est, et qui n'a pu servir à autre chose, qu'à y mettre le corps de quelque mort.» J'ai fait nettoyer le trou jusqu'au fond, et, en effet, quand on y regarde d'en haut, il semble qu'il se termine par une chambre. Mais, malgré son apparence de puits funéraire, ce n'est qu'une fissure agrandie qui va en s'élargissant, et qui se termine par un vide assez spacieux ménagé précisément dans le plein des cuisses."

16   Bauval 2014, chapter 10.

17   Temple and Temple 2009, chapter 2.

18   Hancock and Bauval 1996, pp. 160-162.

19   Schoch and Bauval 2017, p. 205.

20   El-Daly 2005, p. 81.

21   Pliny's Natural History, Book XXXVI, chapter 17.

22   These circumstances are somewhat reminiscent of Balinas' account of how the Emerald Tablet was found in Anatolia. The theme of an Emerald Tablet was copied by Maurice Doreal, a.k.a. Claude Dodgin, founder of the Brotherhood of the White Temple, who in 1939 originally published The Emerald Tablets of Thoth the Atlantean. In this book, he claimed that he had previously been instructed by the Great White Lodge connected to the pyramid priesthood to recover ten lost tablets written by Thoth from South America to return them to the Great Pyramid. During this 1925 adventure, on the details of which Doreal does not elaborate, he claims he was able to make copies and translate the texts. Https://brotherhoodofthewhitetemple.com/the-emerald-tablets/, last accessed March 8, 2021.

23   Mark Lehner has proposed, for example, that the idea of a chamber under the Sphinx may have originated when an access gate to the northern roof court of the Valley Temple of Khafre became visible during excavations by Mariette before the Sphinx ditch was cleared. This, according to Lehner, may have visually suggested to casual observers that an underground access gate exists which leads to the Sphinx. (Lehner and Hawass, 2017, p. 206, Fig. 9.21.

24   Ibid.

25   Hancock and Bauval 1996, pp. 178-181.

26   Ibid., pp. 233-236.

27   Magli and Belmonte 2009, pp. 315-320.

28   For example, Bauval in Schoch and Bauval (2017), pp. 296-317.v

29   Hawass 1997, pp. 17-18.

30   Dobecki and Schoch 1992; Schoch 1992.

31   Schoch in Schoch and Bauval 2017, pp. 234-269.

32   Lehner and Hawass 2017, pp. 240-241.

33   Schoch in Schoch and Bauval, Appendix 7.

34   Reisner 1912

35   NBC 1993

36   YouTube Video "Drilling under the Sphinx," last accessed March 8, 2021.

37   Lehner 1991, p. 159.

38   Robert Schoch, personal communication.

39   Sherbiny 2017, p. 145.

CHAPTER III: HEKA

40   Seyfzadeh and Schoch 2918, pp. 36-37.

41   Helck 1987, pp. 21-30.

42   Allen 2014, p. 75.

43   Gaudard 2010.

44   Helck 1987, pp. 23. The phrase *ḥw swn.f*, "prevent that he may suffer", is a phonetic insinuation of *ḥsf*, an anagram of *ḥfs*, the word for "mosquito". Mosquito is the intended meaning here one of three animal spirits to be invoked by the Shaman priest to aid him in recovering the shadow of the deceased in the afterlife. From the Statuette Making Ritual phonetically, i.e., using Heka Magic, embedded inside the Mouth Opening Ceremony.

45   Allen 2005, pp. 50-52.

46   Vygus 2015, pp. 187; 201.

CHAPTER IV: COFFINS

47   De Buck 1956.

48   Faulkner 2004, Spell 758, p. 290.

49   Vygus 2015, p. 1602.

50   Ibid., p.1573.

51   Ibid., p. 1570.

52   Pyramid Text 506, Pepi and Merenre.

53   Sherbiny 2017, pp. 1-38.

54   https://oi.uchicago.edu/research/publications/oip/oip-87-egyptian-coffin-texts-7-texts-spells-787%E2%80%931185, last accessed March 8, 2021.

55   Sherbiny 2017, chapter 1.

56   Ibid., 2017, p. 283.

57   Hancock and Bauval 1996, p.133.

58   Ibid., pp. 148-151.

59   Ibid., pp. 178-179.

60   Ibid., p. 265, legend to figure 68.

61   Schoch's seismic refraction data suggest an Anomaly under the left fore-paw some 5 meters below the level of the ditch.

62   Faulkner 2004, Spell 1, p. 1.

63   Faulkner 2004, Spell 18, p. 11.

64   Krauss 1997, pp. 14-66.

65   Ibid. p. 64.

66   Ibid. pp. 48-49.

67   Ibid., p. 63.

68   Ibid. pp. 16-17.

69   The ancient Egyptian's cardinal reference cross was north to south. Therefore, west was to their right and east to their left, opposite of our own convention nowadays.

70   Sherbiny 2017, pp. 192-193, 266-267.

71   Ibid., p. 283.

72   Ibid., p. 192, He-who-lives-besides-the-Fledgling-of-the-Lake.

73   Ibid., p. 193 [38], [40].

74   Ibid, p. 193 [39].

75   Ibid., p. 236.

76   Ibid., p. 191 [18].

77   Ibid., p. 429.

78 Ibid., p. 459.

79 Ibid., p. 441.

80 Ibid., p. 443.

81 https://youtu.be/bcruFSQuqEo, last accessed March 8, 2021.

82 Ibid., pp. 272-273., the four basins of *Heqet* and *Khepri* symbolic of the primordial waters of chaos in the *Ogdoad*, *Nun* and *Naunet*.

83 Ibid., p. 193 [44].

84 For example, Spell 75, *Spell for the soul of Shu and for becoming Shu*, where it is written that "...*I am stronger and more raging than all the Enneads.*"

85 Faulkner 2004, Spell 78, p.81.

86 De Buck (1938), p. II 27.

87 Faulkner 2004, Spell 155, p.

88 Krauss 1997, p. 80.

89 Ibid., p. 81.

90 Ibid., p. 82.

91 Ibid., p.83

92 The Egyptian word for to lead astray, to confuse is ***stnm***.

93 https://web.archive.org/web/20080918080211/http://www.gamesmuseum.uwaterloo.ca/Archives/Piccione/index.html, last accessed March 8, 2021.

CHAPTER V: COILS

94 Kendall 2007.

95 Ibid.

96 Allen 2005, p. 49.

97 Krauss 1997, p. 143.

98 The exact cycle is the difference between the time in solar days of a sidereal and a tropical year divided into a sidereal year period. Currently, that computes to a precessional cycle of 25795 years.

99 https://stellarium.org/, last accessed March 8, 2021.

100 A heliacal rising of a star, an asterism, or a constellation is that time of the year when it reappears above the eastern horizon for a moment before sunrise having been absent for a period time during the year after its

cosmic setting. We cannot see a star unless the Sun is sufficiently below the horizon while the star is sufficiently above.

101   Currently, the annual wander is a little over 20 minutes, approximately 1/72 of a day.

102   Bauval and Brophy 2011, chapters 3 and 4.

103   Richter 2012, p. 1.

104   https://www.britishmuseum.org/collection/object/Y_EA1726, last accessed March 9, 2021.

105   Ibid., p. 3.

106   Malville et al. 2007, p. 5.

107   Ibid., p. 5, Figure 5.

108   Bauval and Brophy 2011, pp. 139-142.

109   Belmonte et al. 2005, pp. 3-4.

110   For an excellent analysis of this see Alexander Puchkov's future publication "Multi-star target model for astronomical orientation of the Old Kingdom Egyptian pyramids"; in preparation.

111   Allen 2005, p. 12.

112   Ibid., pp. 5-12.

113   Hawass 1996, pp. 391-394.

114   Dr. Richter's About Page can be accessed at: http://www.barbararichter.com/about.htm, last accessed March 8, 2021.

115   Richter 2008, pp. 79-80.

116   Brendan Crawford, 2021: https://grahamhancock.com/phorum/read.php?1,1273235,1274986#msg-1274986, last accessed March 8, 2021. Brendan Crawford's Academia.edu page can be accessed at https://independent.academia.edu/BrendanCrawford1

117   Wilkinson 2003, 9. 157. Also see the House of the two Ladies on an oil tag dated to Horus-*Djet*, where the Red Crown is phonetically complemented with Gardiner X1 denoting the sound "t" for female gender. The two symbols, Red Crown and "t", thus spell *njt*.

118   Budge 1978, p. 1078a

119   Shockley and Aleff 2013, for example. Personal communication John Lundwall.

120   For an example, see the inscription on the naophorous block statue of a Governor of *Sais, Psamtikseneb* 664–610 BC where the House of the Bee

is the name of a temple of Osiris in Sais. https://collectionapi.metmuseum.org/api/collection/v1/iiif/550755/1219256/main-image, last accessed March 8, 2021.

121 Budge, E. A. W. (1904). *The Gods of the Egyptians*. London: Methuen & Co, p. 452.

122 Gardiner 1927, symbol S3, p. 504; compare also L2 p. 477.

123 Belmonte and Shaltout 2009, p. 162. The crocodile is spatially in the circumpolar star zone next to the Hippopotamus deity **rret**. Horus the *Behedetite* and the axe-like knife *adze* called **nw** which was likely seen in the small dipper constellation Ursa minor. The word **nw** also meant time and moment.

124 Belmonte and Shaltout 2009, p. 164.

125 John Lundwall, personal communication.

CHAPTER VI: COFFERS

126 Sherbiny 2017, p. 136.

127 Billson 2010, p. 12.

128 Ibid., pp. 15-16.

129 Ibid., p. 20.

130 Allen 2006.

131 Billson 2010, pp. 32-37.

132 Ibid., p. 40-41.

133 In the quantum world, time is not a one-way street. Elemental particles are not forbidden to travel back in time based on the known laws of physics. When many particles come together to become big things like us, all of them would have to behave identically in a coherent way for time travel to be possible. This does not happen because of the chaos caused by entropy dictated by the Second Law of Thermodynamics, which explains the random, discohesive motion of elemental particles caused by their encounter with energy. Physicists predict the entanglement of particles can not only occur over vast distances but also across the time barrier. There are also theories which have proposed that messages may have travelled back in time such as that proposed by Jim Penniston and Gary Osborn in the 2019 book *The Rendlesham Enigma*. Another theoretical, as yet unproven mechanism of how information could appear to travel back in time, is the 2003 Simulation Hypothesis proposed by Nick Bostrom.

134   Faulkner 1977, p. 290.

135   Ibid., p. 139.

136   Ibid., pp. 146-147.

137   Ivanov 2017, p. 9. This is based on additional attributes the author discovered besides those previously identified by Aylward M. Blackman.

138   Ibid., Figures 2 and 3.

139   Ibid, p.136.

140   Ibid., pp. 139, 145, 149.

141   Ibid., p. 136.

142   Edgar Cayce Foundation 1971, p. 22.

143   Ibid., 2329-3, 5-1-1941 reading, p. 48.

144   Ibid., 1486-1, 11-26-1937, p. 46; 5748-6, 7/1/1932, p. 65.

145   Ibid., the 10-29-1933 reading, p. 23.

146   Ibid., 378-16, the 10/29/1933 reading, p. 44.

147   Horus of the horizon if read a nisbe, or Horus of the two horizons if read as the dual plural.

148   Faulkner writes **mr.f**, but the hieroglyphic spelling on B1L spells **mrš.f**.

149   Faulkner 1973.

150   The hieroglyphic spelling at CT 695c leaves out the final "t" of the plural and thus only reads **ḥwdw**. However, since the word is feminine, the correct spelling of the plural would have had to be **ḥwdwt** with even more closely resembling the words **ḥw dw3t**.

151   Sherbiny 2017, pp. 139-150.

152   This theme was expanded by Robert and Oliva Temple using other textual sources which refer to the hidden, water-submerged body of jackal and the *Lake of the Jackal*, for example. The authors suggest in their 2009 book *The Sphinx Mystery: The Forgotten Origins of the Sanctuary of Anubis* that the Great Sphinx monument was originally a jackal, not a lion, and that it was partly under water inside of the Sphinx ditch which they proposed to have been a moat.

153   The first instance is when the magician *Djedi* greets *Khufu*'s son *Djedefre* who summons him to come to his father's court to tell him about the sanctuary of Thoth. *Djedi* responds with several blessings. One of these formulaic greetings is the phrase: "and may your soul know the roads [of '*fdt*] to the portal of him who shelters the dead." The second instance

and third instances occur when *Djedi* replies to *Khufu*'s question about the number of chambers in the sanctuary of Thoth: "'There is a casket of flint in a room called the Inventory in Heliopolis; in that casket." All three instances have unique context signs at the end.

154   Sherbiny 2017, p. 489.

155   Ibid., p. 493.

156   Ibid., p. 500. Sherbiny also thinks there is fire and darkness around.

157   Ibid.

158   Ibid., p. 493.

159   Ibid., p. 496.

160   Ibid., p. 501.

161   Faulkner 1973, Spell 1130.

162   Sherbiny 2017, p.565.

CHAPTER VII: ARCHIVE

163   Kurth et al. 2014, pp. 582-583.

164   Ibid. 2014, p. 583.

165   Allen 2014, p. 106.

166   Faulkner 2003, p. 275.

167   The *Edfu* Project was originally launched in 1986 by Professor of Egyptology Dr. Dieter Kurth from the University of Hamburg in Hamburg, Germany.

Dr. Kurth's webpage at H.U.: https://www.kulturwissenschaften. uni-hamburg.de/de/einrichtungen/arbeitsbereich-aegyptologie/personal/ kurth.html, last accessed March 8, 2021.

The homepage of the Edfu Project can be accessed at https://adw-goe. de/forschung/abgeschlossene-forschungsprojekte/akademienprogramm/ edfu-projekt/, last accessed March 8, 2021.

168   Kurth 2014, p. 577.

169   Ibid, p. 564

170   Behedet can refer to both Edfu and a city in the north. For a discussion of this issue, see Gardiner 1944.

171   Sharafeldin et al. 2019.

172   See Gardiner 1944, pp. 32-33, undermining Kees' argument against this idea.

173   Ibid.

174   Gardiner 1938, p. 160.

175   Bárta 2020, p. 48.

176   Ibid., p. 56.

177   Helck 1987, p. 236.

178   Ibid., pp. 232, 237-238, 245.

179   Der Manuelian 2003.

180   Dreyer 1999.

181   Malville et al. 2007, p. 4.

182   Ibid. p. 5.

183   https://www.hebrewversity.com/hebrew-names-ark-covenant/, last accessed March 8, 2021.

184   Helck 1987, p. 171.

185   Ibid., pp. 170-171.

186   Ricke 1970.

187   Ibid., p. 4.

188   Ibid., p.15.

189   Ibid., pp. 4-6.

190   Lehner 1991, p. 150.

191   Sherbiny 2017, p. 113.

192   *Horakhty* is one of the names of the Great Sphinx in the New Kingdom inscribed on the Dream Stele between the forepaws of the monument.

193   The Valley Temple's two gates have niches onto which statues of baboons were place. Uvo Hölscher found one of these during his excavation of the temple front. There are three baboon-like creatures shown on the wooden tablet in Figure 109

194   There is a dock with two piers in front of the Valley Temple presumably a place where boats coming into the Nile-fed basin in front of the temples were mooring.

195   Ricke 1970, p. 37.

CHAPTER VIII: *MEHIT*

196   *Sneferu, Khufu, Djedefre, Khafre, Bakare, Menkaure, Shepseskaf, Khentkaus.*

197   *Hemiunu* may have passed away a few decades at most before *Khafre* came to power.

198   Smith 1963, p. 12.

199   Der Manuelian 2003, p. 32.

200   Petrie 1901, p. 32, referring to Plate XXV. The bent rod is shown as item 4.

201   See endnote 358

202   Helck 1987, chapter 11.

203   Der Manuelian 2003, pp. 32-40.

204   Horvárth 2015, p. 131. The Moon association derives from the fact that this festival was part of a four-day series of other Moon-related festivals near the beginning of the Egyptian civil calendar. There is an interesting visual pun as well, because the hieroglyphs for plummet and beer jug, Gardiner F34 and W22, look similar, especially when written in the cursive Hieratic.

    The theme of the First of Drunkenness was that of the vengeful Sun God sending his emissary eye in its manifestation of a raging lioness to punish rebellious man on Earth. The lioness only relents its epic destruction once subdued from drunkenness, when the Sun God reconsiders his deed, and fools the lioness into drinking a red alcoholic beverage believing it is blood. The conventional astronomical interpretation is the annual inundation of the Nile after months of dry heat and drought roughly coinciding with the summer solstice. The Moon connection may once have been related to a lunar calendar from which some chronologists, like Richard Parker, believe the civil calendar was ultimately devised.

205   YouTube Video "Single Tumbler Bolt Lock," last accessed March 8, 2021.

206   I published one paper with both Schoch and Bauval and two more papers with Schoch which dealt with the Sphinx. All were published in Archaeological Discovery Journal.

207   In Petrie 1901, p.47, he writes "so-called yoke sign" and draws a connection to sealings 115 and 116 on Plate XVI showing *Mehit*.

208   Ibid.

209 According to Strudwick 1985, pp. 214-216, the first title of the tandem title with *Mehit*, *mḏḥ zš nswt*, was supplanted in the mid-Fifth Dynasty by the *jmj r' zš nswt*, which persisted into the Middle Kingdom, and tended to be held by the vizier. It conferred a high-status scribal function. *mḏḥ zš nswt*, on the other hand, persisted, but lost the high status it had conferred in the Third and Fourth Dynasties, during the Fifth and Sixth. There were two bearers after Mery, who held this title without the JAW-*Mehit* part: *dw3 n r'* [Dua-n-rah] and *zṯw* [Ze-thoo]. The JAW-*Mehit* title, on the other hand, disappeared with Mery.

210 Smith 1942, Figure 4.

211 https://www.metmuseum.org/art/collection/search/547737, last accessed March 8, 2021.

212 Vygus 2015, pp. 857, 991, 993, 1250.

213 Ibid., pp. 896, 1250, 1556, 1557, 1607, 1924,

214 Schoch and Bauval 2017, pp. 174-177.

215 Ibid. pp. 221-224.

216 A seal labeled "Seal 1," and impressions from it made by a royal scribe and signed with the name *Mery* next to *Khafre*'s cartouche and banner were found in both an ancient dump at Giza explored by Kromer (1970) and a pottery pile at *Heit El-Gurab* by Mark Lehner's team. See Witsell 2018, p. 6. *Mery*'s name spelled in hieroglyphic can be seen in the left lower corner figure, top pane, at the bottom of the third column from the right.

217 Petrie 1901, Plate XVI, 116. See also comment on p. 31.

218 Helck 1987, p. 180.

219 West and Schoch 1993 (NBC), animation sequence.

220 Ibid.

221 Wilkinson 2003, pp. 176-183.

222 Seyfzadeh, Schoch, Bauval 2017.

223 https://www.robertschoch.com/mehit.html

224 Yoshimura et al. (2005), pp. 389-391.

225 Tallet and Marouard 2014, Figures 3 and 5.

226 Probably to the reign of *Sneferu*; Pierre Tallet, personal communication.

227 Turah is the white, high quality limestone from which the casings of the Giza pyramids and some mastabas were built.

228 Hawass 1994.

229 Hawass 1996, p.394.

230 Hawass 1987, pp. viii-ix; 425.

231 Lehner 2002, p. 15.

232 Bonani et al. 2001.

233 See https://www.unicode.org/L2/L2016/16257-n4751-hieroglyphs-new.pdf, page 193, P10. Last accessed March 8, 2021.

234 Helck 1987, chapter 11.

235 Der Manuelian 2003, pp. 32-40.

236 Petrie 1901 (Extra Plates), LV A. 112-115.

237 In fact, *Baset* may be one of the earliest known written words in hieroglyphic. The German Archaeological Institute under Günter Dreyer discovered bone tags inscribed with Egypt's earliest known written records dated to circa 3200-3100 BC According to his interpretation of the entire set of symbols discovered in Tomb UJ they encode names of kings and places. One of them reads as the name of this town in the Delta, *Baset* (see Dreyer 1999, Tafel 31, 103-104.

238 Vygus 2015, pp. 334-335.

239 Oppenheim 1998, pp. 14-27.

240 Oppenheim 1995, pp. 175-176.

241 Allen 2014, pp. 260-263.

242 Seyfzadeh and Schoch 2018, pp. 138-140.

243 Neyland 2019.

244 Lehner 1991, p. 349.

245 Ibid., pp. 352-353.

246 Kitchen 1975, p. 175.

247 Spencer 1978.

248 Baruch Brandl 2016, for example argues that the predominant animal depicted is the elephant and locates the shrine to Hierakonpolis.

249 Reviewed by Brandl referring to Dieter Arnold who suggested this animal. Herbert Ricke (1944, pp. 30-32) also thought that the horn-like protrusions on the *pr wr* shrine were rhinoceros' horns in *Bemerkungen zur ägyptischen Baukunst des Alten Reiches I.* However also possible is

a canine such as shown in Dreyer 1999, Tafel 30, 73-75 in which case the "horns" are rather ears.

250 It is relevant to note here that in Spell 707 of the Coffin Texts, the speaker there identifies himself with both jackal and lion as if they were equivalent. The same ambivalence on these bone tags suggests that they were both seen as guardians of the animal shrine, the later symbol of royal administration, writing, and archiving. This shared attribute as guardian may explain the confusing equivalence in the later writings and symbols of animal-mounted shrines.

251 Dreyer 1999, Tafel 30, 69

252 Brandl 2016.

253 Helck 1987, p. 178.

254 The *pr wr* name of the shrine is known from the Third Dynasty, where it is inscribed with the symbol of the animal shrine into one of Djoser's Heb Sed reliefs, and from the Fourth Dynasty where inscriptions dated to *Sneferu* show the icon of the structure, together with the phonetic spelling of its name.

255 i.e., as Brandl 2016 proposes.

256 Numen/Numina: Latin for resident divine power

257 Helck 1987, pp. 71-77.

258 Ibid. Chapter 11.

259 Vygus 2015, pp. 1315, 2059, 2065.

260 Ibid. p. 140.

261 This was a Third Dynasty official who also carried the *Master of JAW-Mehit* title. Helck 1987, p. 260.

262 Ibid., p. 257.

263 The astronomical connections of the step-pyramid complex which have been proposed at an orientation to the northern stars in the big dipper, the Sothic Cycle in the enclosure wall, the Metonic Cycle in the colonnade, and gate towards Sirius on the southeast corner.

264 See Hierakonpolis Online.

https://www.hierakonpolis-online.org/index.php/explore-the-predynastic-settlement/hk29-the-ceremonial-center, last accessed March 8, 2021.

Accessed March 2021.

265 Kaplony 1963, Tafel 40-47.

266   Helck 1987, p. 181.

267   Kaplony 1963, Tafel 43, 151.

268   Ibid., Tafel 53, 197.

269   Helck 1987, p. 179.

CHAPTER IX: FISSURE

270   https://opencontext.org/projects/141e814a-ba2d-4560-879f-80f1afb019e9, last accessed March 8, 2021.

271   for example, his well-known tome *The Complete Pyramids.*

272   American Association for the Advancement of Science. This meeting was held in Chicago in February of 1992.

273   NBC 1993.

274   Lehner 1994.

275   This, according to Lehner himself. See Hancock and Bauval 1996, p. 287.

276   Mark Lehner 1974. A.R.E. Press. https://www.goodreads.com/book/show/683648.The_Egyptian_Heritage, last accessed March 8, 2021.

277   Leon Festinger, Henry W. Riecken, Stanley Schachter (1956). *When Prophecy Fails: A Social and Psychological Study of a Modern Group that Predicted the Destruction of the World.* Harper Torchbooks (Harper & Row) - Book Series List.

278   The title of Leon Festinger et al.'s 1956 book he read in 1974.

279   Hassan 1949, pp. 16-17.

280   An account of these beginning written by Mark Lehner in response to an inquiry by Graham Hancock and Robert Bauval can be read in authors' 1996 book *The Message of the Sphinx*, Appendix 2, pp. 287-291.

281   Lehner 1991, pp. 158-159, 202-203.

282   Ibid., p. 203.

283   Lehner 1991, p. 159.

284   Ibid., p. 409.

285   Neyland 2019.

286   Lehner 1991, p. 159.

287   Seyfzadeh and Schoch 2019.

288   Emery, 1954, Fig.'s 140-142

289   Kahl 1994, p. 491.

290   Ibid., p. 496.

291   Dreyer 1999.

292   Boehmer et al. 1993.

293   Morenz and Schmidt 2009.

294   I visited Göbekli Tepe in January 2020 to participate in the start of principle photography for Robert Schoch's upcoming documentary film on the origin of civilizations.

295   https://youtu.be/WUMHftplBIs, last accessed March 8, 2021.

296   Peters and Schmidt 2004.

297   Ibid.: Based on the mismatch between the composition of animal remains and the animals shown in relief, hunting rituals were ruled out as unlikely.

298   Ibid, p. 215.

299   Sidharth 2010.

300   Schoch 2012, pp. 53-57.

301   Magli 2013.

302   Collins 2017.

303   Sweatman and Tsikritsis 2017

304   Morenz and Schmidt 2009.

305   Schoch 2012, p. 41.

306   The French *Centre national de la recherche scientifique.*

307   Processual archaeology focuses on scientific evidence regardless of preconceived mechanisms, such as either purely materialistic or purely anthropological, by which culture evolves. In other words, both, neither, or one or the other, may, at times, be the driving force for cultural advances, or declines.

308   Viera, V. (2010). A Context Analysis of Neolithic Cygnus Petroglyphs at Lake Onega. *Cambridge Archaeological Journal, 20*(2), 255-261. doi:10.1017/S0959774310000260

309   Keynes, J. M. (1936). The General Theory of Employment, Interest and Money. Chapter 12: The State of Long-Term Expectation.

       https://www.marxists.org/reference/subject/economics/keynes/general-theory/ch12.htm, last accessed March 8, 2021.

310   Morenz and Schmidt 2009, p. 25.

311   Fenton 2017.

312   Emery 1954, Plate X X X V b.

313   For example, the Battlefield Palette housed at the British Museum in London, England, dated to 3300-3100 BC.

314   Spelled with the one-symbol word synonymous with her name.

315   This was the time when the king still travelled himself to the regions of the Nile Delta to collect taxes in the form of food and drink provisions as well as jewelry, pottery, and various other luxury items used at the royal court in Thinis.

316   S3507 was discovered in 1938. Walter Emery dates the tomb to the early reign on Horus-Den.

317   Emery 1958, Plate 86.

318   Ibid, p. 84.

319   Then still believed to be the Sphinx Temple, which had not yet been discovered.

320   Hölscher et al. 1912, p. 42.

321   Seyfzadeh and Schoch 2019, p. 19.

322   This is an effort begun in 1986 by Hamburg University's Dieter Kurth to fully translate the massive body of the Edfu Texts. The project has been funded by the Academy of Sciences of Göttingen since 2002. The website is at https://adw-goe.de/forschung/abgeschlossene-forschungsprojekte/akademienprogramm/edfu-projekt/, last accessed March 8, 2021.

323   Inner enclosure wall, north side, west half, second register. P. 241, Edfou VI.

324   Vygus 2015, p. 282. *dšr* means red, *dš* means to separate.

325   Inner north wall, west half, second plate. *Edfou* VI.

CHAPTER X: THOTH

326   Kaplony 1963, Figures 142, 145, 146, 150, 167.

327   Krauss 1997.

328   Sherbiny 2017.

329   Emery 1958, Plate 82, 40.

330   Ibid., pp. 520-523.

331 Wael Sherbiny has recently identified a leather roll in the Cairo Museum containing the same map, not specifically located to Hermopolis indicating that the original composition modelling for the coffins made at Deir El Barsha may have originated elsewhere.

332 Attia 2018.

333 Ibid., p. 523.

334 Schoch, Bauval, and I in Seyfzadeh et al. 2017.

335 Krauss 1997, pp. 67-79.

336 Ibid., pp. 14-66.

337 Helck 1987, pp. 233-235.

338 Ibid., pp. 22-24.

339 tomb 50-60.

340 https://www.hierakonpolis-online.org/index.php/explore-the-predynastic-cemeteries/hk6-elite-cemetery, last accessed March 8, 2021.

341 Hendricks et al. 2010.

342 Pieri 2011, p. 8.

343 Seyfzadeh and Schoch 2018.

344 Vygus 2015, p. 27.

345 Vygus 2015, pp. 1618; 586, 860, 865, 870, 872, respectively.

346 Ibid., p. 1783.

347 A decan is a star asterism or individual star known to have been tracked and named by Egyptian astronomers not later than the Middle Kingdom. For the *smd* family to which *Smd Mḥtj* belongs see https://aea.physics.mcmaster.ca/index.php/en/database/decans/smd-srt, last accessed March 8, 2021.

348 Klotz and Stauder (2020), p. 127.

349 Faulkner 1973, p. 85.

350 Traces of red paint have been found both on the head of the Great Sphinx and some of the blocks used for repair work.

351 Bauval and Gilbert 1994, chapter 10. Hancock and Bauval 1996, chapter 17.

352 Graham Hancock, personal communication.

353   1801-2100 AD. The NASA Eclipse Website can be viewed at https://
       eclipse.gsfc.nasa.gov/LEcat5/LEcatalog.html, last accessed March 8,
       2021.

354   25920 years/12 = 2160 years. Some epochs are longer, some are shorter
       depending on the width of the Zodiac constellation on the ecliptic that
       defines it.

355   Viewed from north, east is left.

356   Vygus 2015, pp. 1712-1713.

357   Ibid., p. 364.

358   Ibid., p. 83.

359   Ibid., pp. 91-92.

360   Belmonte and Shaltout 2009, chapter 8.

361   Ibid., pp. 227-228.

362   Alexander Puchkov, personal communication (January 2021). I reviewed
       Puchkov's prepublication article showing the data which support his con-
       tention. A preliminary draft of this article is on the author's Academia.
       edu page. https://dnu.academia.edu/AlexanderPuchkov, last accessed
       March 8, 2021.

363   Hancock and Bauval 1996, pp. 219 and 296.

364   Ibid., pp. 216-218.

365   The vernal point is that position on the horizon where the Sun can be
       seen to rise due east. This happens when the center of the Sun traverses
       a plane defined by Earth's equator either from celestial south to north
       on the first day of northern hemispheric spring or from celestial north to
       south on the first day of northern hemispheric fall.

366   Hancock and Bauval 1996, p. 218.

367   The vernal point closely coincided with the position of Regulus in Leo
       during the 8800-8700 BC time interval thus commencing the Age of Leo
       according to this definition.

368   Hancock and Bauval 1996, p. 265.

369   The most current estimate is 1.78 milliseconds per century (Stephenson
       et al, 2016, Figure 18). Over 120 centuries, a time error accumulates sig-
       nificant enough to cause the projection to undercount at the level of hours
       and this affects location where eclipses may have occurred. Stellarium
       points out a common source of error arising from extrapolations too far
       into the past or future as follows:

The moon's motion is very complicated, and eclipse computations can be tricky. One aspect which every student of history, prehistory and archaeology should know but as it seems not every does, is at least a basic understanding of the irregular slow-down of Earth's rotation known as ΔT (see section 17.4.3). Eclipse records on cuneiform tablets go back to the 8th century BC, some Chinese records go back a bit further. Experts on Earth rotation have provided models for ΔT based on such observations. These are usually given as parabolic fit, with some recommended time span. Extrapolating parabolic fits to erratic curves too far into the past is dangerous, pointless and inevitably leads to errors or invalid results. Models differ by many hours (exceeding a whole day!) when applied too far in the past. This means, there was certainly an eclipse, and latitude will be OK, but you cannot say which longitude the eclipse was covering. The probability to have seen a total eclipse at a certain interesting location will be very small and should by itself not be used as positive argument for any reasonable statement. This is not a problem of Stellarium, but of current knowledge. To repeat, you may find a solar eclipse in the sixth millennium BC, but you cannot even be sure which side of Earth could observe it!

370   Reliable date range is -1999 to +3000. 10120 BC falls outside of this range which would affect the longitudinal range on Earth where the eclipse would have been observable.

371   Herodotus, *Histories*, Book 1, chapter 30, section 1.

372   Her full name was Cleopatra VII Philopator

373   Alan Green and I travelled to Egypt in 2017.

374   Belmonte and Shaltout 2009, p. 185.

375   For a demonstration see this YouTube video at https://youtu.be/za839cp-wUh0?list=PLeuMeoe3GTgQBkEy8GClieTUfhYN7pmKr, last accessed March 8, 2021.

376   Hancock and Bauval 1996, pp.213-214.

377   Hendrickx and Eyckerman 2012.

378   Ibid., p. 33.

379   Schoch and Bauval 2017, pp. 171-173; 205-206.

380   Petrie 1925. Petrie found three large squares of graves dated to Djer, Djet, and Merneith. He theorized that these were made for court officials close to the king, but not as close as those buried around his own tomb

about a mile higher up in the desert such as members of his harem, for example.

381 Ibid., Plate III, 12. Comments on page 5. Petrie calls this symbol a bundle of tied-up papyrus rolls and compares it to a *diwan*, i.e., a collection of writings. Hence, it can be described as a symbol for an archive.

382 Ibid., pp. 44-51.

383 *Nekhen* is the hieroglyphic name of the predynastic settlement Hierakonpolis situated on the west bank of the Nile about half-way between Luxor and Aswan.

384 This female figurine is displayed at the Brooklyn Museum. https://www.brooklynmuseum.org/opencollection/objects/4225, last accessed March 8, 2021.

385 https://archive.org/details/ERA21/page/n73/mode/2up

Petrie, Wainwright, and Mackey found this palette in the same predynastic archaeological context as Decorated Pottery with motives identical to that shown in Figures 144, 146, 147, and 149. It is dated to *Naqada* II. *El-Gerzeh* is circa 5 miles north of Meydum by the Fayum. The Gerzeh Palette is displayed at the Museum of Egyptian Antiquities in Cairo, Egypt.

386 Hendrickx and Eyckerman 2012, p. 36.

387 Hassan 1953, p.116.

388 Ibid., p. 33.

389 Ibid., pp. 25-32.

390 The Assyrian Dictionary, Oriental Institute University of Chicago, Volume 20, U and W, p. 108b.

391 Hendrickx and Eyckerman 2012, p. 45.

392 Ibid., p. 44.

393 Hancock 2015, pp. 148-165.

394 Ibid. In endnote 8, where Hancock references the sea-faring character of the survivors of an island state which was destroyed.

395 Kurth et al. 2014, pp. 322-324.

396 Vygus 2015, p. 172.

397 Kurth et al. 2014, p. 322.

398 The ending *jw* designates a nisbe-adjective and the plural since they are two.

399   Vygus 2015, p. 1420.

400   Belmonte and Shaltout, M. 2009, p. 83, show a graph adapted from Neu-gebauer plotting Nile inundation data from the 19th century. The interval between two successive floods ranged between 335 and 415 days, i.e., 11-14 months, and consequently 7-10 months between the end of the previous and the beginning of the next inundation.

401   At circa 9,700 B.C., 11,700 years ago, there is a sharp rise in proxy air temperatures as determined with Greenland ice core samples. See https://pubs.usgs.gov/pp/p1386a/gallery2-fig35.html; last accessed March 30, 2021.

402   Going backwards in time using Stellarium, the westernmost five stars of the constellation Virgo (δ, ϵ, γ, η, and ν Vir) become recognizable as horizontally balanced "outstretched arms" or "cattle horns" shaped like the Egyptian hieroglyph Gardiner F13 *wp* above the eastern horizon beginning in the Tenth Millennium B.C., in the same way as the nearby constellation Leo gradually assumes a parallel position above the horizon in the eleventh Millennium B.C. Most Full Moons during this era rise south of Virgo, but there is a window of about a century between 10,000 and 9,000 B.C., when the Full Moon rose in the center of the V-shape formed by these five stars. In the example shown, the Moon is at 98% illumination. In the rare case of a dimmer, eclipsed Moon in Virgo, the constellation would be even more visible.

403   https://escholarship.org/content/qt2vh551hn/qt2vh551hn.pdf; last accessed March 30, 2021.

404   Richter 2012.

405   Reymond 1962.

406   Vygus 2015, p. 2002.

407   Vygus 2015, p. 2004.

408   Petrie 1925.

409   Kahl 1994, p. 553, footnote 964.

410   Green 1998.

411   Case and Payne date Tomb 100 to an overlap period between Gerzean/Naqada II and Egypt's First Dynasty, i.e. the proto-dynastic period. The tomb likely belonged to a chieftain whose status based on the uniqueness of the tomb resembles the kings of dynastic Egypt.

412   Payne 1973, p. 5, Plate XXV.

413   Case and Payne 1962; Jerald Jack Starr 2018. https://sumerianshake-speare.com/748301/855901.html, last accessed March 8, 2021; see also Helck 1987, chapter 10 for a general review of the topic of the extent of Sumerian influence in Egypt.

414   Case and Payne 1962, p. 16.

415   Hendrickx and Eyckerman 2012, p. 34.

416   Dreyer 1999

417   Helck 1987, chapter 11.

418   Ibid.

419   Kromer 1972, pp. 26-27; p. 34

420   Allen 2014, pp. 1-2

421   El-Daly 2005

422   The expected ending in the first-person singular would be "*kw*" or "*kj*", but it can also be just "*k*". See Allen 2014, p. 228.

423   For a complete list of methods used in enigmatic writing see Daniel A. Werning's chapter, pp. 195-247, in Klotz and Stauder (2020).

424   Klotz and Stauder (2020), p. 1.

425   Richter (2008), pp. 82-86; Klotz and Stauder (2020), p. 200.

426   Daniel Werning in Klotz and Stauder (2020), pp. 236-239.

427   Gaudard 2010, p. 174.

428   Fairman 1945, pp. 62-64.

429   Richter 2012, pp. 16-17.

430   Ibid, p. 36.

431   Ibid. p. 16.

432   Allen 2005, p. 269.

Index

A

Aaron Ha-Edut, 166. *See also Ark of the Testimony; Hebrew*

Aaron, biblical, 166. *See also Magical Rod of Aaron*

Aboriginal, 256

Abu Al-Hol, Arabic name of the Great Sphinx, 25

Abusir, pyramid field south of Cairo, 158, 190–191, 205

Abydos, early dynastic cemetery, 111, 135, 168, 183, 198, 215, 220–221, 261–263, 266, 314, 340, 348

Acacia, the tree, 318, 320

acrophonic, the philological principle, 249, 256

Adam, biblical, 6

Africa, the continent, 193, 210, 304

agglomeration, in economics, 253

Aigner, Thomas, 236. *See also Harrell, James A.*

Aker, the conjoined lions of the netherworld, 42, 63, 128, 203, 220, 230, 277–278, 281–285, 289, 309–312, 329. *See also Ruty, double lion*

akh(w), a skillful spirit, 135, 140–141, 197

akhet, zone of the eastern horizon where spirits become skillful, 25, 140–141, 197

Akkadian, ancient Mesopotamian language, 215

Al-Maqrizi, Arab historian, 25

alabaster, 31

alchemist, 235

Algieba, star in the constellation Leo, 202

algorithm, 303

Alkaid, star in Orion, 109

Allen, James Peter, 23, 65, 68, 109, 127, 157, 225, 234, 356

alluvial, 218

Alnilam, star in Orion, 166

Altenmüller, Hartwig, 67

Amarna, region and city in Middle Egypt founded by Akhenaten, 61

Amassis, Egyptian king, 304

Amduat, Middle Egyptian netherworld book, 44, 50, 60, 114–115, 311, 345, 353. *See also Richter, Barbara*

Amenophis, Egyptian king, 44, 50, 345

Amun, Egyptian god, 44, 50, 157, 345, 354–355

B

C

H

Y

Z

Δ

Kappa

Lightning Source UK Ltd.
Milton Keynes UK
UKHW012240310123
416265UK00003B/104